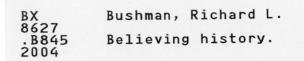
BX
8627
.B845
2004

Bushman, Richard L.

Believing history.

$40.00

DATE			
WITHDRAWN			

BAKER & TAYLOR

BELIEVING HISTORY

BELIEVING HISTORY

Latter-day Saint Essays

Richard Lyman Bushman

Edited by Reid L. Neilson and Jed Woodworth

COLUMBIA UNIVERSITY PRESS
NEW YORK

COLUMBIA UNIVERSITY PRESS
Publisher Since 1893
New York   Chichester, West Sussex
Copyright © 2004 Richard Lyman Bushman

Library of Congress Cataloging-in-Publication Data

Bushman, Richard L.
    Believing history : Latter-day Saint essays / by Richard Lyman Bushman ; edited
by Reid L. Neilson and Jed Woodworth.
    p. cm.
    Includes bibliographical references and index.
    ISBN 0–231–13006–6 (cloth : alk. paper)
    1. Book of Mormon—Criticism, interpretation, etc.   2. Smith, Joseph,
1805–1844.   I. Neilson, Reid Larkin.   II. Woodworth, Jed.   III. Title.

    BX8627.B845 2004
    289.3'09—dc21

2003855289
203055289

∞

Columbia University Press books are printed on permanent
and durable acid-free paper.
Printed in the United States of America
c 10 9 8 7 6 5 4 3 2 1

Contents

Preface vii
Introduction ix

PART I: *Belief*   1

1. Faithful History   3

2. My Belief   20

3. Learning to Believe   30

4. The Social Dimensions of Rationality   37

PART II: *The Book of Mormon and History*   45

5. The Book of Mormon and the American Revolution   47

6. The Book of Mormon in Early Mormon History   65

7. The Lamanite View of Book of Mormon History   79

8. The Recovery of the Book of Mormon   93

9. The Book of Mormon and Its Critics   107

PART III: *Joseph Smith and Culture*   143

10. Joseph Smith and Skepticism   145

11. Joseph Smith in the Current Age   161

12. Making Space for the Mormons   173

13. The Visionary World of Joseph Smith   199

14. Was Joseph Smith a Gentleman?
    The Standard for Refinement in Utah   217

15. Joseph Smith as Translator   233

16. The "Little, Narrow Prison" of Language: The Rhetoric
    of Revelation   248

17. A Joseph Smith for the Twenty-first Century   262

AFTERWORD: *Reflections on Believing History*   279

Index   283

Preface

When Reid Neilson and Jed Woodworth proposed to publish a collection of my Mormon essays, I was surprised and touched. I was complimented that these two young scholars, whom I had come to know through the Joseph Fielding Smith Institute for Latter-day Saint History summer seminar on Joseph Smith, would consider my scattered works, written over many years for many occasions, worth bringing together. At first I was skeptical. Was there enough here to warrant a book? Would the collection amount to anything more than a pile of leaves fallen from a tree? To summarize the available work, they arranged the titles into a tentative table of contents, with the essays grouped into three sections. This conception of the project won me over. The list persuaded me that the collection—and my Latter-day Saint writings—had a semblance of order.

The collection remains, nonetheless, a compilation rather than an integrated study. The essays are perhaps best thought of as the record of a Latter-day Saint historian contemplating his own religious tradition over the last quarter of the twentieth century. They bear the imprint of the intellectual environment in which they were written, which I see as one of skepticism about religion and especially about religion as literal and institutional as Mormonism.

I entered this environment of doubt at age eighteen when I arrived in Cambridge as a Harvard freshman. My sophomore tutor in History and Science, the distinguished historian of science I. B. Cohen, casually mentioned during one of our meetings that many people at Harvard thought Mormon theology was garbage. I think he meant the comment as a kindly effort to educate me away from my primitive beliefs and introduce me to the grownup world of realistic knowledge, but the words came across as a dismissal of my people, my faith, and me. I stuck to my belief partly out of a rebellious desire not to be subdued by this dominating skepticism. I have never forgotten that telling moment and have remained a believing, practicing Latter-day Saint to this day while knowing that my belief and practice are an offense to modern thinking. The essays were written in constant awareness of the doubt at the heart of our intellectual culture.

As I say in the essay "My Belief," I have fought the desire to strike back at the disbelievers. I know that arguments proving the truth of Mormonism are usually fruitless. Argumentation rarely brings about a change of mind, much less conversion. But I have not given up on a desire to show skeptics the richness and compass of Joseph Smith's thought. At least we can ask for respect. The Book of Mormon, in my opinion, has never been examined in its full complexity by outside scholars, nor have the force and originality of Joseph Smith's doctrine been measured. This absence of serious studies pains me. In apparently dispassionate essays such as "The Lamanite View of Book of Mormon History" and "The Book of Mormon in Early Mormon History," I am driving home the point that there is more here than my Harvard critics dreamed.

The doubters are not the only characters in my imagined audience. I sometimes turn toward my brothers and sisters in the Church and ask for their attention. I may feel about them the way Cohen felt about me. Some of the essays seem to say you don't understand how complicated the world is. Living on the East Coast magnifies the temptation to think one is more aware of complexity than westerners, even though I know that sophistication and experience know no geographical bounds. Though my prejudices are probably unjustified, I have an urge to awaken self-satisfied Mormons to the problems we face, both intellectual and cultural. I take this tack in "The Visionary World of Joseph Smith," where I report findings on visionary experiences in Joseph's time, and in certain passages in "Joseph Smith in the Current Age" about Joseph challenging modern corporations. I hope some readers will feel my elbow in their ribs from time to time.

In a peculiar way, then, I am on the attack in most of these essays. My wife, Claudia, insists that all writing is autobiographical. These essays show me defending my position in life—a believing Mormon in an unbelieving world and a historian in the Mormon world. I disguise my aggressiveness as best I can, but the impulse to protect my particular place cannot be concealed. Nor need it be. The work would not be better if my personal campaign for justification were neutralized. The truth is that the essays would never have been written without the motivating force of personal need. One can only hope that thought formed to vindicate one life can be helpful to readers leading other lives.

Richard Lyman Bushman
New York City

Introduction

The seventeen essays reproduced here were not written to be read together. The first was published in 1969, the last in 2001. Each set out to answer a particular question or series of questions. Most of the essays were published in journals with large Mormon readership, but one appeared first as a book chapter, another as a commencement speech. Structurally the essays are miles apart. Some are heavily footnoted, others read as lunch talks. Those in the first section are personal essays, while those in the second and third sections are history with a touch of literary analysis. Though differences exist, the essays share a common theme, Mormonism, and the perspective of an author, Richard Lyman Bushman, who believes in the religion about which he writes.

What does it mean to say Bushman is a believer? He is a believer, first of all, by birth. He was born a fifth-generation Mormon in Salt Lake City, Utah, the headquarters of the Church of Jesus Christ of Latter-day Saints, and was raised in a believing Mormon household in Portland, Oregon. Yet he thinks of himself as a believer by choice. He married a Mormon, raised his children as Mormons, and has served in church leadership positions all his adult life. "I find our Mormon truth good," he says, "and strive to install it at the center of my life."[1] Overlaying those beliefs, and at points intermingling with them, are the habits of mind of a professional historian. A Harvard Ph.D. in the history of American civilization, Bushman has written and edited numerous books and professional articles. In the academic world, he is known primarily as a colonial historian, not as a Mormon historian. In a flourishing career spanning forty years, he has taught in the history departments of Brown University, Brigham Young University, Boston University, and the University of Delaware. He is currently Gouverneur Morris Professor of History Emeritus at Columbia University. An intellectual by temperament and training, he is an active practitioner of the historical craft.

Bushman draws no line of demarcation between his Mormon and his professional beliefs. He does not use history as a shield to protect him from his belief in Mormonism, nor does he use Mormonism as a shield to protect him from the unimpeded pursuit of historical knowledge. His Mormon essays bear the marks of his academic training. Imagining an audience consisting of both Mormon and non-Mormon readers, Bushman takes on the seemingly impossible task of pleasing both. *Believing History*, then, is not only a book about religion and history. It is also about a person who unites them. These essays, brought together under one cover, illustrate how scholarly inquiry can be united with religious conviction. Collectively the essays answer the question, Can a believing historian speak meaningfully about his own belief?

There are several reasons why one might say it cannot be done. The "dream" of objectivity still lingers in the historical profession even though philosophers and literary critics years ago debunked the myth that strict objectivity is possible. In a profession torn between the humanities and the social sciences, most historians have liberalized in allowing Marxist, feminist, and a variety of multicultural perspectives into mainstream debate.[2] Religious perspectives have yet to find acceptance, but there are signs of change. George Marsden's *Soul of the American University*, a book that indicted the academic establishment for suppressing religion, has laid the issues on the table.[3] Marsden's "Concluding Unscientific Postcript," a confession of his evangelical Protestant beliefs, did not invalidate the book's argument in the eyes of reviewers. Even though Marsden claimed that religion doesn't get a hearing at the university, the fact that his book stimulated so much discussion shows a climate more favorable to religious views than in years past. Other books with a confessional tone written by academics have followed. Historians do not bury their subjectivity the way they once did, and some advocate full disclosure of basic beliefs.[4]

Bushman's professional reputation helps neutralize the problem of objectivity. His Mormon essays represent but a fraction of his historical work. Bushman is a prize-winning historian of major works in American history. He won the Bancroft prize for *From Puritan to Yankee: Character and Social Order in Connecticut, 1690–1765*.[5] His most recent book, *The Refinement of America: Persons, Houses, Cities*, a synthetic masterpiece, was called by one reviewer "the most suggestive and delightful American social history we have ever had," a work of "astonishing erudition."[6] His Mormon studies constitute only part of his scholarly interests. One would think an academic with a reputation to lose would not write history that could be charged with partiality.

His reputation among Mormon historians is likewise solid. Bushman helped define the "New Mormon History," which sought understanding over affirmation or rejection. Terryl Givens recently called him the "foremost historian of Mormonism."[7] A past president of the Mormon History Association, Bushman is respected by Mormons in diverse camps. Advocates and dissidents, scholars and laypeople, historians and social scientists all quote his writings. His fair-minded tone appeals to thinkers of various stripes.[8]

The difficulties of his undertaking should not be minimized. Rigor, like objectivity, is a concern for religious history. Can a believer put enough critical distance between personal belief and his work to tell the truth? Will academic tools get checked at the door upon entering discussion on religious subjects? Bias may be admitted, but weak analysis cannot be countenanced. As non-Mormon historian Grant Wacker puts it, "There is no reason that a Thomist or a Mormon spin on the past should be any less acceptable in the academic marketplace than a Freudian or a Marxist one, so long as all of them are able to prove themselves both intellectually plausible and morally consistent." Positivist assumptions go unchecked all the time. The simple fact that a historian subscribes to a particular set of beliefs, or confesses to those beliefs, should not eliminate the historian's writings on the subject from serious consideration. To be plausible within the modern academy, written history must meet standards of professional excellence. Admitting that the standards are contested, Wacker says plausible history is open to historical context, change, and disconfirmation. Parochial history and imaginative literature does not meet these standards.[9]

Like his colonial history, Bushman's Latter-day Saint essays are richly contextual. "The Visionary World of Joseph Smith" situates the founding prophet of Mormonism among other American visionaries of his time. Smith was perhaps the most extravagant and successful of dozens if not hundreds of early-nineteenth-century visionaries who sought contact with the heavens through divination and faith healings. The essay "Joseph Smith and Skepticism," to take another example, views Smith within currents of Enlightenment skepticism, reading the injunctions against seeking miracles found in Smith's early revelations as responses to the Christian rationalist arguments circulating in early national America. Many of these essays, following a trend in the historical profession, were prepared as preliminary studies for his long-term project of writing a "cultural" biography of Joseph Smith.

Bushman's Mormon writings assume the standard historical project of charting change over time. *Joseph Smith and the Beginnings of Mormonism* interprets conflicting accounts of Smith's First Vision by arguing for an evolving self-conception. As Smith grew into his role of prophet, he understood his visions differently. His role in bringing forth a new gospel dispensation intruded into later accounts while his initial concern for personal forgiveness receded into the background.[10] The essay "Making Space for the Mormons" contrasts early Mormon conceptions of sacred space with later diffusionist policies. Smith funneled converts into a single city, while modern Mormonism inverted this scheme by encouraging converts to remain in their native countries. This obvious transition cannot be ignored. "If 'apostasy' isn't the right word," Bushman concluded, "then 'change' certainly is."

Change and contextualism can be linked to a theory of history implicit in Bushman's writings. For Bushman, providential history arises out of human dilemmas. Early-nineteenth-century visionaries, for example, stood on the border between Enlightenment skepticism and medieval magic, yearning for a connection with the divine when mainstream faiths had relegated religious enthusiasm to superstition. Early Mormon conceptions of space changed, he suggests, because Church population increased, making the funneling of converts to a single gathering place impracticable. Smith adapted his telling of the First Vision to his particular audience; the most expansive account appeared as he prepared his history for public consumption. None of these explanations discounts the influence of God, but neither does any overtly posit God's influence. A God who works in history works through human need. This hypothesis enables Bushman to follow secular historians in claiming that "reasonableness and plausibility" are the *sine qua non* of good history. His essay "Faithful History" speculates on the possibility of discerning God's influence in history, but the essay finally concludes that such schemes encounter insurmountable difficulties. Produced in a secular age, Bushman's Latter-day Saint essays account for historical change in broadly humanistic, not providential, terms.

Rigorous history does not subject some ideas to hard scrutiny while exempting others from careful consideration. Wacker says "the possibility that a proposition could be decisively disconfirmed comes as close as any to serving as a wedge by which properly historical texts can be separated from properly imaginative ones."[11] All historical affirmations, even cherished myths, must be available for testing. Bushman was one of the first Mormon historians to acknowledge that the young Joseph Smith engaged in treasure-digging and vernacular magic, long a resisted admission among Latter-day Saints. In the essay "Joseph Smith as Translator," Bushman uses the affidavits sworn out by Smith family neighbors, documents often discounted by believing Mormons, to connect Joseph Smith to a magical culture stretching from Europe to America down through the centuries. Mormons had long downplayed Smith's magical pursuits, thinking them beneath the dignity of one called of God, but Bushman's candor led the Saints to reconsider Smith's early visions. Bushman's history has been called revisionist. In the essay "Was Joseph Smith a Gentleman?" the answer was a somewhat unsettling "no," challenging genteel depictions of the Prophet in contemporary Mormon art. For Bushman, no shibboleth is beyond scrutiny.

Yet there must be evidence. Bushman's "The Recovery of the Book of Mormon" gently chides secular accounts of the Book of Mormon translation for ignoring the historical sources closest to Joseph Smith. Implicit were several non-Mormon reviewers of *Joseph Smith and the Beginnings of Mormonism* who criticized Bushman for affirming a traditional Mormon view. By relying heavily on the primary accounts, all of which seemed to affirm the existence of "golden plates" and angelic visitations, Bushman was viewed as a sympathizer. But that was the evidence, and he used it. Unbelievers wanted Bushman to find a naturalistic explanation for the early visions. When he did not, his own faith was taken as evidence that was pitching softballs.[12] The dispute was typical of those in Mormon historiography. As R. Laurence Moore distilled the problem, "Mormonism is apparently not quite an old enough faith to render irrelevant the question of whether Smith really did translate golden plates that he had, with divine assistance, uncovered on the Hill Cumorah, near Rochester."[13] As Moore implies, the starting point for writing religious history usually begins with sacred origins, a perspective not fully allowed Mormon studies, which continues to be plagued by unrealistic expectations. In effect, reducing a rich religious phenomenon like Mormonism to naturalistic terms is like saying a Beethoven symphony is merely horse hair rubbing across catgut.

Bushman's method in both his secular writings and his Latter-day Saint essays begins with the assumption that historians are no greater than their subjects. The alleged sea of faceless masses, he says in "My Belief," does not exist. If people are carried along by historical forces outside their control, they are also "individual persons, quite idiosyncratic, perverse, and interesting." He assumes that all individuals, and no less religious individuals, have a valid take on the world. He treats self-reports seriously, which is not to say he treats them uncritically ("Some statements about the past can be proven wrong," he says in "Faithful History"). Bushman tries to get inside the skin of historical actors, to see the way they saw. His writing has been called empathetic. His point is not to prove that a Mohammad or a Joseph Smith did or did not have visions but to ask what the visions they claimed meant to them and their followers. The method seeks to make judgments without being judgmental.

Mircea Eliade once described this style of actor-centered history: "There is no other way of understanding a foreign mental universe than to place oneself *inside* it, at its very center."[14] In an effort to understand eighteenth-century religious and political thought, Bushman as a young scholar took seminars from the psychosocial theorist Erik Erikson, a student of Freud's. Psychological theory had entered the writing of historians trained in the generation after World War II, and Bushman found in what later became known as "psychohistory" a way to extend his empathetic approach. Plumbing the depths of mind and soul, Bushman felt, brought him even closer to the experience of the historical figures he was studying. His long-standing interest in psychoanalysis is apparent in his Latter-day Saint essays. "The Lamanite View of the Book of Mormon" draws on Freud to understand the behavior of Laman and Lemuel, the backsliding brothers in the Book of Mormon. Psychological words like "need" and "feeling" and "motivation" sprinkle all the essays. If some have sought to reduce history to logic, Bushman has wanted to reduce it to emotion. His essays are introspective, self-reflective, and psychologically nuanced.[5]

Tying emotion to history impels Bushman to consider the influence of his own belief on his written history. Any theory used to interpret the past must in some measure correspond to the private lives of those who employ that theory. How can someone say texts have inexhaustible interpretations and yet interpret events in their private lives univocally? Wacker wants his- tory to admit what it is doing, laying all cards on the table while "never employing covert methods in the interest of some higher cause."[15] Bush- man's essays "My Belief" and "The Social Dimensions of Rationality" cer- tainly lay out all the cards, frankly admitting the influence of personal belief on historical renderings.

Bushman frequently reasons with his audience by employing the first-person plural "we," the language of consensus history, a word merging pri- vate belief with public interest. His writings assume a soft, not hard, historical determinism. Historians sometimes treat the past as ironclad social construction, overlooking the fact that they do not think of their own lives this way. If historians see themselves as agents, should they not extend the same liberty to others—including the dead? Bushman's essays situate Joseph Smith in history without compressing him into the product of historical forces. No other Jacksonian American produced a book like the Book of Mormon. Must not Smith, then, be credited with unusual originality if not inspiration? Essays such as "The Book of Mormon and Its Critics" and "The 'Little, Narrow Prison' of Language" remind readers that Mormonism cannot be explained away as just another sect arising from the religious revivals of early-nineteenth-century America. There is too much that is exceptional. Harold Bloom's assessment of Joseph Smith as an "authentic religious genius" is a description Bushman is inclined to accept.[16]

Moral consistency can be seen in Bushman's attention to the Book of Mormon, a work standing beside the Bible as scripture in Mormon thought. Smith claimed he translated the book from golden plates hidden in a hill near his home in upstate New York. He said an angel told him where to find the plates. Secular historians, turned off by Smith's super- natural claims, have resisted careful study of the Book of Mormon. Eager to pronounce the work fraudulent, they wave off the book with surface references to warmed-over King James English or theology resembling Smith's environment. They do not probe the text.[17] But Bushman's his- torical method and his Mormon belief compel him to take the book seri- ously. By its own account the Book of Mormon is not a simple text. The essays "The Book of Mormon in Early Mormon History" and "The Book of Mormon and the American Revolution" explore the complexity of the book's narrative.

Bushman's is a reassuring voice as Mormonism seeks acceptance and professional legitimacy. Will the concerns be different a generation from now? Will an essay with a title like Bushman's "Joseph Smith in the Current Age" be written with startlingly different conclusions? Will the categories "believing" and "unbelieving" found in "A Joseph Smith for the Twenty-first Century" be merged and re-divided as Mormonism grows into a sprawling and diverse world religion as sociologists predict? Joseph Smith may one day overflow an American context strictly divided between believers and unbelievers. Until then, there is much to learn from believing history.

We acknowledge the help of many individuals who made this work possible. Thanks first to Richard Lyman Bushman, who saw merit in the idea and volunteered to write headnotes and make light revisions. John W. Welch and Heather M. Seferovich provided steady hands when this project was first contemplated for publication at BYU Press. Anastasia Sutherland scanned and formatted the essays, and Kimberly Chen Pace did the production work. Karen Todd read all the essays and made valuable edits. Jan McInroy's proofreading caught many errors. Wendy Lochner and many others at Columbia University Press, as well as several peer reviewers, improved the collection immensely.

We thank the following publishers for permission to reprint the essays in their present form. "Faithful History," from *Dialogue: A Journal of Mormon Thought* (winter 1969), © 1969 by Dialogue Foundation, P.O. Box 20210, Shaker Heights, OH 44120; "The Book of Mormon and the American Revolution," "My Belief," and "The Visionary World of Joseph Smith," and "A Joseph Smith for the Twenty-first Century," from *BYU Studies,* © 1976, 1985, 1998, and 2001 by BYU Studies, 403 CB, Provo, UT 84602; "Learning to Believe" (formerly "The Quest for Learning: By Study and Also by Faith"), from *BYU Magazine* (formerly *BYU Today*), © 1991 by BYU Magazine, 218 UPB, Provo, UT 84602; "The Social Dimensions of Rationality," from *Expression of Faith: Testimonies of Latter-day Saint Scholars,* edited by Susan Easton Black, © 1996 Deseret Book Co., P.O. Box 30178, Salt Lake City, UT 84130–0178; "The Book of Mormon in Early Mormon History," from *New Views of Mormon History: A Collection of Essays in Honor of Leonard J. Arrington,* edited by Davis Bitton and Maureen Ursenbach Beecher, © 1987 by the University of Utah Press, 1795 E. South Campus Dr., Suite 101, Salt Lake City, UT 84112–9402; "The Lamanite View of the Book of Mormon," from *By Study and Also by Faith: Essays in Honor of Hugh Nibley on His 80th Birthday,* edited by John M. Lundquist and Stephen D. Ricks, © 1990 by Deseret Book and FARMS, Deseret Book Co., P.O. Box 30178, Salt Lake City, UT 84130–0178; "The

Recovery of the Book of Mormon," from *Book of Mormon Authorship Revisited: The Evidence for Ancient Origins*, edited by Noel B. Reynolds, © 1997 by Foundation for Ancient Research and Mormon Studies, P.O. Box 7113, University Station, Provo, UT 84602; "The Book of Mormon and Its Critics," chapter 4 from Richard L. Bushman, *Joseph Smith and the Beginnings of Mormonism*, © 1984 by University of Illinois Press, 1325 S. Oak St., Champaign, IL 61820–6903. Richard Lyman Bushman, *Joseph Smith and Skepticism*, © 1974 by BYU Press, 403 CB Provo, UT 84602; Richard Lyman Bushman, *Making Space for the Mormons*, © 1997 by Richard Lyman Bushman, published by Special Collections and Archives, University Libraries, Utah State University; "Was Joseph Smith a Gentleman? The Standard for Refinement in Utah," from *Nearly Everything Imaginable: The Everyday Life of Utah's Mormon Pioneers*, edited by Ronald W. Walker and Doris R. Dant, © 1999 by BYU Press, 403 CB, Provo, UT 84602; "Joseph Smith as Translator," from *The Prophet Puzzle: Interpretive Essays on Joseph Smith*, edited by Bryan Waterman, © 1999 by Signature Books, 594 W. 400 N., Salt Lake City, UT 84116; "Joseph Smith in the Current Age," from *Joseph Smith: The Prophet, the Man*, edited by Susan Easton Black and Charles D. Tate Jr., © 1993 by Religious Studies Center, 167 HJG, Provo, UT 84602; "The 'Little, Narrow Prison' of Language: The Rhetoric of Revelation," from *The Religious Educator: Perspectives on the Restored Gospel* (spring 2000), © 2000 by Religious Studies Center, 167 HJG, Provo, UT 84602.

Finally, we thank Ronald K. Esplin, former managing director of BYU's Joseph Fielding Smith Institute for Latter-day Saint History, as well as the Smith Institute's faculty and patrons, who introduced us to Richard Lyman Bushman through a summer fellowship program.

Jed Woodworth
Madison, Wisconsin

Reid L. Neilson
Chapel Hill, North Carolina

NOTES

1. On Bushman's church involvement, see his accounts in Susan Buhler Taber, *Mormon Lives: A Year in the Elkton Ward* (Urbana: University of Illinois Press, 1993), 177-82; and *Why I Believe* (Salt Lake City: Bookcraft, 2002), 79–83.
2. The standard source on the American historical profession is Peter Novick, *That Noble Dream: The "Objectivity Question" and the American Historical Profession* (Cambridge: Cambridge University Press, 1988). A defense of objective inquiry is Joyce Old-

ham Appleby, Lynn Avery Hunt, and Margaret C. Jacob, *Telling the Truth about History* (New York: W. W. Norton, 1994). The seriousness with which objectivists approach philosophical critique can be seen in the title by Keith Windshuttle, *The Killing of History: How a Discipline Is Being Murdered by Literary Critics and Social Theorists* (Paddington: Macleay, 1996).

3. George M. Marsden, *The Soul of the American University: From Establishment to Established Nonbelief* (New York: Oxford University Press, 1994).

4. See, for example, Bruce Kuklick and D. G. Hart, eds., *Religious Advocacy and American History* (Grand Rapids, Mich.: William B. Erdmans, 1997); George M. Marsden, *The Outrageous Idea of Christian Scholarship* (New York: Oxford University Press, 1997); and Jane Goodall with Phillip Berman, *Reason for Hope: A Spiritual Journey* (New York: Warner Books, 1999). See also Kelly James Clark, ed., *Philosophers Who Believe: The Spiritual Journey of 11 Leading Thinkers* (Downers Grove, Ill.: InterVarsity Press, 1993).

5. Richard L. Bushman, *From Puritan to Yankee: Character and Social Order in Connecticut, 1690–1765* (Cambridge: Harvard University Press, 1967).

6. Richard L. Bushman, *The Refinement of America: Persons, Houses, Cities* (New York: Alfred A. Knopf, 1992). Michael Zuckerman, review of *The Refinement of America*, in *American Historical Review* 98, no. 2 (1993): 457–58. Zuckerman, also one of *The Refinement of America*'s hardest critics, says the book lacks multicultural perspective.

7. Terryl L. Givens, *"By the Hand of Mormon": The American Scripture that Launched a New World Religion* (New York: Oxford University Press, 2002), 246.

8. See, for example, Ronald W. Walker, David J. Whitaker, and James B. Allen, *Mormon History* (Urbana: University of Illinois Press, 2001), 85, 92–93, 124, 139; Eric A. Eliason, *Mormons and Mormonism: An Introduction to an American World Religion* (Urbana: University of Illinois Press, 2001), 14; Richard L. Bushman, "Faithful History," in George D. Smith, ed., *Faithful History: Essays on Writing Mormon History* (Salt Lake City: Signature Books, 1992), 1–17; Armand Mauss, *The Angel and the Beehive: The Mormon Struggle with Assimilation* (Urbana: University of Illinois Press, 1994), 11, 16 n. 5; D. Michael Quinn, *Mormonism and the Magic Worldview*, 2d ed. rev. and enl. (Salt Lake City: Signature Books, 1998), xvii; and Philip L. Barlow, *Mormons and the Bible: The Place of the Latter-day Saints in American Religion* (New York: Oxford University Press, 1991), 227.

9. Grant Wacker, "Understanding the Past, Using the Past: Reflections on Two Approaches to History," in Bruce Kuklick and D. G. Hart, eds., *Religious Advocacy and American History* (Grand Rapids, Mich.: William B. Erdmans, 1997), 159–78.

10. Richard L. Bushman, *Joseph Smith and the Beginnings of Mormonism* (Urbana: University of Illinois Press, 1984), 56–58.

11. Wacker, "Understanding the Past, Using the Past," 171.

12. See Martin Ridge, "Joseph Smith, Brigham Young, and a Religious Tradition," in *Reviews in American History* 14, no. 1 (1986): 28–29; and David Brion Davis, "Secrets of the Mormons," *New York Review of Books*, August 15, 1985, 16–17. Mormon historian Marvin Hill calls Bushman an apologist in "Richard L. Bushman—Scholar and Apologist," *Journal of Mormon History* 11 (1984): 125–33. But Klaus Hansen says Bushman and non-Mormon historian Jan Shipps "write the same kind of history." "Jan Shipps and the Mormon Tradition," *Journal of Mormon History* 11 (1984): 137.

13. R. Laurence Moore, "Prophets in Their Own Country," *New York Times Book Review*, July 21, 1985.

14. Mircea Eliade, *The Sacred and the Profame: The Nature of Religion*, trans. Willard R. Trask (New York: Harcourt Brace, 1987), 162, 165.

15. Wacker, "Understanding the Past, Using the Past," 173–75.

16. Harold Bloom, *The American Religion: The Emergence of the Post-Christian Nation* (New York: Simon and Schuster, 1992), 80; and Richard L. Bushman, "The Mysteries of Mormonism," *Journal of the Early Republic* 15, no. 3 (1995): 501–8.

17. Exceptions include Paul C. Gutjahr, *An American Bible: A History of the Good Book in the United States, 1777–1880* (Stanford: Stanford University Press, 1999), 151–60; Jan Shipps, *Mormonism: The Story of a New Religious Tradition* (Urbana: University of Illinois Press, 1985); and Thomas F. O'Dea, *The Mormons* (Chicago: University of Chicago Press, 1957).

PART ONE

Belief

1

Faithful History

This essay is the fruit of my six years at Brigham Young University. During that BYU period, I felt a compelling pressure to orient my historical work toward religious questions like the ones raised here. In the Mormon atmosphere, religion seemed to dwarf conventional studies of politics or culture. I began to feel that historical inquiries had to relate to God or salvation to be significant. For a moment I wondered if I was better described as an "intellectual" rather than as a "historian," meaning I was less interested in digging up new historical facts than in interpreting them in a religious spirit.

"Faithful History" was written in Arlington, Massachusetts, after I had left BYU. During a year away from Provo on a sabbatical leave, I accepted a position at Boston University, and we settled in Arlington and later Belmont. Away from Utah, the need to connect everything to religion gradually diminished. In Boston's more secular environment, I began to think of myself as a historian again, but the question of how to write about the religious dimensions of history still intrigues me.

The essay now has an antiquated flavor. Over the past quarter century, the issue it discusses—the pliability of historical knowledge—has been treated with great sophistication and sometimes baffling complexity. (One need only read two books to get a sense of the problem. Peter Novick, That Noble Dream: The "Objectivity Question" and the American Historical Profession [Cambridge: Cambridge University Press, 1988], and Joyce Oldham Appleby, Lynn Avery Hunt, and Margaret C. Jacob, Telling the Truth about History [New York: Norton, 1994].) Had the essay been written after the postmodern explosion of interest in representation, it would have required reference to an immense literature.

I include it here now in its initial naive rendering to illustrate the way religious belief in an unbelieving world drives the mind toward skepticism and relativism. The separation between one's own convictions and the standard common sense of the time forces one to doubt the validity of received wisdom. A modern believer lives in a kind of postmodern time warp where religious reality is constantly overlaid on conflicting secular reality, making everything seem relative and indeterminate. In the modern world, faith is a choice. One has to choose to believe over against the reigning common sense. This leads to the liberating but disconcerting realization that historical truth is also molded to suit our assumptions and desires.

Written history rarely survives the threescore and ten years allotted those who write it. Countless histories of the French Revolution have moved onto the library shelves since 1789, and no end is in sight. The same is true of any subject you care to choose—the life of George Washington, the medieval papacy, or Egyptian burial rites. Historians constantly duplicate the work of their predecessors, and for reasons that are not always clear. The discovery of new materials does not satisfactorily account for the endless parade of books on the same subject. It seems more that volumes written even thirty or forty years before fail to persuade the next generation. The same materials must constantly be recast to sound plausible, the past forever reinterpreted for the present.

The books on the framing of the Constitution written over the past hundred years illustrate the point. Through most of the nineteenth century, Americans conceived of the framers as distinguished statesmen, if not demigods, who formulated a plan of government which embodied the highest political wisdom and assured freedom to Americans so long as they remained true to constitutional principles. Near the end of the century, however, when certain provisions of the Constitution were invoked to prevent government regulation of economic excesses, reformers began to think of the Constitution less as a safeguard of liberty than as a shield for greed and economic domination. Proposals for drastic revision began to circulate. Among the advocates of reform was a young historian, Charles Beard, who set out in a new mood to rewrite the story of the Constitution. As reported in *An Economic Interpretation of the Constitution,* Beard discovered that most of the framers were wealthy men who feared popular attempts to encroach on property rights.[1] Quite naturally they introduced provisions that would forestall regulation of business by the democratic masses. The deployment of the Constitution in defense of business interests in the late nineteenth century was only to be expected. The framers themselves were businessmen who had foreseen the popular tendency to attack property and had written a document that could be brought to the defense of business. Far from creating a government for all the people, they constituted the power of the republic so as to protect property. Their interests were narrow and by implication selfish.[2]

That interpretation caught on in the early twentieth century when the main thrust of reform was to regulate business. For nearly twenty years, historians found Beard's interpretation of the Constitution true to life as they knew it and faithfully taught his views to their students. Shortly after World War II, however, the temper of the times changed. Business interests no longer appeared so malevolent as before; the Supreme Court took a brighter view of government regulation; and constitutional principles were invoked on behalf of civil rights and other libertarian causes. All told, the provisions protecting property did not stand out so prominently as before, and the broader import of the document was seen once again. A number of historians then began to attack Beard. They argued that all the political leaders of the eighteenth century were men of property, and that wealth did not distinguish those who favored the Constitution from those who opposed it. Rather than being protectors of class interest, the framers were seen to be seeking a balance in government that would keep order while preserving liberty, and they were generally acknowledged to have succeeded. Now the consensus of historical opinion has swung around once more to honor the framers as distinguished statesmen of unusual political wisdom who framed a constitution for which we can be thankful.

Presumably we are closer to the truth now than thirty years ago when Beard's views held sway. And yet it is disconcerting to observe the oscillations in historical fashion and to recognize how one's own times affect the view of the past. Anyone unfamiliar with the writing of history may wonder why historians are such vacillating creatures. Are not the facts the facts and is not the historian's task no more than to lay them out in clear order? Why the continual variations in opinion? It seems reasonable that, once told, the story need only be amended as new facts come to light.

The reason for the variations is that history is made by historians. The facts are not fixed in predetermined form, merely awaiting discovery and description. They do not force themselves on the historian; he selects and molds them. Indeed, he cannot avoid sculpturing the past simply because the records contain so very many facts, all heaped together without recognizable shape. The historian must select certain ones and form them into a convincing story. Inevitably scholars come up with differing accounts of the same event. Take the following vignette, the individual components of which we will assume are completely factual.

> Having come from a broken home himself, Jack yearned for a warm and stable family life. For many years he went out with different girls without finding one whom he could love. At age thirty-four he finally met a girl who won his heart completely, and in his delirious happiness he dreamed of creating the home he had missed in his own childhood. In the fall of 1964, one month before their wedding, the girl withdrew from the engagement. Jack was heartbroken and deeply distressed. Two months later he entered the hospital and in three months was dead.

No causes for the death are explicitly given, but we surmise a tangled psychic existence connected with Jack's ambivalence about marriage. He yearned for a wife and a happy home life, and yet his experience as a boy prevented him from risking it until long after most men are married. When he finally found the girl, the long pent-up desires were promised fruition. Her withdrawal from the engagement shocked his nervous system and induced a psychosomatic ailment serious enough to kill him. Admittedly we have to read a lot into the story to reach that conclusion, but it is not implausible. If the historian gave us only those facts and we were of a psychological bent, we would probably believe the account.

But listen to a briefer narration from the same life:

> Beginning in his last year in high school, Jack smoked two packs of cigarettes a day. In the winter of 1965, his doctor diagnosed lung cancer, and three months later he was dead.

Aha, we say, now we have the truth. We do not have to resort to far-fetched psychological theories to explain what happened. We all know what cigarettes do to you.

But as careful historians we cannot yet close the case. The most obvious diagnosis is not necessarily the true one. Only a small fraction of those who smoke two packs of cigarettes a day contract lung cancer at age thirty-four. Smoking alone does not explain why Jack was one of them. Can we rule out the possibility that psychic conflicts broke his resistance and made him susceptible? I do not think we can, though most people may prefer the more straightforward explanation. The point is that, given the multitude of facts, historians can pick and choose to make quite different and plausible stories, and it is difficult to demonstrate that just one of them is true. There is room for debate about the cause of Jack's death even when all the facts are in, including a medical autopsy. When so simple a case refuses to yield an indubitable result, think how interpretations of broad, complex events can vary: the motives of a presidential candidate, the causes of a war, or the origins of the Book of Mormon.

Notice also that neither of these explanations would have convinced reasonable people thirty or forty years ago. After the demise of romantic notions of brokenhearted lovers, and before the currency of psychoanalytic ideas about psychosomatic disease, a death by a broken engagement would have sounded outlandish indeed. In the same period, the connection of smoking and cancer was not yet established. The juxtaposition of two packs a day and the doctor's diagnosis would have been thought irrelevant, like linking the ownership of cats or a taste for bright neckties to tuberculosis. Nowadays, however, both theories make sense. New outlooks in our own time demand that past events be surveyed anew in search of relationships overlooked by earlier scholars. Reasonableness and plausibility, the *sine qua non* of good history, take on new meanings in each generation.

I doubt if any practicing historian today thinks of history as a series of beadlike facts fixed in unchangeable order along the strings of time. The facts are more like blocks that each historian piles up as he or she chooses, which is why written history is always assuming new shapes. I do not mean to say that historical materials are completely plastic. The facts cannot be forced into just any form at all. Some statements about the past can be proven wrong. But historians themselves have much more leeway than a casual reading of history books discloses. The historians' sense of relevance, their assumptions about human motivation and social causation, and the moral they wish readers to draw from the story—what they think is good and bad for society—all influence the outcome.

Perhaps the most important influence is the sense of relevance—what the historian thinks is worth writing about. For that sense determines what part of the vast array of facts the historian will work with. When you consider all that has happened in the world's history—children reared, speeches given, gardens planted, armies annihilated, goods traded, men and women married, and so on and on and on—more important than how you answer a question is what question you ask in the first place. Not until you decide that you want to know the history of child-rearing or oratory or gardening do you even bother to look at all the facts on those subjects stored away in the archives. A large part of creativity in the writing of history is the capacity to ask new questions that draw out arrays of facts previously neglected.

Fashions in historical questions come and go like other fashions, and these changes in the sense of relevance require that old stories be told anew. Beard's generation took a great interest in economic forces. They wished to know (and we still do today) the wealth and sources of income of historical figures, the distribution of wealth through society, price levels, and the volume of trade and production. Earlier generations, particularly those before 1800, did not even think such facts important enough to record them properly. Economic historians today are hard-pressed to answer the questions that interest them most. The same is true of demographers, who bewail the failure of colonial Americans to take even a rude census before 1754. The present generation would also dearly love to know the opinions and feelings of the poor and the slaves. One hundred and fifty years ago, hardly anyone thought it worth the effort to record their thoughts. Now we must laboriously collect materials from scattered sources, speculate on the implications of the skimpy materials we do have, and try to answer questions our generation is asking in order to make the past relevant for us.

To sum it all up, written history changes simply because history itself brings change. Were we exactly like our ancestors, their history would satisfy us just as their houses and clothes would. But time has altered our concerns, our beliefs, our values, just as it has changed our taste and technological skill. We need new histories that appeal to our views of causation, our sense of significance, and our moral concerns. Since the materials out of which histories are made are so vast and flexible, historians are forever rearranging old facts and assimilating new ones into accounts that will help those in the present understand the past.[3]

II

Historians nowadays are philosophical about the frailty of their work. Most of my contemporaries realize the next generation's books will supersede their own and are content to write for their own times. They know their work will pass into obsolescence just as architects build knowing their structures will come down. Looking at the matter realistically, we can probably hope for nothing more. So long as we change, our understanding of the past must also change. Even from a religious perspective, at least from a Mormon point of view, there can be no lasting history for mortals. So long as we progress, we will enjoy ever broader horizons, and these must inevitably reflect on our understanding of what went before. As our wisdom enlarges, we will see more deeply into all of our experiences. Only when we come to the limits of knowledge and intelligence will we reach the final truth about history.

Recognizing the contingency of written history does not mean we can dismiss it as trivial. No human activity, including the physical sciences, escapes these limitations. We must try to speak the truth about the past as earnestly as we try to tell the truth about anything. Accepting the inevitable role of beliefs and values in history simply compels us to examine more closely the concerns that influence us and to make sure that we write history with our truest and best values uppermost.

Given these premises, it seems to me that Mormon historians, if they are given to philosophizing about their work, must ask themselves what values govern their scholarship. What determines their views of causation, their sense of significance, and their moral concerns? One might think that their religious convictions, their deepest personal commitments, would pervade their writing. But in my own experience, religious faith has little influence on Mormon historians for an obvious reason: we are not simply Mormons but also middle-class American intellectuals mostly trained in secular institutions.

It is perfectly clear that all Mormons live by varying values and outlooks, not all of them religious. When we sell cars, we act like most used-car salesmen, for they are our teachers in selling automobiles. When we preside over a ward or teach a gospel lesson, we act in another frame of mind, more in accord with what we have learned at church. The two are not entirely separable, but we all sense the different spirit of the two situations—a used-car lot and a church classroom. Obviously different ideas and assumptions about life prevail in each place. Similarly, historians who are Mormons write history as they were taught in graduate school rather than as Mormons. The secular, liberal, establishmentarian, status-seeking, decent, tolerant values of the university govern us at the typewriter, however devoted we may be as home teachers. Indeed, this viewpoint probably controls our thinking far more than our faith does. The secular, liberal outlook is the one we instinctively think of as objective, obvious, and natural, even though when we think about it we know it is as much a set of biases as any other outlook.

The values learned in modern universities are not without merit, and I do not intend to disparage the work produced under their auspices. But given a choice, would not most Latter-day Saints agree that their religious faith represents their best selves and their highest values? Is it not the perpetual quest of the religious man or woman to have religious principles regulate all conduct, the selling of automobiles and the writing of history as well as Sunday preachments—in short, to do all things in faith? Now that we have abandoned the naive hope that we can write objective history, I think Mormon historians should at least ask how we might replace our conventional, secular American presuppositions with the more penetrating insights of our faith.

I am not contending for orthodox history in the sense of adherence to one opinion. Gospel principles do not point toward one way of describing the past any more than they specify one kind of human personality. The Lord does not intend that we all be exactly alike. The possible styles of history in a Mormon spirit are as varied as the persons who write it. The authentic forms of Mormon-style history will emerge in the works of Mormon historians. They cannot be deduced from theological doctrines. All we can do in a theoretical vein is to speculate on some of the leads the gospel opens up, the directions Mormon historians might take. And that is what I intend to do in the remainder of this essay.

III

The Book of Mormon is a source of insight about the nature of history, a source that Mormons have only begun to mine. Since it was written by prophets, we can assume that extraneous cultural influences were largely subordinated to faith (although Mormon's interest in military tactics must have affected his decision to include the war episodes in the latter part of Alma). What clues does the Book of Mormon offer about appropriate concerns for a Mormon historian?

As I read the book, one pervasive theme is the tension between humans and God. Class struggles, dynastic adventures, technological change, economic forces are all subordinated to this one overriding concern. Human obedience and divine intervention preoccupied the prophets who told the story. Where is God leading the Nephites? Will he help Nephi get the plates of Laban? Will Laman and Lemuel repent? Will God protect the Nephites on the voyage? Will they serve him in the new land? The prophets are most interested in what God does for his people and their willingness in turn to serve him. All events take on meaning as they show God's power or as they depict people coming to him or falling away. The excitement of the story often lies in finding out what God will do next or how the people will respond. As would be expected of prophet-historians who had experienced God's glory, the fundamental axis of every story stretches between earth and heaven.

Presumably Mormon historians today might concentrate on the same relationship. Just as the concerns of the Progressive Era led its historians to focus on economic forces, our concerns interest us in God. Nothing could be of more lasting importance. As we examine our best selves in moments of faith, God's presence seems to fill our consciousness and seems to be the ultimate source of meaning in life. Inevitably, we must ask how God has shaped human experience generally, just as the historians overawed by industrialization and business power asked how economic forces affected the past.

Admittedly, we are not as gifted as the prophets in discerning the hand of God or even the consequences of sin. Who can say where he intervened in the lives of Charlemagne or Napoleon or even in the formation of the Constitution? Belief in God is not a simple guide to relevant history. But our faith certainly compels us to search for God as best we can, and the scriptures suggest some avenues to follow. We know from our doctrine that God enters history in various ways: revelation to the prophets, providential direction of peoples and nations, and inspiration through the Spirit of Christ to all men and women. Each of these offers an interpretive structure that puts God to the fore and suggests a strategy for the Mormon historian. Someone someday may work out more systematically the implications of each of these perspectives and perhaps even approach a Mormon philosophy of history. But even on first inspection some of the possibilities—and problems—can be seen.

1. Revelation to the Prophets. We are most certain of divine intervention when the prophets, whose judgment we trust, tell us God has spoken or acted. The most obvious subject for Mormon historians is the history of the Church, the story of God's revelation to his people and the implementation of his will on the earth. Mormons are drawn to their own past not merely out of ethnocentrism, but because they see it as part of the Lord's work.

Faith in the revelations does not, however, determine how the story is told, not even its basic structure. The fundamental dramatic tension can be between the Church and the world, or it can be between God and the Church. In the first, the Lord establishes his kingdom on earth, and the Saints struggle to perform his work against the opposition of a wicked world. Joseph Fielding Smith's *Essentials in Church History* rests on this structure.[4] In the second, the Lord tries to establish his kingdom, but the stubborn people whom he favors with revelation ignore him much of the time and must be brought up short. I know of no modern Mormon who has written in this vein, but it is common in the Bible and the Book of Mormon. The prophets mourn the declension of faith within the Church itself more than they laud the righteousness of the Saints. In the first, the Saints are heroes and the world, villains. In the second, the world is wicked, but so are the Saints much of the time.

Unfortunately, the polarization between Mormon and anti-Mormon has foreclosed this latter kind of history for the time being. Virtually everyone who has shown the "human side" of the Church and its leaders has believed the enterprise was strictly human. To defend the faith, Mormon historians have thought they must prove the Church to be inhumanly righteous. We need historians who will mourn the failings of the Saints out of honor for God instead of relishing the warts because they show the Church was earthbound after all.

However we write our own story, we cannot, of course, content ourselves with the history of the Church because, statistically speaking, it is such a small part of world history. We must find some way of bringing a larger portion of mankind within our field of vision. The most common device among Mormons for comprehending the whole of world history within the scope of revelation has been the concept of dispensation. The revelation of knowledge and the bestowal of priesthood power is seen as a pattern repeated through history to various people in many places. Usually an apostasy follows each dispensation of divine blessings so that history follows the path of an undulating curve. Each dispensation raises men toward God, and then they fall away, only to be lifted by the succeeding dispensation.

The archetype of this pattern was the "Great Apostasy," from the dispensation of Christ to the restoration of the primitive Church through Joseph Smith. B. H. Roberts and James Talmage have most vividly explicated this period of history for Mormons with the liberal assistance of Protestant scholars, who were equally committed to belief in the apostasy of the Roman Church. (Indeed, it would be interesting to know if Roberts, Talmage, or James Barker added anything to the findings of Protestant scholars.[5]) On this framework Mormons have hung the course of Western civilization since Christ. Milton Backman's *American Religions and the Rise of Mormonism* has filled in the picture with a more detailed account of the Protestant Reformation and the growth of tolerance in preparation for the Restoration.[6] Together these works tell of the Church's glory under the original Twelve, declension under Roman influence, upward movement with Protestantism and religious liberty, and climax in Joseph Smith and the Restoration.

Beyond this one period, the dispensation pattern is more difficult to apply because the scriptural and historical materials are much thinner.

Milton Hunter's *Gospel Through the Ages* briefly tells the whole story from Adam to the present, relying almost entirely on the scriptures.[7] But clearly the most significant advances in this area have been achieved by Hugh Nibley. Nibley's great innovation is to argue that the influence of revelation in the dispensation cycle does not end with apostasy. Revelation leaves its mark long after people cut themselves off from God. The Gnostics go on yearning for revelation and even counterfeiting it; medieval Christians envy the temple when temple ceremonies are long forgotten. In short, the structure and aspirations of uninspired religion are derived from the revealed religions from which they once sprang. Even in non-Christian ritual, remnants of the temple ceremony can be glimpsed.[8]

The dispensation pattern thus does not restrict itself to the people who figure in the scriptures. Revelation to the prophets more or less directly influenced vast portions of world civilization, perhaps all of it. A number of anthropologists today argue that rather than arising independently, civilization diffused from some cultural center in the Near East. Nibley, himself a diffusionist of a sort, seems to be hinting that a revelation started it all, and the divine original still shows up in the distorted worship of apostate religions.

I can only suggest the scope and richness of Nibley's thought. One certainly cannot accuse him of unduly narrowing the span of time or space which he encompasses. It will require teams of scholars to match his erudition in a large number of complex fields and to follow up on his insights. I hope the immensity of the task will not discourage the young scholars he has inspired. He very well may have opened up the most promising approach to a religiously oriented understanding of world history.

My only misgiving about this method is its limited sympathy. Nibley's gospel framework may brilliantly illuminate some aspects of a people's culture. The Gnostics' frenetic search for mysteries and ineffable experience makes sense when seen as a quest of recovery, an effort to regain the Holy Ghost. But at distant removes, the gospel frame may also distort a culture's values and purposes. The temple ceremonies may indeed have shaped the form of the Roman liturgy or of Icelandic sagas, but does not time alter a culture until it means something quite different to the people absorbed in it than was originally intended? Should we not be sensitive to what the mass means today as well as to the remnants of the ordinances from which it was derived? If nothing else, our love for all people as part of God's progeny should caution us against stuffing them into our own categories, however cosmically significant. At its best, Nibley's analysis would show the interplay of what a religion was originally and what history made of it.

Far the larger part of all the history written with an identifiable Mormon twist falls into these two categories: history of the Church or history of the dispensation cycle. The reason for this concentration is obvious. In both cases, the prophets tell us where God intervened. We do not have to rely on our own insight to make this most difficult of judgments. The revelations themselves guide us. The historian has only to work out the implications of divine action. God's part in the other forms of history I wish to discuss is far more conjectural, and historians have understandably shied away from them. Until we develop more-precise techniques, these categories will probably remain empty, mere theoretical possibilities.

2. **Providential Direction of Peoples and Nations.** The large plan of three scriptural histories falls into this division: the Old Testament, the Book of Mormon, and the Book of Ether. Day by day, the dramatic tension in all of the scriptures resembles that of the Book of Mormon: God acting and man responding. But the collection of small events in these three national histories is not a shapeless heap of successes and failures; they form a Providential pattern. Each of the peoples in these books was chosen by God, guided, chastised when they wandered, and eventually rejected— though not forever; ultimately the Lord will restore them (except for the people of Ether, who were obliterated).

This divinely supervised rise and fall is related to the dispensation cycle but stands above it as a pattern of its own. The history of a nation or people forms the next larger historical unit after the dispensation. It tells the whole story of a people, following the long curve of their history along the ups and downs of various dispensations and apostasies that occur within the larger cycle of national ascent and decline. Presumably this scriptural structure could guide scholarly study today as it did the work of Old Testament historians.

Practically speaking, the history of the Jews is the only area that will prove fruitful for the time being. The absence of non-scriptural sources compels us to rely mainly on the Book of Mormon for the history of Lehi's and Ether's people. So long as we are unable clearly to identify which of the pre-Columbian remains connect up with the Book of Mormon, we have no materials to enlarge the scriptural accounts. Not that we should neglect early American history; Mormons certainly should be involved. But as far as I know we are as yet a long way from writing Providential history of pre-Columbian America that would in any way add to the Book of Mormon. We simply have no way of telling where God intervened. We are less in the dark about the Jews. Scriptural events and non-scriptural sources have been connected at a number of points. We could write their history and that of their predecessors in the light of the concept of Providence. Doubtless that is partly the fascination of Cleon Skousen's ambitious works.[9] Certainly it is sufficient reason to attract serious Mormon scholarship.

But beyond the application to these two peoples, the scriptural model of Providential history raises questions for other nations. Does God have a plan for them as well? Does their history follow a Providential pattern? It seems to be a fact that all civilizations rise and fall much as Israel did. Could it be for similar reasons? Nibley discovered that the dispensation cycle could be enlarged to include many peoples; perhaps Providence also has a wider compass than we have imagined.

The possibility of broadening the scope of Providential governance leads us back to examine more carefully the causes of Israel's ascent and decline. The Old Testament leads one to believe that God rejected the Jews because the Jews rejected God. The tribes of Israel entered into a covenant at Sinai, and when they consistently refused to honor it, God's patience wore thin. Finally, he cast them aside. If that is all there is to it, Israel's case would apply only to covenanted nations. Egyptian and Hellenic civilization would be another matter entirely. Not having been chosen, they could not be rejected. Providence must govern them according to another plan, and the Old Testament does not tell us what that plan is.

Just possibly the Book of Mormon does. Much less is said there of the original covenant, and more of the righteousness of the people. The general impression one receives is that righteousness brought peace and prosperity, while war and misery came close on the heels of sin. The people of Lehi declined when they persistently broke the commandments. Their fate was less dependent on a personal quarrel with God than on refusal to comply with his laws. By extrapolation, righteous behavior and the well-being of a civilization may be linked in some lawful relationship among gentiles as well as among covenanted people. The historian who understood the laws well enough could explain the course of a nation's development just as Arnold Toynbee tried to do, except that divine principles would be seen to underlie events.

A simplistic form of such a history could model itself after David McClelland's study of the achievement motive.[10] McClelland worked out a measure of people's desire for concrete achievements and used it to assess the presence of this need in popular literature over the past two or three centuries. To his delight, the production of iron and steel, a rough indicator of economic growth, followed the ups and downs of the need-achievement curve. Presumably when people got worked up about getting things done, that desire ultimately got the economy to perking. A need for righteousness or for religion might yield similar results. Could it be when the level of pride goes up so does civil strife, or when a nation humbles itself it enjoys peace?

The difficulties of the program are obvious. How does one measure righteousness, and what kind of righteousness is most critical? And what are the historical consequences of goodness? Wealth? Peace? An artistic flowering? Military power? Imperial conquest? I doubt very much that the relationship will be the simple one that seemingly held for McClelland. However, it would be a mistake to give up on the scriptures as a source of historical understanding. We still might be able to derive a religious sociology and psychology from the Book of Mormon that would illuminate all national histories. We sense in our bones that virtue affects the quality of social life. The prophets have expressed the same sentiment rather emphatically. Can that insight be worked out in concrete historical instances? I think it deserves a try. We may not be able to plot the course of a people through all of their history as the scriptures do for Israel and as Toynbee does for his civilizations. But perhaps we can penetrate lesser events or epochs to show Providence at work governing the world by divine law.

    3. Inspiration Through the Spirit of Christ. Mormons have long entertained the vague belief that God was guiding all good men and women everywhere to various triumphs of the spirit in art and government and science. In general we have attributed the appearance of "the finer things" to the activity of the Spirit of Christ, thereby reconciling our gospel convictions with our commitment to middle-class American culture. I have no serious objection to this comforting belief so long as we do not fall prey to secularization of the worst sort—that is, to clothe worldly values in religion. But what I have in mind as a program of historical research has a different purpose than the sanctification of culture heroes.

    The program rests on two doctrines: spiritual death at the Fall and spiritual life through the light of Christ. The assumption is that our separation from God wounded us, and we desire to be healed. We are not whole without God, and we seek completion. The truest and only completely satisfying course is to yield to the Spirit of Christ, which God sends into the world in lieu of his own presence. Following that Spirit brings us eventually to the gospel and to God, where we enter once again into the rest of the Lord. But en route most humans are waylaid or deceived. They accept counterfeit gods, mere idols, and fruitlessly seek fulfillment in them. Rarely are individuals entirely defeated, for the Spirit continues to strive with man, and men as a whole, however badly misled for a time, will always back away from their false gods and start again on a more promising path. Thus the search is perpetual, driven by man's deepest need. In this sense, all of human history can be thought of as *heilige Geschichte,* a quest for salvation.

    The model for this mode of history, I must confess, is not the scriptures (though they too tell of the quest for salvation) but Reinhold Niebuhr's Gifford Lectures published as *The Nature and Destiny of Man.*[11] Niebuhr's categories were human finitude and divine infinitude. Man is limited and contingent but, because of a divine component, yearns to be infinite and free. His quest has taken two major forms, romantic and classical, which roughly correspond to emotion and reason, loss of self in the senses and exaltation through the mind. The romantics are Dionysians, giving themselves over to feeling and seeking union with the All through sense and emotion. Classical figures are Apollonians. They seek order and perfect control. The scientist is a classical man who tries to reduce all of life to laws of which he is perfectly certain and that afford complete control. Both the romantic and the classical styles are idols, Niebuhr argued, false and misleading efforts to be God, that eventually lead to tyranny and death. The only true way to reach the infinite is through worship, which permits men to reach God without claiming to be God themselves. I do not subscribe entirely to Niebuhr's categories, although they are immensely useful, but his model of incomplete man striving for completion does accord with the scriptural view of the human situation.

Furthermore, I find that the model works in historical research. I am currently studying religious and political thought in America in the early eighteenth century. Without forcing the issue, I see people in this period attempting two things in their ideological discourse. The first is to describe life as it should be. This generation was vexed by their own greed and contentiousness. The self was forever getting in the way, venting bitter and rancorous emotions, or pursuing its private interests at the expense of the whole. These people yearned for peace and union, ways of keeping the self in check or of giving themselves to noble causes that would make them forget self. Union, tranquillity, peace, harmony were among their most prominent values, and these, I think, represent in some way a response to the Spirit of Christ, a form of the desire for the rest of the Lord.

The second quest is for moral justification. We yearn to prove ourselves right, that is, to reconcile what we are with what we think we should be. I am willing to work on the assumption that conscience is somehow related to the Spirit of Christ. Warped as moral standards sometimes appear to be, usually we find behind the specific standards of behavior an intention we can recognize as admirable in our own terms. What I am arguing is that conscience is not entirely relative, though in detail it varies immensely. And that when we find men justifying themselves or setting standards for others, we see them wrestling with the influence of heaven. These eighteenth-century figures, living as they did in a rapidly expanding society, were forever contending with one another and following naked self-interest in contradiction to what they believed ought to be. Their tortured efforts to justify their actions open a window on an authentic religious struggle.

All of this becomes interesting historically when we see various ideals, sometimes disparate ones, working against a reality that drives people to fight with themselves. The ideals and the actual situation create a dynamic interplay that goes far to explain specific events and to account for changes in ideology. In eighteenth-century America, the ideal of harmony and the reality of conflict moved people toward a new view of the social order that envisioned life as compartmentalized, each person secluded and safe within the bounds of his own rights—in short, an order more like our present pluralistic society. That minimized contention and unleashed ambition, but it also separated men from each other and required another ideal to give moral significance to life: the free individual progressing toward his own destiny. Nineteenth-century Americans sought their salvation by pursuing that ideal.

Again without forcing the issue, I am convinced that we require a moral setting for our lives. We want to measure ourselves against some ideal standard, however grotesque, inarticulate, or irrational it may be. Life has to have purpose and meaning, to operate within a structure that describes existence as it should be and permits people to justify their exertions by some standard outside themselves. In some respects, these moral frameworks are godly, and rightly attributed to the Spirit of Christ. They seem to be among the chief means by which people undertake to save themselves.

The advantage of the history of salvation (or man's attempt at it) over the history of revelation or the history of Providence, the two other categories I have discussed, is that the first applies to all people and permits, even demands, full sympathy with them. There is no danger of narrowness, which is inherent in concentration on the locus of revelation or on the vicissitudes of covenanted nations. Its disadvantage is that it may blend imperceptibly with secular history. I confessed my indebtedness to Niebuhr, no Mormon, though a Christian. At the moment I am impressed with the work of Carl Schorske, who has no religious convictions at all so far as I know. If these men write history as I aspire to write it, can I still claim to be working out of a Mormon heritage in response to the self I encounter in moments of faith?

IV

The query brings me to my final point, one I touched on when I said we will know what Mormon history is only when Mormons write it. There is a paradox in the very discussion of the subject of Mormons writing history. On the one hand, I wish to encourage Mormon historians, like Mormon psychologists and Mormon physicians, to think about the relationship of their faith and their professional practice. We are still too much merely Sunday Christians. On the other hand, I do not wish my categories to be thought of as prescriptive. I think it would be a mistake to set out to prove that nations rise and fall according to principles of righteousness outlined in the Book of Mormon. The outcome would probably be no more convincing than the books that try to show principles of psychoanalysis governing novels. Such works always seem stilted, forced, and artificial. You feel the author was trying to prove an ideological point rather than tell you what he thinks actually happened.

Scriptural principles will guide us toward more powerful works of history only when those principles are fully and naturally incorporated into our ways of thinking, so that when we look at the world we see it in these categories without lying to ourselves or neglecting any of the evidence. We must believe in our framework as sincerely as the Progressive historians believed in economic forces or as any of our secular contemporaries believe in their theories of motivation or social change. It must be part of us, so much so that we will not consciously write as Mormons, but simply as men who love God and are coming to see the world as he does.

Thus it is that my history of the eighteenth century as a quest for salvation may indeed partake of secular strains of thought. But I also know that for me it is religious as well. It is faithful history. As I look at the world in my best moments, this is how I see it. I am not lying to any part of myself, neither the part that prays nor that which interprets documents. If I am still the victim of secularism, the recourse is not to a more obviously Mormon approach but to repentance. Merely altering technique or a few ideas will not make the difference. My entire character, all the things that shape my vision of the world, must change.

The trouble with wishing to write history as a Mormon is that you cannot improve as a historian without improving as a person. The enlargement of moral insight, spiritual commitment, and critical intelligence are all bound together. We gain knowledge no faster than we are saved.

NOTES

1. Charles A. Beard, *An Economic Interpretation of the Constitution of the United States* (New York: Macmillan, 1913).

2. For an analysis of Beard's work and its intellectual milieu, see Richard Hofstadter, *The Progressive Historians: Turner, Beard, Parrington* (New York: Alfred A. Knopf, 1968), chaps. 1, 5–8.

3. The questions I raise are explored more fully in E. H. Carr, *What Is History?* (New York: St. Martin's, 1961).

4. Joseph Fielding Smith, *Essentials in Church History: A History of the Church from the Birth of Joseph Smith to the Present Time* (Salt Lake City: The Church of Jesus Christ of Latter-day Saints, 1922).

5. B. H. Roberts, *The "Falling Away": Or, the World's Loss of the Christian Religion and Church* (Salt Lake City: Deseret Book, 1931); James E. Talmage, *The Great Apostasy Considered in the Light of Scriptural and Secular History* (Salt Lake City: Deseret News, 1909); James L. Barker, *Apostasy from the Divine Church* (Salt Lake City: Kate Montgomery Barker, 1960).

6. Milton V. Backman Jr., *American Religions and the Rise of Mormonism* (Salt Lake City: Deseret Book, 1965).

7. Milton R. Hunter, *The Gospel Through the Ages* (Salt Lake City: Stevens and Wallis, 1945).

8. Nibley's articles in Church and secular journals, as well as his books, are listed in Louis Midgley, "Hugh Nibley: A Short Bibliographical Note," *Dialogue: A Journal of Mormon Thought* 2 (spring 1967): 119–21.

9. W. Cleon Skousen, *The First 2000 Years* (Salt Lake City: Bookcraft, 1953); *The Third Thousand Years* (Salt Lake City: Bookcraft, 1964); *The Fourth Thousand Years* (Salt Lake City: Bookcraft, 1966); *Fantastic Victory: Israel's Rendezvous with Destiny* (Salt Lake City: Bookcraft, 1967).

10. David C. McClelland, *The Achieving Society* (Princeton, N.J.: Van Nostrand, 1961).

11. Reinhold Niebuhr, *The Nature and Destiny of Man: A Christian Interpretation*, 2 vols. (New York: C. Scribner's Sons, 1941–43).

2

My Belief

Like so many of the essays in this volume, "My Belief" was written in response to a request. Phil Barlow, a Latter-day Saint whom I came to know while he was studying at Harvard Divinity School, wanted to publish the thoughts of Latter-day Saint academics on the reasons for their faith. By the time he came to me, I had stabilized my belief, and turning the struggle into a story for Barlow's book helped me gain control over questions that had been on my mind since my first Harvard years.

The essay has been surprisingly useful in talking to people about religious belief. I have given offprints to dozens of people. I think Mormons like the essay because it acknowledges the existence of doubt in Mormon lives. Many people wrestle with unbelief while remaining true to the Church. They are happy to know their uncertainties do not disqualify them. The essay offers hope that resolution can come in time.

When I was growing up in Portland, Oregon, in the 1930s and 1940s, I always thought of myself as a believing Latter-day Saint. My parents were believers; even when they were not attending church regularly, they still believed. All of my relatives were Latter-day Saints and, so far as I could tell, accepted the gospel like eating and drinking, as a given of life. In Sunday School I tried to be good. I answered the teachers' questions and gave talks that brought compliments from the congregation. From the outside, my behavior probably looked like the conventional compliance of a good boy. But it went deeper than mere appearance. I prayed faithfully every night, and whenever there was a crisis I immediately thought of God. I relied on my religion to redeem me. I often felt silly or weak, and it was through prayer and religious meditation that I mustered my forces to keep on trying. As a sophomore and junior in high school, I was a thoroughbred wallflower, at least as I remember it now, with no close friends. At lunchtime, I often ate all by myself because no one noticed me, and I had no idea how to insinuate myself into a circle of people. At the end of my junior year, a Mormon friend in the class beyond mine said it was my obligation, for the honor of the Church, to run for student-body president. One thing I had learned in church was to speak, and a good speech could win an election. I prayed that God would help me for the sake of the

Church, got my speech together, and was elected. That made redemption very real.

Partly because of the student government responsibilities that fell to me as a senior, I was admitted to Harvard and left my family and Portland for Cambridge in the fall of 1949 (fig. 1). I loved everything about Harvard—the people, the studies, the atmosphere. I was more myself there than I had ever been in my whole life. Harvard helped redeem me, too, but it also eroded my faith in God. I went to church regularly and made good friends with Latter-day Saint graduate students, a faculty member or two, and the small circle of Mormon undergraduates.

Courtesy Claudia Lauper Bushman

FIG. 1. Richard Lyman Bushman as a Harvard undergraduate.

The undergraduates met Sunday afternoons to discuss the scriptures. We debated everything about religion, but we all were believers. I do not know why it was that by the end of my sophomore year my faith had drained away. Logical positivism was at a high tide in those days, trying to persuade us that sensory evidence was the only trustworthy foundation for belief. At the end of my freshman year, I wrote a paper comparing Freud and Nietzsche and confronted the assertion that Christian morality is the ideology of servile personalities who fear to express their own deepest urges. Up until then I had prided myself on being a servant of God. Was I also servile? These ideas and perhaps the constant strain of being on the defensive for believing at all must have eaten away at my belief. The issue in my mind never had anything to do with Latter-day Saint doctrine specifically. I was not bothered by the arguments against the institutional Church, which so trouble people today, or the problems of Mormon history, another current sore spot. I was not debating Mormonism versus some other religion; the only question for me was God. Did he exist in any form or not? I was not worried about evil in the world, as some agnostics are. I suppose Mormon theology had made the existence of evil perfectly plausible. I simply wondered if there was any reason to believe. Was all of religion a fantasy? Were we all fooling ourselves?

These doubts came on strongest in the spring of my sophomore year. During the preceding Christmas holiday, I had been interviewed for a mission and received a call to New England, to serve under the mission president who attended the same sacrament meeting as the students in Cambridge.

Did I have enough faith to go on a mission? I debated the question through the spring, wondering if I were a hypocrite and if fear of displeasing my parents was all that carried me along. And yet I never really considered not going. It may be, I think looking back, that my agnosticism was a little bit of a pose, a touch of stylish undergraduate angst. It was true enough that my bosom did not burn with faith; on the other hand, I was quite willing to pledge two years to a mission. So I went.

The mission president was J. Howard Maughan, an agricultural professor from Utah State and former stake president (fig. 2). In our opening interview in the mission home in Cambridge, he asked if I had a testimony of the gospel. I said I did not. He was not at all rattled. He asked if I would read a book, and, if I found a better explanation for it than the book itself gave, to report it to him. Then he handed me the Book of Mormon. The next day I left North Station in Boston for Halifax, Nova Scotia. For the next three months, while trying to learn the lessons and the usual missionary discipline, I wrestled with the book and wrote long entries in my journal. I thought a lot about the Three Witnesses: Were they liars? Had they been hypnotized? Were they pressured? I believe it was at that time I read Hugh Nibley's *Lehi in the Desert*.[1]

I also read the Book of Mormon and prayed, sometimes in agnostic form— "if you are God. . . ." After three months, President Maughan came up for a conference, and when it was my turn to speak, I said with conviction that I knew the Book of Mormon was right. The reasons that I had concocted for believing were not the difference—though Nibley made a great impression. It was more the simple feeling that the book was right.

The mission left me with another impression. At Harvard in those days we talked a lot about the masses, envisioning a sea of workers' faces marching into a factory. Tracting in Halifax, we missionaries met the masses

Courtesy Claudia Lauper Bushman

FIG. 2. J. Howard Maughan (1893–1976). Maughan directed several hundred missionaries during his volunteer tenure (1951–55) as president of the New England Mission. Here he stands in front of the mission headquarters, in Cambridge, Massachusetts, with three former missionaries. *Left to right*: Don Lind, James Sandmire, J. Howard Maughan, and Richard Lyman Bushman.

every day, and they did not exist. There were a great number of individual persons, quite idiosyncratic, perverse, and interesting. They were no more a mass than the Harvard faculty or the United States Congress. That realization planted a seed of doubt about formal conceptions. Did they conform to the reality of actual experience? After the mission, I never again felt that the issues debated in the academy were necessarily the issues of real life. This skepticism grew, especially after I entered graduate school in history and learned how formulations of the past had continually altered, each generation of historians overturning the conceptions of its predecessors and making new ones for itself. Rational discourse came more and more to seem like a kind of play, always a little capricious and unreal—and in the end, compared to the experience of life itself, not serious. To confuse intellectual constructions with reality, or to govern one's life by philosophy or an abstract system came to seem more and more foolhardy. My attitude as it developed was not precisely anti-intellectual. Ideas did not strike me as dangerous; they were too weak to be dangerous. I was depreciating intellectual activity rather than decrying it. But whatever the proper label for this attitude, it put distance between me and the intellectuals whom I so admired and whom, as it later turned out, I would aspire to emulate.

Paradoxically, in my own intellectual endeavors, I have benefited from this skepticism engendered in the mission field, for it has led me to trust my own perceptions and experience over the convictions of my fellow historians, considered individually or *en masse*. I have always thought it possible that virtually anything taught and believed in the academy could be wrong. Repudiation of God by every intellectual in creation did not mean God was nonexistent. By the same token, any of the certainties of historical interpretation could be perfect errors. However fallible I might be myself, however much subject to influences and illusions, I had to trust my own perceptions above everything else.

After I returned from the mission field, I no longer had doubts, but I did have questions. They were not specific questions about the meaning or validity of specific doctrines, the wholesome kind of questions that enlarge understanding. They were the questions of some unknown interlocutor who asked me to justify my faith. "Why do you believe?" the masked stranger asked. This was the old question of my sophomore year, asked now, however, of one who did believe, who had faith and was being called upon to justify it. I suppose there was nothing complicated about the questioning. At Harvard I studied in the midst of people who made a business of defending their convictions. It was an unwritten rule that you must explain why you took a position or supported a proposition. "Why do you believe in God?" was a question that all of Harvard whispered in one's ears without prompting from any skeptical inquisitors. In fact, when I returned to Harvard in 1953, the religious atmosphere was much more favorable to believers. The president, Nathan Pusey, was himself a believing person, and he had seen to the hiring of Paul Tillich as a university professor and to the rejuvenation of the Divinity School. Even the agnostics listened respectfully to Tillich, and undergraduates talked more freely of their religious convictions. In my senior year, I headed a committee sponsored by the student council on "Religion at Harvard," and our poll of undergraduates turned up a majority who said they had a religious orientation toward life. Even so, the mood did not quiet my faceless questioner. I still wanted to justify my convictions.

How those questionings came to an end is beyond my powers of explanation. For an undergraduate reader today, still fired by fierce doubts and a desperate need to know for sure, one word may seem to explain all—complacency. But I myself do not feel that way. My questions have not simply grown dim over the years, nor have I answered them; instead, I have come to understand questions and answers differently. Although I cannot say what truly made the difference, a series of specific experiences, small insights, revelations, new ideas, all addressing the same issue and coming over a period of thirty years, have caused me to change my views. I now have a new sense of what constitutes belief.

For a long time, twenty-five years or more, I went on trying to answer the questioner. I received little help from religious philosophers. The traditional proofs for God never made an impression on me. I did not find flaws in them; they simply seemed irrelevant. My empirical temperament and suspicion of grand systems worked against any enthusiasm for arguments about a prime mover. I never studied those arguments or made the slightest effort to make them my own. My chief line of reasoning was based on the Book of Mormon. It was concrete and real and seemed like a foundation for belief, not merely belief in Joseph Smith but in Christ and God. Joseph Smith and Mormonism, as I said before, were never the issues; it was God primarily. Although it was a lengthy chain from the historicity of the Book of Mormon, to Joseph's revelations, to the existence of God, it was a chain that held for me. I felt satisfied that, if that book were true, my position was sound. Without it, I do not know where I would be. I have imagined myself as a religious agnostic were it not for the Book of Mormon. That is why Hugh Nibley's writings played a large part in my thinking. Although I recognized the eccentricities of his style and was never completely confident of his scholarship, there seemed to me enough there to make a case. 1 Nephi could not be dismissed as fraudulent, and so far as I know no one has refuted the argument Nibley made in *Lehi in the Desert*. He offered just the kind of evidence I was looking for in my pursuit of answers: evidence that was specific, empirical, historical.

Nibley's style was important enough that I made one attempt myself to prove the Book of Mormon in the Nibleyesque manner, and this effort came about in such a way as to confirm my belief. When I was asked to give some talks in Utah during the bicentennial of the American Revolution, I decided to examine the political principles embodied in the Book of Mormon and make some application to our Revolution and Constitution. I thought this would be simple enough because of the switch from monarchy to a republic during the reign of Mosiah. I was sure that somewhere in Mosiah's statements I would find ideas relevant to the modern world. With that in mind, I accepted the invitation to talk, but not until a few months before I was to appear did I get down to work. To my dismay I could not find what I was looking for. Everything seemed just off the point, confused and baffling. I could not find the directions for a sound republic that I had expected. Gradually it dawned on me that the very absence of republican statements might in itself be interesting. I long ago learned that it is better to flow with the evidence than to compel compliance with one's preformed ideas. So I asked, instead, what does the Book of Mormon say about politics? To my surprise, I discovered it was quite an unrepublican book. Not only was Nephi a king, and monarchy presented as the ideal government in an ideal world, but the supposedly republican government instituted under Mosiah did not function that way at all. There was no elected legislature, and the chief judges usually inherited their office rather than being chosen for it. Eventually I came to see that here was my chance to emulate Nibley. If Joseph Smith was suffused with republican ideas, as I was confident he was, then the absence of such sentiments in Nephite society was peculiar, another evidence that he did not write the Book of Mormon. Eventually, all of this came together in an article, "The Book of Mormon and the American Revolution," published in *BYU Studies* in 1976.[2]

While circumstances and my predilection to justify belief influenced me up to that point and beyond, my commitment to this kind of endeavor gradually weakened. Perhaps most influential was a gradual merger of personality and belief. By 1976 I had been a branch president and a bishop and was then a stake president. Those offices required me to give blessings in the name of God and to seek solutions to difficult problems nearly every day. I usually felt entirely inadequate to the demands placed upon me and could not function at all without some measure of inspiration. What I did, the way I acted, my inner thoughts, were all intermingled with this effort to speak and act religiously for God. I could no longer entertain the possibility that God did not exist, because I felt his power working through me. Sometimes I toyed with the notion that there could be other ways of describing what happened when I felt inspired, but the only language that actually worked, the only ideas that brought inspiration and did justice to the experience when it came were the words in the scriptures. Only when I thought of God as a person interested in me and asked for help as a member of Christ's kingdom did idea and reality fit properly. Only that language properly honored the experience I had day after day in my callings.

Church work more than anything else probably quieted my old questions, but there were certain moments when these cumulative experiences precipitated new ideas. Once in the early 1960s, while I held a postdoctoral fellowship at Brown University and was visiting Cambridge, I happened into a young adult discussion, led, I believe, by Terry Warner. He had the group read the Grand Inquisitor passage in *The Brothers Karamazov*. The sentences that stuck with me that time through were the ones having to do with wanting to find reasons for belief that would convince the whole world and compel everyone to believe. That was the wish of the Grand Inquisitor, a wish implicitly repudiated by Christ. The obvious fact that there is no convincing everyone that a religious idea is true came home strongly at that moment. It is impossible and arrogant, and yet that was exactly what I was attempting. When I sought to justify my belief, I was looking for answers that would persuade all reasonable men. That was why I liked Nibley: he put his readers over a barrel. I wanted something that no one could deny. In that moment in Cambridge, I realized the futility of the quest.

I was moved still further in this direction by a lecture Neal Maxwell invited me to give at Brigham Young University in 1974 as part of the Commissioner's Lecture Series. I cannot for the life of me recall why I turned to the topic of "Joseph Smith and Skepticism," but that was the subject.[3] In that lecture I sketched in the massive effort to demonstrate rationally the authenticity of the Christian revelation. The effort began in the early eighteenth century, when Deism first took hold in earnest, and continued through the nineteenth century. The Christian rationalists assembled all the evidence they could muster to prove that biblical miracles, such as the parting of the Red Sea, were authentic and therefore evidence of God's endorsement of Israel. In the course of the nineteenth century, as agnosticism waxed strong among intellectuals, the volumes on Christian evidences proliferated. I can still remember sitting on the floor in the basement of the Harvard Divinity School library, flipping through these books, each one almost exactly like the others. I realized then that the tradition of seeking proof was very strong in the nineteenth century and that Mormons had been influenced by it. B. H. Roberts, a man troubled by questions as I had been and a great apologist for the Latter-day Saint faith, borrowed these methods. His *A New Witness for God* was a replica of the books in the Harvard Divinity School basement, except with Mormon examples and conclusions.[4] Hugh Nibley dropped the nineteenth-century format for works of Christian evidences, but his mode of reasoning was basically the same.

Awareness of the affinity of Nibley with these Protestant works did not dilute my own interest in evidences. The study of Book of Mormon republicanism, my own contribution to the genre, came along two years later. But the contradictions were taking shape in my mind and readied me, I suppose, for a personal paradigmatic shift. It occurred in the early 1980s at the University of Indiana. Stephen Stein of the religion department had some Lilly Endowment money to assemble scholars and religious leaders from various denominations to discuss their beliefs. With Jan Shipps's help, he brought together a handful of Mormon historians, some historians of American religion, a local stake president, a regional representative, and a seminary teacher. The topic was Joseph Smith. The historians among us made some opening comments about the Prophet, and then over a day and a half we discussed the issues that emerged. It was a revelatory assemblage from my point of view because it brought together in one room representatives of the various groups involved in my religious life—Church leaders, non-Mormon scholars, and Mormon scholars. Although all of these people had been represented in my mind symbolically before, they had never been together in person before my face, talking about Joseph Smith.

Their presence brought together notions that previously had been floating about separately in my head. Sometime in the middle of the conversations, it came to me in a flash that I did not want to prove the authenticity of Joseph Smith's calling to anyone. I did not want to wrestle Stephen Stein to the mat and make him cry "uncle." It was a false position, at least for me, and one that I doubted would have any long-range good results. I recognized then that the pursuit of Christian evidences was not a Mormon tradition; it was a borrowing from Protestantism and not at a moment when Protestantism was at one of its high points. At any rate, it was not my tradition, and I did not want to participate in it. There was no proving religion to anyone; belief came by other means, by hearing testimonies or by individual pursuit or by the grace of God, but not by hammering.

By the time of the conference, I had completed the manuscript of *Joseph Smith and the Beginnings of Mormonism.*[5] The Book of Mormon chapter in that book hammered at readers. My urge had been to show that the common secular explanations of the Book of Mormon were in error and to imply, if not to insist, that only a divine explanation would do. In the revision, I tried without complete success to moderate the tone. I did not wish to dissipate the basic argument, which is that the counterexplanations are inadequate to the complexity of the book, but I sincerely did not want to push readers into a corner and force them to come out fighting. The desire to compel belief, the wish of the Grand Inquisitor, was exactly what I had abandoned.

At the present moment, the question of why I believe no longer has meaning for me (fig. 3). I do not ask it of myself or attempt to give my reasons to others. The fact is that I do believe. That is a given of my nature, and whatever reasons I might give would be insufficient and inaccurate. More relevant to my current condition is a related question: How do

Courtesy Claudia Lauper Bushman

FIG. 3. Richard Lyman Bushman.

others come to believe? I would like to know if there is anything I can do that will draw people to faith in Christ and in the priesthood. My answer to this question is, of course, related to my personal experiences. I no longer think that people can be compelled to believe by any form of reasoning, whether from the scriptures or from historical evidence. They will believe if it is in their natures to believe. All I can do is to attempt to bring forward the believing nature, smothered as it is in most people by the other natures that culture forms in us. The first responsibility is to tell the story, to say very simply what happened, so that knowledge of those events can do its work. But that is the easy part, the part that could be done by books or television. The hard part is to create an atmosphere where the spiritual nature, the deep-down goodness in the person, can react to the story honestly and directly. Some people can create that atmosphere quite easily by the very strength of their own spiritual personalities. It is hard for me. There are too many other natures in me: the vain aspirer formed in childhood, the intellectual fostered at Harvard, the would-be dominant male created by who knows what. But I do believe that when I am none of these and instead am a humble follower of Christ who tells the story without pretense to friends whom I love and respect, then they will believe if they want to, and conversion is possible. Questions may be answered and reasons given, but these are peripheral and essentially irrelevant. What is essential is for a person to listen carefully and openly in an attitude of trust. If belief is to be formed in the human mind, it will, I think, be formed that way.

NOTES

1. Hugh Nibley, *Lehi in the Desert and The World of the Jaredites* (Salt Lake City: Bookcraft, 1952). The book was composed of articles that ran in the *Improvement Era* from 1948 to 1952.

2. Richard L. Bushman, "The Book of Mormon and the American Revolution," *BYU Studies* 17 (autumn 1976): 3–20. The essay is reprinted in chapter 5 below.

3. The essay is reprinted in chapter 10 below.

4. B. H. Roberts, *A New Witness for God* (Salt Lake City: George Q. Cannon and Sons, 1895).

5. Published as Richard L. Bushman, *Joseph Smith and the Beginnings of Mormonism* (Urbana: University of Illinois Press, 1984).

3

Learning to Believe

The invitation to deliver the summer 1991 commencement address at Brigham Young University presented an opportunity to offer my opinions on open discussion at an LDS university. I have long been aware of the tension between classic academic freedom doctrines and the imperatives of belief. The Church has the responsibility of preserving faith, while intellectual culture thrives on questioning. How the two contradictory cultures cohabit at BYU is a miracle in itself.

I have always believed that the BYU faculty's chief responsibility is to emphasize faith, not to suppress doubt. Faith has to overcome doubt not by censoring, but by strengthening itself. This means we cannot shield students from conflicting opinions. We have to trust young people to find belief just as their teachers have done. Sheltering students in college only weakens them for the blasts they will encounter after graduation.

As I prepared the address, I kept thinking of Elder Boyd K. Packer's frequent counsel for Latter-day Saints to seek individual inspiration from God. Students have to find their way to faith through personal inspiration rather than by closing their minds.

We call the occasion of our meeting today a commencement to recognize the new lives you are about to begin. You are scattering in a thousand directions and within a short time will be caught up in new worlds, some of them far from here and quite different from the lives you have known in Provo. But beginnings must also be endings, and today you are ending something, too. You are ending your lives as students, leaving familiar places, good friends, and a particular kind of community, the community of scholars. My thoughts on this occasion might better be called an ending rather than a commencement address, for I wish to ask what it means to have been a member of the community of scholars. How will your time at BYU affect the new lives you are beginning today?

College teachers are sometimes criticized for trying to make little scholars of undergraduates when very few of you will go on to become academics. But in my opinion that is precisely what we should do: make scholars of you. For the time you are at the university, we should try to involve you in the scholarly life. Students should sense the immense pleasure of pursuing knowledge and know its pride, its rigor, its confusion, and its reassurances. If your education has been successful, you have been scholars. While scrambling for grades to make a good record, you now and then felt the pure happiness of knowing something exactly and truly, and in those moments you were scholars.

Now you are leaving us, and what will become of you? Many of you are Latter-day Saints, as I am, and during your sojourn among the scholars, you may also have experienced the ambivalence of the scholarly life. Is scholarship good from an eternal perspective, or is it bad? "To be learned is good," the scriptures say, "if . . ." (2 Ne. 9:29). There is an *if* in the passage. Scholarship is not endorsed unconditionally. There are reservations and uncertainties and, in fact, dangers. "When they are learned they think they are wise, and they hearken not unto the counsel of God, for they set it aside, supposing they know of themselves, wherefore, their wisdom is foolishness and it profiteth them not. And they shall perish." (2 Ne. 9:28–29) These hazards of learning are part of the life of your teachers, and in joining us for the past few years you have been exposed to the same dangers. In this respect you will not leave us. For you have eaten of the apple and gained knowledge and henceforth will never be entirely out of jeopardy, never entirely free from the dangers of scholarship. These hazards are what I wish to talk about today.

From one point of view, no modern religion more warmly supports learning than the Latter-day Saints. It would be difficult to match the classic scriptures: "Seek ye out of the best books words of wisdom; seek learning, even by study and also by faith" (D&C 88:118). "Study and learn, and become acquainted with all good books, and with languages, tongues, and people" (D&C 90:15). In some places, we sense a ravenous hunger for knowledge in Joseph Smith. In the midst of the Saints' poor and arduous beginnings, he organized schools and universities and spent days and days in the classroom himself. Learning was given the best possible endorsement in the scriptures and in Joseph's life: it was made part of God's work.

Those first seeds have borne fruit in our culture. The passages on learning are not empty words. Years ago when I was teaching at BYU, Kenneth Hardy, a psychologist on the faculty, reported research on the impact of cultural values on educational achievement. Researchers who studied undergraduate colleges to determine which produced the most Ph.D.'s found that certain factors such as the academic ability of the student body and field of study predicted most of the achievement, just as you would expect. Colleges that admitted students with the highest academic talent produced the most Ph.D.'s. However, there were two clusters of colleges that produced far more high achievers than predicted. The two groups were four New York City colleges with large Jewish populations and three Utah universities with heavily Mormon populations. In these institutions, the researchers concluded, particular cultural values motivated people to pursue scholarship. The implication was, of course, that Mormon culture, like Jewish culture, inspires people to learn.[1]

Shortly after this study was completed, David McClelland, the distinguished Harvard psychologist, visited BYU, and the author of the article mentioned his findings. How would McClelland account for these unforeseen results? McClelland said that it was obvious to him. In essence he said, "You think it is your responsibility to save the world. That's what makes you want to learn." Strangely enough, that is what Joseph Smith said, too. We are to learn, not to rise to fame and glory, but to carry forward our mission of saving the world.

I observe the Mormon heartland from a safe distance on the eastern seaboard. But even there I am aware of the impact of Mormon educational values on our young people. During the bicentennial of the Revolutionary War in 1976, the Mormon Tabernacle Choir toured the East and visited Boston. I was then teaching at Boston University, and Chase Peterson (then dean of admissions at Harvard and a fellow member of the Church) and I decided we would invite John Silber, the illustrious and controversial president of Boston University, to the concert. Silber had spoken at BYU and knew quite a few Latter-day Saints. At the dinner before the concert, Silber turned to my wife, Claudia, and asked, "When are you going to send the missionaries?" Jaws dropped around the table, and Silber, who loves the dramatic effect, went on to say, "When are you going to send the missionaries to Boston University?" What our student body needs, he said, is an influential core of returned missionaries. My wife, never at a loss for words, replied, "When are you going to set up a scholarship fund for them?" Then it was his turn to drop the jaw (fig. 1).

Courtesy Claudia Lauper Bushman

We have had the same experience at Columbia. The associate dean of the law school became aware of the twenty or thirty Latter-day Saints at

FIG. 1. Claudia Lauper Bushman and Richard Lyman Bushman, ca. 1989.

Columbia Law School, many of them BYU graduates, and asked our stake president, a member of the Columbia law faculty, to help him recruit more. Now the same man is dean of Columbia College and has asked Claudia and me to help recruit LDS undergraduates. When asked why he wants Mormons, he said because they are so "centered."

I think the fact is that Latter-day Saints, apart from any native ability, do well in educational settings. They are clearheaded, they work hard, and they value learning. All of that comes from our culture. And you, the latest generation of graduates, must, and most certainly will, carry it on—simply because you are Latter-day Saints. It is your heritage and your destiny.

All of this is on the positive side of learning. Here we see learning and our faith coming together as the scriptures say they should. On the negative side are the hazards where learning and faith part company or go to war. Not everything in scholarship sustains our faith or wears a godly countenance. Those of us who live in the community of scholars do not experience it as a community of belief. While there are numerous individual believers among scholars, the mien of scholarship, its public countenance, is agnostic. It does not profess belief in God and is in fact ostensibly godless.

A few years ago, an editor at *Life* magazine conceived of a volume devoted to the meaning of life. He asked people from many fields and vocations to sum up in a hundred words their understanding of the meaning of life. The contributors were not a cross-section of the population. They asked a few religious people like me to contribute, but mainly they were notables of one sort or another—scientists, entertainers, novelists, philosophers, artists. When the book came out, I was surprised at how little faith I found in the statements. A few respondents said there was no meaning to life; a person just lived it. Others found meaning but mainly in some kind of harmony—with other people or with nature. Very few mentioned anything that bore a resemblance to the God that we know.[2]

The book made me realize how little faith there is among the men and women who control our public culture—the writers, the media leaders, the intellectuals. However much the polls show everyday Americans professing belief in God, our cultural leaders do not profess that kind of faith. And that is true for scholars and teachers as well. A friend recently proposed a book of essays by believing historians about their faith and asked me to list possible contributors. I searched through the names of the hundreds of historians whom I know and could think of very few who, so far as I can tell, worship God.

We all live our lives in this prevailing atmosphere of unbelief, but scholars live that way more than most. From my undergraduate years at Harvard on, I have always felt myself to be a little bit of an outsider because of my belief. Not that I am not at home with my fellow scholars and do not love and admire many of them, but I recognize that my belief sets me apart in their eyes, that there is an intellectual quirk in my makeup that they do not understand.

Soon after I was hired at the University of Delaware, I went to lunch with one of the members of the search committee who had hired me for the new job. As we drove along, just to make conversation, I mentioned that I was working on a biography of the young Joseph Smith. Something must have clicked in his head, because he turned to me with a warm smile and said, "Dick, we took all that into account and decided it didn't matter."

I had a similar experience after writing the book. When I submitted the manuscript to Richard Wentworth at the University of Illinois Press, he received favorable readings from four or five scholars, but one reader, a key figure, thought the book was too sympathetic to Joseph Smith. After analyzing how the belief of the author shaped the work on every page, the reader finally concluded that the book should be published anyway. We publish books from the viewpoint of Marxists and homosexuals, he said; why not from a Mormon viewpoint?

We should not underestimate the influence of living in an atmosphere of unbelief such as this. Strong as we may be, the awareness of doubt and skepticism all around us will have its effect. I was an undergraduate in the heyday of logical positivism, the philosophical doctrine that only the experience of the senses provides a foundation for sound reasoning. As an undergraduate, I was deeply troubled by doubts and went into the mission field not at all sure the Church was true. When I returned I took a class on American intellectual history from Arthur Schlesinger Jr. Mark Cannon, a graduate student in government at the time, went to Schlesinger's lecture on Joseph Smith with me. Schlesinger began by saying that he knew that there were sensible people who believed in the Mormon religion—Ezra Taft Benson had just been appointed secretary of agriculture, and Schlesinger was made newly aware of Mormons in high places. But then he launched into his lecture with his classic smirk and was unrelenting in his sarcasm. As we walked from the lecture hall, Mark observed that at least Schlesinger got more laughs per minute from Joseph Smith than from any of the historical figures he discussed during the semester.

For years I felt that I had to answer these scholars. I had to come up with a reply to every doubt, every jibe, every question, every argument; and my own faith would not be secure until I did. I held imaginary dialogues with these people in an effort to subdue them. And I did find things to say in reply, for we have been given a great deal of concrete evidence for our beliefs. But in the end I recognized that I could not answer them all. There were far too many of them, and I could not win the doubters over anyway. Furthermore, it did not matter to me. I had to recognize a simple fact about myself. I am a believer. I believe in God and Christ and want to know them. My relations with scholarship and scholars have to begin there.

What of you who now have eaten of the fruit of knowledge and for a time have been part of this world of scholarship? Will you come out where I have? Will you be believers twenty years from now? We take a great risk when we invite you here to join the world of scholarship. As you have heard so often, you, more than any other single group, will make up the pillars of the coming Church. As you scatter across the world, you are the ones on whose shoulders the Kingdom will rest. How, then, can we invite you, our precious hope for the future, to learn of doubt as well as faith, to encounter minds, if only through books, who contend that reason leads in the end to disbelief and the repudiation of morality.

The university does its best to attract the most competent, well-trained, faithful men and women possible to be your teachers, and has succeeded admirably. But it cannot and does not attempt to remove from the shelves every book that attacks the Church, casts doubt on the existence of God, or criticizes traditional standards of conduct. Those books are in the BYU library as they are in every other university library in the land.

My son and daughter-in-law, who were in Riyadh, Saudi Arabia, during the Iraqi war, were issued gas masks and instructed on how to create a safe room sealed off from poison gas. You saw the scenes of people putting tape around windows and doorjambs. The gas masks for their four- and two-year-old children were essentially transparent bags with rubber strips that went around their necks with a small electric pump to pull the air through a purifying device. Their new baby boy, born on the night of one of the last SCUD attacks, had a mask with a rubber belt around his abdomen. The masks and safe rooms were meant to keep the children free of toxic fumes delivered on a warhead. Our son said that their two children could not abide the gas masks and would not keep them on for a minute. Likewise, there is no way you can be sealed off against ideas that oppose the gospel. It cannot be done. You would not tolerate such treatment in this university either, and furthermore, it would not be right to subject you to it. You were not sent here to be isolated from evil. It would be wrong to attempt to create a safe room, and it would not work.

But if, on principle, you cannot be protected against error, what can we your teachers, your believing teachers, say to you about the unbelief in the world of scholarship? How could we have asked your parents to send you to the university where you learn about error as well as about truth?

We can say only one thing: you will, with God's help, find the path. Having taught you what we believe and what we know, we trust you. That is the only way: trust.

My son, the one in Saudi Arabia, went off to Harvard as an undergraduate the way I did. I was very much aware as he went that now he was free to choose—to believe or not, to obey or not. He could continue faithful, or he could put all that we had taught him away and become someone who was not LDS, who was not a believer.

Contemplating all this, about January of his first year I wrote him a letter. I was thinking of the mission that should figure into his plans soon. I told him that I knew he would have to make the basic decisions about the Church on his own. I asked only one thing of him. I asked that he keep himself worthy, that he live the commandments so that there would be no guilt to cloud his thinking. I wanted him to make a perfectly free decision, and guilt would constrain his freedom. I am happy to say that he went on a mission, and now he and his wife are doing their parts in the Riyadh Ward.

In my view, it is one of God's miracles that most of you, perhaps all, will follow the same course, and be faithful and serve. In the midst of the doubt and uncertainty all around us, you will choose the LDS way. We go against the grain of the public culture in our simple, direct faith in a God who loves us and hears our prayers. But contrary to the prevailing opinion, our faith is not at war with scholarship. In my experience, quite the opposite is true. If you decide like me that you are a believer, that you worship God and want to enjoy his spirit, you will love learning. Your mind will clear. You will absorb and understand. You will work hard and enthusiastically. You will grow in intelligence. You will enter into your rightful intellectual inheritance as Latter-day Saints.

That believers will value and enjoy scholarship was prophesied long ago, when all I have been saying was said much better: "To be learned is good if they hearken unto the counsels of God" (2 Ne. 9:29).

NOTES

1. Kenneth R. Hardy, "Social Origins of American Scientists and Scholars," *Science* 185 (1974): 498.

2. David Friend and the Editors of *Life, The Meaning of Life: Reflections in Words and Pictures on Why We Are Here* (Boston: Little, Brown, 1991).

4

The Social Dimensions of Rationality

This essay germinated while I was driving the New Jersey Turnpike one evening between Delaware and New York. I had occasional business in Delaware after we moved to Manhattan in 1989, and the drive provided an uneventful two hours for thinking. I had in mind family members who were not believers and graduate students who occasionally engaged me in religious conversation. The thoughts were another answer to the old question of how to justify belief.

The essay takes advantage of the postmodern moment when the Enlightenment was under attack. Unlike some Latter-day Saints, I welcomed postmodern criticism because it undermined my old bugaboo, positivist science. Since my college days, I had felt that the scientific requirement of accurate sensory evidence for every conviction presented the greatest challenge to religious faith. I cheered when that shibboleth was questioned. In this essay, I don't completely buy into postmodern thinking; I was too much a child of the fifties for that. But I invoke enough doubts about the Enlightenment to shake the tree. My main points are the necessity of deciding on the good for ourselves and the impossibility of reaching a conclusion without help from our friends. We always make a social decision when we decide on truth. Even hermits imagine a community of some kind when they decide what is good and true.

I recently attended a conference on religious advocacy sponsored by a group of Christian scholars who feel that religious belief is unduly restricted in academic discourse. The starting point for the conference was the evident fact that political convictions are freely advocated in classrooms and scholarly writing. These political positions are ideological and value laden, so why not introduce religious views too? If history can be taught from a Marxist perspective, why not from a Christian viewpoint?

At the conference, scholars with a wide range of personal outlooks, some religious, some not, addressed the question of how their personal beliefs affected their teaching and writing. The paper of one of the less-believing participants reminded me of how academics commonly think of Mormon belief. He was looking for an outer limit to what rational people would dare bring into serious academic conversation, and the example he chose was Joseph Smith. Forgetting that I was a Latter-day Saint, he proposed the idea of an angel delivering gold plates as an example of a religious phantasm so far beyond the boundaries of plausibility as to preclude any consideration in college classrooms or scholarly writing.

When we got to the discussion segment of that session, I reminded him that I had written a book on Joseph Smith founded on the very assumption that an angel delivered golden plates on a New York hillside.[1] The writer did not press his point and generously acknowledged in private conversation that he should read my study of Joseph's early life. Neither of us suffered embarrassment, but his candor brought out an attitude that I know many of my colleagues share. Belief in angels is outside the pale of academic conversation. After all, what can be said about events so far beyond the bounds of ordinary experience?

Belief in angels and golden plates apparently does not disqualify a person for other kinds of scholarly activity. I am asked to give papers and review books and have never felt that my religion prevents me from engaging in all the usual routines of modern academic life. Apparently, the crazy Mormon side of my mind is envisioned as sequestered in some watertight compartment where it cannot infect my rational processes. Beliefs inhabit a realm of feeling and traditional loyalties where we are not called to rational account and where eccentricities and bizarre ideas can be tolerated. Probably my colleagues have peculiar notions of their own that they would not want to defend before a panel of academic critics.

When a graduate student or a colleague does ask about my beliefs, I am often asked if I was reared a Mormon. The question is, of course, a hypothesis. They are explaining my belief not as a rational choice made in the face of other choices but as one component of an elaborate cultural system intertwined with my family, the culture of my home, loyalty to old friends, the fundamentals of my personal identity. They think I am Mormon the way other people are Jewish or Polish; they think that's simply me. My belief in the angel and the plates cannot be extricated from my personal culture. I am a Mormon, they implicitly presume, not because I *believe* in Mormonism. I believe in Mormonism because I *am* a Mormon—by upbringing, affection, and cultural construction.

I accept this explanation and go one step further. I believe in the doctrine and the miraculous events because they sustain life. I need them to carry on from day to day. The God whom I worship and who dwells in the midst of Mormon scriptures is the God who heals me when I am wounded, who corrects me when I err, who restores me to good when I fall into evil. My religion is a crutch, an absolutely necessary crutch that I need to hobble on through life. Far from rationally judging every historical event in the fabulous life of Joseph Smith or weighing the worth of each doctrine, I believe in the God of the Mormon scriptures because I need that God. My beliefs grow in the dark, warm realm of feelings, the place of fears and agonizing human needs, of desires beyond naming, the place where my soul has its roots.

All this is a simple fact of my religious life, perhaps of all religious life. Does this mean, therefore, that all religious doctrine is irrational, that all the events of Mormon history are beyond discourse, that one cannot make an argument for Mormon beliefs? Obviously not. Those arguments are made constantly. I have myself made a historical case for the authenticity of the Book of Mormon. Hugh Nibley has devoted his life to assembling evidence in rational support of Mormon scriptures. The Foundation for Ancient Research and Mormon Studies (FARMS) has mobilized an army of people who publish hundreds of pages a year in support of our beliefs. This scholarship is not generally acknowledged outside of Mormon circles, but that does not mean it is trivial. The people at FARMS are trained in accredited graduate schools, learned in languages, informed about current scholarship, and careful in argumentation. They abide by all the canons of rational discourse. Nor can it be claimed that they are emotionally unbalanced or congenitally stupid. They bear every evidence of psychological stability and intellectual acuity. These people, and many others not directly associated with FARMS, have brought their considerable powers to bear in support of Mormon beliefs about history and God. If my colleagues consider my beliefs outside the realm of rational discourse, these Mormon apologists do not. They maintain, and I concur, that a more persuasive argument can be made for belief in God and Christ through the Book of Mormon than through any of the arguments of conventional Christianity.

The cultural position of Mormon belief, then, is strangely anomalous. For me it grows out of family culture, a thousand personal associations, and deep human needs. At the same time, it is girded up with forceful (though never unassailable) rational arguments based on conventional scholarly methods and the rules of rational discourse. My colleagues are correct in placing my beliefs in the realm of feeling and deep loyalties, where it is tactful not to call for rational explanation; on the other hand, if they wished to take the trouble, I could provide them with shelves of scholarship in support of the Book of Mormon and Joseph Smith's story. Belief is irrational and rational at the same time.

My academic colleagues would explain away the apologist scholarship in the way they account for my belief. In their view, all the other Mormon scholars argue on behalf of their faith for the same reasons I do: because they are personally grounded in Mormon society, where they live and move and have their being. Social environment has made Mormons of these people, and they devote their lives to a defense of the faith in order to sustain their own social and personal identities.

This explanation has served to put believing Mormon scholars in their place largely in contrast to another kind of scholarship that is thought to be beyond social loyalties or deep personal needs: the scholarship of science and objective reason, best exemplified by the physical sciences. Over the past four centuries, scientific scholarship has developed rigorous methods for screening out personal preferences and arriving at conclusions based on objective, measurable reality and cool, disinterested reasoning. This kind of scholarship is responsible for breathtaking advances in physics, chemistry, and biology, and it inspires a hope that the study of history and sociology, the sciences of the human spirit, can make comparable progress.

By the standards of this rigorous scientific inquiry, Mormon scholars with their obvious personal commitments do not measure up. To practitioners of objective science, the findings of Mormon scholars are necessarily polluted by their personal interest in the outcome. Mormon scholars have a form of scholarship but deny the power thereof, and hence can be dismissed as special pleaders rather than as serious claimants to objective truth.

That is where Mormon scholarship was located, anyway, until about twenty years ago. Now, that perspective on belief is undergoing a fundamental shift, not because of changes in Mormon scholarship but because of the way modern thinkers are conceiving scholarship as a whole. We live at a moment in history when the Enlightenment dream of scientific scholarship has been eaten away by doubts about the possibility of scholarly objectivity. A host of thinkers, many of them French, have called into question the very possibility of dispassionate inquiry. They are arguing not merely that objectivity is an impossible achievement for human beings, who can never detach their minds from the rest of their being, but that the pretense of objectivity is an exercise in self-aggrandizement. Objectivity disguises a play for power by those who pretend to the authority of objective scholarship when they are every bit as self-interested in the outcome as any religious apologist. The scientific authorities of an era, according to current theory, claim to speak only for truth against error, when in actuality they stand to benefit by promoting their particular truth and vanquishing all others. No truth, not even the most rigorously scientific, is objective. All truth is colored by personal interest of some sort.

That is harsh criticism of the scientists whom we have all learned to admire, and I, for one, am loath to go all the way with postmodernist thinkers. It is very hard to relinquish faith in some measure of objective scholarship. We all can think of utterly biased and self-serving scholarship that we are sure would not hold up under scrutiny, or history writing that is filled with factual errors. We want to reserve the right to correct this corrupted work in the name of some kind of objective truth.

But if we cannot go all the way with the critics of the Enlightenment, we must at least acknowledge that no scholarship, no truth, exists in a social vacuum. Though it is rarely mentioned in the work itself, all scholarship is tied to a community of some kind and bears the marks of that community's influence. Scholarship is the product of people who are located in institutions—universities, research institutes, or circles of like-minded thinkers. They publish their work and want to have it read by others. Their reputations, promotions, pay raises, and appointments depend on how that work is received. When they write, they use the language, the mannerisms, the forms of their scholarly community. In taking an intellectual position, they silently, but inevitably, associate themselves with people of a similar outlook. Scholars take pleasure in hearing references to their work at scholarly meetings or seeing it mentioned in publications. They can imagine being part of a distinguished community of learned people whose intelligence and character are admired. In the scholarly work itself, a conclusion is presented as the outcome of careful scrutiny of the facts and rigorous analysis; but the assumptions, the perspective of the work, the fundamental attitude come from some community, from a society with which the scholar is implicitly and probably quite hopefully associating.

Every form of scholarship is rooted in a society, an imagined community of scholars in which the teachers or writers live and move and have their being. We cannot take a position on a scholarly issue without implicitly forming or breaking a social relationship. Everything we write and say links us to other people, with all the tangled consequences for our self-esteem, our personal identities, our hopes and aspirations. There is a social and personal dimension to every form of rational discourse, which means that all beliefs, not merely religious beliefs, are both rational and irrational. We may indeed become persuaded rationally that the Book of Mormon is a nineteenth-century production. There may be hundreds of facts we can invoke to sustain this position. But in making that assertion we are forming and breaking human relationships that unavoidably influence our thinking, just as the memories of a religious upbringing (or of a transforming conversion) coil around the work of the Mormon apologists.

The explanation for faith that I imagine in the minds of my academic colleagues has never intimidated me. I acknowledge my subjectivity and the influence of a million personal associations. But this recognition of my own limitations has made me deeply skeptical of all who claim to escape their subjectivity, who think they have rid themselves of the prejudices of their tribe. We all have our tribes. The desire to form tribes, to join tribes, to triumph within our tribes drives and shapes our scholarship. Every form of discourse, every rationality is rooted in a society and serves social purposes. However much we enjoy the pursuit of truth for its own sake, these social purposes are preeminent. Without a society behind the scholarship, we would never do the research or write the books. Every truth is socially conditioned and socially motivated. When we take an intellectual position, we are announcing the society to which we wish to belong and the kind of people we want to be. The very explanation that my academic colleagues offer for my belief is what I use to understand theirs. All truth,

Mormon and scientific, is of necessity social truth and profoundly conditioned by human associations. The pretenses of Enlightenment scholarship have been torn away in recent decades, and the inescapable contingencies of this profoundly human endeavor have been laid bare.

In what, then, can we put our trust? If truth always grows from a particular society, how do we choose among the perplexing confusions of multiple and conflicting truths? If the Enlightenment quest has faltered and the pursuit of knowledge seems mired in subjectivity, if scholarship is entwined in the corrupting pursuit of power, what can we cling to? What can replace objective scientific truth as a foundation for culture and personal identity? Where do we go when we are post-Enlightenment, post-modern, post-everything?

I begin with an insistent question that shoulders aside even truth in demanding our attention: How should we live a life? It may take a long time to discover the truth, especially if we follow the tortuous path of scientific rigor. But we must answer the question of how to live a life every second of every day. We may have only tentative answers, to be replaced from day to day, but some answer we must find for the inescapable queries: What is good? What is worth pursuing? What should we give our time to? How should we treat other people? How should we think of them? How should we feel and act? These questions thrust themselves insistently upon us and demand immediate answers in our actions and thoughts. We cannot wait to hear from science or the universities about these matters. We are in the middle of the fray the minute we open our eyes each morning.

We sometimes think that if we knew the true, then we would know the good. The right way to live should grow out of the right way to understand. A goodness based on falsehood would be faith built on the sand. The true and the good should come together, we want to think, and indeed may be close to equivalent. In the pragmatic tradition that has influenced my thinking, I carry that hope one step further to say that what we find to be truly good is the truth. The only truth we can know is the truth that works.

One of the perplexities of academic scholarship is how it shies away from goodness. Classroom teachers make a point of saying that they have no intention of telling students how to live their lives. It is true that a certain set of moral precepts grows out of scholarship—accuracy of expression, an honest reading of evidence, clarity of reasoning, diligence, empathy. But objective scholarship will not reveal what it means to be a good husband or wife, how to learn to be generous, how to bless people. Those who are academics have values, of course, but they bring these political and ethical principles into their teaching from other sources—from their religious backgrounds, their families, their communities. Except in the narrow realm of scholarly methods, the Enlightenment pursuit of truth does not provide answers to the question of how to live a life. In fact, it explicitly denies responsibility for finding the good. Scholarship has no doctrine of repentance because it has no doctrine of good. I consider that a damning lack.

Scientific scholarship is the official truth of our culture. The government will grant you money to investigate questions by scientific methods; you will never get money to answer inquiries by spiritual means. And yet, that official culture holds no promise of ultimately discovering what is good or of helping people attain it. We are left on our own to discover the truth that teaches us what is worth doing in life and how to be a good person.

As I said at the outset, I find goodness in the God of the Mormon scriptures. There I find truth to live by, which to my way of thinking is the most significant, the most useful, the most compelling kind of truth. But is this Mormon truth real? We cannot help asking, Is it anything more than a hopeful fabrication? That question comes from the ghost of the Enlightenment, the ghost that tells us we can escape our subjectivity and find a truth above human frailty, a truth that all reasonable people will be forced to accept. But it is a ghost that speaks to us; the hope of objective truth has been slain. No one is capable of finding that dreamed-of reality by scholarly methods. Objectivity is the claim of people who think they are gods now, not of persons worshipping God and striving to be like him, nor of persons who understand the reality of finite human life without God. It is a magnificent phantasm, a blind and futile aspiration—futile not just because we can never escape ourselves, but because in the end the Enlightenment project fails us. Even when science has done its work to perfection, it fails to tell us how to live a life.

The Mormon truth, above all, tells us how to be good and helps us to get there. Faith and repentance are wrapped up together. The goodness that I see in Mormon lives, and day after day in my own life when I construct myself as the scriptures direct, is every bit as real as the abstractions of scientific scholarship. I can, if I wish, cast an aura of rationality over this belief in an effort to explain and justify myself to my academic colleagues. Our valiant apologists will go on defending the faith with scholarly evidence, to keep up our connection with the academic establishment. But I hold to my beliefs not because of the evidence or the arguments but because I find our Mormon truth good and yearn to install it at the center of my life. After losing many followers when he taught an especially hard doctrine, Jesus asked his disciples, "Will ye also go away?" Then Simon Peter answered, "Lord, to whom shall we go? thou hast the words of eternal life" (John 6:67–68).

NOTES

1. Richard L. Bushman, *Joseph Smith and the Beginnings of Mormonism* (Urbana: University of Illinois Press, 1984).

PART TWO

The Book of Mormon and History

5

The Book of Mormon and the American Revolution

During the bicentennial of the American Revolution, every historian of early America was asked to give innumerable talks. One of my invitations was from a Federal Heights LDS congregation in Salt Lake City that sponsored a lecture series to fulfill the Church's charge to mark the nation's birth. I have explained in "My Belief" how I backed into the essay by realizing that Book of Mormon political practice did not correspond to government in the United States in the early nineteenth century. Instead of a deliberation about politics, the essay turned out to be an argument for the historical authenticity of the Book of Mormon. Lucybeth Rampton, a member of the congregation, brought her husband, Utah governor Calvin Rampton, to the lecture, and I am sure both were disappointed. The lecture offered very little to interest a participant in American politics. When my colleague John W. Welch read it, however, he liked it and helped me get it ready for publication in BYU Studies, *a multidisciplinary academic journal in Provo, Utah.*

The Book of Mormon, much like the Old Testament, was written to show Israel "what great things the Lord hath done for their fathers" and to testify of the coming Messiah.[1] Although cast as a history, it is history with a high religious purpose, not the kind we ordinarily write today. The narrative touches only incidentally on the society, economics, and politics of the Nephites and Jaredites, leaving us to rely on oblique references and occasional asides to reconstruct total cultures. Government is dealt with more expressly than other aspects, however, perhaps because the prophets were often rulers themselves and because the most significant reforms in the history of Nephite government were inspired by a prophet-king. From their comments and Mormon's editorial interjections, it is possible to get a rough idea of the theory and practice of politics in Nephite civilization.

While we value these scraps of information, the political passages, it must be recognized, expose the book to attack. The more specific the record, the more easily its verity can be tested. Details about government make it possible to ask if the political forms are genuinely ancient, or if they bear the marks of nineteenth-century creation. The late Thomas O'Dea, a sympathetic but critical scholar, thought that "American sentiments permeate the work."

In it are found the democratic, the republican, the anti-monarchial, and the egal-
itarian doctrines that pervaded the climate of opinion in which it was conceived
and that enter into the expressions and concerns of its Nephite kings, prophets,
and priests as naturally as they later come from the mouths of Mormon leaders
preaching to the people in Utah.[2]

That kind of indictment would be precluded were the Book of Mormon
exclusively and narrowly religious. As it is, O'Dea purports to find evidence
of nineteenth-century American political culture in the Book of Mormon—for example, the prophecy of the American Revolution early in
Nephi's narrative, and later, the switch from monarchy to government by
elected judges. On first reading, both have a modern and American flavor.
O'Dea, to be sure, wrote in the mode of higher criticism, which assumes
that an accurate prophecy of a specific event can occur only after the event.
Even if one discounts for that assumption, however, the question remains
whether the spirit and content of some of the political passages in the Book
of Mormon do not partake more of American republicanism than of
Israelite or ancient Near Eastern monarchy.[3]

O'Dea's observations comport with the widely accepted view of the
Book of Mormon which holds that it "can best be explained, not by Joseph's
ignorance nor by his delusions, but by his responsiveness to the provincial
opinions of his time."[4] One of the first critics of the Book of Mormon,
Alexander Campbell, noted in 1831 that the record incorporated, among
other conventional American ideas, commonplace sentiments about
"freemasonry, republican government, and the rights of man."[5] A comparison of the political cultures of the Nephites and of Joseph Smith's America
thus bears on the larger question of the origin of the English text of the Book
of Mormon.

The Political Milieu of Joseph's Smith's New York

There is little reason to doubt that however the book originated,
Joseph Smith must have absorbed the ordinary political sentiments of his
time. The air was thick with politics. The Revolution, by then a half century
old, still loomed as the great turning point in American and world history.
Americans annually celebrated the nation's birthday with oratory, editori-
als, and rounds of toasts. In 1824 and 1825, Lafayette, absent from the
United States for thirty-eight years, toured all twenty-four states with his
son George Washington Lafayette. The following year, 1826, was the jubilee
anniversary of the Declaration of Independence, and Fourth of July orators
exerted themselves as never before. A few days after the celebration, news
spread that on the very day when the nation was commemorating its
fiftieth birthday, two of the most illustrious heroes of the Revolution, John

Adams and Thomas Jefferson, had died within six hours of one another. A new round of patriotic rhetoric poured forth to remind the nation of its history and the glories of republicanism. All this was reported in the *Wayne Sentinel*, Palmyra's weekly, along with coverage of yearly electoral campaigns and debates on current political issues. Joseph Smith could not easily have avoided a rudimentary education in the principles of American government and the meaning of the American Revolution before he began work on the Book of Mormon in 1827.[6]

Patriotic orations served various purposes for the politicians who delivered them, but certain conventional usages recur: a set of attitudes and rhetorical patterns apparently shared by Americans of all persuasions. The patterns varied little from region to region, probably because newspaper editors commonly reprinted orations and essays from other areas, but we can be assured of sampling the political atmosphere in Joseph Smith's immediate environment if we rely primarily on three sources: the *Wayne Sentinel*, upstate New York oratory, and the schoolbooks for sale in Palmyra's bookstore.[7] Young Joseph may not have spent much time with any of them, but if any provincial sources influenced Joseph Smith, these must be the ones. They shaped, or expressed, the ideas of his neighbors, local politicians, and those who gathered in taverns and stores to talk politics. Presumably, O'Dea would see such sentiments to be at the root of Book of Mormon political ideas.

My purpose is to test that conclusion by comparing some of the most obvious contemporaneous ideas about government and the American Revolution with political ideas and practices in the Book of Mormon. There are three that were prominent in the political literature of the 1820s: first, the depiction of the American Revolution as heroic resistance against tyranny; second, the belief that people overthrow their kings under the stimulus of enlightened ideas of human rights; and third, the conviction that constitutional arrangements such as frequent elections, separation of powers, and popularly elected assemblies were necessary to control power.

Heroic Resistance or Divine Deliverance

The most common of all conventions in orations, essays, and editorial columns was the dramatic structure of the Revolution, still familiar today. The Revolution was a struggle of heroes against oppressors, a brave people versus a tyrant king or corrupt ministry. That theme was rehearsed whenever the orators honored the Revolutionary veterans in the audience. A large portion of his hearers, one speaker said, were too young to know "the divine enthusiasm which inspired the American bosom; which prompted her voice to proclaim defiance to the thunders of Britain." It was from the soldiers themselves, the venerable asserters of the rights of mankind, that we are to be informed, what were the feelings which swayed within your breasts, and impelled you to action; when, like the stripling of Israel, with scarcely a weapon to attack, and without a shield for your defence, you met, and undismayed, engaged with the gigantic greatness of the British power.[8]

The greatness of Jefferson was that

on the coming of that tremendous storm which for eight years desolated our country, Mr. Jefferson hesitated not, halted not. . . . He adventured, with the single motive of advancing the cause of his country and of human freedom, into that perilous contest, throwing into the scale his life and fortune as of no value.[9]

Similarly, Lafayette "shared in the dangers, privations and sufferings of that bitter struggle, nor quitted them for a moment, till it was consummated on the glorious field of Yorktown."[10] For many Americans, the courage of the heroes in resisting oppression was the most memorable aspect of the Revolution. The editors of the "Readers" and "Speakers," the textbooks of that generation, consistently favored passages that dwelt on that theme.[11]

The narrative conventions are worth noting because of the Book of Mormon's brief description of the American Revolution. While Joseph Smith might alter costumes and the locale of the narrator, the spirit of the event was less malleable. A responsive young provincial, it would seem, would absorb this first and retain it longest. Yet coming to Nephi's prediction of the Revolution after reading Fourth of July orations, an American reader even today finds the account curiously flat. Just before the Revolution prophecy, Nephi tells of "a man among the Gentiles," presumably Columbus in Europe, who "went forth upon the many waters" to America (1 Ne. 13:12). And it came to pass that the Spirit of God then "wrought upon other Gentiles; and they went forth out of captivity, upon the many waters" (1 Ne. 13:13). The gentiles did "humble themselves before the Lord; and the power of the lord was with them" (1 Ne. 13:16). Then the Revolution is depicted in this fashion:

[The] mother Gentiles were gathered together upon the waters, and upon the land also, to battle against them.

And I beheld that the power of God was with them, and also that the wrath of God was upon all those that were gathered together against them to battle.

And I, Nephi, beheld that the Gentiles that had gone out of captivity were delivered by the power of God out of the hands of all other nations. (1 Ne. 13:17–19)

By American standards, this is a strangely distorted account. There is no indictment of the king or parliament, no talk of American rights or liberty, nothing of the corruptions of the ministry, and most significant, no despots or heroes. In fact, there is no reference to American resistance. The "mother gentiles" are the only warriors. God, not General Washington or the American army, delivers the colonies.

The meaning of the narrative opens itself to the reader only after he lays aside his American preconceptions about the Revolution and recognizes that the dramatic structure in Nephi's account is fundamentally different from the familiar one in Independence Day orations. The point of the narrative is that Americans escaped from captivity. They did not resist, they fled. The British were defeated because the wrath of God was upon them. The virtue of the Americans was that they "did humble themselves before the Lord" (1 Ne. 13:16). The moral is that "the Gentiles that had gone out of captivity were delivered by the power of God out of the hands of all other nations" (1 Ne. 13:19). The theme is deliverance, not resistance.

The theme of deliverance by God is more notable in Nephi's prophecy because it recurs in various forms throughout the Book of Mormon. Three times a people of God suffer from oppressive rulers under conditions that might approximate those in the colonies before the Revolution: Alma under King Noah, the people of Limhi under the Lamanites, and once again Alma under the Lamanites. In none do revolutionary heroes in the American sense emerge.[12] In each instance the people escaped from bondage by flight.[13] They gathered their people, flocks, and tents and fled into the wilderness when their captors were off guard. When they learned that the corrupt and spiritually hardened King Noah had dispatched an army to apprehend them in their secret meeting place, Alma's people "took their tents and their families and departed into the wilderness" (Mosiah 18:34). Limhi's people, an exploited dominion of a Lamanite empire, departed "by night into the wilderness with their flocks and their herds" (Mosiah 22:11). Alma's people, after escaping King Noah, fell into the hands of the Lamanites who "put tasks upon them" and "taskmasters over them" (Mosiah 24:9). When they cried to the Lord for succor, they were told to "be of good comfort, for I know of the covenant which ye have made unto me; and I will covenant with my people and deliver them out of bondage" (Mosiah 24:13). The deliverance came in due course, but not by way of confrontation. "The Lord caused a deep sleep to come upon the Lamanites. . . . And Alma and his people departed into the wilderness" (Mosiah 24:19–20). The point seemed to be that the people obtained their liberty by obedience rather than by courage or sacrifice. After successfully eluding their captors, the people thanked God because he had "delivered them out of bondage; for they were in bondage, and none could deliver them except it were the Lord their God" (Mosiah 24:21).

Godly people in the Book of Mormon defended themselves against invaders—in that sense they resisted—but they never overthrew an established government, no matter how oppressive. When we step back to look at the larger framework, we can see that their actions were consistent. The deliverance narrative grew out of the Nephites' conception of history as naturally as resistance in the American Revolution sprang from Anglo-American Whig views. Book of Mormon prophets saw the major events of their own past as comprising a series of deliverances beginning with the archetypal flight of the Israelites from Egypt. Alma the Younger pictured the Exodus from Egypt and Lehi's journey from Jerusalem as the first of a number of bondages and escapes.

> I will praise him forever, for he has brought our fathers out of Egypt, and he has swallowed up the Egyptians in the Red Sea; and he led them by his power into the promised land; yea, and he has delivered them out of bondage and captivity from time to time.
>
> Yea, and he has also brought our fathers out of the land of Jerusalem; and he has also, by his everlasting power, delivered them out of bondage and captivity, from time to time even down to the present day. (Alma 36:28–29)

Among those bondages reaching "down to the present day" were those of his father and Limhi, who, like their illustrious predecessors, were

> delivered out of the hands of the people of king Noah, by the mercy and power of God.
>
> And behold, after that, they were brought into bondage by the hands of the Lamanites in the wilderness . . . and again the Lord did deliver them out of bondage. (Alma 5:4–5)

Understandably the prophet-historians delighted in Alma's and Limhi's deliverances because they illustrated so perfectly the familiar ways of God with his people. Events took on religious meaning and form as they followed the established pattern of divine intervention.

Nephi's prophecy of the Revolution, therefore, makes sense in terms of its own culture as an act of divine deliverance. Any other rendition of the prophecy would have offended later Nephite sensibilities just as its present form puzzles us. In the context of the Book of Mormon, heroic resistance could not give revolution moral significance. Only deliverance by the power of God could do that.[14] Once the pattern of Nephite interpretation of history comes into focus, Nephi's account of future events becomes comprehensible.

There are two points to be made here. The first is that Book of Mormon accounts of the Revolution and of the behavior of godly people in revolutionary situations differ fundamentally from American accounts of the Revolution. The second is that there is a consistency in the Book of Mormon treatment of these events. Each deliverance fits a certain view of providential history. The accounts disregard a significant convention of

American patriotic oratory of the late 1820s in order to respect one of the book's own conventions.

Enlightenment and Popular Opposition to Monarchy

Heroic resistance did not exhaust the meaning of the Revolution for the orators of the 1820s. Beyond their display of sheer courage, the patriots of 1776 were honored for adopting the true principles of government. "This is the anniversary of the great day," the *Wayne Sentinel* editorialized on July 4, 1828, "which commenced a new era in the history of the world. It proclaimed the triumph of free principles, and the liberation of a people from the dominion of monarchial government." The adoption of free principles, namely the end of "monarchial government," and the institution of "a government, based upon the will of the people, free and popular in every feature," effected a "sublime and glorious" change in the "civil and moral condition" of the United States and the world.[15] The Revolution was "the glorious era from which every republic of our continent may trace the first march of that *revolutionizing* spirit, which, with a mighty impetus has disseminated the blessings of free governments over so large a portion of our globe."[16] Revolutionary principles were shaking all the nations of the earth. "Whole states are changed, and nations start into existence in a day," the jubilee orator in Palmyra declared. "Systems venerable for their antiquity have been demolished. Governments built up in ages of darkness and vassalage, have tottered and fallen."[17]

And why had this political earthquake occurred? "Knowledge and a correct estimate of moral right have opened the eyes of men to see the importance of free institutions, and the only true, rational end of existence."[18] The principles of the Revolution were awakening people everywhere and moving them to throw down their masters. The *Sentinel*, a month after the jubilee celebration, quoted Jefferson's aspiration that the Declaration of Independence would "be to the world what I believe it will be; the signal of arousing men to burst the chains under which the monkish ignorance and superstition had persuaded them to bind themselves, and to assume the blessings of free government." The American Revolution was the beginning of a world revolution in which "man, so long the victim of oppression, awakes from the sleep of ages and bursts his chains."[19]

Does any of that struggle seep into the Book of Mormon? Do enlightened people in its pages overthrow monarchs enthroned in ignorance? The most famous passage on monarchy in the Book of Mormon does in a general way echo the American aversion to monarchy. Jacob, brother of the first Nephi and son of Lehi, prophesied that "this land shall be a land of liberty unto the Gentiles. . . . For he that raiseth up a king against me shall perish, for I, the Lord, the king of heaven, will be their king" (2 Ne. 10:11, 14). Yet when we examine more closely the Nephites' own attitude toward kings, principled opposition to monarchy is scarcely in evidence. Enlightened people in the Book of Mormon do not rise up to strike down their kings as the Fourth of July scenario would have it. In fact, the opposite is true. The people persistently created kings for themselves, even demanded them. Shortly after their settlement in the New World, the followers of Nephi asked him to be their king. Nephi demurred, being "desirous that they should have no king," but they continued to look on Nephi as "a king or a protector" and by the end of his life he had acquiesced (see 2 Ne. 5:18; 6:2). As he approached death, "he anointed a man to be a king and a ruler over his people," thus initiating the "reigns of the kings" (Jacob 1:9).[20] Nephi's establishment of monarchy set the precedent followed throughout Nephite political history with respect to kingmaking. When a segment of the nation migrated to another part of the continent under the leadership of the first Mosiah, they made him king over the land (see Omni 1:12). This process was repeated not long afterward following another migration: Zeniff, the leader of the migrants, "was made a king by the voice of the people" (Mosiah 7:9; see also Mosiah 19:26). It was quite natural that when Alma broke away with yet another band, his people should be "desirous that Alma should be their king, for he was beloved by his people" (Mosiah 23:6). Unlike Nephi, Alma firmly declined, and a few years later, kingship among the people of Nephi at large was ended.

The abandonment of monarchy, however, did not occur by revolution nor at the instigation of the people. The occasion for the change was the refusal of the sons of Mosiah II to accept the kingship. Mosiah feared the contention that might ensue from an appointment outside the royal line and proposed the installation of judges chosen by the voice of the people (see Mosiah 29). Mosiah's lengthy argument against monarchy, written down and distributed through the countryside, persuaded the people and

> they relinquished their desires for a king. . . .
>
> . . . They assembled themselves together in bodies throughout the land, to cast in their voices concerning who should be their judges. . . .
>
> And thus commenced the reign of the judges . . . among all the people who were called the Nephites. (Mosiah 29:38–39, 44)[21]

There is nothing in these episodes of an enlightened people rising against their king. The people did not rise nor were they enlightened about the errors of monarchy. Quite the contrary. In every instance, the people were the ones to desire a king, and in three of five cases they got one. The aversion to kingship was at the top. Nephi, Alma, and Mosiah were reluctant, not the people. When monarchy finally came to an end, it was because the king abdicated, not because the enlightened people overthrew him. In the American view, despot kings held their people in bondage through superstition and ignorance until the true principles of government inspired resistance. The Book of Mormon nearly reversed the roles. The people delighted in their subjection to the king, and the rulers were enlightened.

Book of Mormon opposition to monarchy was not a matter of fixed principle either. Americans believed the patriots of 1776 had broached "a new theory" and discovered the "first principle" of government, which was "diametrically opposed" to the inequalities of monarchy. "There is no neutral ground, no mid-way course," a Boston orator said in 1827.[22] That was far from the case in the Book of Mormon. Alma and Mosiah's opposition to kingship was no theoretical breakthrough, nor was it advocated as a fundamental political truth. It was simply that wicked kings had the power to spread their iniquity.

> He enacteth laws, and sendeth them forth among his people, yea, laws after the manner of his own wickedness; and whosoever doth not obey his laws he causeth to be destroyed . . . and thus an unrighteous king doth pervert the ways of all righteousness. (Mosiah 29:23)

A good king was another matter. "If it were possible that you could always have just men to be your kings," Alma said, "it would be well for you to have a king" (Mosiah 23:8). Mosiah made the same point.

> If it were possible that you could have just men to be your kings, who would establish the laws of God, and judge this people according to his commandments . . . then it would be expedient that you should always have kings to rule over you. (Mosiah 29:13)

There was nothing intrinsically wrong with monarchy. It was not "diametrically opposed" to good government. It was simply inexpedient because it was subject to abuse.

The Reign of the Judges and American Constitutional Government

The Nephite government was no more resistant to monarchy in practice than it was in theory, and in fact came to occupy the very middle ground that, according to the Boston orator, could not exist. The institution of judgeships, rather than beginning a republican era in Book of Mormon history, slid back at once toward monarchy. The chief judge much more resembled a king than an American president. Once elected, he never again submitted himself to the people. After being proclaimed chief judge by the voice of the people, Alma enjoyed life tenure. When he chose to resign because of internal difficulties, he selected his own successor (see

Alma 4:16).[23] That seems to have been the beginning of a dynasty. In the next succession, the judgeship passed to the chief judge's son and thence "by right" to the successive sons of the judges (see Alma 50:39; Hel. 1:13). Although democratic elements were there—the judges were confirmed by the voice of the people—the "reign of the judges," as the Book of Mormon calls the period, was a far cry from the republican government Joseph Smith knew.[24] Life tenure and hereditary succession would have struck Americans as only slightly modified monarchy. The citizens of Palmyra in the middle 1820s were urged to "remember that at all times the terms of office should be short—an account to the public certain and soon."[25] A point urged in favor of Jackson in 1828 was that

> his election will break the chain of succession which has been so long practically established, and by which the presidents have virtually appointed their successors, and which if not interrupted, will render our elections a mockery, and our government but little better than a hereditary monarchy.[26]

Book of Mormon government by Jacksonian standards was no democracy. Had they examined the matter closely, Joseph Smith's contemporaries would certainly have called the elections a mockery and the government little better than a hereditary monarchy.[27]

Looking at the Book of Mormon as a whole, it seems clear that most of the principles traditionally associated with the American Constitution are slighted or disregarded altogether. All of the constitutional checks and balances are missing. When judges were instituted, Mosiah provided that a greater judge could remove lesser judges and a number of lesser judges try venal higher judges, but the book records no instance of impeachment. It was apparently not a routine working principle. All other limitations on government are missing. There was no written constitution defining rulers' powers. The people could not remove the chief judge at the polls, for he stood for election only once. There were not three branches of government to check one another, for a single office encompassed all government powers. The chief judge was judge, executive, and legislator rolled into one, just as the earlier kings had been (see Mosiah 29:13). In wartime he raised men, armed them, and collected provisions (see Alma 46:34; 60:1–9). He was called interchangeably chief judge and governor (see Alma 2:16; 50:39; 60:1; and 3 Ne. 3:1). He was also lawmaker. There is no ordinary legislature in the Book of Mormon. When the editor said in the heading of Mosiah 29 that Mosiah "recommends representative form of government," he could not have meant representatives elected by the people to enact laws. The only representation was in the choice of judges, not in the selection of legislators. In the early part of the Book of Mormon, the law was presented as traditional, handed down from the fathers as "given them by the hand of the Lord," and "acknowledged by this people" to make it binding (see Mosiah

29:25; Alma 1:14). But later the chief judge assumed the power of proclaiming or at least elaborating laws. Alma gave Nephihah the "power to enact laws according to the laws which had been given" (Alma 4:16). Any major constitutional changes, such as a return to formal kingship, required approval of the people, but day-to-day legislation, so far as the record speaks, was the prerogative of the chief judge (see Alma 2:2–7; 51:1–7). Perhaps most extraordinary by American standards, the Book of Mormon said nothing about taxation by a popular assembly.[28] The maxim "no taxation without representation" had no standing in Nephite consciousness.[29] These salient points in enlightened political theory, as nineteenth-century Americans understood it, were contradicted, distorted, or neglected.[30]

Ancient Precedents

In the context of nineteenth-century political thought, the Book of Mormon people are difficult to place. They were not benighted Spaniards or Russians, passively yielding to the oppression of a monarch out of ignorance and superstition, nor were they enlightened Americans living by the principles of republican government. The Book of Mormon was an anomaly on the political scene of 1830. Instead of heroically resisting despots, the people of God fled their oppressors and credited God alone with deliverance. Instead of enlightened people overthrowing their kings in defense of their natural rights, the common people repeatedly raised up kings, and the prophets and the kings themselves had to persuade the people of the inexpediency of monarchy. Despite Mosiah's reforms, Nephite government persisted in monarchical practices, with life tenure for the chief judges, hereditary succession, and the combination of all functions in one official.

In view of all this, the Book of Mormon could be pictured as a bizarre creation, a book strangely distant from the time and place of its publication. But that picture would not be complete. A pattern running through the apparent anomalies provides a clue to their resolution. Book of Mormon political attitudes have Old World precedents, particularly in the history of the Israelite nation. Against that background its anomalies become regularities. The Hebrews, for example, cast their history as a series of deliverances. Moses was not a revolutionary hero from an American mold. His people fled just like Alma's and Zeniff's, and the moral of the story was that God had delivered them from captivity. Moses was not lauded for courageous resistance. The Book of Mormon deliverance narrative, incongruous amid Fourth of July orations, is perfectly conventional biblical discourse.

The same is true for the popular demand for kings. Biblical people, too, raised up kings among themselves, sometimes successfully, sometimes not. The most famous instance was the anointing of Saul. There the Book of Mormon prototypes are laid down precisely. The people demanded a king of Samuel, who tried to persuade them otherwise, warning them of the iniquities a king would practice on them, just as Alma and Mosiah warned their people (see 1 Sam. 8:1–22; 10:18–25; Deut. 17:14).[31] This basic plot was not singular to Saul, either. Earlier, the Israelites had requested Gideon to be their king, and he had refused because "the Lord will rule over you" (Judges 8:22–23). On another occasion, the Israelite army, after hearing of the assassination of their king, "made their commander Omri king of Israel by common consent," much as the voice of the people confirmed kings among the Nephites (see 1 Kings 16:16, NEB).[32] Whereas the Book of Mormon practice of making kings at the behest of the people clashed with American assumptions, it fit the biblical tradition.

The same holds for reliance on traditional law instead of a representative legislature and for indifference to the separation of powers.[33] Not every biblical political tradition reappeared in the Book of Mormon, but there are biblical precedents for most of the Nephite practices that are not at home in provincial upstate New York. The templates for Book of Mormon politics seem quite consistently to have been cut from the Bible.[34]

With so many similarities before us, it is tempting to conclude that Joseph Smith contrived his narrative from the biblical elements in nineteenth-century American culture and leave it at that. But the problems of interpretation are not so easily dismissed. Biblical patterns work differently in the Book of Mormon than in the culture at large. While American orators blessed God for delivering them from British slavery, they never permitted their gratitude to shade the heroism of the patriots. The acknowledgment of divine aid was more a benediction on America's brave resistance. Similarly, Americans believed God inspired the Constitution, but no one suggested that it was patterned after the government of ancient Israel. No one proposed to eliminate an elected legislature or to make the presidency hereditary because a king ruled the Jews. In fact, no Americans, including the Puritans of Massachusetts Bay, followed biblical political models as closely as Book of Mormon people. Biblical language was used to sanctify American history and American political institutions, but Hebrew precedents did not deeply inform historical writing nor shape political institutions. The innermost structure of Book of Mormon politics and history are biblical, while American forms are conspicuously absent.

How does all this affect the interpretation of the book—the problem raised at the outset? At the very least, the dictum that the Book of Mormon mirrored "every error and almost every truth discussed in N[ew] York for the last ten years" should be reassessed.[35] Scholars confine themselves unnecessarily if they derive all their insight from the maxim that Joseph Smith's writings can best be explained "by his responsiveness to the provincial opinions of this time." That principle of criticism obscures the Book of Mormon, as it would any major work read exclusively in that light. It is particularly misleading when so many of the powerful intellectual influences operating on Joseph Smith failed to touch the Book of Mormon, among them the most common American attitudes toward a revolution, monarchy, and the limitations on power. The Book of Mormon is not a conventional American book. Too much Americana is missing. Understanding the work requires a more complex and sensitive analysis than has been afforded it. Historians will take a long step forward when they free themselves from the compulsion to connect all they find with Joseph Smith's America and try instead to understand the ancient patterns deep in the grain of the book.

NOTES

1. The quotation is from the title page of the Book of Mormon. The Lord's opening words to Moses on Sinai as recorded in Exodus were: "I am the Lord thy God, which have brought thee out of the land of Egypt, out of the house of bondage" (Ex. 20:2), and the memory of that event was used ever after to recall Israel to its covenant obligations.

2. Thomas F. O'Dea, *The Mormons* (Chicago: University of Chicago Press, 1957), 32.

3. O'Dea's evidence is cited at *The Mormons*, 268, nn. 19–21. Many of his references are to choices made by the "voice of the people." For a comment on the function of popular consent in monarchies as well as republics, see note 24 below. The same note also contains observations, on Moroni's war for liberty, that indicate his fight did not follow an American pattern. See Alma 43:48–49; 46:35–36; 48:11; 51:7. The antimonarchical sentiments that O'Dea cites are shown in this essay to be strangely un-American. See, for example, 2 Nephi 5:18; Mosiah 2:14–18; 5:7; 23:6–14; 29:13–18, 23, 30–31; Alma 43:45; 46:10; 51:5, 8; 3 Nephi 6:30; Ether 6:22–26. For a comment on the idea of equality, see note 30 below.

4. Fawn M. Brodie, *No Man Knows My History: The Life of Joseph Smith, the Mormon Prophet*, 2nd ed., rev. (New York: Alfred A. Knopf, 1971), 69.

5. Alexander Campbell, *Delusions: An Analysis of the Book of Mormon; With an Examination of Its Internal and External Evidences, and a Refutation of Its Pretences to Divine Authority* (Boston: Benjamin H. Greene, 1832), 13; reprinted from Alexander Campbell, "Delusions," *Millennial Harbinger* 2 (February 7, 1831): 85–96.

6. An account of Lafayette's visit is found in Nathan Sargent, *Public Men and Events, From the Commencement of Mr. Monroe's Administration, in 1817, to the Close of Mr. Fillmore's Administration, in 1853*, 2 vols. (Philadelphia: J. B. Lippincott, 1875), 1:89–94. The 1824 *Wayne Sentinel* reported on Lafayette's progress almost weekly. For representative accounts, see the issues of July 7; September 1, 8, 15, 29; October 6 and 20; November 3 and 24, 1824. When news of the deaths of Adams and Jefferson reached Palmyra, the July 14, 1826, issue of *Sentinel* edged all its columns in black. Political interest in New York reached a high in the election of 1828 when 70.4% of adult white males voted. See Richard P. McCormick, "New Perspectives on Jacksonian Politics," *American Historical Review* 65 (January 1960): 292.

7. The relevant schoolbooks most frequently advertised in the *Wayne Sentinel* were *American Speaker, American Reader, American Preceptor, Columbian Orator*, and *English Reader*. For illustrative ads, see *Sentinel* issues of June 30 and November 10, 1824; October 27 and November 24, 1826; May 18, 1827; and September 26, 1828.

8. Caleb Bingham, *The American Preceptor; Being a New Selection of Lessons for Reading and Speaking, Designed for the Use of Schools*, 2nd ed. (New York: B. and J. Collins, 1815), 144.

9. "Eulogy for Thomas Jefferson," *Wayne Sentinel*, August 11, 1826.

10. As quoted in "La Fayette," *Wayne Sentinel*, September 1, 1824.

11. Mark A. Noll discusses the idea of the American Revolution as deliverance in *Christians in the American Revolution* (Washington D.C.: Christian University Press, 1977), 71–72. This theme, voiced during the Revolution, faded by Joseph Smith's day.

Among the favorite selections in textbooks were passages from the Boston Massacre orations of Joseph Warren, Benjamin Church, and John Hancock. See William B. Fowle, *The American Speaker, or Exercises in Rhetorick; Being a Selection of Speeches, Dialogues, and Poetry, from the Best American and English Sources, Suitable for Recitation* (Boston: Cummings, Hilliard, 1826), 74–90.

The deliverance theme can be seen in Fourth of July orations. The orator at Albany in 1817 observed that forty-one years had passed

> since the dauntless representatives of an oppressed but high minded people, having exhausted the gentle spirit of entreaty, and become persuaded of the utter uselessness of all further attempts at conciliation, dared to raise the arm of independence. . . . The country, bleeding at every pore, but not disheartened, reciprocated the lofty sentiment, and confiding in the equity of their cause, looked to heaven, and then aimed a death-blow at the head of tyranny. 'Twas one of the sublimest spectacles earth ever witnessed.

"PATRIOTS of '76," he said in the customary address to the veterans, "to you the scene must be most animating. You toiled, you suffered, you were willing to bleed and die in the glorious cause." Hooper Cummings, *An Oration, Delivered July 4th, 1817* (Albany: I. W. Clark, 1817), 5, 14.

12. In one instance, an individual not numbered among the people of God attempts to assassinate King Noah, but the wily monarch escapes by subterfuge. See Mosiah 19:2–6.

13. Hugh Nibley discusses flight as part of the tradition of escape from crumbling societies in *An Approach to the Book of Mormon*, 2nd ed. (Salt Lake City: Deseret Book, 1964), 106–14.

14. There is no evidence that Book of Mormon people believed revolution to be sinful. The people of Limhi considered delivering "themselves out of bondage by the sword," but gave up the idea because of the superiority of Lamanite numbers. See Mosiah 22:2. The point is that resistance was not necessary to make a compelling story. Flight and deliverance had a greater moral impact.

15. Editorial, *Wayne Sentinel*, July 4, 1828.

16. Editorial, *Wayne Sentinel*, July 18, 1828.

17. "Oration," *Wayne Sentinel*, July 21, 1826.

18. Ibid.

19. Jefferson, quoted in "Eulogy on Thomas Jefferson," *Wayne Sentinel*, August 11, 1826. The orator who pronounced the eulogy on Adams and Jefferson at nearby Buffalo in 1826 elaborated the same themes.

> Looking retrospectively through the lapse of half a century, we behold those stern patriots ardently engaged in the great work of political reformation. Until then, the human mind, shackled and awed by the insignia of power, had remained unconscious of its own noble faculties. Until then, man had failed to enjoy that exalted character designed in his creation. Until

then, he had yielded to the dictates of usurpation and the arrogant pretensions of self-created kings. . . . Here and there the rays of mental light had burst upon the earth; but like the flashes of the midnight storm, they had passed away, and all again was darkness. . . .

To them and a few worthy compatriots, were reserved the signal honors of broaching a new theory; of solving that, until then mysterious problem of self government; of opposing successfully the blasphemous doctrine of the divine right of kings; of redeeming the rights of man from the chaotic accumulations of ignorance, superstition and prejudice; of unfolding to the world the true source of temporal enjoyment, and the legitimate object of restoring man to his proper dignity in the great scale of being. (Sheldon Smith, "Eulogy, Pronounced at Buffalo, New-York, July 22d, in 1826," in *A Selection of Eulogies, Pronounced in the Several States, in Honor of those Illustrious Patriots and Statesmen, John Adams and Thomas Jefferson* [Hartford, Conn.: D. F. Robinson, Norton and Russell, 1826], 92, 95)

Orators enjoyed taking inventory of democracy among the nations of the earth and analyzing the reasons for the continuance of tyranny. Why despotism in nations where conditions were otherwise favorable? asked the speaker at Troy in 1825. "If they were not debased in spirit—if they were not groping in the darkness of ignorance, or faltering in the twilight of the mind, no tyrant would strip them of their rights—no despotic throne would cast its portentous and chill shadow over the land of their birth." O. L. Holley, *An Address, Delivered before the Mechanics of Troy, at their Request, on the 4th of July, 1825* (Troy, N.Y.: Tuttle and Richards, 1825), 7. For the most part, Americans were optimistic about the principles of democracy. William Duer at Albany in 1826 predicted that before another jubilee, the principles of the Declaration "will take root and flourish in every soil and climate under Heaven! The march of Light, of Knowledge, and of Truth, is irresistible, and Freedom follows in their train." Duer, as quoted in L. H. Butterfield, "The Jubilee of Independence, July 4, 1826," *Virginia Magazine of History and Biography* 61 (April 1953): 138. "The old monarchies of Europe must be entombed in some great political convulsion, if they listen not in season to the low but deep murmur of discontent, among their subjects, which is growing louder and louder with the progress of intellectual light." William Chamberlain Jr., *An Address Delivered at Windsor, Vt., Before an Assembly of Citizens from the Counties of Windsor, Vt., and Cheshire, N. H. on the Fiftieth Anniversary of American Independence* (Windsor, Vt.: Simeon Ide, 1826), 24.

20. Mormon reported much later that "the kingdom had been conferred upon none but those who were descendants of Nephi" (Mosiah 25:13), implying hereditary monarchy. Jacob, Nephi's brother, said that to honor the first Nephi, subsequent rulers "were called by the people, second Nephi, third Nephi, and so forth, according to the reigns of the kings" (Jacob 1:11).

21. Hugh Nibley suggests that rule by judges was familiar to Nephites because of precedents in Israel.

In Zedekiah's time the ancient and venerable council of elders had been thrust aside by the proud and haughty *judges*, the spoiled children of frustrated and ambitious princes. . . . Since the king no longer sat in judgment, the ambitious climbers had taken over the powerful and dignified—and for them very profitable—"*judgment seats*," and by systematic abuse of their power as judges made themselves obnoxious and oppressive to the nation as a whole while suppressing all criticism of themselves—especially from the recalcitrant and subversive prophets. (Nibley, *An Approach*, 82)

The provision for impeachment of corrupt judges in Mosiah's time could have reflected the trouble these judges had given the Israelites. Compare Hugh Nibley, *Lehi in the Desert and The World of the Jaredites* (Salt Lake City: Bookcraft, 1952), 20–26.

22. William Powell Mason, *An Oration Delivered Wednesday, July 4, 1827, in Commemoration of American Independence, Before the Supreme Executive of the Commonwealth, and the City Council and Inhabitants of the City of Boston* (Boston: N. Hale, 1827), 17.

23. There was a democratic element in the transmittal of authority. Alma "selected a wise man who was among the elders of the church, and gave him power according to the voice of the people" (Alma 4:16). But Alma's selection was the major part of it: "Now Alma did not grant unto him the office of being high priest over the church, but he retained the office of high priest unto himself; but he delivered the judgment-seat unto Nephihah" (Alma 4:18).

24. The confirmation of the chief judges by the voice of the people is the only element of the Nephite constitution that comes close to republicanism, and in the context of life tenure and hereditary succession, this "election" is closer to the traditional acclamation of the king than to a popular plebiscite. We forget that kings have usually been thought to rule by the consent of their people and that at the ascent of a new king to the throne this consent is normally exhibited anew. Sometimes the election is merely ritualistic; in other cases, such as the selection of William III by the Convention Parliament in 1688, the consent of the people's representatives was as essential as the popular election of an American president. There was a popular element in Nephite monarchy, too. While still monarch, Mosiah had sent "among all the people, desiring to know their will concerning who should be their king" (Mosiah 29:1). Zeniff was earlier "made a king by the voice of the people" (Mosiah 7:9; see also Mosiah 19:26). The army of Israel "made their commander Omri king of Israel by common consent" (1 Kings 16:16, NEB).

Marc Bloch, in his study of medieval European society, asks,

> How was this monarchical office, with its weight of mixed traditions, handed on—by hereditary succession or by election? Today we are apt to regard the two methods as strictly incompatible; but we have the evidence of innumerable texts that they did not appear so to the same degree in the Middle Ages. . . .
>
> . . . Within the predestinate family . . . the principle personages of the realm, the natural representatives of the whole body of subjects, named the new king. (Marc Bloch, *Feudal Society*, tr. L. A. Manyon [Chicago: University of Chicago Press, 1961], 383–84)

One episode that may to a casual reader have a republican flavor is General Moroni's elevation of the "title of liberty," on which he wrote: "In memory of our God, our religion, and freedom, and our peace, our wives, and our children" (Alma 46:12). Around this emblem he rallied the people against a movement to raise up a king. While the word *liberty* and the opposition to monarchists strike a familiar note, the details of the story, beginning with the peculiar designation "the title of liberty," are strangely archaic.

Moroni made the scroll in the first place by rending his coat, and proceeded to enlist the people in the cause by "waving the rent part of the garment in the air" and crying, "Behold, whosoever will maintain this title upon the land let him come forth in the strength of the Lord, and enter into a covenant that they will maintain their rights, and their religion, that the Lord God may bless them" (Alma 46:19–20). Responding to the call, the people "came running together with their armor girded about their loins, rending their garments in token, or as a covenant, that they would not forsake the Lord their God" (Alma 46:21). "They cast their garments at the feet of Moroni" and covenanted that God "may cast us at the feet of our enemies, even as we have cast our garments at thy feet to be trodden under foot, if we shall fall into transgression" (Alma 46:22). Whereupon Moroni launched into an elaborate comparison with Joseph, "whose coat was rent by his brethren into many pieces," and expressed hope for the Nephites' preservation in similitude of Joseph's (Alma 46:23).

It is difficult to see where Joseph Smith could have encountered precedents for that ritual in his American environment. Hugh Nibley has suggested that the title of liberty resembles the battle scroll of the Children of Light in the Qumran community. See Nibley, *An Approach*, 169–80; Hugh Nibley, *Since Cumorah: The Book of Mormon in the Modern World* (Salt Lake City: Deseret Book, 1967), 273–75.

25. As quoted in "Cincinnatus, No. 1," *Wayne Sentinel*, November 3, 1826.

26. As quoted in "Voice of the People," *Wayne Sentinel*, September 5, 1828. See also Editorial, *Wayne Sentinel*, September 12, 1828. A common argument against an incumbent was the danger of aristocratic pretensions occurring in men held in office too long. In 1826 the party opposing the reelection of Governor Clinton resolved "that the continuance of the office of governor in one family, for a period longer than twenty-eight years, out of forty-nine, in a state containing a population of nearly two millions, is at war with the republican principle upon which our government is founded, and would tend to the establishment of an odious aristocracy." "Address," *Wayne Sentinel*, October 20, 1826. Jacksonians in 1828 argued that one of the evils of the election of 1824 was that it established a system for passing on the presidency. Were it perpetuated, "the sovereignty of the people would be an idle name. . . . The president and his successor would save us [from] the trouble of an election—the heir-apparent would create the king—the king would nominate the heir-apparent to the crown." "Politics," *Wayne Sentinel*, October 10, 1828.

27. Under the influence of their own cultural conditioning, Mormons and non-Mormons alike have read American principles into the Book of Mormon, even though closer analysis will not sustain that view. Alexander Campbell saw republicanism in the book as did B. H. Roberts. Campbell, *Delusions*, 13; and B. H. Roberts, *New Witnesses for God*, 3 vols. (Salt Lake City: Deseret News, 1909), 2:209, 212.

28. Despite abuses of the taxing power, no recommendation was ever made for an elected assembly. See Mosiah 11:3, 6, 13; and Ether 10:6.

29. The nonrepublican forms of Book of Mormon government compel us to recognize that the "just and holy principles" that protect human rights can be embodied in various constitutional arrangements.

30. The word *inequality* in Mosiah 29:32 catches the eye of modern Americans, but in context the word assumes a meaning foreign to American thought. In the preceding verses, Mosiah explains the thinking behind his image, namely, that wicked kings enact iniquitous laws and compel their people to submit, thus causing them to sin. See Mosiah 29:17–18. A good king like Mosiah would enact no laws of his own, but rather would judge the people by the law handed down from the fathers, which ultimately came from God. See Mosiah 29:15, 25. Under bad monarchs, the king was responsible for the people's sins; under good ones, the people were responsible for themselves. One of the reasons for eliminating kings was to ensure "that if these people commit sins and iniquities they shall be answered upon their own heads. For behold I say unto you, the sins of many people have been caused by the iniquities of their kings; therefore their iniquities are answered upon the heads of the kings" (Mosiah 29:30–31). Then Mosiah makes the reference to inequality. "And now I desire that this inequality should be no more in this land" (Mosiah 29:32). It seems clear that *inequality* refers to the disproportionality of one sinful man, the king, having power to lead his people into iniquity.

This must be kept in mind when reading Mosiah 29:38, where it is reported that the people became "exceedingly anxious that every man should have an equal chance." An equal chance to do what? As Americans, we immediately assume an equal chance to get ahead in the world or to have a voice in government. The verse actually reads, "Every man should have an equal chance throughout all the land; yea and every man expressed a willingness to answer for his own sins" (Mosiah 29:38). Having so committed themselves, the people went out to choose judges "to judge them according to the law which had been given them." With a twist of mind we can scarcely understand today, the privilege of being judged according to the traditional law was a major part of the "equality" and "liberty" in which the Nephites "exceedingly rejoiced" (Mosiah 29:39; see also Mosiah 29:25, 41). A similar principle underlies the American Constitution. The Lord suffered it to be established, he says in the Doctrine and Covenants, so that "every man may be accountable for his own sins in the day of judgment" (D&C 101:78).

The discourse of Mosiah, viewed against the practice of hereditary descent of the chief judgeship, raises the possibility that the major distinction between judge and king was the lawmaking power. Mosiah did not contest the right of the king to make laws, only to make iniquitous ones. A judge, however, could not even claim legislative powers and thus perforce governed by the divine law passed down from the fathers. See Mosiah 29:15, 25. Seemingly by definition, a lawmaker was suspect because he usurped the power of God, the maker of the traditional law. When the prophets said that the Lord should be king, they meant, at least in part, that he should make the laws.

31. There was another biblical tradition that credited God with instituting kings among the Israelites. Roland de Vaux, *Ancient Israel: Its Life and Institution*, tr. John McHugh, (New York: McGraw-Hill, 1961), 94.

32. See also Judges 9:1–6; 2 Samuel 2:4; 1 Kings 16:21–22; 2 Kings 11:12; 8:20.

33. de Vaux, *Ancient Israel*, 149–52.

34. This construction of the Book of Mormon is confirmed by the recent discovery that certain sections of the book follow the intricate patterns of chiasmus characteristic of Hebrew writing. See John W. Welch, "Chiasmus in the Book of Mormon," *BYU Studies* 10 (autumn 1969): 69–84. In many other details, which Hugh Nibley more than any other scholar has mastered, the Book of Mormon follows Hebrew and Near Eastern forms. See Nibley, *An Approach*; Nibley, *Since Cumorah*; and Nibley, *Lehi in the Desert*. Nibley points out similarities to the Egyptian as well as the Jewish culture. At the time of Lehi's exodus, the Jewish nation was under the political shadow of Egypt and was soaking in Egyptian patterns of thought and behavior.

35. Campbell, *Delusions*, 13.

6

The Book of Mormon in Early Mormon History

This essay, written as the 1986 presidential address for the Mormon History Association, was meant to engage two questions: first, the relevancy and, second, the intricacy of the Book of Mormon. At that time, I was puzzled by Joseph Smith's apparent neglect of the Book of Mormon once it was in print. After laboring arduously on the translation, he did not seem to build on the book in the way you would expect. He appeared to set it aside while turning to other activities. The essay attempted to link Joseph with his first major scriptural production.

The other question was how to convey the complexity of the Book of Mormon plot, my long-running campaign. Rather than prove the book true, I wanted to reveal its intricacy. It thrilled me to discover how historical texts, the fate of peoples, and translation were interwoven through the long history of Book of Mormon peoples—interwoven more thoroughly, I would say, than in any other historical writings, including the Bible. The book is extraordinarily self-conscious about its own construction. I thought it marvelous that a theme so foreign to Joseph Smith's own experience would be inserted into the inner structure of the narrative.

Was Joseph Smith a magician? That question has always lingered over the early history of Mormonism, but in recent years interest in the issue of magic has been renewed. The flurry of excitement over the short-lived Hofmann letters, with their evidence of a magical outlook in the 1820s, turned the attention of Mormon historians as never before to the broader scholarship on folk magic. There we have found a growing literature on an underground world of magical practices among Christians throughout the western world. Keith Thomas's massive work *Religion and the Decline of Magic* demonstrated beyond question the prevalence of magical beliefs in early modern England, and scholars working in the American field have found ample evidence of such beliefs persisting into the nineteenth century.[1] Alerted by the Hofmann letters and these studies of American religion, historians of Mormonism who reviewed the record with magic in mind discovered here and there many signs of magic among early Mormons. Even with the Hofmann letters out of the picture, magic is now entrenched in the story of Mormonism's founding. The excitement of the new discoveries, sustained by the general scholarly interest in magic, has even tempted some to toy with the idea that Joseph Smith was essentially and above all a magician and that magical beliefs lay at the very heart of nineteenth-century Mormonism.²

In the midst of the interest aroused by the new discoveries, we must not lose sight of other, more familiar materials that bear on the question of Joseph Smith's development and the mission of the early Church. Specifically, we should not forget the Book of Mormon. In that volume, we have over five hundred pages of source material, bearing on Joseph's character and culture. This is the book he dictated day after day for months. While most of the evidence about magic comes from the minds of others, the Book of Mormon came from Joseph Smith's own lips, giving it a special claim on our attention. There seems to be little question that Joseph Smith did follow practices that we would call magic, but before we sum him up in that one idea, we should weigh the few hundred words on that theme against the tens of thousands of words in the Book of Mormon. What do they imply for the Prophet's character? If believers object that the Book of Mormon does not contain Joseph's own words, they would surely agree that something to which he gave so much effort affected his thinking and provides insight into his mental world. By the same token, nonbelievers must agree that writing the Book of Mormon raises Joseph Smith above the ranks of ordinary folk magicians.

My purpose then is to reflect on the relationship of the Book of Mormon to the young Joseph Smith and to early Mormonism. Unfortunately, the relationship is far from clear, one reason perhaps for the neglect of the book's meaning in the early life of the Prophet. One connection is beyond dispute: the mission to the Lamanites in 1830 and 1831 obviously emerged directly from the Book of Mormon conception of the gathering of Israel in the last days. Otherwise, the interplay of the book, the Prophet, and the early Church is not easily described. Book of Mormon themes that we think should have resonated in Joseph Smith's life or in the early Church came to nothing. One would think that the passages on the Gadianton secret society would have aroused Joseph and his followers to active involvement in Antimasonry, but the early Mormons apparently avoided the movement, even when the Antimasonic party was at its peak. Or why was not Alma the Younger's conversion made the model for early Mormon conversions? Alma's experience of conviction of sin and reliance on Christ for redemption from the pains of hell followed the standard evangelical pattern closely enough for any nineteenth-century American to recognize the similarities. Yet Mormons never sought conversions of that sort. Mormons tried to instill belief in the Book of Mormon, faith in Christ, and repentance, quite a different thing from the ubiquitous revival preaching of the day. Grant Underwood has found that Mormons quoted the Book of Mormon far less than the Bible, even in sermons among themselves. Apart from the mission to the Lamanites, the Book of Mormon seems to stand apart from Joseph Smith and the early Church, complicating the task of determining what it reveals about the character of the young Prophet.[3]

Rather than search for specific doctrines or ideas linking the Book of Mormon to Joseph and early Mormonism, we are better advised, I believe, to consider the Book of Mormon in its broadest outlines. We should look for connections at a slightly higher level of abstraction. It is important to recognize that the Book of Mormon was more than a patchwork of theological assertions, or a miscellany of statements about the Indians, like Ethan Smith's *View of the Hebrews*.[4] We may miss the point if we treat the Book of Mormon as if it were a kind of hodgepodge. Some critics employ a proof text method in their analyses, taking passages out of context to prove a point. They pick out passages sounding like Masonry or republican ideology or evangelical preaching and link them to Joseph Smith's culture. While that kind of analysis may have its uses, it has had disappointing results. The danger is that we will lose sight of the larger world which the book evokes.

The genius of the Book of Mormon, like that of many works of art, is that it brings an entire society and culture into existence, with a religion, an economy, a technology, a government, a geography, a sociology, all combined into a complete world. For purposes of analysis, we must, of course, call forth one thread, one theme, one idea at a time, but we must also bear in mind the existence of this larger world and relate individual passages to greater structures if we are to find their broadest meaning. Perhaps by stepping back and considering this larger world of the Book of Mormon, we will perceive connections with early Mormonism that otherwise remain invisible.[5]

In this spirit, I turn to a particular aspect of Book of Mormon culture: its involvement with records. I wish to relate this single theme to the larger structures of Book of Mormon culture, in the hope that a connection with Joseph Smith and the early Church will come into view. The fundamental question for this inquiry is: Why is there a Book of Mormon? A record was made, hidden, discovered, translated, and published. Why did that happen? The question of why a Book of Mormon can be asked from many perspectives, but I wish to pose the question from the perspective of the book itself. Within the story's larger frame, why all the record-keeping? Why the immense effort lasting over centuries? Why the care to convey the records from one generation to the next? Why did Mormon, in the midst of his many troubles, work through the voluminous records to write a history? And going from the record-keepers themselves to their theology, what kind of a God makes so much of records? Why open a dispensation of the gospel with the translation of an ancient book? Since Mormon himself answered the question on the first page, we may conclude that nothing further need be said. But the title page of the Book of Mormon is only the beginning, or perhaps more accurately, it is the culmination and end. By re-creating the Book of Mormon world of records, we may catch a glimpse of how Joseph fits into the picture.[6]

The narrative involves readers with records in the very first sentence. Nephi introduces himself as a record-maker—"therefore I make a record of my proceedings in my days"—and goes on to testify of the record's truth before telling a single event (1 Ne. 1:1–3). We learn in the first chapter that Nephi's father, Lehi, also keeps a record, and we are given a complicated explanation of how Nephi will abridge his father's record as well as keep his own (see 1 Ne. 1:16–17). Besides launching us into the story of the family's visions and adventures, Nephi self-consciously informs us about the mechanics of getting it all down and of managing the various records being made.

Once the family has abandoned its home for the wilderness, the first major incident has to do with records. The return for Laban's plates lets the reader know that records loom large in this culture. Lehi asks his sons to accomplish a seemingly impossible task—to get the brass plates from a powerful, armed, truculent official who has no desire to give them up. The father knows he places his sons' lives at risk, yet insists. They not only jeopardize their lives but offer all the family's gold, silver, and precious things for the plates. In the end, Nephi, against all his instincts, kills for the record. He explains the murder of Laban by saying, "I knew that the Lord had delivered Laban into my hands for this cause—that I might obtain the records according to his commandments" (1 Ne. 4:17). The reasoning is that "it is better that one man should perish than that a nation should dwindle . . . in unbelief" (1 Ne. 4:13). In the Book of Mormon world, religious culture depends on records.

It should come as no surprise that at the end, Mormon, the redactor for whom the book is named, introduces himself as a record-keeper just as Nephi had. Mormon's introductory line is, "Now I, Mormon, make a record of the things which I have both seen and heard," and he tells at once how Ammaron, his predecessor, informed him of the plates' location in Shim and charged him to continue the record (Morm. 1:1–4). In the course of battling the Lamanites as Nephite civilization came to an end, Mormon moved the plates from one safe location to another, and in the midst of all his troubles managed to write a history from the beginning (Morm. 4:23; 6:6). The records pass to Moroni, who opened his account with the familiar tag, "Behold I, Moroni, do finish the record of my father" (Morm. 8:1).

In between Nephi and Moroni, we never lose sight of the records. Their descent is meticulously accounted for. In the first portion of the history, before King Benjamin, the kings, the descendants of Nephi, passed down one set of records; the other set went through descendants of Nephi's brother Jacob (see Jacob 7:27; Omni 1:11, 35; Mosiah 25:13). We lack the kingly record, but the Jacobean record tells us step by step of the passage from one record-keeper to another. For a time in Omni, the transmission of the records was nearly all that was written about (see Omni 1:8–12).[7] Throughout the Book of Mormon, there is a recurrent clanking of plates as they pass from one record-keeper to another. To my mind, it is noteworthy that there is nothing like this explicit description of records and record-keeping either in the Bible or in books current in nineteenth-century America.[8]

Looking back, we explain this interest in records teleologically, that is, by the final result. The Book of Mormon had a foreordained mission to fulfill before the end of the world. The record had to be kept, we say to ourselves, to accomplish the purposes outlined by Mormon on the title page. But that is only half the story. Records were intricately interwoven into the structures of Nephite society. Records had an ongoing function, apart from their ultimate purpose, making the process significant in the record-keeper's own times, not in the future alone.

We catch a glimpse of this function in an exchange between two groups of Nephites in the Book of Mosiah. Around 120 B.C., the Nephites occupied two regions, one around the city of Zarahemla and another in the land of Nephi. At the prompting of his people, King Mosiah in Zarahemla commissioned Ammon and sixteen men to find the other group, which Ammon succeeded in doing (see Mosiah 7:1–2, 6–7). At the point of contact, records came into play. Once King Limhi recognized Ammon as an emissary of the Zarahemla Nephites, he called his people to a meeting at the temple. Before the combined audience, Limhi read from two histories. One was the history of his own people since their arrival in the land of Nephi, and the other was the history of the people in Zarahemla to the point where his people departed (see Mosiah 7:17–33; 8:1). Then Limhi turned to Ammon and asked him to tell the history of the Zarahemla people since the separation, which Ammon did, including King Benjamin's famous address (see Mosiah 8:2–3). That ceremony concluded, Limhi dismissed the people, but the telling of histories was not yet at an end. Limhi also brought to Ammon the written records of the people to be read. The reunion of the two long-separated peoples apparently required a recitation of their histories, involving not only the two leaders, Limhi and Ammon, but the entire people.

Eventually Limhi's people reunited with Mosiah's people in Zarahemla, and once again the exchange of histories took place. The way Mormon put it is that "Mosiah received them with joy; and he also received their records," as if the joining of two peoples entailed the joining of their records (Mosiah 22:14). Mosiah, like Limhi earlier, then called all of the people together. The people from Nephi sat in one body and those from

Zarahemla in another, and Mosiah read the record of Limhi's people from the time they left Zarahemla until their return. Another record was read as well. Part of Limhi's people, under the leadership of Alma, had earlier splintered off and made their way back to Zarahemla about the same time. Though pursued and harried by enemies, Alma's small band had kept a record, which Mosiah read aloud before all the people (Mosiah 25:1–6). Once again the reunion of the three groups entailed the recitation of their various histories in a large public ceremony.

In Mormon's account, we are given a glimpse of what the ceremony meant to the people. The recitations went beyond mere ritualistic formality. Hearing them, the people "were struck with wonder and amazement" (Mosiah 25:7). A great variety of emotions played over them. They "were filled with exceedingly great joy" at the deliverance of their brethren (Mosiah 25:8). On the other hand, "they were filled with sorrow, and even shed many tears of sorrow" at the thought of the people killed by the Lamanites (Mosiah 25:9). The "goodness of God" exemplified in the stories caused them to give thanks, while the "sinful and polluted state" of the Lamanites filled the people "with pain and anguish" (Mosiah 25:10–11). Far from a boring lesson in history, the rehearsal of the stories thrilled the listeners. The recorded histories entered into their imaginations, stirring and instructing them.

The two kings, Limhi and Mosiah, apparently desired their peoples to know the stories of other groups, and formal procedures had been worked out for conveying this knowledge. At the same time, the people themselves wanted the knowledge and delighted in the poignant emotions the histories evoked. This was the pattern again when it came to translating the Jaredite record on the twenty-four gold plates. King Limhi early on had asked Ammon about translation, and Ammon had told the king about Mosiah's gift of seership. But when Limhi and Mosiah were united, Mosiah's people were the ones to urge immediate translation. Mosiah had to work on the plates "because of the great anxiety of his people; for they were desirous beyond measure to know concerning those people who had been destroyed" (Mosiah 28:12). When Mosiah finished, the "account did cause the people of Mosiah to mourn exceedingly, yea, they were filled with sorrow; nevertheless it gave them much knowledge, in the which they did rejoice" (Mosiah 28:18). In the Book of Mormon world, histories nourished and instructed people. Records were the bread and meat of their conceptual lives.

This process of passing histories from one people to another went beyond the immediate value to the hearers. Records were tied to a broad conception of human society and world history. Records did not come into being as an isolated phenomenon but as a necessary component of an elaborate historical pattern. To begin with, it must be recalled that the

Nephites, far more than the Israelites, conceived of "global" societies. The Bible refers to scores of "ites," the various tribal peoples and nations living in the lands bordering Canaan. But the Israelites' geographical images did not stretch much beyond the Middle East and the Mediterranean. Only obscurely did the prophets call up faint pictures of America or the Orient. Not so with the Nephites. Consistent with their own migration, they had a more extended image of the earth. The Nephites conceived of human society as consisting of many peoples scattered across the earth, many of these nations keeping records. There were many nations and many records, and the records were the means by which the nations defined their roles in world history.

The Nephite conception of multiple nations began with Israel. In his effort to explain the meaning of their lives to his little band washed ashore in a strange land, Nephi enlarged upon Isaiah's idea of Israel scattered to the isles of the sea. Their own condition, Nephi insisted to his people, was not aberrant but typical. "For it appears that the house of Israel, sooner or later, will be scattered upon all the face of the earth, and also among all nations" (1 Ne. 22:3–5). Already "the more part of all the tribes have been led away; and they are scattered to and fro upon the isles of the sea" (1 Ne. 22:4–5; see also 3 Ne. 15:20). And the rest were soon to follow. The Nephites were but one fragment among many of the original Israel, and as a dispersed fragment were prototypical. In time all of Israel would be spread about the earth.

Each of these fragments, Nephi told his people, kept its record of God's revelations. God spoke to the Jews just as he did to the Nephites and, as the scripture said, "I shall also speak unto the other tribes of the house of Israel, which I have led away, and they shall write it" (2 Ne. 29:12). Each fragment of scattered Israel had its written record, and that was not all. Nephi envisioned other nations, not sprung from Israel, each with revelations, each with a record. "For I command all men, both in the east and in the west, and in the north, and in the south, and in the islands of the sea, that they shall write the words which I speak unto them" (2 Ne. 29:11). Every people had its revelation and its record. "I shall also speak unto all nations of the earth and they shall write it" (2 Ne. 29:12; see also Alma 29:8).[9] World history was creating a river of bibles cascading down through time from the diverse peoples of the earth.

The ultimate value of this great library of records went beyond their use by each individual people. In time the records would come together just as the people themselves would be gathered. The ritual of exchanging histories practiced in miniature by Limhi, Mosiah, Alma, and Ammon would be replicated on a grand scale. Nephi gave it as a general principle that "when the two nations shall run together the testimony of the two nations shall run together also" (2 Ne. 29:8). At the concluding gathering at the end of the earth, all of these various records would be joined, and each people would learn the others' histories. "The Jews shall have the words of the Nephites, and the Nephites shall have the words of the Jews; and the Nephites and the Jews shall have the words of the lost tribes of Israel; and the lost tribes of Israel shall have the words of the Nephites and the Jews" (2 Ne. 29:13). It would be a complicated and time-consuming ceremony, but Nephi insisted that the exchange of histories among the various peoples must be complete. Each must know the history of the others as part of the final assemblage of Israel. Just as the Lord's peoples were to become one, so his "word also shall be gathered in one" (2 Ne. 9:14).

Records, then, in the Nephite conception of the world, were, in effect, surrogates of peoples. They encompassed their revelations and their experience, and when Providence in the end assembled and united all peoples, bringing history to a conclusion, the records stood for the people. At that final day, their records would give the Nephites a part in the grand orchestra of the nations.[10]

The central place given records at the end grew out of their function all through the course of history. We have seen how peoples exchanged records when they met, whether in the course of events or at the final restoration. The ritual was important: the records were powerful forces shaping and directing their culture. Consider the poor people of Zarahemla who left Jerusalem in the days of Zedekiah without records, no one having had the foresight to wrest them from a Laban. When they met Mosiah, all they could offer by way of history was a genealogy, recited from memory by their leader, Zarahemla. Without a record, within three or four hundred years their language was corrupted, and they had lost their religion, not even believing in God anymore. When they met Mosiah, they yielded at once to the superior culture of the Nephites, learning their language and making Mosiah king in place of Zarahemla (see Omni 1:14–19).

Something of the same sort was true for the Christian church. Nephi saw the apostasy of Christianity in his wilderness vision and explained why the church stumbled. They began with the record of the Jews containing "the fulness of the gospel of the Lord" (1 Ne. 13:24). People fell after there were "many plain and precious things taken away from the book" (1 Ne. 13:28). The perversion of the scriptural record brought on apostasy. "Because of these things which are taken away out of the gospel of the Lamb, an exceedingly great many do stumble, yea, insomuch that Satan hath great power over them" (1 Ne. 13:29). Records guided and sustained culture; without a true record, religion and the social order fell apart. Within the world of the Book of Mormon, it was perfectly consistent for the resurrected Christ to examine the Nephite records and require their amendment when an omission was found (see 3 Ne. 23:7–13). The maintenance of culture depended on accurate records.

If poor records led to the deterioration of culture, by the same token, true records had the power to revive and redirect a people. Since the loss of plain and precious truths from the record of the Jews caused the gentile Christian church to stumble, what better means to restore it than a true and accurate record? In fact, what other means? Without a true record there was no hope for a true religion. The ultimate role of Nephi's record was to "make known the plain and precious things which have been taken away" from the Jewish record and thus bring people back to Christ. The Nephite record was to speak from the dust, especially to the Lamanites, establishing their true identity as the covenanted people of Israel (1 Ne. 13:35–40).

What was true for the Lamanites was true for all of Israel. One of Nephi's central themes, taking a cue from Isaiah, was the ultimate restoration of Israel. And by what means was God to accomplish this great recovery? "He shall bring forth his words unto them," the words recorded in the Book of Mormon (2 Ne. 25:17–18). The great work of God in restoring lost Israel was to be accomplished by the production of a record, the written history and revelations of an ancient people.[11] In the world of the Book of Mormon, confidence in the power of words far exceeds the comparable faith of our own supposedly literate culture.

So we can see that records wind their way in and out of Nephite culture, not superficially but profoundly. They lay at the foundation of the Book of Mormon world as depicted by its prophets. The practice of exchanging histories suggests the Nephite assumption that every people must have its record, and that one people relates to another by presenting its testimony, that is to say its history. The exchange of records facilitates relationships from time to time in the course of ordinary events, but also at the culmination of world history when all people will come together and join in one, exchanging histories and testimonies as part of the concluding restoration.

Beyond the articulation of relationships among the nations, in the Book of Mormon world, records sustain the identity and culture of a people. Without records a people degenerate, lose their religion and their language, and forget their covenants with God. By the same token, records have the power to revive culture, to restore religion, and to reaffirm a people's identity and remembrance of covenants. Records are the primary instrument of restoration. Hence the Book of Mormon's mission to inform Israel of the covenant of the Lord and to convince Jew and Gentile that Jesus is the Christ. Within the world of the Book of Mormon, a historical record was the natural instrument to accomplish grand purposes.

The Book of Mormon works out this schema of world history down to the brass-tack details. From a practical standpoint, the exchange of diverse records entails serious technical difficulties. Multiple languages require translations from one tongue to another. Otherwise how are people to understand one another at the last day? Rather than finesse the technical problems, leaving them to be settled in some vague, unspecified fashion, the Book of Mormon focuses on them. It brings forward the issue of multiple languages, exalts translators, and makes translation a holy process.

From the very outset, record-keeping and the problem of language were joined. In the same opening statement where he announced himself as a record-keeper, Nephi informed his readers of the characters in which he wrote—Egyptian (1 Ne. 1:2). At the end of Nephite history, Moroni again raised the language question, mentioning that the record-keepers used reformed Egyptian (Moro. 9:32).[12] How was a record in reformed Egyptian to be read? Moroni believed that "none other people knoweth our language," leading to problems when the Nephite records written in a lost language reached the Gentiles and the latter-day Lamanites (Morm. 9:34). That, of course, is all worked out in the story. God had long before foreseen the need and given the Brother of Jared stones for interpreting language (see Ether 3:23). But that was not all. The interpreters were associated with a person and a calling. A new religious office emerges in the world of the Book of Mormon, one to my knowledge unknown in other religious cultures, the office of translator, a person granted the "high gift," as Ammon said, of translating records (Mosiah 8:13–14). The first Mosiah, the father of King Benjamin, was the first man in the record to actually exercise the gift when he translated the engraved stone that told of Coriantumr, the Jaredite (see Omni 1:20). Although not commonly exercised thereafter, the translating powers of the seers were nonetheless well known. When Ammon heard about the twenty-four gold plates, he knew at once how to get them interpreted. "I can assuredly tell thee, O king, of a man that can translate the records" (Mosiah 8:13). Ammon knew that King Mosiah, grandson of the previous translator, could perform the task because Mosiah had the interpreters. The power of seership and thence of translation passed with the records and the interpreting stones. Even Ammon, a soldier and explorer who counted himself unworthy to baptize, was aware of the gift. It was likely part of common lore, known to Ammon and many others, that whoever possessed the stones "is called seer, after the manner of old times" (Mosiah 28:13–16).[13]

Which brings us at last to Joseph Smith and the modern Church of Christ. I wrote at one time that the Book of Mormon had peculiarly little influence on Mormonism, considering the great effort that went into the book's translation.[14] I now see I was mistaken. In the early years of the Church, Joseph Smith was to a surprising degree absorbed into the world of the Book of Mormon. The Book of Mormon had a peculiar power to draw readers into its world. Its authors continually turn from the world in which they themselves lived toward their modern readers. "I speak unto you as if ye were present," one said, and virtually all wrote in that spirit, looking us right in the eye (Morm. 8:35). Moroni carries this connection with the modern world to an extreme. He acts like the explorer in the Woody Allen movie *The Purple Rose of Cairo.* He steps off the screen into the audience, shows up in the bedroom of Joseph Smith, and invites him to join the story going on inside the movie.

And Joseph Smith did, in one portion of his life, become a character in the Nephite drama. The mission to the Lamanites was part of the story, but not all. Hints of Joseph's role appear in the book itself, in the prophetic description of the modern Joseph. He is there defined primarily as a seer, and as one who would bring forth records (see 2 Ne. 3:7, 12, 19). The modern revelations to Joseph Smith picked up that theme. They made clear that his great gift, the one first to define his religious vocation, was the gift of translation. Prominent among the titles given him at the organization of the Church were those of "a seer, a translator" (D&C 21:1). It did not suffice at the beginnings of the Church for Smith to receive revelations like the prophets who preceded him. He was also to translate, the role given him by prophecy in the Book of Mormon (see D&C 3:11–12; 10:1–3, 46–53; 20:8).

Naturally the title fit, because Joseph Smith's first great call was to translate the Book of Mormon. But his license to translate did not lapse once he completed the book. In the Book of Mormon, translation had lasting importance. It was not a fleeting assignment that ended when a single job was done. The Book of Mormon filled history with sacred records, all requiring translation to complete the work of restoration and the unification of the earth's peoples. Though the gift of translation might lie dormant, as it did periodically in the Book of Mormon itself, the gift could never lapse completely while records in diverse tongues yet remained. Especially at the end of the world, in the time of restoration, the seer must repeatedly exercise his powers. In keeping with the requirements of the age, the revelations assigned the title of translator to Joseph to the end of his life, and permanently attached it to the office of President of the High Priesthood (see D&C 107: 91–92; 124:125).

In the Prophet's own time, the powers of translation did not remain dormant. The modern revelations took up where the Book of Mormon left off with intimations of additional ancient records to be translated. At one point, a revelation promised Oliver Cowdery the prized gift of translation (see D&C 6:25–26; see also 8:1, 11). When he failed to translate from the Book of Mormon plates, a revelation told him not to worry. He would have another chance with "other records" yet to come forth (D&C 9:2). The revelations referred to "all those ancient records which have been hid up, that are sacred" (D&C 8:11). Although Cowdery remained on the margins of the work, Joseph soon was deeply immersed in the recovery of such records. The Book of Moses, revealed through the latter half of 1830, contained scriptures lost "because of wickedness" from Moses' original record (Moses 1:23). Soon after, Smith began retranslating the Bible, and in 1835 started on the Book of Abraham. In the midst of organizing the Church, sending out missionaries, establishing Mormon settlements, and directing migrations, Joseph Smith did not forget his crucial role as translator. Though harried with demands of every kind, for days at a time he worked away on one record or another to fulfill his divine calling.[15]

There is not then a gap between the Book of Mormon and the early latter-day Church, as I once thought. Jan Shipps has argued that the Book of Mormon was one of the great foundation pillars of early Mormonism, and I agree.[16] Far more than the folk magic that soon receded into the background, the translation of ancient records was Joseph Smith's central religious vocation from 1827 until the organization of the Church. In 1830 he was above all a seer and a translator. The work of translation occupied much of his time, the gift of translation attracted followers, and the role distinguished him. And the role, the gift, and the underlying conception of historic peoples keeping sacred records to be recovered in the last day all emerged from the world of the Book of Mormon.

The Book of Mormon in fact gave to the word *restoration* its peculiar Mormon flavor. Restoration was more than the recovery of true doctrine, or even the bestowal of priesthood keys. Restoration in the Book of Mormon sense meant the recovery of the entire experience of all the world's peoples through the translation and absorption of their histories. Nothing less than the restoration of world history was the charge given to Joseph Smith when he accepted the responsibilities of seer and translator prophesied of him in the Book of Mormon.

NOTES

1. Keith Thomas, *Religion and the Decline of Magic* (New York: Scribner, 1971); Herbert Leventhal, *In the Shadow of the Enlightenment: Occultism and Renaissance Science in Eighteenth-Century America* (New York: New York University Press, 1976); Jon Butler, *Awash in a Sea of Faith: Christianizing the American People* (Cambridge: Harvard University Press, 1990), 225–38; Alan Taylor, "The Early Republic's Supernatural Economy: Treasure Seeking in the American Northeast, 1780–1830," *American Quarterly* 38 (spring 1986): 6–33.

2. D. Michael Quinn, *Early Mormonism and the Magic World View*, rev. ed. (Salt Lake City: Signature Books, 1998); Richard L. Bushman, *Joseph Smith and the Beginnings of Mormonism* (Urbana: University of Illinois Press, 1984), 69–72; Marvin S. Hill, "Money-Digging, Folklore and the Beginnings of Mormonism: An Interpretive

Suggestion," *BYU Studies* 24 (fall 1984): 473–88; Ronald W. Walker, "Joseph Smith: The Palmyra Seer," *BYU Studies* 24 (fall 1984): 461–72; Ronald W. Walker, "The Persisting Idea of American Treasure Hunting," *BYU Studies* 24 (fall 1984): 429–59; and Alan Taylor, "Rediscovering the Context of Joseph Smith's Treasure Digging," *Dialogue: A Journal of Mormon Thought* 19 (winter 1986): 18–28.

3. Bushman, *Joseph Smith and the Beginnings of Mormonism,* 128–31, 140–42; Grant Underwood, "The Earliest Reference Guides to the Book of Mormon: Windows into the Past," *Journal of Mormon History* 12 (1985): 69–89; Grant Underwood, "Book of Mormon Usage in Early LDS Theology," *Dialogue: A Journal of Mormon Thought* 17 (autumn 1984): 35–74.

4. Ethan Smith, *View of the Hebrews* (Poultney, Vt.: Smith and Shute, 1823).

5. The best Book of Mormon analysis has always looked at the large picture, of course. An excellent example is John L. Sorenson, *An Ancient American Setting for the Book of Mormon* (Salt Lake City and Provo: Deseret Book and FARMS, 1985).

6. John L. Sorenson makes astute and revealing comments about Book of Mormon record-keeping in his *Ancient American Setting,* 50–56.

7. For an analysis of the motives of these record-keepers, see John W. Welch, "The Father's Command to Keep Records in the Small Plates of Nephi," unpublished typescript, FARMS, 1984.

8. From time to time, records came to the fore in Israelite history, as in 2 Chronicles 34:29–30 and 35:26–27 in the reign of Josiah. Emphasis on records was not inconsistent with events in the Bible; records simply received much more attention in the Book of Mormon.

9. The "all nations" must have had some qualifications, as John Sorenson has pointed out to me, since the people of Zarahemla and the Lamanites were known not to keep written records.

10. Ezekiel 37:15–20 is one passage in the Old Testament suggesting a similar process. For comments on this passage from a Latter-day Saint point of view, see Keith H. Meservy, "Discoveries at Nimrud and the 'Sticks' of Ezekiel 37," *Newsletter and Proceedings of the Society for Early Historical Archaeology* 142 (November 1978): 1–10; Hugh Nibley, "The Stick of Judah," *Improvement Era* 56 (January 1953): 16–17, 38–41; and the subsequent parts entitled "The Stick of Judah and the Stick of Joseph," *Improvement Era* 56 (February 1953): 90–91, 123–27; (March 1953): 150–52, 191–95; (April 1953): 250, 266–67; (May 1953): 331–32, 334, 336, 338, 341, 343–44.

11. See 2 Nephi 3:12; 29:2, 30:3–6; Mormon 5:14–15; 7:1, 9–10, 19.

12. Since an altered form of Hebrew was the vernacular language of Nephite society, according to Moroni, the record-keepers had to learn a second language. Benjamin taught his sons language, presumably Egyptian, to enable them to read the prophecies (see Mosiah 1:2). All of the record-keepers must have received the same instruction. Moroni said the reformed Egyptian was handed down from generation to generation to the very end (see Morm. 9:32). Assumption of responsibility for the records included mastery of a priestly language. Apparently the high place afforded record-keeping in the culture sufficed to sustain this arduous requirement over a thousand-year period.

13. The Nephites believed the stones were "prepared from the beginning, and were handed down from generation to generation, for the purpose of interpreting languages" (Mosiah 28:14, 20). Alma the Younger received the interpreters as did his son Helaman (Alma 37:21). Although the gift went unused for generations, Alma said the "gift of translation" was one of the gifts granted to the Nephites (Alma 9:21). Moroni, for example, translated the Jaredite record anew, rather than going back to Mosiah's previous translation (Ether 1:2). For the seers who possessed the interpreters, the translation of ancient records was a matter of course.

14. Bushman, *Joseph Smith and the Beginnings of Mormonism*, 141–42.

15. On the translation of other texts, see Richard P. Howard, *Restoration Scriptures: A Study of Their Textual Development*, 2d ed., rev. (Independence, Mo.: Herald Publishing House, 1995); Robert J. Matthews, *"A Plainer Translation": Joseph Smith's Translation of the Bible, a History and Commentary* (Provo: Brigham Young University Press, 1975); and James R. Clark, *The Story of the Pearl of Great Price* (Salt Lake City: Bookcraft, 1955).

16. Jan Shipps, *Mormonism: The Story of a New Religious Tradition* (Urbana: University of Illinois Press, 1985), 25–39.

7

The Lamanite View of Book of Mormon History

I cannot recall why I originally wrote this essay; it was not for the Hugh Nibley festschrift where it eventually appeared. I had the essay in my files for years before an opportunity to publish arose.

The essay shows the influence of my work on the American Revolution and my years working in psychohistory. Anyone who investigates the historiography of the Revolution learns about the fate of the Tory view in the aftermath of the American victory. The Loyalists' understanding of the Revolution was simply abolished for a century until a later generation of Anglophiles rediscovered it. In a sense, I wanted to do for the Lamanites what the "imperial" historians did for the Tories. The essay's other influence is Freud. The passages on Laman's frustrated wish for pleasure without submission echo my two-year postdoctoral study under the tutelage of Erik Erikson, the famous psychoanalyst and author of Young Man Luther *(New York: Norton, 1958), a psychosocial biography. The idea of a conflict between the desire for sensory gratification and the need to submit to authority comes right out of Freudian psychodynamics of the id and superego.*

History is one of the spoils of war. In great conflicts, the victors almost always write the history; the losers' story is forgotten. We remember the patriots' version of the American Revolution, not the loyalists'; the Northern account of the Civil War, not the Southern story of the War between the States; the Allies' story in World War II, not the Axis's. Ordinarily the winners' account of events commands our memories as completely as their armies controlled the battlefield. The reverse is true of the Book of Mormon. The Lamanites vanquished the Nephites and survived; yet by virtue of a record that went into the earth with them, the Nephites' version of the history is the one we now read. We think of the Nephites as the superior nation because they wrote the history, even though in the end the Lamanites won on the battlefield. How would the story go if the Lamanites had kept the records and their view were in our hands today? We cannot say in any detail, of course, but there are enough clues scattered through the Nephite record to offer a few conjectures about a Lamanite history of Lehi's descendants. Since the way we write history is tied closely to fundamental cultural values, in recovering the Lamanite perspective, we obtain a clearer view of the two cultures, and, as it turns out, a deeper understanding of Nephite religion.

One fact would surely figure as prominently in the Lamanite record as the Nephite: the frequent wars between the two peoples. Especially in their first six hundred years, the Lamanites exerted relentless pressure on the Nephites, driving or causing them to move farther and farther north, to the lands of Nephi, Zarahemla, and Bountiful, and at last the land northward. Why did the Lamanites fight? More often than not in the first six hundred years, they lost the wars with the Nephites. They sent vast armies into Nephite territory,.won a battle or two, and then were defeated with a huge loss of life and driven back to their own lands. For hundreds of years these attacks and defeats succeeded one another with no apparent gain. What brought the Lamanites back year after year to be outmaneuvered and out-fought by the Nephites?

The Nephite record says little more than "they delighted in wars and bloodshed, and they had an eternal hatred against us, their brethren" (Jacob 7:24). Without questioning the essential truth of that judgment, as moderns we wish to know more. Were not the Lamanites seeking more substantive gains for themselves than mere vengeance? We could under-stand the wars if the Lamanites suffered from a land shortage and wished to capture new territory. While that was possibly the case, there is no men-tion of a land shortage, and there is evidence of a plenitude of land. The Lamanite king welcomed the people of Zeniff when they migrated into Lamanite territory as if there were enough land to go around (Mosiah 9). Why would a Lamanite king clear out his people from a broad valley to make room for Nephites if he lacked land? The king did benefit from Zeniff's presence in one respect: he exacted tribute. Traditionally that has been a powerful motive for imperial expansion, and whenever a Nephite people came under Lamanite control, the Nephites paid heavy tribute. But the Lamanite armies failed so consistently for eight hundred years, never actually conquering a Nephite people for more than a few years at any one time so far as can be known, it is difficult to believe that the expectation of tribute sustained the Lamanites through all their losses.

The Nephite record gives a further explanation for those wars, in words directly quoted from Lamanite documents. In 63 B.C.E., Ammoron, the Lamanite king, wrote to Moroni about a prisoner exchange and explained why they fought: "For behold, your fathers did wrong their brethren, inso-much that they did rob them of their right to the government when it rightly belonged unto them" (Alma 54:17). The war would stop, Ammoron said to Moroni, if you "lay down your arms, and subject yourselves to be governed by those to whom the government doth rightly belong" (Alma 54:18). Ammoron referred, of course, to Laman's complaint that Nephi "thinks to rule over us," when Laman claimed the right of rulership. "We will not have him to be our ruler; for it belongs unto us, who are the elder brethren, to rule over this people" (2 Ne. 5:3). Ammoron represents the war as a continuation of an ancient feud between the two sets of brothers in Lehi's family.

That hardly makes sense to us. Would countless thousands of men hundreds of years later throw themselves into battle simply to reclaim an ancient right? It is all the more puzzling because after the landing in America, Nephi and his descendants made no claims that we know of to rule the Lamanites. Quite to the contrary, Nephi withdrew from the site of the first landing by command of the Lord, leaving the area to his brothers (2 Ne. 5:57). The first King Mosiah also withdrew by command of the Lord (Omni 1:12–13), pulling back from the Lamanites and not forcing his rule on them. Until near the end, the Nephites never fought aggressive wars. The Lamanites were the ones to attack, not the Nephites. How could such an abstraction as this ancient hurt motivate people over so many centuries? We have to credit the Book of Mormon explanation for the wars, coming as it does from both sides, but the source of its power remains a puzzle. Why should Nephi's onetime claim to rule arouse the wrath of the Lamanites generation after generation for hundreds of years?

In attacking this puzzle, we are best advised, I believe, to begin where the evidence points, with the story of the brothers in the opening pages. In summing up Lamanite animus against the Nephites, Ammoron attributed it to the original contest between Laman and Nephi, and that is probably reason enough for recognizing its primal importance to Lamanite culture. But there is another reason for taking these stories seriously. The Book of Mormon, like other ancient narratives, blends family history and national history. The story of a whole people grows out of the story of a single family, as the history of Israel begins with the family of Abraham. Israel thought of itself as the descendants of Abraham, Isaac, and Jacob, and what the patriarchs did to a large extent determined what Israel was for thousands of years. In our day, a revolution and the work of a convention in the Philadelphia statehouse determine our national identity. In ancient times, families founded nations and determined their character ever after. That is why the story of the competing brothers requires close analysis.

The most powerful impression we get from the family story is of Laman's and Lemuel's complaining natures. They were forever raising objections to Lehi or Nephi, becoming first sullen, then angry, and finally violent. We have to allow for Nephi's stern, exacting judgments of his brothers, but there is no reason to question the reality of their complaints. We too may have objected to the sacrifice of a comfortable life in Jerusalem for an arduous trek in the desert toward an unknown destination. Nor is there reason to question Laman's and Lemuel's resort to violence. At least five times, they physically punished Nephi or threatened his life. After the second visit to Laban, when they left all their property behind as they fled, Laman and Lemuel took out their anger on their younger brothers, smiting them with a rod (1 Ne. 3:29). A little later, on the way back from Jerusalem with Ishmael's family, Laman and Lemuel and a few of Ishmael's children grew so angry with Nephi's preaching that they bound him with cords and planned to kill him (1 Ne. 7:16). After the broken bow incident and Ishmael's death, Laman and Lemuel planned to kill both Lehi and Nephi (1 Ne. 16:37). When they arrived at the sea and Nephi proposed to build a ship, his brothers' patience wore thin again, and they tried to throw him "into the depths of the sea" (1 Ne. 17:48). Finally, aboard ship on the way to the promised land, Nephi reproached them for merrymaking, and Laman and Lemuel bound him with cords and treated him with "much harshness" (1 Ne. 18:11). By that time, Nephi's reproaches, the brothers' murmuring, and the violence had fallen into a pattern that characterized their relationship, establishing the recurring subplot of First Nephi.

On the other hand, a frequent result of the brothers' assaults on Nephi was a rebuke from the Lord. Once an angel appeared to chastise them, and on another occasion they heard the voice of the Lord. They gave way in the face of these rebukes, but on one occasion they did more than relent. When Nephi was about to construct a ship and the brothers in anger tried to throw him into the sea, Nephi was given the power to shock them physically with a touch. This show of power so overwhelmed Laman and Lemuel that they swung to the opposite extreme. Nephi says they "fell down before me, and were about to worship me," and he had to reassure them he was still only their brother (1 Ne. 17:53–55). This reaction, combined with the brothers' repeated violent assaults on Nephi, suggests that force was their characteristic reaction to crisis, the only language they understood in such situations. It seemed to be a matter of smite or be smitten.

There is another element in the founding story along with the complaints and the violence, namely deprivation. That theme is most evident on the ship. Laman and Lemuel, the sons of Ishmael, and their wives made themselves merry—dancing, singing, and speaking with much rudeness. Nephi, ever fearing the Lord would be displeased, spoke to them soberly, and they grew angry. Immediately his brothers came forth with the classic complaint: "We will not that our younger brother shall be a ruler over us," and bound him with cords (1 Ne. 18:9–11). In this case it seems that the denial of pleasure and the objections to Nephi's rule are closely linked. The attempt to stop the merrymaking aroused the thought of his unfounded claims to govern. The connection is most clear on the ship, but it has a place throughout the narrative. The brothers' complaint from the beginning is that Lehi and Nephi cause them needless physical suffering. Laman and Lemuel did not want to leave their home and leave behind "their gold, and their silver, and their precious things, to perish in the wilderness"

(1 Ne. 2:11). Then it was the loss of their precious things to Laban that set off the first physical attack—they beat Nephi with a rod (1 Ne. 3:24–28). Once on their way in the desert, suffering and deprivation became their common lot. The loss of the steel bow brought the problem to a head when "they did suffer much for the want of food," causing the brothers to "murmur exceedingly" (1 Ne. 16:19–20). The death of Ishmael made things worse, his daughters complaining that "we have suffered much affliction, hunger, thirst, and fatigue; and after all these sufferings we must perish in the wilderness with hunger" (1 Ne. 16:35). Even amid the abundance of Bountiful by the sea, the brothers held a grudge against Nephi for the eight years of wandering with their oftentimes pregnant wives, suffering in the desert when all along they might "have enjoyed [their] possessions and the land of [their] inheritance" (1 Ne. 17:20–21).

Basic deprivation underlay their truculence throughout. Nephi's intervention to stop the shipboard merrymaking was the straw that broke the camel's back. They had undergone untold afflictions in the wilderness—hunger, thirst, raw food—and now when they sought a little pleasure for themselves, he wanted to prevent them once more. To Laman and Lemuel, all the deprivations they suffered could be blamed on Nephi. It was not merely that he claimed rulership unjustly. His governance became unbearable when it was driven home that he used his power to cause them suffering. Nephi was the cause of their deprivation. Deep down they may have believed Nephi sought his own pleasure at their expense. They said once that they suspected him of leading them away to make himself king "that he may do with us according to his will and pleasure" (1 Ne. 16:38).

Combining these clues, then, we can reconstruct events as the Lamanites probably understood them. Initially they were living a pleasurable life amid their treasures and precious things in the land of Jerusalem. Their father's vision and subsequently Nephi's God-given claim to rule and teach them tore them away from these pleasures and subjected them to danger, affliction, and hunger. They grew angry time after time whenever events brought their fundamental grievance to the surface: they were made to suffer deprivations because of Nephi's attempts to rule. It is noticeable in this reconstructed plot that force plays a large part. The brothers feel that Nephi and Lehi are compelling them; Laman and Lemuel use force to stop Nephi; and it is divine force that breaks their will and compels submission. The Freudians would say that Laman and Lemuel had archaic superegos—that is, the internal monitors that controlled their desires used terror rather than persuasion to exact obedience.

With this plot before us, we can begin to understand the dilemma of existence as Laman and Lemuel understood the world. They felt compelled to choose between two unfortunate alternatives. On the one hand, they could enjoy pleasure and comfort by refusing submission to their father and brother, and since these two spoke for the Lord, refusing submission to God, too. Or on the other hand, they could yield abjectly to the superior power of the two prophets and their God, giving up all claims to pleasure and even to honor. Judging from the stories, Laman and Lemuel felt driven by events to choose between rebellious pleasure and fearful self-denial and submission. They could not envision a middle ground where obedience was joined with love and pleasure, and where a flourishing of their egos was in a happy harmony with God's will.

Nephi tried to cope with Laman's and Lemuel's legitimate complaints. There is no reason to believe that he was dedicated to a puritanical repression of the desire for pleasure. He was the one, when the steel bow broke, to make another from a straight stick and slay game for the group. He came into the camp with the beasts, and "when they beheld that I had obtained food, how great was their joy!" That was an understandable reaction, of course, but Nephi goes on to say, "They did humble themselves before the Lord, and did give thanks unto him" (1 Ne. 16:32). One catches a brief, pitiful glimpse of boys deprived of simple pleasure and eager to be compliant when for the moment they felt provided for. But the humility did not last. At the next trouble, their hearts hardened again, and they were plotting once more to slay Nephi. They acted as if force alone could be relied on. When Nephi said the party must leave Bountiful, the mysterious haven by the sea with its "much fruit and also wild honey" (1 Ne. 17:5), the brothers were at his throat immediately. With every call for a sacrifice they fell into the familiar pattern of murmuring and violence. Hovering in the distance was the promised land, enough to sustain Nephi and the faithful members of the party through the afflictions of the journey, but this was thin gruel for the suspicious and perhaps constitutionally deprived brothers.

Nephi's and Lehi's theology offered more enduring sustenance to Laman and Lemuel as a way to resolve the conflict between submission and pleasure. In the brothers' characteristic plot, submission meant deprivation, and pleasures came only through rebellion and violence. In their view of events, God's superior power forced them to submit and drove them into the sufferings of the wilderness. The family's theology and faith in Christ, by contrast, offered supreme pleasure and happiness, not through rebellion but through submission to God. Lehi's vision made the point most graphically with the tree "whose fruit was desirable to make one happy." When Lehi partook, he "beheld that it was most sweet, above all that I ever before tasted" (1 Ne. 8:10–11). Christ was presented as the resolution of the troubling conflict. The image of divine love in the form of luscious fruit should have appealed directly to Laman's and Lemuel's most fundamental need. But an understanding of Christ's love was beyond them. They were too firmly fixed in another pattern. Lehi regretfully reported that in the dream Laman and Lemuel did not take the fruit (1 Ne. 8:35).

In the ensuing centuries, the saga of the founding family formed the framework for the descendants of Laman and Lemuel to interpret events. Judging from the Lamanites' frequent references to the story, it remained as vivid in their national memory as the Revolution and Declaration of Independence do in ours. The relationship between the two peoples paralleled the relationship between Nephi and his brothers. The Nephites were accused of unjust rule and suspected of schemes to deprive the Lamanites of their possessions just as Laman and Lemuel believed Nephi deprived them of their rightful pleasures. Zeniff's people, who came into bondage to the Lamanites around 160 B.C.E., learned that the Lamanites still taught their children that Nephi robbed their fathers, that all Lamanites should hate the Nephites, "and that they should murder them, and that they should rob and plunder them" (Mosiah 10:16–17). The immediate reaction of the father of Lamoni when he discovered his son fraternizing with Nephites was to suspect them of robbery. They are sons of a liar, he charged, who "robbed our fathers; and now his children are also come amongst us that they may, by their cunning and their lyings, deceive us, that they again may rob us of our property" (Alma 20:13). The Lamanites seemed to believe that the old story of deprivation would be played out whenever Nephites appeared on the scene.

And by the same token, the Lamanite response followed the line of the ancient story. How were the Nephites to be stopped from their habitual robbery of their brethren? Bind them, smite them, kill them. The father of Lamoni turned on Ammon with a sword, and that was always the way. Nephi said his brothers' hearts were like flint, and the most common Nephite characterization of the Lamanites described them as ferocious. They were a "wild and a hardened and a ferocious people; a people who delighted in murdering the Nephites, and robbing and plundering them" (Alma 17:14). It was nearly impossible for many of the Nephites to see anything gentle or loving in Lamanite life, because the boundary between the two peoples was defined by the founding saga as one of perpetual war. To his credit, Jacob recognized that national traditions distorted the Nephite view. He told the Nephites in his sermon on chastity that Lamanite "husbands love their wives, and their wives love their husbands; and their husbands and their wives love their children." They were not implacably ferocious in every relationship. Lamanite violence toward the Nephites grew out of tradition, not innate viciousness. "Their hatred towards you is because of the iniquity of their fathers," Jacob said (Jacob 3:7). And yet that hatred was so unrelenting, and the resulting violence so intense, that Jacob himself could only think that Lamanites "delighted in wars and bloodshed, and they had an eternal hatred against us, their brethren" (Jacob 7:24).

One of the most troubling occurrences in the Book of Mormon, for some modern readers, is the cursing of the Lamanites. It took place after the separation of the peoples when the cultural divide widened. Nephi apparently ruled over all the brothers when they first landed in America, but, chafing under his government, the Lamanites made an attempt on his life, forcing Nephi to flee with his people into the wilderness. The Lord explained that, in consequence of the brothers' refusal to follow Nephi, they would be cut off. The curse of blackness came because the Lamanites "hardened their hearts against him, that they had become like unto a flint" (2 Ne. 5:21). The purpose of the sign accompanying the curse, the dark skin, was to prevent the Nephites from mixing with the Lamanites; under the curse they would not be enticing. That idea troubles us because it makes skin color divisive in a way that we dislike. But in a later incident, we learn more about the inner meaning of the curse. In the time of Alma a group of dissident Nephites called Amlicites joined the Lamanites in an attack on the Nephites. The Amlicites marked their foreheads with red paint to distinguish friends from enemies in battle. The marking led Mormon (presumably the editor of Alma's records) to comment on the curse. Mormon explained the reason why the Lord did not wish the Lamanites and Nephites to mix. It was not because of their contrasting skin colors. The curse was pronounced "that they might not mix and believe in incorrect traditions which would prove their destruction" (Alma 3:8). At issue was the story of their founding, deeply embedded as it was in Lamanite culture. The danger was not a mixture of races or skin colors but a mixture of false traditions with true ones. Mormon said the very identity of the Nephites lay in their acceptance of the true history of their origins.

> Whosoever would not believe in the tradition of the Lamanites, but believed those records which were brought out of the land of Jerusalem, and also in the tradition of their fathers, which were correct, who believed in the commandments of God and kept them, were called the Nephites. (Alma 3:11)

The two peoples were defined by their contrasting explanations of the enmity between Nephi and Laman, and the crucial issue was how to keep the true version intact. We may object to the selection of skin color as a means of separating the people and call these passages racist, but we should understand that in God's mind, and in the minds of his people, correct traditions, not skins, were the issue. The people of God would have objected just as heartily to a Nephite marriage with an Amlicite as to one with a Lamanite, when the only Amlicite mark was a painted forehead. The important thing was the Amlicite false belief and enmity to the Nephites. By accepting the false tradition, the curse fell on them as surely as upon the Lamanites. Mormon says the Amlicites fulfilled the wish of Providence in painting their foreheads, for in rebelling against God "it was expedient that the curse should fall upon them" (Alma 3:18). They were cursed, without receiving a dark skin, because they rebelled against God and embraced a false tradition. Presumably a dark skin on a person who embraced the true tradition would have no significance. Skin color was only skin deep; what mattered was the history one believed—and the hatred or love that went with each version.

It may be that the hatred against the Nephites polluted Lamanite society more than they desired themselves. The Nephites thought the Lamanites were idle. Instead of working for riches, "they sought to obtain these things by murdering and plundering, that they might not labor for them with their own hands" (Alma 17:14–15). The customary violence against the Nephites spilled over into the treatment of each other; they fought for goods rather than working for them. We have to treat the charge of indolence with a little skepticism, considering that the Nephites mainly saw the Lamanites from a distance or up close in a murdering and plundering mode. But it is also true that King Lamoni suffered from a band of rustlers who drove off the king's herds from the watering place. These were not a hostile group of outsiders, but some of his own subjects. Rather than work to assemble their herds, they used force (Alma 17:26–27). The use of violence against the Nephites may have legitimized plundering within Lamanite society, just as veterans returning from wars in some instances settle personal quarrels with guns. National myths and practices can affect the limits of personal behavior, and, in Lamanite history, force was made a virtue.

However much the founding saga influenced individual Lamanites, there is no question that it definitively established Lamanite policy toward the Nephites. "Their hatred was fixed," Enos said (Enos 1:20). Even when circumstances acted to moderate the hatred, it only subsided; it was never wholly extinguished. In a sense it was a great national resource, a source of energy and resolve that malicious rulers could call upon to serve their selfish interests. The Book of Mormon frequently speaks of the Lamanites being stirred up to anger. With mostly primitive governmental mechanisms at their disposal, Lamanite rulers governed with oratory. The people had to be aroused in order to mobilize them for their massive war efforts against the Nephites. In such times, the tradition of the fathers was a resource like money or food. Zerahemnah, an especially vicious king, made a special effort among his people to "preserve their hatred towards the Nephites, that he might bring them into subjection to the accomplishment of his designs" (Alma 43:7). A national heritage, whether benign or malign, can fade from time to time, and must be revived if leaders are to use it to their advantage. After an especially disastrous defeat, a large group of exhausted and fearful Lamanites refused to go into battle again (Alma 47:2). The response of the king was to undertake a campaign to "inspire the hearts of the Lamanites against the people of Nephi." And how did he accomplish that? "He did appoint men to speak unto the Lamanites from their towers, against the Nephites" (Alma 48:1). We can easily guess at the message spoken from the towers, and the results were predictable. He "hardened the hearts of the Lamanites and blinded their minds, and stirred them up to anger" (Alma 48:3).

Lamanite resolve presented the Nephites with a nearly insoluble problem. There was seemingly no way to stop the Lamanite attacks permanently. If the problem had been a land shortage or the imbalance of wealth in the two societies, an agreement might have been worked out. But Lamanite hatred of the Nephites was far more profound than that. It was ingrained in their national identity. Their founding story depicted them as a people who had been robbed and therefore whose destiny it was to destroy those who had wronged them. Wars against the Nephites were to the Lamanites like fighting for freedom and equality is to us. Fighting wars maintained fundamental values of the society that were rooted in the mythic account of their national beginnings and were essential to their identity as a people. One could not expect them to stop the wars any more than we can be expected to renounce the idea of equality enunciated in the Declaration of Independence. They would not be Lamanites, nor we Americans, if this occurred.[1]

Because war was part of the Lamanite identity, there was no resolution of the conflict—unless the Lamanites could be persuaded to forgo their own tradition. It seemed like a hopeless undertaking, like persuading the United States to return to monarchy and its attendant arbitrariness. But one valiant attempt was made. We think of the sons of Mosiah as giving up statecraft when they unitedly yielded their rights to the throne. Their abdication in advance of Mosiah's death compelled the king to introduce a major constitutional change in Nephite government, altering it from a monarchy to a rule by judges. We admire the young men for giving up the throne to preach the gospel, but we may question their judgment. Was it not irresponsible to refuse the duty that always falls on the sons of the king? Could not one of them have stayed behind to occupy the throne? But our doubts are quieted when we look closely at the reasons for the mission, for it appears that they went to the Lamanites for reasons of state as well as to right themselves with the Lord. The sons of Mosiah had been converted along with Alma and desired to "impart the word of God to their brethren, the Lamanites." But besides bringing them to a knowledge of God, they wished to "convince them of the iniquity of their fathers." It was not enough to teach Christ. They also had to attack the story of Laman and Lemuel as the Lamanites understood it—in other words, the tradition of their fathers. The reason for doing that was simple. The missionaries hoped that "perhaps they might cure them of their hatred towards the Nephites." That would permit them all to rejoice in the Lord their God, that they too "might become friendly to one another, and that there should be no more contentions in all the land" (Mosiah 28:1–2). It was a long shot, but by 92 B.C.E., after five hundred years of warfare, it may have been apparent to the king's sons that Lamanite warfare could be halted only by attacking its foundation, the tradition of their fathers.

The marvel is that they succeeded as well as they did. Traveling in the wilderness toward Lamanite lands, the missionaries prepared themselves by much fasting and prayer, beseeching the Lord to enable them to bring the Lamanites "to the knowledge of the truth, to the knowledge of the baseness of the traditions of their fathers, which were not correct" (Alma 17:9). And their prayers were answered. The method by which they achieved their purpose is inspiring as well as interesting. They did it by simple acts of love and generosity. The ease with which the Lamanites gave way before the missionaries belies the Nephite images of flinty and ferocious Lamanites. Instead, some of the Lamanites appear remarkably vulnerable. Lamoni's men bound Ammon when he entered their land, as they always did with Nephite intruders, but when he announced his wish to live with them, perhaps until the day he died, Lamoni was so touched he offered Ammon a daughter for a wife (Alma 17:20–24). Lamoni's tender heart was deeply moved by Ammon's faithful service, which prepared the king to be converted soon thereafter.

Lamoni's father reacted like Laman of old in drawing his sword against his son and then Ammon, and when Ammon overpowered him, the old king cowered before the missionary's greater power, again as Laman did before Nephi (Alma 20:20–24). But it was not Ammon's physical superiority that impressed the king; it was the love for the king's son that astonished him exceedingly (Alma 20:26). When another set of missionaries offered to serve Lamoni's father, he remembered this love and wanted to listen. Ammon's generosity, as well as his words, troubled the king, and he was ready to hear more (Alma 22:3). The willing service and acts of generosity and love, so contrary to the Lamanite stereotypes of the Nephites, got through the armor and touched the hearts of the two kings.

These stories remind us of the time when Laman and Lemuel pulled back from their plan to slay Nephi as they returned from Jerusalem with Ishmael and his family. Instead of a show of force halting the attempt, one of Ishmael's daughters, along with her mother and a son, pleaded for Nephi. We see in the incident the beginning of a romance, but what may be far more significant is that a womanly appeal, from a mother as well as a daughter, softened the flinty hearts of the brothers. They responded as fully to this appeal as to the later shock of power from Nephi. The record says that "they were sorrowful, because of their wickedness, insomuch that they did bow down before me, and did plead with me that I would forgive them of the thing that they had done against me" (1 Ne. 7:20). At the outset, gentleness succeeded where harsh rebukes failed, and in later history kindness and love again exercised influence where the Nephites' militant resistance bred only more warfare. Force may not have been the only language some of the Lamanites understood.

The conversions fulfilled the missionaries' hopes far more completely than they had any reason to expect. The two kings and many of the people believed. And it was not just the gospel they accepted. They were convinced that "the traditions of [their] wicked fathers" were wrong (Alma 24:7). That meant Laman and Lemuel were wrong and Nephi was right, a deep and profound reversal of their whole identity as a people that required an upending of old values. Their acceptance of this new tradition went hand in hand with their acceptance of the gospel. When the old king conferred the kingdom on his son, he gave him a new name, Anti-Nephi-Lehi, as if to recognize that a new set of founding fathers had to be embraced. The word sounds to us like opposition to Nephi and Lehi, but Hugh Nibley has told us it probably means the opposite, which the story itself of course strongly suggests. Anti-Nephi-Lehi and his brother Lamoni seemed to understand that some heroic effort would be required to root out the old tradition and set their people on a new course. They accomplished this reorientation by asking of their people an incredible sacrifice that directly attacked the besetting sin of Lamanite culture. The kings asked the people to give up violence. They agreed to bury their swords in the belief that Christ had removed the blood of many killings; for to fight again might leave a stain that could not be cleansed. That was the only way, they believed, to repent sincerely of their "many sins and murders." When the king had offered this covenant to the people, "they took their swords, and all the weapons which were used for the shedding of man's blood, and they did bury them up deep in the earth" (Alma 24:9–17). An attack of their unbelieving brethren did not cause them to waver. They knelt before the oncoming warriors and submitted to the slaughter. The reversal of old values was sealed with the converts' blood.

The missionary effort thus accomplished all that the sons of Mosiah had hoped for. Lamanites were converted to Christ, they gave up the tradition of their fathers, the spirit softened their hearts, and they "opened a correspondence with [their] brethren, the Nephites" (Alma 24:8). Having relinquished violence and plundering as the way to riches, the converts changed their living habits. "Rather than spend their days in idleness they would labor abundantly with their hands" (Alma 24:18). Peace with this transformed people was now perfectly natural. The Nephites welcomed the converts into their midst and gave them a land of their own.

These conversions did not permanently end the Lamanite wars by any means. The unconverted, still enmeshed in the tradition of their fathers, came up against the Nephites year after year, bent on their destruction. But the sons of Mosiah showed how peace was to be achieved—by conversion to Christ and to the correct story of the nation's founding (see Alma 25:6). Their work set the pattern for later conversions by Nephi and Lehi, the sons of Helaman. The converts from this later proselytizing effort also "did lay down their weapons of war, and also their hatred and the tradition of their fathers" (Hel. 5:51). With the false tradition out of the way, once more peace came to the two nations, commerce opened between them, and they enjoyed greater prosperity than at any time in their history to that point. This second missionary episode strengthens the implication that conversion to the gospel and repudiation of false traditions was the only workable basis for permanent peace.

Having reviewed this evidence, are we now in a position to rewrite the Book of Mormon from the Lamanite perspective? Perhaps we could sketch in some basic themes and a bare outline. But even in skeletal form, the history we might piece together would not be all we would like it to be. Our first impulse would be, perhaps, to vindicate the Lamanites, to lift them up and justify them. We may think that Nephi in all his grandeur is so hard on his brothers, so pitiless in his reproaches, and so sure of his mission that we should right the balance and find good in his rebellious brothers and their descendants, making a place for weaker souls in the annals of God's people. But our sympathy can go only so far. Lamanite history would be a bitter story, of a people obsessed with a perpetual sense of deprivation, wronged at the beginning, so they thought, and wronged ever after, living for vengeance, with blood on their swords. Lamanite history would honor valor and resolution in the face of repeated defeats, but in a cause we can hardly admire.

On the other hand, we would gravely err to consider the Lamanites hopelessly benighted and persistently ferocious, hardened, and indolent in nature. Jacob warned against that error when he told his own people, speaking of the Lamanites, to "revile no more against them because of the darkness of their skins; neither shall ye revile against them because of their filthiness" (Jacob 3:9). The Lamanites who turned to Christ are among the most faithful and self-sacrificing in the Book of Mormon, giving themselves to be slaughtered rather than return to their sins. Even before conversion, they were faithful to each other in their families, at a time when the Nephites had taken up concubinage. Building on that foundation, the first Lamanite converts raised a generation of righteous offspring unmatched in the Book of Mormon. The source of Lamanite failings was not their natures but their tradition. Alma said it was "the traditions of their fathers that caused them to remain in their state of ignorance" (Alma 9:16). The Lamanites understood their national past erroneously, and so they misconstrued their national purpose. Their history taught them that they had been wronged and that it was their destiny to right that wrong through relentless war on the Nephites. The incorrect tradition of their fathers was the cause of the misspent effort, the untold suffering, and the rivers of blood. The moral of the Lamanite story has nothing to do with their depravity but with the terrible consequences of misunderstanding the past.

There may be a moral for later generations of Book of Mormon readers, too. The story speaks to all who face implacable enemies, ones who are committed to aggressive incursions on peaceful peoples. The Book of Mormon tells us we may indeed have to defend ourselves with force in the face of an enemy onslaught, but it just as clearly states that militant defense will not ultimately end wars. Aggressive people, when meeting resistance, will come back generation after generation, century after century, even though soundly defeated time after time. Force, however benevolently intended, will not stop force permanently. As Christ said, he who lives by the sword dies by the sword; violence begets violence. In national as in personal affairs, kindness, truth, and service are the only avenues to lasting peace.

NOTES

1. For a similar perspective on Lamanite traditions, see Noel B. Reynolds, "The Political Dimension in Nephi's Small Plates," *BYU Studies* 27 (fall 1987): 15–37.

8

The Recovery of the Book of Mormon

When he was well along in the preparation of Book of Mormon Authorship
Revisited *(Provo, Utah: FARMS, 1997), Noel Reynolds, then the president of the
Foundation for Ancient Research and Mormon Studies (FARMS), realized that
he needed an essay on finding the "golden plates" to go along with the more technical essays on authorship. He asked me to provide a brief summary, which I
decided to use as an occasion for discussing how historians use sources in telling
this contested story. This essay is one of the occasions when I try to score a few
points on unbelieving historians by claiming they repress material coming from
eyewitnesses close to Joseph Smith. The historians' problem is that the people
around Joseph consistently wrote and acted as if he had the Book of Mormon
plates. Emma Smith and Oliver Cowdery, who both lived in the house where
Joseph worked, never questioned the existence of plates. Nor did Joseph Smith Sr.,
Lucy Smith, or David Whitmer. Skeptics have to minimize quotations from the
participants or else the plates take on all too real a life.*

All the events connected with the recovery, translation, and publication of the Book of Mormon took place in a six-and-a-half-year period
from September 1823 to March 1830. The time of most intense activity was
even shorter. During the four years from September 1823 to September
1827, the only significant happenings were the annual visits to the site
where Joseph Smith first saw the plates. The bulk of the important occurrences—the removal of the gold plates from their hiding place, the struggle
to preserve them from thieves and the curious, the consultation with scholars in New York City, the translation with the aid of various secretaries, the
loss of the first batch of copy, the application for copyright, the search for a
printer, and the publication of the manuscript—all happened in two and a
half years, from September 1827 to March 1830. At the end of that time,
Joseph Smith offered to the public a volume of 590 pages that has since
been a subject of study, controversy, and devotion.

Unlike some events in Church history—such as the First Vision and
the restoration of the Melchizedek Priesthood—the chronology and main
outlines of the recovery story are not much in question. We are not likely to
be blindsided by a clever researcher who shows a lack of evidence for a

FIG. 1. Lucy Mack Smith (1775–1856). Lucy recounted the doings of the Smith family in a history published before her death. Engraving by E. Roffe, from sketches by Frederick Piercy. Frontispiece in James Linforth, ed., *Route from Liverpool to Great Salt Lake Valley* (Liverpool: Franklin D. Richards, 1855).

major occurrence. The sources on events before 1827 are limited; we are largely dependent on the accounts of Joseph Smith himself and his mother, Lucy Mack Smith (fig. 1).[1] But after the plates were removed from the stone box in the hill and neighbors learned about them, plenty of people, hostile and sympathetic, gave their versions of events.

Chronologically, the first published account appeared in a newspaper, the *Wayne Sentinel*, a Palmyra weekly, on June 26, 1829, and others followed on August 31, 1829, and September 5, 1829, in two Rochester papers, the *Advertiser and Telegraph* and the *Gem*. The main points of the story, as Francis W. Kirkham demonstrated many years ago, can be found even in the hostile affidavits that Doctor Philastus Hurlbut collected for E. D. Howe and published in *Mormonism Unvailed* [*sic*] in 1834.[2] The editor of the *Wayne Sentinel*, Pomeroy Tucker, recorded everything he could remember in a volume on Mormonism published in 1867.[3] Of course, Joseph Smith himself is the primary source, supplemented by Lucy Smith, and their narrations are elaborated in firsthand accounts by Oliver Cowdery, Joseph Knight, Emma Smith, Martin Harris, and David Whitmer. If there remain uncertainties about details and contradictions on some points, the basic chronology of happenings is well grounded in friendly and unfriendly sources.

How these sources are used to retell the story of recovery varies greatly according to the inclinations of the teller. Mormon historians, for example, emphasize the rapidity of the translation. John Welch and Tim Rathbone estimate that there were sixty-three translating days available from Oliver Cowdery's start as secretary on April 7, 1829, to the end of June 1829, when the title page was published in the *Wayne Sentinel*. That comes to eight pages of printed text a day[4]—a marvelous production rate for any writer and a stupendous one for an uneducated twenty-three-year-old who, according to his wife, could scarcely write a coherent letter.[5] During the translation period, Joseph was hard-pressed to put food on the table and had to take time off to scavenge. To avoid interruptions from hostile neighbors, he moved his entire household from Harmony, Pennsylvania, to Fayette, New York. Yet, through it all, he dictated the Book of Mormon text without hesitation day after day.

Unbelieving writers pass over this achievement, usually by simply acknowledging Joseph Smith's genius; one author has attributed the book to a freakish capacity for automatic writing.[6] Secular historians pay less attention to the circumstances of translation, such as the amazing production rate, and instead look for the sources of the book's content. They play down the miraculous and play up the conventional material from Joseph's own culture that they think shows up in the Book of Mormon. Ethan Smith's *View of the Hebrews,* published in Poultney, Vermont, in 1823, for example, is credited with supplying the main idea of Israelites migrating to the Western Hemisphere. Masonry and Antimasonry, the Bible, local theological controversies, and Joseph Smith's own family dynamics are all said to have played a part.[7] Secular accounts thus attempt a cultural biography of Joseph Smith, scouring the intellectual landscape for possible sources of Book of Mormon ideas and speculating on how those sources might have made their way into Joseph Smith's mind. Day-to-day happenings are neglected to make room for this wide-ranging search.

Courtesy Library-Archives, Community of Christ

FIG. 2. Emma Smith (1804–79). At age seventy-four, Emma recalled husband Joseph translating the Book of Mormon. Her answers to questions posed by their son, Joseph Smith III, were published in 1879, several months after her death.

Mormon writers are more inclined to put reports from people close to Joseph Smith into the story. Because the recovery of the Book of Mormon is a sacred story, every detail is relished. Mormons are interested in the futile efforts of Lucy Harris, Martin's tempestuous wife, to see the plates, or in Emma's father's refusal to allow an object in his house that he was forbidden to look at. We love Emma Smith's comment that she never saw the plates but "moved them from place to place on the table, as it was necessary in doing my [house]work" (fig. 2).[8] The way the divine work played on the lives of the various actors— perplexing, frustrating, thrilling, and enraging them—captures the Mormon imagination. These everyday details are beside the point for secular historians who want to run down the elusive sources of Book of Mormon ideas and who do not want to make the protection of the plates, the gathering of converts, and the laborious work of translation seem too real. Most of the detailed sources were written by believers, and to follow them too closely infuses a narrative with their faith. Secular historians are, therefore, more inclined than Mormons to suppress source material from Joseph's closest associates.

Joseph Smith did not record all the details about recovering the Book of Mormon in his first attempt at autobiography in 1832. He had not yet found his full voice as a writer and historian. At that point he seemed more concerned with promoting the idea of a divine work breaking forth. The exact appearance of Moroni, the contents of his instructions, and the circumstances of the vision were played down; he told the whole story in one breathless sentence!

> When I was seventeen years of age I called again upon the Lord and he shewed unto me a heavenly vision for behold an angel of the Lord came and stood before me and it was by night and he called me by name and he said the Lord had forgiven me my sins and he revealed unto me that in the Town of Manchester Ontario County N.Y. there was plates of gold upon which there was engravings which was engraven by Maroni & his fathers the servants of the living God in ancient days and deposited by the commandments of God and kept by the power thereof and that I should go and get them and he revealed unto me many things concerning the inhabitants of the earth which since have been revealed in commandments & revelations and it was on the 22d day of Sept. A.D. 1822 and thus he appeared unto me three times in one night and once on the next day and then I immediately went to the place and found where the plates was deposited as the angel of the Lord had commanded me and straightway made three attempts to get them and then being excedingly frightened I supposed it had been a dreem of Vision but when I considred I knew that it was not therefore I cried unto the Lord in the agony of my soul why can I not obtain them behold the angel appeared unto me again and said unto me you have not kept the commandments of the Lord which I gave unto you therefore you cannot now obtain them for the time is not yet fulfilled therefore thou wast left unto temptation that thou mightest be made acquainted with the power of the advisary therefore repent and call on the Lord thou shalt be forgiven and in his own due time thou shalt obtain them for now I had been tempted of the advisary and saught the Plates to obtain riches and kept not the commandment that I should have an eye single to the glory of God.[9]

This abbreviated narration goes a long way to win over a reader to Joseph's sincere struggle to discover his mission. The passage has an endearing candor to it. Joseph admits his teenage transgressions and his hope for forgiveness. He comes across as a learner trying to understand what he is to do. He is baffled when he cannot get the plates and wonders for an instant if he had just dreamed the vision. He is terrified that he has done something wrong. The angel at times frightens him. When he is rebuked, Joseph recognizes that he had been thinking of gold and riches, not the glory of God. He is relieved to record the assurance that by repentance he could be forgiven and get the plates eventually. Like every other text, this one could be read for signs of extraneous cultural influences, such as a magical belief in visions in threes, and probably turned to other interpretive purposes. But however cleverly managed, the passage captivates a reader, making it hard to doubt Joseph's sincerity. Inserting too much language like this into a secular account would diffuse the search for Book of Mormon sources and turn attention to Joseph's desire to comply with the will of heaven. Mormons, on the other hand, love every word of it. In this sense, believing historians are more inclined to be true to the basic sources than unbelieving ones.

In the 1832 account, Joseph leapt in a single phrase from age seventeen to age twenty-one, when he recovered the plates. The only interim event that figured in the story was his marriage to Emma Hale, daughter of Isaac Hale, on January 18, 1827. Actually, the Smith family suffered considerable adversity during the four years from 1823 to 1827. They lost their eldest son and major breadwinner, Alvin, in 1823. In a futile attempt to raise money, Joseph Smith Sr. involved Joseph Jr. in an abortive search for Spanish treasure that was to employ Joseph's powers as a seer. (Joseph had found a seer stone while digging a well for Willard Chase in 1822 and became adept at finding lost objects.) The Smiths failed to make the last payment on their farm and lost it, with all improvements, in 1825. Joseph was brought to trial in 1826 in South Bainbridge on charges of disorderly conduct, presumably because he had used his seer stone in a treasure search. All of this, however, was tangential to the narrative of the Book of Mormon recovery, and Joseph left it out.[10]

Marriage to Emma Hale, however, was relevant to the story; she became a copartner in the enterprise from that point on. Emma went with Joseph to the Hill Cumorah in the dark early hours of the morning of September 22, 1827, to get the plates (fig. 3). She was the one to rush to him with a report that thieves were hunting for the hiding

FIG. 3. Hill Cumorah. Joseph Smith came here, on the early-morning hours of September 22, 1827, to retrieve Book of Mormon plates. John Barber and Henry Howe, *Historical Collections of New York* (New York: S. Tuttle, 1845), 582.

place of the plates in a fallen tree where Joseph had left them that night. She arranged for a place to translate on her father's property in Harmony and was Joseph's first secretary. When Martin Harris lost 116 pages of manuscript, Joseph thought first of Emma: "Must I . . . return to my wife with such a tale as this? I dare not do it, lest I should kill her at once."[11] After all her troubles with the doctrine of plural marriage and long after her break with Brigham Young, Emma held on to her belief in the Book of Mormon. For Emma, Joseph could not have authored the Book of Mormon. With a wife's realistic assessment of her husband's abilities, she told her son that "it would have been improbable that a learned man could do this; and, for one so ignorant and unlearned as he was, it was simply impossible."[12]

Among the enlarging circle of friends and enemies who were drawn into the story after the recovery of the plates was Joseph Knight of Colesville, New York, a farmer, miller, and carding machine operator who employed Joseph in 1826 during the months when Joseph was courting Emma. Probably by design, Knight made a point of being at the Smiths', on September 22, 1827, and wrote about what he observed. Although a believer from the start, Knight's "Recollection" has bothered some Mormon readers because of its rough-cut style and its unembarrassed reports of familiar relations with neighborhood money diggers. Knight recorded a warning Joseph sent to Samuel Lawrence, a conjurer, to stay away from the hill on September 22 or Joseph would "thrash the stumps with him." Knight talked to Joseph soon after the return from the hill on the morning of September 22 and reported the impression that Joseph "seamed to think more of the glasses or the urim and thummem then he Did of the Plates, for, says he, 'I can see any thing; they are Marvelus.'" Knight also tells of pressure from the money diggers to see the plates, resulting in Joseph's and Emma's retreat from Manchester in December 1827 to a quieter haven on Emma's father's place in Harmony.[13]

Knight's "Recollection" is now more widely accepted in standard Mormon narrations of the recovery story. We are coming to appreciate the homely details and the skirmishes with the money diggers. Knight's account seems all the more authentic because it is so candid. His close observation helps us understand how an increasing number of people were caught up in the drama of the gold plates. Joseph did not carry on his work alone.

Martin Harris entered the story when Joseph and Emma left Manchester for Harmony (fig. 4). Fascinated by the accounts of the gold plates circulating in Palmyra, Harris was both believing and doubtful. In spurts he was immensely helpful and was filled with misgivings. He told his story to the editors of *Tiffany's Monthly*, a spiritualist publication that speculated that Joseph Smith was indeed inspired supernaturally but by low-grade spirits who foisted inferior doctrines on him. Mormon scholars have

FIG. 4. Martin Harris (1783–1875). This prosperous Palmyra farmer lent valuable aid during Book of Mormon translation. Etching by C. B. Hill, New York. Courtesy LDS Church Archives.

mistrusted the *Tiffany's* report on Harris because of the magazine's bias, but some parts are too good to resist and have made their way into Mormon narrations.[14]

Harris is famed for a number of interventions. He played a major role in the recovery story because he was a prosperous farmer who had money. He lent Joseph Smith fifty dollars to pay for the trip to Harmony in December 1827, and then during the winter, he came down himself. Joseph had been translating with the help of Emma and her brother Reuben Hale and had copied some of the characters on a sheet of paper. Harris took the transcription to various learned men— most notably to Samuel Mitchill, then at Rutgers Medical School, and Charles Anthon of Columbia University. Joseph said that Harris himself received the inspiration to make the trip. It may be that, in a doubting mood, he wanted confirmation that Joseph had the plates. I have speculated that Joseph wanted reassurance that he was doing the translation properly, considering the daunting difficulty of the task laid upon him. In the outcome, Harris was satisfied, even though Anthon himself later wrote that he tried to disillusion his visitor. Anthon could not translate the characters; he reportedly said that they were a scrambled mélange of various languages. But Harris, who interpreted the encounter differently, came away reassured that they were authentic.[15]

The incident made an impact on Joseph. He received no confirmation of his accuracy as a translator, but soon after this incident, he realized that Harris, Anthon, and he had fulfilled prophecy. As he retold the story in his 1832 account (and again in 1839), Harris's experiences with Anthon conformed with the verses in Isaiah 29 about the learned man being unable to read a sealed book and an unlearned person succeeding despite his ignorance.[16] While we think it obvious that Joseph stood in the middle of the prophetic stream concerning the last days, we must remember that he was only twenty-two, truly unlearned, with no worldly standing, living in an obscure rural backwater, and with only a few visionary glimpses of what lay ahead. It was anything but obvious that he was to be a major figure in divine history, despite the extraordinary visions he had received. To find himself tied into the grand tradition of biblical prophecy must have thrilled Joseph and given him a larger understanding of his role.

Harris went back to his Palmyra farm after reporting on the Anthon visit but returned in April with his wife, Lucy. Lucy Harris was a nuisance, at least in Lucy Smith's telling. Lucy Harris would not rest until she saw the plates. She rummaged through everything, forcing Joseph to extreme measures to conceal their whereabouts. After she left in the late spring of 1828, Joseph and Martin got down to translating, the first protracted period of work on the plates since Joseph had received them the previous September. After 116 pages were written, Harris asked if he could show them to his wife. The gold plates were dividing his household, and he must have hoped that sight of the manuscript would reassure Lucy Harris of their reality. Joseph inquired of the Lord and was told no. Martin importuned. On the third request, permission was granted under close restriction as to the persons who were to see the pages.

After Harris left with the 116 pages, Joseph turned his attention to Emma, who, on June 15, 1828, bore a son who died the same day. For two weeks Joseph tended her until she urged him to return to Manchester to check on the manuscript. To his dismay, the worst had happened. Martin had shown the manuscript to more than the agreed-on number, and finally, one day when he went to retrieve it, the pages were gone. Lucy Smith blamed the loss on Lucy Harris, suspecting her of stealing the manuscript with the intention of altering it. A retranslation, even if exactly the same, would make Joseph look like a fraud who was making up the text rather than translating it.

Lucy Smith reported that when Joseph got the news, "the most bitter lamentations filled the house."[17] Joseph's own regrets were then underscored by a revelation that chastised him for giving way to Harris and threatened him with losing the gift of translation (see D&C 3). Joseph had to give up the interpreters and the plates. At the same time, he was promised forgiveness if he repented, and on September 22, 1828, the plates and interpreters were returned (see D&C 3).

Joseph still had to deal with the consequences of losing the manuscript. For the next year and a half, he lived in fear that an altered text would appear to discredit his translation. He was warned of the danger in a revelation, and in the preface to the published Book of Mormon, he cautioned readers about the possibility of a doctored manuscript turning up. He worried that "Satan would stir up the hearts of this generation, that they might not receive this work."[18]

The incident marked the end of Martin Harris's term as secretary for the translation. For the next six months, little was accomplished until

FIG. 5. Oliver Cowdery (1806–50). A school teacher from Vermont, Cowdery was primary scribe during the three months when the Book of Mormon was translated. Etching by C. B. Hill, New York. Courtesy LDS Church Archives.

Oliver Cowdery arrived in Harmony on April 5, 1829 (fig. 5). Cowdery was a twenty-two-year-old Vermonter who had kept store, blacksmithed, and taught school. He came from a family with a taste for the supernatural and apparently had tried water witching himself.[19] In 1834 he attempted a history of Joseph's visions and the rise of the Church in a series of eight letters to the Mormon newspaper, the *Messenger and Advocate*, in Independence, Missouri. Although close to Joseph Smith and a participant in many critical events, Cowdery is less than satisfactory as a historian. His wordy style and his proclivity to run off into meditations about the meaning of events keep getting in the way of the story. But he does tell us clearly that he arrived in Harmony on Sunday evening, April 5, helped Joseph with business matters on Monday, and began to write Book of Mormon dictation on Tuesday.[20]

They labored together for three months, from April through June 1829. During that time they had to scramble for food; at one point they were saved from going out to work by Joseph Knight, who arrived from Colesville with nine or ten bushels of grain, five or six bushels of potatoes, a pound of tea, and a barrel of mackerel. In mid-May a passage in the Book of Mormon manuscript got them wondering about baptism. When they prayed, John the Baptist appeared and restored the Aaronic Priesthood.[21]

Besides translating, Joseph received revelations for his brother Hyrum and the helpful Joseph Knight, and was instructed by the Lord to translate the small plates of Nephi rather than go back again to Lehi's longer record. But through all of the ambient events, the main project ground on, the words coming relentlessly from Joseph's mouth and going onto paper under Cowdery's pen.

In early June, Joseph and Cowdery left Harmony for Fayette, New York, and the Peter Whitmer household (fig. 6). Joseph saw signs of an impending mobbing, and Cowdery had asked his friend David Whitmer, son of Peter, if the family could make room while the translation was finished up. Many of the Whitmers—but David particularly—were

Courtesy Museum of Church History and Art

FIG. 6. Peter Whitmer Sr. Farmhouse, Fayette, New York. This reconstruction of the original house shows the site where Joseph Smith lived during the summer of 1829 while completing Book of Mormon translation.

interested in the gold plates. David took time away from the spring farm work to go down to Harmony to pick up the pair. Like Cowdery, Whitmer gave his own account of events in these years, but only long after he had soured on the Church and had lived in religious isolation for many years (fig. 7). Whitmer was most happy with Joseph during his time at the family farm and just after the Church was organized. In Whitmer's view, these were the times of recurrent miracles involving him and his family, a time when Joseph was in touch with God through his seer stone, and when priesthood and organization played a lesser role.[22]

Joseph and Cowdery got back to work the day after they arrived in Fayette. They translated in a room at the top of the house in the heat of early summer. David Whitmer said, "It was a laborious work for the weather was very warm, and the days were long and they worked from morning till night."[23] Occasionally Emma and one or two of the Whitmers spelled Cowdery, but Joseph labored on day after day. Sometime before June 11, they applied for a copyright. By then they had finished the plates of Mormon and translated Mormon's title page. The small plates of Nephi and Ether kept them busy probably until near the end of June.

Around June 20, 1829, possibly prompted by passages in Ether 5:2–4 and 2 Nephi 27:12 about others who would see the plates, the three men closest to Joseph—Oliver Cowdery, David Whitmer, and Martin Harris—asked if the privilege might be theirs. The testimonies of the three, along with a similar statement by eight others who saw and touched the golden plates, appeared in the first edition of the Book of Mormon. It was the only attempt at providing proof for the plates and the divine inspiration behind the translation. In answer to Martin Harris's earlier request for a witness, the revelation had said that "they would not believe you, my servant Joseph, if it were possible that you should show them all these things which I have committed unto you" (D&C 5:7). That June, however, the three were told they would see the plates, the breastplate, Laban's sword, the "miraculous

directors," and the Urim and Thummim (see D&C 17:1). Then after they
had "seen them with [their] eyes,
[they should] testify of them, by the
power of God" (D&C 17:3). The witnesses' statements were an effective
demonstration of authenticity for a
skeptical age, including modern doubters
who have found no plausible cause
for the elaborate vision. Fawn Brodie
could only hypothesize Joseph's "positive talent at hypnosis"; in a more recent
study, John Brooke makes no attempt
at explanation.[24] Secular historians have
never adequately explained why none
of the eleven who saw the plates (in
addition to Joseph Smith) ever recanted.

With the completion of the book
by the end of June 1829, Joseph was at
last relieved of his arduous labor. He
turned now to the search for a pub-

FIG. 7. David Whitmer (1805–88).
Whitmer offered a place where translation could proceed free from local persecution. Etching by C. B. Hill, New
York. Courtesy LDS Church Archives.

lisher. The printer in Palmyra, Egbert B. Grandin, refused the job, apparently feeling religious compunctions in keeping with many in the village.
In July, Joseph and Martin went to Rochester in search of a printer and
were turned down by Thurlow Weed, publisher of a Rochester newspaper,
before winning the cooperation of another Rochester printer, Elihu Marshall. Before signing with him, however, they went back to Grandin and
persuaded him to take the contract, since the book was to appear anyway.
Grandin required a $3,000 security in case the books did not sell, and Mar-
tin Harris mortgaged his farm to raise the money. Cowdery meanwhile
began recopying the manuscript for the printer's use. Typesetting commenced in August.

Joseph left Harris, Cowdery, and Hyrum Smith to see the manuscript
through the press while he returned to his little farm in Harmony. He had
to return to Palmyra in January 1830 when the publisher of a new Palmyra
weekly, the *Reflector*, began printing pirated excerpts from the Book of
Mormon. The publisher was Abner Cole, a former justice of the peace,
who, under the pseudonym Obediah Dogberry, began the paper the previous September. He set the type in Grandin's office on Sundays and apparently in that way got Book of Mormon passages in advance of publication,
hoping to take advantage of the local notoriety in order to sell newspapers.
Hyrum's warnings to Cole had no effect, and the family decided Joseph Sr.
should go to Harmony for Joseph. Returning to Palmyra in a blizzard,

Joseph caught Cole on Sunday afternoon hard at work and reminded him of the consequences of stealing copyrighted material. Cole heated up and challenged Joseph to a fight—a dangerous proposition against an adept wrestler like Joseph Smith. Joseph waved him off, and eventually Cole agreed to stop after his January 22 issue, closing the case.[25]

As the book neared completion and news of its actual contents began to leak out, opposition mounted. Lucy Smith said that people from the county called a meeting to mobilize resistance. They resolved not to purchase the book and went directly to Grandin, the printer. Hoping he would stop work, they told him the printing expenses would never be paid. Harris and Joseph calmed Grandin down, and the work went on. The incident may have occurred around January 16, 1830, when Joseph Smith Sr. signed an agreement that Harris would have an equal chance to sell copies of the book along with Joseph Sr. and his friends.[26] The pressure from the villagers may have worried Harris as much as it did Grandin. When the book came off the press in late March 1830, Harris was still panicky. Bringing Joseph up from Harmony in that month, Joseph Knight came across Harris on the road with a pile of books in his arms. He told the two of them, "The Books will not sell for no Body wants them."[27] Refusing to be reassured, Harris told Joseph, "I want a Commandment," meaning another revelation. Joseph told him to obey the commandments he had, but Harris insisted.[28] The next day Joseph received the revelation in Doctrine and Covenants 19 in which Harris was sorely rebuked and admonished to "not covet thine own property, but impart it freely to the printing of the Book of Mormon, which contains the truth and the word of God" (D&C 19:26).

Grandin announced in the March 26, 1830, edition of the *Wayne Sentinel* that the Book of Mormon was now for sale, wholesale and retail, at the Palmyra bookstore. After all the effort that had gone into the translation over the past two and a half years, it should have been a high moment for Joseph Smith and the small circle of believers. But none is recorded. Neither Lucy nor Joseph nor anyone close to them expressed exhilaration at the accomplishment. The book was launched, and the Prophet went on to other matters. Within two weeks, the Church was organized.

Nothing in the newspaper reviews gave the translator any cause for celebration. The Book of Mormon was noticed, to be sure. Within a year, James Gordon Bennett could write in the *New York Morning Courier and Enquirer:* "You have heard of MORMONISM—who has not?"[29] But the press response was universally scornful. Within a week after the March 26 publication date, the *Rochester Daily Advertiser* described the book under the headline "BLASPHEMY": "The 'Book of Mormon' has been placed in our hands. A viler imposition was never practised. It is an evidence of fraud, blasphemy and credulity, shocking to the Christian and moralist."[30] Those words were picked up in Boston and Vermont within weeks. Thus was the Book of Mormon greeted when it came into the world.

Joseph seems to have given the reviews no notice, never mentioning the bad press. He had not translated the book to win acclaim in the newspapers, and he saw no need to answer the attacks. The revelation to Martin Harris, when the Book of Mormon was published, said he was to carry it to Jew and Gentile "with all humility, trusting in me, reviling not against revilers" (D&C 19:30). Rather than reply to the revilers, Joseph contented himself with writing an account of events as he had experienced them, to which were added reports from many friends and family members. Together they constitute the bulk of the historical record, the original source material for the story of the Book of Mormon's recovery. Narrations that balk before the miraculous events and try to tell another story must suppress these sources and disregard the consistent and detailed accounts from the people who knew Joseph Smith best.

NOTES

1. The two major versions of his own history by Joseph Smith are in Joseph Smith Letterbook 1:1–10, Joseph Smith Collection, Church Archives, The Church of Jesus Christ of Latter-day Saints, Salt Lake City, and in History of the Church, also in the Church Archives. Both are superbly edited in volume 1 of Dean C. Jessee, ed., *The Papers of Joseph Smith*, 2 vols. (Salt Lake City: Deseret Book, 1989–92). The best readily available edition of Lucy Mack Smith's account is her *Biographical Sketches of Joseph Smith, the Prophet, and His Progenitors for Many Generations*, vol. 6 in Prominent Works in Mormon History (1853; Orem, Utah: Grandin, 1995). Her preliminary manuscript, housed in the Church Archives, and recently published in Lavina Fielding Anderson, ed., *Lucy's Book: A Critical Edition of Lucy Mack Smith's Family Memoir* (Salt Lake City: Signature Books, 2001), contains material omitted from *Biographical Sketches*.

2. Francis W. Kirkham, *A New Witness for Christ in America: The Book of Mormon*, 2 vols. (Independence, Mo.: Zion's Printing, 1942), 1:129–37, 146–52. After all these years, Kirkham's work is still useful and for most readers provides the easiest access to a large body of source material such as complete reprints of these key newspaper articles. The affidavits were recently republished in Dan Vogel, ed., *Early Mormon Documents*, 3 vols. (Salt Lake City: Signature Books, 1996–2000), 2:13–77.

3. Pomeroy Tucker, *Origin, Rise, and Progress of Mormonism* (New York: D. Appleton, 1867).

4. John W. Welch and Tim Rathbone, "The Translation of the Book of Mormon: Preliminary Report on the Basic Historical Information," unpublished typescript, FARMS, 1986, 38–39.

5. Joseph Smith III, "Last Testimony of Sister Emma," *Saints' Herald* 26 (October 1, 1879): 290.

6. Scott C. Dunn, "Spirit Writing: Another Look at the Book of Mormon," *Sunstone* 10 (June 1985): 16–26.

7. For two recent comments on the sources of the Book of Mormon, see John L. Brooke, *The Refiner's Fire: The Making of Mormon Cosmology, 1644–1844* (Cambridge:

Cambridge University Press, 1994), 149–83; and Richard S. Van Wagoner, *Sidney Rigdon: A Portrait of Religious Excess* (Salt Lake City: Signature Books, 1994), 462–67.

8. Joseph Smith III, "Last Testimony," 290.

9. Jessee, *Papers of Joseph Smith*, 1:7–8. The scribe was Frederick G. Williams.

10. A basic narrative of events in the recovery years is available in Richard L. Bushman, *Joseph Smith and the Beginnings of Mormonism* (Urbana: University of Illinois Press, 1984), 79–114. A useful chronology that adds and modifies details is Welch and Rathbone, "Translation of the Book of Mormon," 3–32.

11. Lucy Smith, *Biographical Sketches*, 121–22.

12. Joseph Smith III, "Last Testimony," 290.

13. Dean Jessee, "Joseph Knight's Recollection of Early Mormon History," *BYU Studies* 17 (autumn 1976): 33.

14. Martin Harris, interviewed in "Mormonism—No. II," *Tiffany's Monthly* 5 (1859): 163–70; reprinted in Kirkham, *New Witness*, 2:376–83.

15. Bushman, *Joseph Smith*, 86–89.

16. Jessee, *Papers of Joseph Smith*, 1:9, 284–85; Isaiah 29:11–12.

17. Lucy Smith, *Biographical Sketches*, 121.

18. Book of Mormon, 1830 edition, iii–iv.

19. See Larry E. Morris, "Oliver Cowdery's Vermont Years and the Origins of Mormonism," *BYU Studies* 39, no. 1 (2000): 106–29.

20. Oliver Cowdery's historical letters are included in Jessee, *Papers of Joseph Smith*, 1:27–96. He describes his arrival in Harmony on page 29.

21. Bushman, *Joseph Smith*, 100–1.

22. The longest of David Whitmer's accounts is *An Address to All Believers in Christ* (Richmond, Mo.: David Whitmer, 1887), but published or recorded interviews with him were collected in Lyndon W. Cook, ed., *David Whitmer Interviews: A Restoration Witness* (Orem, Utah: Grandin Book, 1991).

23. Quoted in Bushman, *Joseph Smith*, 103–4.

24. Fawn M. Brodie, *No Man Knows My History: The Life of Joseph Smith, the Mormon Prophet*, 2nd ed., rev. (New York: Vintage, 1995), 77; Brooke, *Refiner's Fire*, 180.

25. Bushman, *Joseph Smith*, 108–9.

26. The text of the agreement, from an original in the Historical Society of Pennsylvania, is reproduced in Welch and Rathbone, "Translation of the Book of Mormon," 31.

27. Quoted in Jessee, "Joseph Knight's Recollection," 37.

28. Ibid.

29. "Mormonism," *New York Morning Courier and Enquirer*, August 31, 1831, quoted in Leonard J. Arrington, "James Gordon Bennett's 1831 Report on the 'Mormonites,'" *BYU Studies* 10 (spring 1970): 357.

30. "Blasphemy—'Book of Mormon,' Alias the Golden Bible," *Rochester Daily Advertiser and Telegraph*, April 2, 1830; reprinted in Kirkham, *New Witness*, 2:40.

9

The Book of Mormon and Its Critics

In a sense, this essay is a period piece. Written as a chapter for my Joseph Smith and the Beginnings of Mormonism *(Urbana: University of Illinois Press, 1984), the essay was partially outdated even when it appeared. I did not deal with the literature on ancient parallels already coming from the Foundation for Ancient Research and Mormon Studies (FARMS), and a rising generation of critics would soon raise a host of new questions. If I were to write about the Book of Mormon today, the essay would take another form.*

But the topic it discusses is not dated. How the Book of Mormon was received from the time it was published in 1830 until the late twentieth century is a subject anyone interested in Joseph Smith wants to know about. The questions raised here have not lost their pertinence. They are still being debated, though within the context of a much more elaborate Book of Mormon scholarship. How elaborate that scholarship has become one quickly discovers by reading Terryl L. Givens, By the Hand of Mormon: The American Scripture that Launched a New World Religion *(New York: Oxford University Press, 2002). To give an idea of the newer work, a sampling has been added to the notes in the essay.*

By any standard, the Book of Mormon is a narrative of unusual complexity. Scores of characters such as Ether and Moroni, Jared and the brother of Jared, move through the story. The pronunciation guide in the current edition lists 344 proper names: Paanchi, Pachus, Pacumeni, Pagag, Pahoran, Pathros, Pekah, Rahab, Ramath, Rameumptum, and on and on. Intricate and shattering events are compressed into a few sentences. Migration, war, and intrigue alternate with prophecy, sermon, and conversion. Mormon, as warrior, historian, and prophet himself, interweaves political and military events with the history of salvation.[1]

Besides the intricacy of plot, the narrative perspective is complicated. The first six books are pure source material, written by early prophets and untouched by later editors. With only a slight introduction, Mormon then takes up the story himself. His narrative, comprising the bulk of the book, is derived from the source materials available to him—records left by previous prophets. He quotes other prophets and sometimes quotes them quoting still others. Moroni injects a letter from his father, and Nephi inserts lengthy passages from previous scriptures. Mormon moves in and

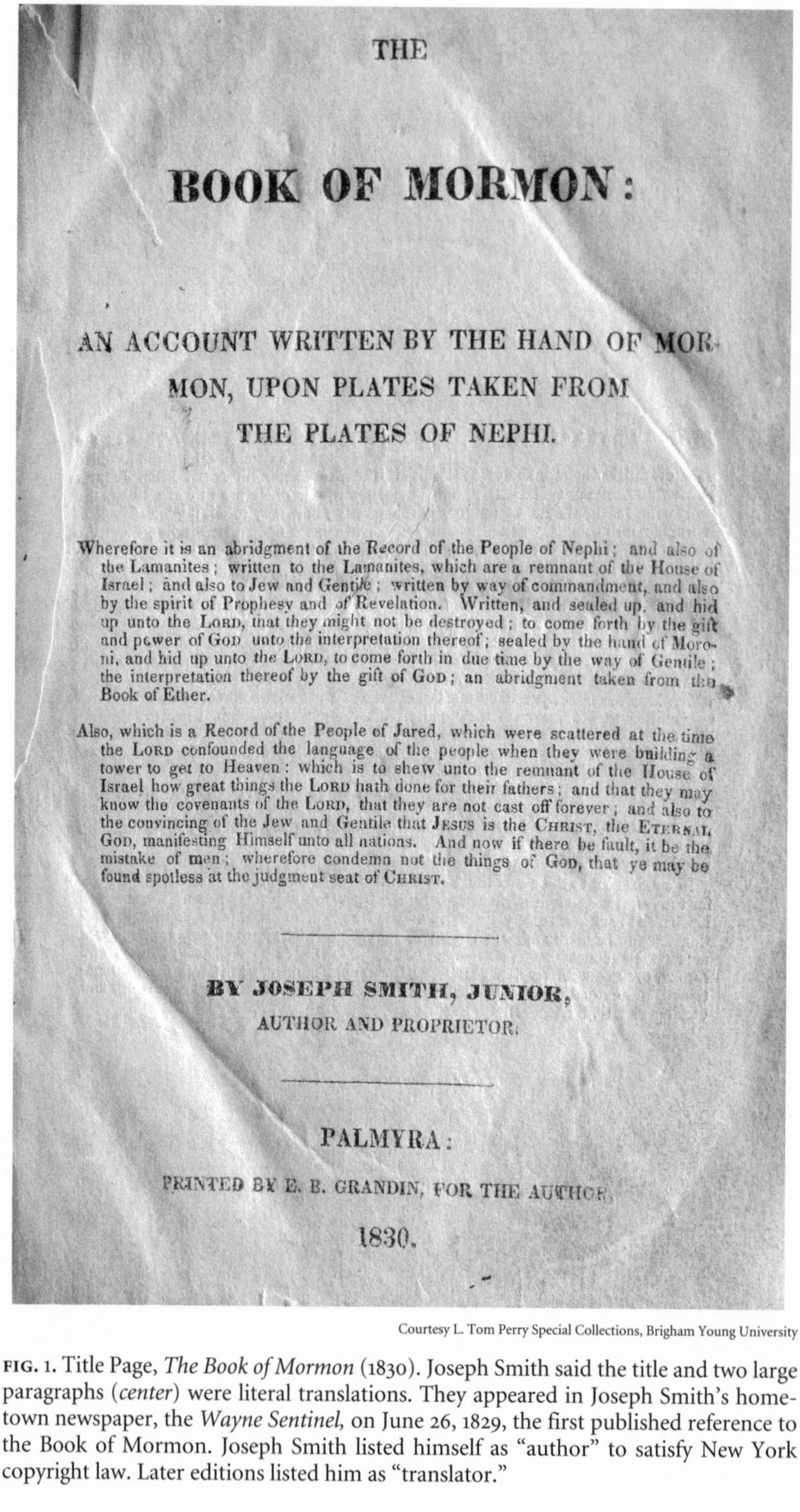

THE

BOOK OF MORMON:

AN ACCOUNT WRITTEN BY THE HAND OF MORMON, UPON PLATES TAKEN FROM THE PLATES OF NEPHI.

Wherefore it is an abridgment of the Record of the People of Nephi; and also of the Lamanites; written to the Lamanites, which are a remnant of the House of Israel; and also to Jew and Gentile; written by way of commandment, and also by the spirit of Prophesy and of Revelation. Written, and sealed up, and hid up unto the LORD, that they might not be destroyed; to come forth by the gift and power of GOD unto the interpretation thereof; sealed by the hand of Moroni, and hid up unto the LORD, to come forth in due time by the way of Gentile; the interpretation thereof by the gift of GOD; an abridgment taken from the Book of Ether.

Also, which is a Record of the People of Jared, which were scattered at the time the LORD confounded the language of the people when they were building a tower to get to Heaven: which is to shew unto the remnant of the House of Israel how great things the LORD hath done for their fathers; and that they may know the covenants of the LORD, that they are not cast off forever; and also to the convincing of the Jew and Gentile that JESUS is the CHRIST, the ETERNAL GOD, manifesting Himself unto all nations. And now if there be fault, it be the mistake of men; wherefore condemn not the things of GOD, that ye may be found spotless at the judgment seat of CHRIST.

BY JOSEPH SMITH, JUNIOR,

AUTHOR AND PROPRIETOR.

PALMYRA:

PRINTED BY E. B. GRANDIN, FOR THE AUTHOR.

1830.

Courtesy L. Tom Perry Special Collections, Brigham Young University

FIG. 1. Title Page, *The Book of Mormon* (1830). Joseph Smith said the title and two large paragraphs (*center*) were literal translations. They appeared in Joseph Smith's hometown newspaper, the *Wayne Sentinel,* on June 26, 1829, the first published reference to the Book of Mormon. Joseph Smith listed himself as "author" to satisfy New York copyright law. Later editions listed him as "translator."

out of the narrative, pointing up a crucial conclusion or addressing readers with a sermon of his own. Almost always two minds are present and sometimes three, all kept account of in the flow of words.[2]

This was the book that Joseph Smith published and Martin Harris began to sell in late March 1830 (fig. 1). The Book of Mormon was more than the citizens of Palmyra were prepared to comprehend. The volume still receives slight attention in cultural histories of the United States. The origin of the Indians, the similarities of Masonry to Book of Mormon robber bands, and the apparent republican tone in certain spots have been noted as connecting with America in 1830, but the whole Book of Mormon, with its multiplicity of stories and characters, its sketches of an ancient civilization, its involved conception of history, and its unrelenting religious message, has eluded analysis.[3] Small wonder that the citizens of Palmyra and village newspaper editors dealt with it summarily and superficially.

How did people make sense of this creation, suspended in its web of marvelous stories and yet entirely tangible and real itself, printed on E. B. Grandin's press just like the weekly newspaper? Joseph Smith said the book "was accounted as a strange thing" and caused "no small stir."[4] Obediah Dogberry, editor of the short-lived *Palmyra Reflector,* more than anyone else, tried to characterize the Book of Mormon for the public in the first few months after publication. The two satires he attempted under the heading "Book of Pukei," published in June and July 1830, give an idea of what Palmyra thought should result when someone of Joseph Smith's background attempted a history of America's ancients. Dogberry had the figure of a little old man appear to Joseph Smith dressed "in Egyptian raiment, except his Indian blanket, and moccasins," and announce he was sent by Mormon, "the great apostle to the Nephites" and "chief among the last [*sic*] ten tribes of Israel." This same apostle conducted the Nephites "to these happy shores in bark canoes," where smallpox "killed two thirds of them, and turned the rest into Indians."[5] Dogberry's reference to Egyptian came from the Book of Mormon. A description of Nephite language as "reformed Egyptian" (1 Ne. 1:2; Morm. 9:22) intrigued many readers. Dogberry's other common symbols of Indians—the bark canoes, the blankets and moccasins, decimation by smallpox—should have been in the story but for some reason were not. In their absence, Dogberry fabricated them himself. He had the Nephites descend from the lost ten tribes when the Book of Mormon perversely overlooked this common explanation for Indian origins. Dogberry made the book comprehensible by adding all the elements Palmyra readers expected and were disappointed to find missing.

Dogberry handled the whole business scornfully and humorously. Without making a direct accusation, he surmised that Joseph worked under the inspiration of "Walters the Magician," apparently an actual person who had earlier caused a stir in Palmyra. As Dogberry told the story, the Book of Mormon was the latest production of a talented money digger working in the tradition of vernacular magic. In Dogberry's imaginary scenario, Walters dubbed Joseph "the *ignoramus*," and promised him the title of greatest of the money diggers.[6] Dogberry ridiculed the healing of Newel Knight, Joseph Smith's friend who was afflicted by an evil spirit, by saying that "no prophet, since the destruction of Jerusalem by Titus, has performed half so many wonders as have been attributed to that *spindle shanked* ignoramus JO SMITH."[7]

After the first flurry of attention, Dogberry said little about the "Gold Bible" until events in the fall of 1830 made the Mormons newsworthy again. Oliver Cowdery, Peter Whitmer, and two other missionaries left New York in October 1830, heading west to teach Indians on the border of the United States. On the way, the missionaries stopped at Kirtland, Ohio, to tell friends of one of the missionaries about the new church, and made a number of converts. The *Painesville Telegraph,* published just nine miles from Kirtland, noted on November 16 that twenty or thirty had been baptized.[8] Two weeks later, there was a "rising of 100 in this and an adjoining county who have embraced the ideas and assertions of Joseph Smith, Jr. many of them respectable for intelligence and piety."[9]

Mormon success put the Book of Mormon in a new light. The *Telegraph* liberally sprinkled the word *pretended* through its reports and warned that, if a fabrication, the Book of Mormon was of "infamous and blasphemous character," but admitted it would be useless to condemn it out of hand. "Time will discover in it either something of vast importance to man, or a deep laid plan to deceive many."[10] The *Telegraph* editor quickly decided in favor of the deception thesis, but in the meantime Mormon numbers were growing. Thomas Campbell, father of Alexander Campbell and a well-known minister through middle America, took Mormonism seriously enough to publish a lengthy letter to his former friend Sidney Rigdon, a recent Mormon convert, challenging him to a debate. No scorn or ridicule tinctured Campbell's arguments. He was intent on proving the Book of Mormon to be a fraud.[11]

News of the Ohio conversions caused Obediah Dogberry to look at the "Gold Bible" with new eyes. Besides using Mormonism to sell the *Reflector* in the vicinity of Palmyra, he saw an opportunity to become a source of information for a much wider audience. A letter from "Plain Truth" in the January 6, 1831, issue observed that "this most clumsy of all impositions, known among us as Jo Smith's 'Gold Bible,' is beginning to excite curiosity abroad." Since the other Palmyra papers refused to print anything on the subject, "Plain Truth" advised, "to you, and you alone, do we look for an expos[é] of the principal facts, and characters, as connected with this singular busines[s]."[12] In that very issue, Dogberry began a six-part series on the Book of Mormon to satisfy the "curiosity of our friends at a distance."[13] Although he did not change his scornful tone, and never quite brought his material under control, Dogberry did replace satire with argument and attempted to make a case against Joseph Smith that would appeal to his enlarged readership.

In this second round of comments, Dogberry took a position commonly assumed by Enlightenment Christians when confronted with supernatural phenomena. Like so many other subsequent writers on Mormonism, Dogberry began "by way of introduction, and illustration" with "brief notices and sketches of the superstitions of the ancients," the "pretended science of alchymy," "Mahomet" and "other ancient impostures" down to more recent legends, "the Morristown Ghost, Rogers, Walters, Joanna Southcote, Jemima Wilkinson, &c."[14] To make sense of unwanted claims to divine power, Christian apologists had adopted the practice of grouping religious frauds together and dismissing them all as the products of human ignorance. Alexander Campbell, in his critique of the Book of Mormon, started off with a similar string of bogus miracle workers.[15] The *Painesville Telegraph* elaborated on the seventeenth-century French prophets.[16] Joseph Smith could be accounted for more readily if it was understood that people had always believed in religious imposture. "The page of history informs us, that from time immemorial, MAN has more or less been the dupe of superstitious error and imposition." Mormons were one more example of human gullibility.[17]

The impostures were believed to succeed because of ignorance. "Where ignorance is found to prevail, superstition and bigotry will abound."[18] Reason was the only antidote. In the modern era, people were less susceptible because enlightenment had steadily spread its beneficent influence. It was a little surprising that Joseph Smith should win converts in the enlightened age, but then Joanna Southcote, the London prophetess, had won adherents not long before. If she could enjoy success "in the greater metropolis of England, and spread over a considerable portion of that kingdom, it is not surprising that one equally absurd, should have its origin in this neighborhood."[19]

Dogberry identified himself and his readers, of course, as people of reason who penetrated the absurdities of Joseph Smith's pretensions. The Smiths, on the other hand, were the epitome of ignorance. Dogberry described Joseph Smith as "having but little expression of countenance, other than that of dullness; his mental powers appear to be extremely limited." The same held true for the rest of the Smiths. "We have never been able to learn that any of the family were ever noted for much else than ignorance and stupidity." Dogberry felt no need to provide evidence of the Smiths' limitations. They had to be dull because it was axiomatic that superstition flourished in ignorance.[20]

This disdain for superstitious belief in supernatural happenings, though convenient for disposing of Joseph Smith, presented a problem to enlightened Christians. What about Christianity itself? How was Christ to be distinguished from Mohammad and innumerable other impostors? An answer had been developed over the past century by Christian apologists who were compelled by skeptics and deists to defend the Bible against the same criticism that Dogberry directed against the Book of Mormon. The critics depicted biblical happenings as the superstition of ignorant and credulous primitives. What could be said in reply? Enlightened Christians chose to place their reliance on miracles, amazing events like the opening of the Red Sea that could not be explained without positing divine intervention. The Bible was to be believed because its prophets worked genuine miracles. That basic outlook affected the reaction to the Mormons. The *Painesville Telegraph,* upon first discussing the Book of Mormon, noted that "we have not been able to discover testimony which ought to elicit faith in any prudent or intelligent mind."[21] By contrast, "when Jesus sent his disciples to preach, he gave them power against all unclean spirits, to cast them out, to heal all manner of diseases, and to raise the dead." Not so with the Mormons. "These newly commissioned disciple[s] have totally failed thus far in their attempts to heal, and as far as can be ascertained, their prophesys [*sic*] have also failed."[22] When Rigdon told a correspondent to the *Telegraph* that the new revelation was not to be confirmed by miracles, the man wanted to know, "How then are we to obtain faith?"[23]

Both Dogberry and the editor of the *Telegraph,* Eber D. Howe, were particularly alert to miracles, because for enlightened Christians miracles were evidence separating true faith from imposture. But miracles alone did not suffice. There were countless claims to miracles attested by witnesses. Healings, appearances, miraculous transformations studded Roman Catholic history. As Christian apologists honed their arguments, they worked down to a single fine point: Christianity was *founded* on miracles. The first disciples believed solely because the evidence of their senses—the miracles of Jesus—first persuaded them. The disciples were not previously committed, nor did they foresee personal advantage. Prevailing belief and established religious authority opposed Jesus; the disciples were bound to suffer by following him. As William Paley, the classic exponent of rational Christianity, put it, "Miraculous pretensions, and miraculous pretensions alone, were what they had to rely upon." The disciples had no other incentive, while fraudulent miracle workers and their witnesses already had established a religion or had something to gain from miraculous proofs. The hope for personal advantage polluted their testimonies. In no case except Christianity did "miraculous evidence [lie] at the bottom of the argument."[24]

False religions, even those that claimed miracles, began with a hope for gain and then later assumed a more religious demeanor. Dogberry's presentation of Joseph Smith was shaped to fit this pattern. The Mormon prophet developed his claims just like that other false prophet, Mohammad. Dogberry pointed out that "Mahomet had a regular plan from the beginning." Only later did he claim miracles, and even those were suspect. Dogberry's Joseph Smith had his plan also. He was a money digger and did not even pretend "to have any communion with angels." The search for treasure preceded any claim to miracles, so Dogberry said. Joseph Smith's whole design from the beginning was to make money, and the Book of Mormon witnesses and other claims to miracle working were added afterward when the scheme was well under way. The witnesses were all in on the design. If not conspirators themselves, they were strongly inclined to believe already. By establishing the timing of the visions to fit the pattern, Dogberry discredited Mormonism and at the same time preserved Christianity's unique claim to a miraculous beginning.[25]

At first oblivious to newspaper attacks, Joseph Smith refused to rise to the challenge to produce miracles. The public questions were no different from the private requests of Martin Harris and Oliver Cowdery. Their desires for proof had been met with the vision of the Three Witnesses, and that was all Joseph offered in support of the Book of Mormon. In a revelation of July 1830, giving instructions to Oliver Cowdery as he went out to preach, Joseph was told to "require not miracles, except I shall command you" (D&C 24:13). A year later, in Kirtland, after the newspaper attacks had stepped up, a revelation warned, "There are those among you who seek signs, and there have been such even from the beginning; But, behold, faith cometh not by signs, but signs follow those that believe" (D&C 63:8–9). Miracles were the reward of faith, not its foundation. "I, the Lord, am not pleased with those among you who have sought after signs and wonders for faith, and not for the good of men unto my glory" (D&C 63:12). The Mormon revelations had no sympathy for the perplexity of Alexander Campbell, who thought it absurd that "*I must believe first, and then ask God if it be true!*"[26]

While Book of Mormon critics complained about the absence of miraculous proof, they had some explaining of their own to do. How did these 584 pages of text come to issue from the mind of an untaught, indolent ignoramus, notable only for his money-digging escapades? That caricature had to be reconciled with the large, complex, intense volume that Mormons carried in their satchels. W. W. Phelps, a Canandaigua, New York, newspaper editor, said in a letter to E. D. Howe, January 15, 1831, that Joseph Smith was certainly a person of "limited abilities in common learning—but his knowledge of *divine things*, since the appearance of his book, has astonished many."[27]

Obediah Dogberry attributed the idea of a book to Walters, the "vagabond fortune-teller" from the town of Sodus, who was reputed to have shown his followers a copy of Cicero's *Orations* in Latin and claimed it was a "record of the former inhabitants of America," telling where the inhabitants deposited their treasures.[28] Dogberry could not make an actual connection between Walters and the Smith family, but he surmised there must have been one. Under the license of satire, Dogberry said that "the mantle of Walters the Magician" fell on Joseph.[29] In a more sober account for the *Painesville Telegraph*, a letter from Palmyra said that "the first idea of a 'Book' was doubtless suggested to the Smiths by one Walters."[30]

The contents were another matter. The Palmyra critics simplified the task by saying that the Book of Mormon was almost entirely borrowed from the Bible. "The book is chiefly garbled from the Old and New Testaments," the Palmyra letter to the *Telegraph* observed, "the Apocraphy having contributed its share." "A quarto Bible now in this village, was borrowed and nearly worn out and defaced by their dirty handling. Some seven or eight of them spent many months in copying, Cowdrey [*sic*] being principal scribe." The letter implied wholesale plagiarizing by a committee of authors who produced a cheap imitation of scripture. Nephi and his brothers did insert seventeen chapters of Isaiah and the resurrected Christ repeated the Sermon on the Mount, but the copying theory fell short because it left so much of the text unaccounted for.[31]

As the months went by, others offered more likely hypotheses. Alexander Campbell read at least part of the book and suggested an explanation that became the kernel of modern critics' view (fig. 2). Campbell was founder of the Disciples of Christ and one of the country's most notable theologians and preachers. When his father, Thomas Campbell, challenged Sidney Rigdon to debate Mormonism in early February 1831, Thomas specified that both contestants should be allowed "every assistance that can be contributed by the friends on each side."[32] His son Alexander, well known for his debating ability from a famous encounter with the atheist Robert Owen, had already begun a study of the Book of Mormon. The young Campbell published his critique on February 7, 1831, in his own paper, the *Millennial Harbinger*, based in Bethany, Virginia. The *Painesville Telegraph* reprinted the essay, and it appeared again as a pamphlet in Boston in 1832 under the title *Delusions: An Analysis of the Book of Mormon; with an Examination of Its Internal and External Evidences, and a Refutation of Its Pretenses to Divine Authority.*[33]

Alexander Campbell proved his knowledge of the Book of Mormon by summarizing about half of the plot, enough to give his readers a sense of the narrative. Dismissing Joseph Smith as "as ignorant and as impudent a knave as ever wrote a book," Campbell saw no need for a committee of authors. Joseph Smith definitely wrote it himself.[34] "There never was a

book more evidently written by one
set of fingers, nor more certainly
conceived in one cranium since the
first book appeared in human language, than in this same book."[35] "It
is as certainly Smith's fabrication as
Satan is the father of lies."[36] Campbell found signs of Joseph's culture
scattered through the book, a touch
of Masonry and republican government, a few characteristic Yankee
phrases, and opinions on many of
the theological controversies of the
day: "infant baptism, ordination,
the trinity, regeneration, repentance, justification, the fall of man,
the atonement, transubstantiation,
fasting, penance, church government, religious experience, the call
to the ministry, the general resurrection, eternal punishment."[37] Still
more revealing were the grammati-
cal errors, which Campbell noted
down in great number and copied

FIG. 2. Alexander Campbell (1788–1866).
A vocal critic of the Book of Mormon,
Campbell was an early leader of the Dis-
ciples of Christ, a restorationist offshoot
of the Baptists. Engraving by H. B. Hall,
in Selina Huntington Campbell, *Home
Life and Reminiscences of Alexander
Campbell* (St. Louis: John Burns, 1882).

into his essay, gaffes like "Ye are like unto they" and "We did arrive to the
promised land." "Smithisms," as Campbell called them, were sure evidence
of human composition.[38]

In contrast to the Palmyra critics, Campbell downplayed the similarity
to the Bible. What most impressed him was how unbiblical the Book of
Mormon was. Partly it was style. "I would as soon compare a bat to the
American eagle, a mouse to a mammoth . . . as to contrast it with a single
chapter in all the writings of the Jewish or Christian prophets."[39] More
striking still was theology. He did not like the fact that Nephi and his brothers exercised the priesthood when they were not descendants of Levi or
Aaron, that another land besides Palestine was a promised land, or that
descendants of tribes other than Judah became kings.[40] What most
appalled him was that the Book of Mormon "represents the christian institution as practiced among the Israelites before Jesus was born."[41] The
Nephites preached "baptism and other christian usages hundreds of years
before Jesus Christ was born!"[42] There was no regard for the divide
between Old and New Testaments. Joseph Smith's "Jews are called christians while keeping the law of Moses, the holy sabbath, and worshipping in
their temple at their altars, and by their high priests." Campbell has Joseph

writing the Book of Mormon in simpleminded ignorance of the basic facts of Jewish and Christian history, and spreading across its pages "every error and almost every truth discussed in N[ew] York for the last ten years."[43]

As for the intricate plot and the huge array of characters, Campbell dismissed all that as "romance."[44] Subsequent critics had more trouble disregarding what every reader of the book could not help noticing: the Book of Mormon was a complex story. In 1833, Eber D. Howe, one of Mormonism's most devoted critics, and an excommunicated Mormon named Doctor Philastus Hurlbut thought they had stumbled across the answer. While preaching in Pennsylvania, Hurlbut learned that some residents of Conneaut, Ohio, saw in the Book of Mormon resemblances to a manuscript written by Solomon Spaulding, a former resident of their town. When interviewed, they swore that the Spaulding story told of lost tribes of Israel moving from Jerusalem to America led by characters named Nephi and Lehi. One deponent remembered the names Moroni and Zarahemla.[45] Hurlbut pursued Spaulding's widow to Massachusetts and eventually located a manuscript that told of a migration to America, but the migrants were Romans, and the story bore slight resemblance to the Book of Mormon. Hurlbut concluded there must have been another manuscript. Piecing together one surmise after another, he and Howe eventually decided that Sidney Rigdon had obtained Spaulding's now lost manuscript while in Pittsburgh, where Spaulding had submitted his work to a publisher. Rigdon transformed the novel into the Book of Mormon by adding the religious parts. Believing the Palmyra critics' characterization of Joseph Smith as a lazy ignoramus, Howe and Spaulding were sure "that there has been, from the beginning of the imposture, a more talented knave behind the curtain."[46] Sidney Rigdon, a formidable preacher, a colleague of Alexander Campbell's, and a close student of the Bible, was the only one qualified for the task. "If there was a man in the world that could successfully spread and give a name to the vagaries of the Smiths, it was Rigdon." He was "the Iago, the prime mover of the whole conspiracy." Somehow or other Rigdon conveyed the manuscript to Joseph without being detected, and then pretended to be converted when the missionaries brought the Book of Mormon to Kirtland in 1830.[47]

The critics thus explained the Book of Mormon by handling it piecemeal, perceiving a portion at a time, accounting for that, and then struggling to comprehend more as ingenuity enabled them to construct more elaborate explanations. The most surprising fact to the Palmyra townspeople was that Joseph Smith, the supposedly lazy son of a money digger, should even pretend to write a book. Dogberry took care of that fact with Walters's recitations from Cicero's Orations. The letter from Palmyra to Painesville (perhaps written by Dogberry in a sober mood) saw the book as a copy of the Bible and credited a group of Joseph's cronies with originating the "Gold Bible." Campbell, while still calling Joseph ignorant, at least acknowledged the Book of Mormon's treatment of theological issues and gave it credit for attempting to decide "all the great controversies" troubling New York for the past ten years. Campbell made it strictly a local production, a reflection of Joseph's knowledge and ignorance. Campbell prepared the way for Howe and Hurlbut, who added recognition of narrative complexity. They solved the problem of the involved theology and the intricate narrative by specifying two authors, one a theologian and the other a novelist.

Although built on slight evidence and an abundance of speculation, the Howe-Hurlbut hypothesis, or Spaulding theory, as it became known, encompassed more of the actual content of the book than any of its predecessors. It remained the standard explanation of non-Mormon critics well into the twentieth century.[48] The fact that Howe and Hurlbut contradicted Alexander Campbell was overlooked. Anti-Mormon writers felt no obligation to explain why the learned Bible student Rigdon would make all the elementary theological blunders Campbell identified, or why Rigdon's grammar should be so faulty. The view that Joseph wrote the book out of his own experience was cast aside until the Spaulding theory failed and a revival of Campbell's environmentalist hypothesis became necessary once again.

Perhaps the most serious failing in all the critiques of the Book of Mormon was an inability to deal with text in any detail. Howe and Hurlbut acknowledged the story by hypothesizing a novelist as coauthor but did not discuss the story itself. Campbell referred to the Book of Mormon positions on theological issues but failed to say what they were or how they related to religion of the time. Dogberry saw similarities to the Bible but made no actual comparisons. The outsiders' contempt for the book caused them to hurry their work. Their aim was always to explain away the Book of Mormon rather than understand it. Failing to ground their view in the actual contents of the book, the critiques did not do justice to the work's actual complexity, and their conclusions were unstable, even ephemeral.[49]

The New Critics

After the turn of the twentieth century, a historicist explanation of the Book of Mormon gradually replaced the Spaulding theory among non-Mormon scholars. In 1902, I. Woodbridge Riley, a Yale Ph.D. and the author of *The Founder of Mormonism*, pointed out the many flaws in Howe and Hurlbut's hypothesis, and in 1945, Fawn Brodie delivered the fatal stroke in *No Man Knows My History*.[50] Though Spaulding still surfaces in critical works from time to time, Alexander Campbell's 1831 analysis has returned to favor. All but a few critics credit Joseph Smith with authorship, as did Campbell. According to these historicists, Joseph absorbed images, attitudes, and conceptions from upstate New York rural culture and wove them into the Book of Mormon story.

While historicist scholarship has illuminated the Book of Mormon's relationship with American culture, these analyses suffer from the same shortcomings as the work of their predecessors. The determination to explain the Book of Mormon's origins (and to explain away the angel stories) has limited the capacity to understand the book on its own terms. The presumed cultural influence—Antimasonry, republicanism, the theories of Indian origins, and romantic nationalism, for example—do roughly resemble certain elements in the Book of Mormon, but the environmental theories leave too many other elements unexplained.

Alexander Campbell first cited Antimasonry as one of the elements of New York culture thought to be an influence on the Book of Mormon. Campbell thought that a certain group of Book of Mormon people called Gadiantons, who "began to bind themselves in secret oaths to aid one another in all things, good or evil," were a reflection of Masonry.[51]

Western New Yorkers had particular reason to respond to the sinister Gadianton bands because of the furor caused by the famous Morgan case. William Morgan, a renegade Mason who had threatened to publish Masonic secrets in the years immediately preceding publication of the Book of Mormon, was mysteriously abducted from jail in Canandaigua in September 1826 and never heard from again. Popular opinion blamed the abduction on the Masons. Trials held in January 1827 brought light sentences to the defendants, although they pled guilty to a "conspiracy to kidnap" the victim. The mercy shown the conspirators angered many who followed the trial. They attributed the result to Masonic influence on the bench and in the jury. Pamphlets reviewing the abduction and trial began to appear in large numbers. A corpse that washed ashore from Lake Ontario in October 1828 was first thought to be Morgan, though later identified as a drowning victim.[52] Strangely the furor did not die down. From October 1826 through the middle of 1831, eighteen trials of Masonic conspirators took place in five western counties, and in the fall of 1827 fifteen candidates were elected to the state legislature on Antimasonic principles.[53] Antimasonry soon became a national political force. In the 1828 presidential election, much was made of the facts that John Quincy Adams was not a Mason and Andrew Jackson was. Antimasonic parties sprang up in Pennsylvania, Massachusetts, Connecticut, Maine, Vermont, Ohio, Indiana, and Michigan. In 1830 and 1831, the Antimasonic party held national conventions and in 1832 ran a presidential candidate, William Wirt of Maryland. John Quincy Adams ran for the governorship of Massachusetts in 1833 on an Antimasonic ticket.[54]

The interest in Masonry provided a large market for Antimasonic books and audiences for speakers who traveled from town to town to divulge Masonic secrets. The pamphlets rehearsed in great detail the lengthy Masonic initiation rites, elucidating the initiations into each of the degrees and going on to describe the specialized orders in Masonry's many branches. Besides playing to the public's fascination with hidden rituals, the Antimasonic literature dwelt on a phrase in the rites pledging initiates to protect their Masonic brothers in difficulty whether they were right or wrong.[55] Above all else, the exposés emphasized the threat of death to any who divulged Masonic secrets. Morgan's abduction proved the oaths were deadly serious. How could the nation be safe when thousands of Masons, many in positions of great influence, were bound to shield their brothers from prosecution no matter what the offense, and to destroy any who divulged secrets?

The association of Gadianton bands and Masonry arose from a few obvious similarities that Campbell might have noticed in a single reading of the Book of Mormon. The members of the Gadianton bands took oaths to conceal one another's crimes, they identified each other with signs and passwords, and they conspired to subvert government. All these understandably sounded to Campbell like an Antimasonic view of Masonry. Expanding on his insight, an early-twentieth-century psychologist thought the similarities in the names Mormon and Morgan proved conclusively that only a western New Yorker, saturated with Antimasonry, could have composed the Book of Mormon and only between 1826 and 1834, when Antimasonry was at its peak.[56] Joseph Smith's later initiation into the Masons when a lodge was organized in Nauvoo in 1842 seems to confirm the idea of a fascination with Masonry, even though in Nauvoo Joseph was for the Masons instead of against them.

What the critics neglect in their preoccupation with American influences is the broader picture of Gadianton growth in the Book of Mormon society, raising the question of whether concentration on the resemblances alone is an adequate method of interpreting the bands. The groups labeled by Mormons as Gadiantons were not one continuing society, like the Masons, but five distinct combinations that sprang up among the Nephites and Jaredites. Three of the five bands took shape in the eighty-five years between 52 B.C.E. and the coming of Christ in 33 C.E., during a period of severe social and political instability. The original band came into being around 52 B.C.E. and lasted until 17 B.C.E. The immediate occasion for its formation was competition among the three sons of a chief judge for succession to their father's office. The supporters of one of the defeated sons refused to accept the voice of the people and conspired with one Kishkumen to assassinate Pahoran, the successful son. The conspirators "entered into a covenant, yea, swearing by their everlasting Maker, that they would tell no man that Kishkumen murdered Pahoran" (Hel. 1:11). Gadianton rose to influence among this group because he was "exceeding expert in many words, and also in his craft, to carry on the secret work of murder and robbery" (Hel. 2:4). Gadianton aspired to the judgment seat himself and promised his followers "power and authority" in return for their support (Hel. 2:5).

A subsequent group of Gadiantons was a collection of Lamanites and Nephite dissenters. Around 12 B.C.E., they infested mountain hideaways, descending to plunder and murder and then retreating again. Nephite dissenters continued to join them until the group became "an exceeding great band of robbers" (Hel. 11:24–26). These roving bands were powerful enough to withstand "the whole armies of the Nephites," and did "cause great fear to come unto the people upon all the face of the land" (Hel. 11:32). The Gadiantons laid cities to waste and were presumptuous enough to demand that one of the chief judges relinquish the government to them (see 3 Ne. 2:11–12; 3:1–9). Not until the Nephites scorched the earth and relinquished their land could they defeat the Gadiantons. Without farms to plunder, the robbers lost their strength, and around 21 C.E. they suffered defeat (3 Ne. 4:1–14, 27).

One can see why Alexander Campbell thought he saw Masons in the Book of Mormon. Conditioned by Antimasonic rhetoric, he understandably reacted to familiar elements in the story. But readers approaching from another perspective might have noted quite different aspects of the Gadianton bands. They could with equal ease be perceived as modern terrorist guerrillas, dissenters at war with the old order, penetrating villages on the margins of official control, undermining from within, and attacking openly when they had strength. Viewed in context, the Masonic-like oaths and covenants were secondary to direct attacks on government through assassinations and military raids.[57]

The similarities noted by the critics, rather than constituting an explanation of the Gadianton bands, speak more for the difficulties the Book of Mormon presented to American readers. Only limited portions were intelligible as expressions of American culture. Critics concentrated on selected proof texts and neglected the context.[58] Their method necessarily obscured differences between American and Book of Mormon culture. In the supposed Antimasonic passages in the Book of Mormon, nothing was said about Masonic degrees or elaborate initiation rituals. Masonry was noted for rituals that raised an initiate from one degree to the next; acceptance of a simple oath of secrecy and allegiance admitted a person to the Gadianton bands and that was only one of a string of omissions. The Gadiantons failed to connect with Solomon's temple, the Masonic craft, or Hiram, builder of the great temple. Perhaps most important, the crucial event in the Antimasonic campaign, the abduction of the Masonic traitor William Morgan, had no equivalent in the Book of Mormon.[59]

The differences may explain why critics in Joseph Smith's own day made so little of Antimasonry in the Book of Mormon. In his 1831 critique, Alexander Campbell mentioned Masonry only briefly and passed on. Subsequent 1830s critics neglected the point entirely, since they credited Solomon Spaulding with authorship. Alexander Campbell himself in time subscribed to the Spaulding theory and dropped the point about Masonry.[60]

Likewise, converts paid no attention to Antimasonry. With the Antimasonic party growing rapidly after 1829 in New England, New York, and Ohio, Mormon converts might be expected to join the campaign to rid the nation of secret combinations. Insofar as early Mormons had political preferences, they likely were Antimasons, but these sentiments were entirely overshadowed. Lucy Mack Smith said nothing about Masonry, Morgan, or Antimasonry in her autobiography. Joseph was equally neglectful. At the height of the Antimasonic excitement from 1829 to 1833, Masonry was scarcely mentioned among the Mormons. The people who knew Antimasonry and the Book of Mormon in the 1830s made less of the connection than later critics.[61]

Book of Mormon republicanism was another item briefly noted by Alexander Campbell and expanded by later scholars. Midway in their history, the Nephites ended monarchy and instituted a government based on the "voice of the people" (Mosiah 29:25). To signify the importance of the change, they numbered their years from what was called the "reign of the judges," until the birth of Christ established a still more fundamental baseline for their calendar (Mosiah 29:44; Alma 1:11; 3 Ne. 2:8). Lehi seemed to associate democracy with the very nature of the American continents when he declared that "this land shall be a land of liberty unto the Gentiles, and there shall be no kings upon the land" (2 Ne. 10:11). "He that raiseth up a king against me shall perish, for I, the Lord, the king of heaven, will be their king" (2 Ne. 11:14). These were presumably reassuring words for a newly minted republic, one of a tiny handful among the formidable monarchies of the earth.[62]

And yet the reign of the judges in the Book of Mormon bears little resemblance to nineteenth-century American republicanism. Nephite culture was never republican insofar as the Book of Mormon describes government. The first prophet, Nephi, allowed himself to be made a king and established a line of kings that lasted 500 years (2 Ne. 5:18; 6:2; Jacob 1:9; Mosiah 29:44). Around 92 B.C.E., King Mosiah gave up his throne and established a system of judges chosen by the voice of the people, but the resulting government was a far cry from the American pattern. By democratic standards, the chief judge was more king than president, as suggested by the Book of Mormon phrase "the reign of the judges." After the first judge, whose name was Alma, was proclaimed by the voice of the people, he enjoyed life tenure. When he chose to resign because of internal difficulties, he selected his own successor, the founder of a dynasty of judges (Alma 4:16). In the next succession the judgeship passed to the chief judge's son and thence, according to his "right," as the book says, to the successive sons of the judges (Alma 50:39; Hel. 1:13). The "voice of the people" entered only marginally into the appointment of an officer who essentially enjoyed life tenure and hereditary succession.[63]

Furthermore, all of the constitutional checks on Nephite rulers, whether kings or judges, are missing. The standard three branches of government do not appear. The chief judge was judge, executive, and legislator combined. In wartime he raised men, armed them, and collected provisions (Alma 46:34; 50:1–7). His titles were interchangeable: chief judge and governor (Alma 60:1–9; 3 Ne. 3:1). He was also lawmaker, for no conventional legislature can be found in the Book of Mormon. In the early part of the book, the law was presented as traditional, handed down from the fathers as "given them by the hand of the Lord," and "acknowledged by this people" to make it binding (Mosiah 29:13–25; Alma 1:14; 2:2–7). Later the chief judge assumed the power of proclaiming, or at least elaborating, laws. Alma gave his successor Nephihah the "power to enact laws according to the laws which had been given" (Alma 4:16). Any major constitutional changes, such as a return to formal kingship, required approval of the people, but day-to-day legislation, so far as the record speaks, was the prerogative of the chief judge. Perhaps most extraordinary by American standards, nothing was made of taxation by a popular assembly. Oppressive kings overtaxed the people, but the remedy never lay in a representative body of any kind. The maxim "no taxation without representation" had no standing in Nephite consciousness.

Latter-day Saints themselves have mistaken the reign of judges for republicanism. In one edition of the Book of Mormon, a twentieth-century editor's chapter heading to Mosiah 29, where Mosiah established judgeships, says the king "recommends representative form of government."[64] The preconceptions of the modern age led Mormons as well as critics to see things in the Book of Mormon that are not there. It has been difficult for Mormon and non-Mormon alike to grasp the real intellectual problem of the Book of Mormon, briefly summed up by one of Joseph Smith's non-Mormon contemporaries in a New York magazine in the early 1840s. Speaking of the Book of Mormon, one Josephine observed that "the style is a close imitation of the scriptural, and is remarkably free from any allusions that might betray a knowledge of the present political or social state of the world. The writer lives in the whole strength of his imagination in the age he portrays."[65] That the Book of Mormon portrays another world in many ways alien to our own is the hardest point for modern readers to deal with.

The critics cannot be faulted for saying that the Book of Mormon was a history of the Indians. The book was that, and early Mormons told the world it was. Samuel Smith asked a New York innkeeper at the end of the first day of missionary work in June 1830 "if he did not wish to purchase a history of the origin of the Indians."[66] Five months later in Ohio, the four missionaries to the Indians presented the Book of Mormon as "an account of their origin, and a prophecy of their final conversion to Christianity."[67] In 1831 Lucy Smith, on her way to visit her brother Stephen Mack's family in Detroit, told a fellow passenger that the Book of Mormon was "a record of the origin of the Aborigines of America."[68]

The missionaries had good reason to cast the Book of Mormon in that light. Settlers in New York and Ohio had a natural curiosity about Indians. The Palmyra newspapers occasionally ran items about Indians and Indian ruins in the miscellaneous information section.[69] The Manchester Rental Library purchased Josiah Priest's *The Wonders of Nature and Providence,* which included materials on the Hebraic origins of the Indians.[70] Priest, a popularizer rather than a student of Indian origins, wrote another such volume for publication in 1833, *American Antiquities and Discoveries in the West,* which sold 22,000 copies in thirty months. The mysterious mounds of Ohio provoked a steady stream of speculation about the cultures that created them.[71] Samuel Smith probably hoped the innkeeper would read the Book of Mormon out of curiosity, if nothing else.

Writers could not agree among themselves on where the Indians came from. Priest's popular 1833 volume speculated that Noah's Ark came to rest in America, and that Polynesians, Egyptians, Greeks, Romans, Scandinavians, Jews, Welsh, Scots, and Chinese migrated to America and contributed to Indian stock. His eclecticism satisfied the public, which apparently was willing to accept supposition in lieu of an authoritative explanation.[72] Scholars could offer nothing better. In 1875 a conference of the world's experts broke up in confusion over attempts to sort out the evidence.[73]

The Book of Mormon offered as reasonable an explanation as any for the time. From the seventeenth century on, ministers in Europe and America had argued that the Indians were Israelites on the grounds of similarities in Hebrew and Indian culture. Increase Mather, Samuel Sewall, Samuel Willard, Jonathan Edwards, and Ezra Stiles had published such opinions, borrowing in part from European sources such as Thomas Thorowgood to prove their point. The idea received fresh impetus from James Adair's *The History of the American Indians,* published in London in 1775. Adair lived for forty years among the Indians as a trader before retiring to write his observations.[74] Excited by Adair's evidence, Elias Boudinot, founder and first president of the American Bible Society, introduced a wide American audience to the theory of Israelite origins in his *A Star in the West,* which

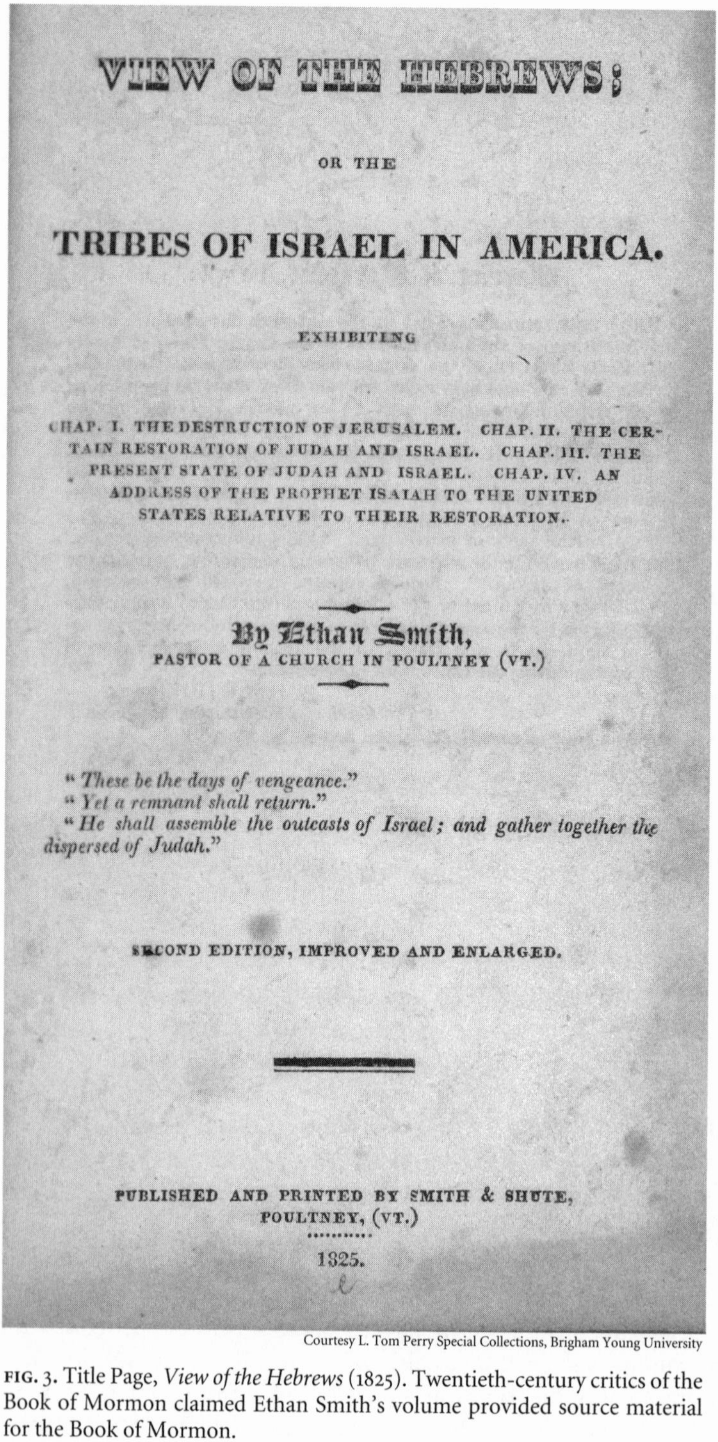

VIEW OF THE HEBREWS;

OR THE

TRIBES OF ISRAEL IN AMERICA.

EXHIBITING

CHAP. I. THE DESTRUCTION OF JERUSALEM. CHAP. II. THE CERTAIN RESTORATION OF JUDAH AND ISRAEL. CHAP. III. THE PRESENT STATE OF JUDAH AND ISRAEL. CHAP. IV. AN ADDRESS OF THE PROPHET ISAIAH TO THE UNITED STATES RELATIVE TO THEIR RESTORATION.

By Ethan Smith,

PASTOR OF A CHURCH IN POULTNEY (VT.)

"These be the days of vengeance."
"Yet a remnant shall return."
"He shall assemble the outcasts of Israel; and gather together the dispersed of Judah."

SECOND EDITION, IMPROVED AND ENLARGED.

PUBLISHED AND PRINTED BY SMITH & SHUTE,
POULTNEY, (VT.)

1825.

Courtesy L. Tom Perry Special Collections, Brigham Young University

FIG. 3. Title Page, *View of the Hebrews* (1825). Twentieth-century critics of the Book of Mormon claimed Ethan Smith's volume provided source material for the Book of Mormon.

appeared in 1816.[75] Spurred by his work, other authors began combing accounts of Indian life in search of evidence. Ethan Smith, a Congregational minister in Poultney, Vermont, in *View of the Hebrews*, published in 1823, reviewed the findings of Adair and Boudinot and added evidence from many other sources. The reviews of *View of the Hebrews* (and presumably the sales), warranted an enlarged second edition in 1825.[76] Josiah Priest, a man with his eye on the main chance, further complimented Smith by excerpting scores of pages in his own *The Wonders of Nature and Providence.*[77]

From one perspective, the Book of Mormon was one more account of Israel in America. But it would be a mistake to see the book as an imitation of these earlier works. Nor is there evidence of heavy borrowing from *View of the Hebrews*, as some critics have said. Comparison of the two works reveals too many fundamental differences.[78]

Ethan Smith's reconstruction of Indian history had one purpose: to identify Indians with the lost ten tribes. The full title of Smith's book is *View of the Hebrews; or, The Tribes of Israel in America* (fig. 3). He derived his inspiration from Elias Boudinot's *A Star in the West; or, A Humble Attempt to Discover the Long Lost Ten Tribes of Israel, Preparatory to Their Return to Their Beloved City, Jerusalem.* The argument turned heavily on a few biblical passages purportedly written about the tribes. Amos 8:11–12, for example, was believed to describe their migration in prophesying of a people who would "wander from sea to sea, and from the north even to the east." Smith conjectured that the ten tribes had moved northward from Assyria, where they had been taken captive, and then east to the ocean. The words "sea to sea" meant the Mediterranean and the Pacific. The tribes crossed North America, possibly via the Bering Straits, and moved south to fill both American continents. Ethan Smith argued that all of the lost tribes remained together because the Bible spoke of dispersed Judah and the "outcasts" of Israel. "It inevitably follows," he insisted, "that the ten tribes of Israel must now have, somewhere on the earth, a distinct existence in an *outcast* state."[79]

Ethan Smith believed that God kept the American continents vacant as a reservoir for the tribes during their long apostasy. Smith had little to say about their history in America, except that a civilized group built the well-known mounds and fortifications before extermination by a degenerate branch. For the most part, God paid no heed to the tribes in their American home. Their original religion steadily deteriorated until only fragments remained to recall the savages' biblical origins. In Ethan Smith's view, investigators understandably found only traces of Mosaic religion. When the time for the fulfillment of God's ancient covenant with Israel arrived, the Indians would convert to Christ and a number of them would return to their ancient promised land.[80]

The excitement in Ethan Smith's book lay in the light it shed on an old puzzle: Where were the lost ten tribes, that mysterious group who dropped out of history after their captivity in Assyria? And on this point, the Book of Mormon was a disappointment. Lehi and his family were not the ten tribes. Lehi left for the new world 125 years after the Assyrian captivity and from Jerusalem, not Assyria. His people were never identified as the lost tribes. The ten tribes were mentioned, as Parley Pratt noted, by the Savior when he said he would visit them after he left the Nephites, but nothing was said of an American home for the tribes.[81] They were another group, located in another part of the world. By the Book of Mormon account, the Indians, rather than being the other half of ancient Israel, were descendants of a tiny band that slipped out of Jerusalem long after the ten tribes had disappeared.[82]

Moreover, the Book of Mormon version of Indian origins contradicted much of Ethan Smith's scriptural evidence. One of the key proof texts in Ethan Smith's treatise did not work for the Book of Mormon. Lehi went south, not north, as Amos 8 prescribed. Nor were the cultural similarities of Indians and Hebrews entirely relevant. Ethan Smith piled up proofs of Indian practice of Mosaic ritual and law. Book of Mormon people abided by the Mosaic law until the coming of Christ, but Mormon buried the fact as if it were of little importance. Nephite prophets taught Christ and the resurrection. Sacrifices, feasts, temple worship—all the material evidence in *View of the Hebrews*—received scant attention amid the outpouring of sermons on salvation through Christ. After the appearance of the Savior, the Mosaic law was abandoned altogether and presumably sifted out of Nephite culture. Almost everything Ethan Smith worked so industriously to prove, the Book of Mormon disproved or disregarded.[83]

The critics have mistakenly searched too hard for specific parallels in the Book of Mormon and *View of the Hebrews*, while neglecting the moral purpose of Ethan Smith's work. Before he was historian or anthropologist, Smith was a preacher. The burden of his message was that the Indians were Israel, a branch of God's chosen people. The great promises made to them in the ancient covenants were soon to be fulfilled. The point for modern Americans was to pay attention to this benighted people. As a reviewer expressed it, the moral of the book was "the weight of obligation which now rests on Gentile Christians, and eminently on American Christians to extend the gospel to the Jews."[84]

If we are to ask where the Book of Mormon converged with the American culture of the 1830s, the theme of Israel's restoration is a better contact point than Ethan Smith's theory about the lost tribes. Smith attached the Indians to the destiny of the Jews to make proselyting among the tribes an aspect of the promised conversion of all Israel, and so did the Book of Mormon.

In this effort, Ethan Smith worked in a well-established tradition. The association of Jews and Indians went back at least as far as the sixteenth century. Elizabethan divines came to believe that the future of the Jews was foretold in Romans 11 and Revelations 16:12, as well as in Isaiah and Ezekiel. A number of seventeenth-century Puritans urged Parliament to readmit Jews to England (they had been expelled in 1290 by royal decree) so as to facilitate their conversion. At the same moment, the great seventeenth-century Amsterdam rabbi Manasseh Ben Israel petitioned Parliament for readmission for his own reason: to complete the dispersion of Israel through the entire world. The Bible prophesied that the Jews would be scattered into every land, and presumably the return to Palestine would not begin until the dispersion was complete. Ben Israel's comprehensive view of Israel's history encompassed America and the Indians as well. His conviction that Israel must be dispersed to the four corners of the globe required that he identify the Indians as among the chosen people. He published his views in 1650, in *Hope of Israel*, which became a touchstone for subsequent investigators. His Puritan allies in the movement to readmit Jews to England shared his belief. Thomas Thorowgood wrote *The Jews in America*, and Increase Mather interspersed sermons on Indian origins with tracts on Jewish conversion.[85]

At the end of the eighteenth century, the French Revolution set off another wave of speculation about Israel's return. Napoleon, the Antichrist of the era, startled millennialists when he convened a Jewish Sanhedrin in Paris in 1807. Speculation ran wild, especially among those who interpreted prophecy to say that the Jews would ally with the Antichrist just prior to their break with evil and their conversion to Christ.[86] As the fury of the revolution mounted, religious leaders in England and America began to make specific preparations. The pastor of the Presbyterian Church in Elizabethtown, New Jersey, David Austin, broke with the church in 1791 and constructed houses for the Jews, who he believed would soon need shelter en route to the Holy Land.[87] In 1809 Joseph S. F. C. Frey, a converted Jew, formed the London Society for Promoting Christianity among the Jews. In 1820, after migration to New York City, Frey organized the American Society for Meliorating the Condition of the Jews. Within four years, the society claimed 200 auxiliaries and a circulation of 20,000 for its paper, *Israel's Advocate*. By the mid-1820s, the restoration of the Jews was a major question for Christians attempting serious explication of the millennial calendar.[88]

When Joseph Frey wanted assistance with a plan to organize a refuge for ostracized Jewish converts, he went to Elias Boudinot, author of *A Star in the West*, the 1816 volume on Indians as Israelites, and probably the most distinguished Christian layman in America. As president of the American Bible Society, Boudinot approved the scheme for a refuge and recommended a revival of the society for evangelizing Jews. In his will, Boudinot left a tract of land to start a Jewish colony.[89] Probably through Boudinot, Frey met Ethan Smith. In the second edition of *View of the Hebrews*, Smith announced that

> the Rev. Mr. Frey, the celebrated Jewish preacher, and Agent for the American Meliorating Society, upon reading *View of the Hebrews*, and warmly approving the sentiment in it, with the others, that the American Indians are the ten tribes, informed the writer of these sheets, that he owned a pamphlet, written by the earl of Crawford and Linsey, (England,) entitled "*The Ten Tribes.*"[90]

Apparently Frey had long taken an interest in the Indians, for he remembered that Crawford, a British army officer in the Revolution, had argued that the Indians were descendants of the ten tribes. Later in life, Frey tried his own hand at proving that the Indians were the lost tribes of Israel.[91]

The nineteenth century, like the seventeenth, saw a blending of Jewish and Christian interest in the return of the Jews and the conversion of Indians. Mordecai Noah, a New York promoter and publicist, petitioned the New York assembly in 1820 to permit him to purchase Grand Island in the Niagara River near Buffalo as a gathering place for the Jews preceding their return. Despite the annoyance and embarrassment of many American Jews, Noah bravely renamed the island Ararat, proclaimed himself "Governor and Judge of Israel," and dedicated Grand Island in an extravagant ceremony in 1825. In the spirit of Manasseh ben Israel, Noah invited the Indian tribes of America, as remnants of the lost ten tribes, to join their Jewish brethren on the island.[92]

The dedication on the title page of the Book of Mormon struck a familiar note in 1830. The record was "to shew unto the remnant of the House of Israel how great things the LORD hath done for their fathers; and that they may know the covenants of the LORD, that they are not cast off forever; and also to the convincing of the Jew and Gentile that JESUS is the CHRIST, the ETERNAL GOD, manifesting Himself unto all nations."[93] Like Ethan Smith's *View of the Hebrews*, the Book of Mormon directed its readers to attend to lost Israel, whether Jew or Indian. The descendants of Lehi were not the lost ten tribes, as Indians were conventionally thought to be, but they were part of the diaspora. Jacob, Nephi's brother, spoke of many groups whom "the Lord God has led away from time to time from the house of Israel," now scattered on "the isles of the sea" (2 Ne. 10:21–22). "Yeah, the more part of all the tribes have been led away," Nephi said, "and they are scattered to and fro upon the isles of the sea; and whither they are none of us knoweth, save that we know that they have been led away" (1 Ne. 22:4). Lehi was of the tribe of Joseph through his son Manasseh, and America, Lehi's promised land, was the isle to which God led him (1 Ne. 5:14–16; Alma 10:3; 46:23). The Book of Mormon's mission was to convert the

Indian fragment of Israel along with all the other dispersed remnants, including Jews and the lost ten tribes. Many Americans besides Ethan Smith understood that mission and could believe in it. Here the book and its American environment did come together.[94]

Despite the convergence, the potential alliance of Mormons with other advocates of the Jews and of Indian Israel never became a reality. The reason was that Mormons and a Congregational minister like Ethan Smith could never agree on the role of the gentile Christian church. The Book of Mormon made very clear that every church in the last day would fall into apostasy, carried away by pride and lost in a tangle of false teachings. "They have all gone astray save it be a few, who are the humble followers of Christ; nevertheless, they are led, that in many instances they do err because they are taught by the precepts of men" (2 Ne. 28:11–14). Rather than a moment of triumph for gentile Christianity, Israel's restoration was an hour of judgment. The gentiles' last act in the closing hour of their dispensation was to bring forward the Book of Mormon to Lamanites and Jews. The restoration of the Book of Mormon was actually a watershed in sacred history, when Israel was to be restored, and the gentiles, who had abused the Christian Gospel, were rejected. In their apostate condition, the gentiles needed the Book of Mormon as much as Israel. The book was a test and separation. If the gentiles believed, they would join Israel and "be a blessed people upon the promised land forever" (1 Ne. 14:2). If they turned away, they would be scourged, driven, and cast off (3 Ne. 20: 15–17; 21:11–21). In either event, the last days belonged to Israel. The early Mormons could not join forces with the gentile Christian churches to convert Israel, for Christians, in Mormon eyes, were as benighted as Jews.[95]

The fate of the American population thus hung in the balance, leaving the United States as a whole in a precarious position. The Book of Mormon fails to express the enthusiasm for the nation that some critics have read into its pages. The belief of one author that the Book of Mormon enshrined "the romantic nationalism of the new republic and the optimism and expectation that characterized the third decade of the nineteenth century" hardly seems to comport with the text.[96] The American land was given an honored place in Book of Mormon sacred history; American civilization was not. The false teachers in the churches, the Book of Mormon said of modern times, "rob the poor because of their fine sanctuaries; they rob the poor because of their fine clothing; and they persecute the meek and the poor in heart, because in their pride they are puffed up" (2 Ne. 28:11–14). The Book of Mormon, Moroni wrote, would come to light in a day when "there shall be great pollutions upon the face of the earth; there shall be murders, and robbing, and lying, and deceivings, and whoredoms, and all manner of abominations" (Morm. 8:31). Mormons showed more affinity for premillennialist disillusionment with contemporary society and the belief that the "deterioration in religion and culture had now reached crisis proportions" than for American optimism and romantic nationalism.[97]

The same pessimism darkened the Smith family's private views of the world. Father Smith's dream of the contemporary religious situation presented a picture of dead fallen timber in a landscape dreary, silent, and devoid of life.[98] In keeping with their reservations, half the family stayed away from church altogether, and others followed their mother into Presbyterianism only after holding back for nearly twenty years. Joseph Jr., wrote to his St. Lawrence County cousins before translating the Book of Mormon to tell them "that the sword of vengeance of the Almighty hung over this generation and except they repent and obeyed the Gospel, and turned from their wicked ways, humbling themselves before the Lord, it would fall upon the wicked, and sweep them from the earth."[99] The lessons Lucy learned from the Book of Mormon, as she wrote her brother Solomon in 1831, were "that the eyes of the whole world are blinded, that the churches have all become corrupted, yea every church upon the face of the earth that the Gospel of Christ is no where preached."[100]

Similar disillusionment had overtaken the men who were attracted to the Prophet. Martin Harris told Charles Anthon during the consultation concerning the characters that the Book of Mormon would "produce an entire change in the world and save it from ruin."[101] After the translation was completed, Oliver Cowdery wrote Joseph that "some times I feel almost as though I could quit time and fly away and be at rest in the Bosom of my Redeemer for the many deep feelings of sorrow and the many long struglings in prayr of sorrow for the Sins of my fellow beings."[102] Mormon optimism arose not from romantic hope for America but from the faith grounded in the Book of Mormon that God would redeem the land from the evil that prevailed there.

Believers

While Dogberry, Campbell, Howe, and Hurlbut worked at discrediting the Book of Mormon, a few people believed in it. Roughly a hundred individuals were baptized in New York by the end of 1830, and as many more in Ohio. The converts read the Book of Mormon with great interest. Thomas Marsh, a resident of Charlestown, Massachusetts, visiting in nearby Lyons, heard of the "Golden Book" while it was still in press. He was "highly pleased" with the report of Oliver Cowdery and Martin Harris, and took home sixteen pages of proof to study with his family. Marsh soon joined the Church and moved west. The Smith cousins in St. Lawrence County were likewise immediately attracted. George A. Smith and his mother spent all one Saturday and Sunday poring over the Book of Mormon. George noted down objections as he read, but when he defended the volume against detractors, he found that he answered all of his own questions.[103] Parley Pratt said that when the Book of Mormon first fell into his hands, he "read all day; eating was a burden, I had no desire for food; sleep was a burden when the night came, for I preferred reading to sleep."[104]

Unfortunately, very few said what it was in the book that caught their attention and finally convinced them. Parley Pratt said that "as I read, the spirit of the Lord was upon me, and I knew and comprehended that the book was true, as plainly and manifestly as a man comprehends and knows that he exists."[105] Ezra Thayre heard Hyrum Smith preach at a meeting in the yard of the Smith house. After the meeting, Hyrum handed Thayre a copy of the Book of Mormon. "I said, let me see it. I then opened the book, and I received a shock with such exquisite joy that no pen can write and no tongue can express." All this without reading a word. When he opened the book again, he felt "a double portion of the Spirit." "I did not know whether I was in the world or not. I felt as though I was truly in heaven."[106] A copy of the Book of Mormon came to Jared Carter through the brother of a convert. "After reading a while in the Book of Mormon and praying earnestly to the Lord that he would show me the truth of the Book I became immediately convinced that it was a revelation of God and it had such an influence on my mind that I had no mind to pursue my business."[107]

The experience of reading the book transcended the specific contents. Samuel Smith, who carried books to some of the towns around Palmyra shortly after publication, made no arguments on its behalf. When he gave a copy to Rhoda Greene, wife of John P. Greene, a Methodist preacher in Bloomington, Samuel explained "the most profitable manner of reading the book . . . , which was to ask God, when she read it, for a testimony of the truth of what she had read, and she would receive the Spirit of God, which would enable her to discern the things of God."[108] Mr. and Mrs. Greene followed his directions and soon joined the Church, followed not long thereafter by Mrs. Greene's brothers, Phineas and Brigham Young. From all reports, the converts seem to have acted on their spiritual feelings more than their sympathy with specific ideas.[109]

It is no easier to deduce the appeal of the Book of Mormon from the influence it exercised in the Church after its organization in 1830. A rapid adoption of certain Book of Mormon teachings would suggest what early Mormons valued most. But, strange to say, the book had far less apparent influence than one would expect, given Joseph Smith's investment of effort in the translation. A few things are clear about the Book of Mormon's role. Early Mormon preachers cited Book of Mormon texts in their sermons, stimulated perhaps by passages of Doctrine and Covenants where the restored

Church was admonished to "become even as Nephi of old" (D&C 33:8) or to "beware of pride, lest ye become as the Nephites of old" (D&C 38:39). Parley Pratt remembered speaking "the word of God with power, reasoning out of the Scriptures and the Book of Mormon" a week after his baptism.[110] The early revelations repeatedly characterized the Book of Mormon as containing "the fulness of the gospel of Jesus Christ" (D&C 20:9). It was a book to be laid alongside the Bible. "The Book of Mormon and the holy scriptures are given of me," a revelation said, "for your instruction" (D&C 33:16).[111]

On the other hand, the Book of Mormon did not become a handbook for doctrine and ecclesiastical practice. It was not as if a new truth had been laid out in the teachings of the ancient Nephites and the restored Church was to pore over the record to extract policy and teachings. From the outset, doctrine came day by day in revelations to Joseph Smith. Those revelations comprised the backbone of belief, the doctrine and covenants for the Church. The teachings of the Book of Mormon were never repudiated, nor did they fail to inspire and instruct their readers. The modern Saints avoided infant baptism just as Mormon had instructed the church in the fourth century (Moro. 8:5–24; D&C 68:25). The sacrament prayers in the Book of Mórmon were repeated word for word in the restored Church (Moro. 4:3; 5:2; D&C 20:77, 79). But most of the applicable Book of Mormon doctrines and principles were revealed anew to Joseph Smith, and derived their authority from the modern revelation as much as from the Book of Mormon. After establishing a principle of the forgiveness of enemies, one revelation declared, "Behold, this is the law I gave unto my servant Nephi, and thy fathers, Joseph, and Jacob, and Isaac, and Abraham, and all mine ancient prophets and apostles" (D&C 98:32). The Book of Mormon citation confirmed modern revelations just like a biblical reference.[112]

Alexander Campbell thought the Book of Mormon was Joseph Smith's attempt to decide "all the great controversies,"[113] but neither Joseph nor the early Mormons used the book that way. Mormons were much more likely to seek revelation through their Prophet. Despite the effort that went into the translation, Joseph Smith did not make the book the foundation of Church doctrine. The Book of Mormon was more like an additional book of scripture that, as one revelation said, did "throw greater views upon my gospel" (D&C 10:45).

When converts said little, and the Church as a body did not conspicuously adopt distinctive Book of Mormon teachings, how is the appeal of the Book of Mormon to be understood?[114] Judging from the recorded responses, we must be prepared to believe that the very idea of a new revelation inspired people. They touched the book, and the realization came over them that God had spoken again.[115] Apart from any specific content, the discovery of additional scripture in itself inspired faith in people who were looking for more certain evidence of God in their lives.

NOTES

1. *The Book of Mormon* (1981), 532–35. On the structure of the book, see John A. Tvedtnes, "Composition and History of the Book of Mormon," *New Era* 4 (September 1974): 41–43.

2. In their wordprint analysis of Book of Mormon authors, Wayne A. Larsen, Alvin C. Rencher, and Tim Layton observe that source authorship shifts approximately 2,000 times in the text of the Book of Mormon. "Who Wrote the Book of Mormon? An Analysis of Wordprints," *BYU Studies* 20 (spring 1980): 229. For further wordprint analysis, see John L. Hilton, "On Verifying Wordprint Studies: Book of Mormon Authorship," *Book of Mormon Authorship Revisited: The Evidence for Ancient Origins,* ed. Noel B. Reynolds (Provo, Utah: FARMS, 1997).

3. Scholarship on the Book of Mormon from a believing perspective can be followed in *Journal of Book of Mormon Studies* (1992–), *Review of Books on the Book of Mormon* (1989–95), and *FARMS Review of Books* (1996–). A collection of critical essays is assembled in Brent Lee Metcalfe, ed., *New Approaches to the Book of Mormon: Explorations in Critical Methodology* (Salt Lake City: Signature Books, 1993). A useful summary of the issues as they were joined in 1996 appears in John Wm. Maddox, "A Listing of Points and Counterpoints," *FARMS Review of the Books* 8, no. 1 (1996): 1–26. The scholarship is brought up to date in Terryl L. Givens, *By the Hand of Mormon: The American Scripture that Launched a New World Religion* (New York: Oxford University Press, 2002).

For efforts in the direction of a literary analysis, see Richard Dilworth Rust, *Feasting on the Word: The Literary Testimony of the Book of Mormon* (Salt Lake City and Provo: Deseret Book and FARMS, 1997); Mark D. Thomas, *Digging in Cumorah: Reclaiming Book of Mormon Narratives* (Salt Lake City: Signature Books, 1999); Alan Goff, "A Hermeneutic of Sacred Texts: Historicism, Revisionism, Positivism, and the Bible and Book of Mormon" (master's thesis, Brigham Young University, 1989); Noel B. Reynolds, "Nephi's Outline," *BYU Studies* 20 (winter 1980): 131–49; Steven C. Walker, "More Than Meets the Eye: Concentration of the Book of Mormon," *BYU Studies* 20 (winter 1980): 199–205; Stan Larson, "Textual Variants in Book of Mormon Manuscripts," *Dialogue: A Journal of Mormon Thought* 10 (autumn 1977): 8–30; John W. Welch, "Chiasmus in the Book of Mormon," *BYU Studies* 10 (autumn 1969): 69–84; Douglas Wilson, "Prospects for the Study of the Book of Mormon as a Work of American Literature," *Dialogue: A Journal of Mormon Thought* 3 (spring 1968): 29–41. No one has exceeded Hugh Nibley's appreciation of the complexity of the Book of Mormon. See Hugh Nibley, *Lehi in the Desert and the World of the Jaredites* (Salt Lake City: Bookcraft, 1952); *An Approach to the Book of Mormon,* 2d ed. (Salt Lake City: Deseret Book, 1964); and *Since Cumorah: The Book of Mormon in the Modern World* (Salt Lake City: Deseret Book, 1967). A collection of essays that shows the difficulty of explaining the Book of Mormon as Joseph Smith's production is Noel B. Reynolds, ed., *Book of Mormon Authorship: New Light on Ancient Origins* (Provo, Utah: Religious Studies Center, Brigham Young University, 1982).

4. Quoted in Joseph Smith Jr., *History of the Church of Jesus Christ of Latter-day Saints,* ed. B. H. Roberts, 2d ed., rev., 7 vols. (Salt Lake City: Deseret Book, 1973), 1:84 (hereafter cited as *History of the Church*).

5. "Book of Pukei.—Chap. 1," *Palmyra Reflector,* June 12, 1830, and "Book of Pukei.—Chap. 2," *Palmyra Reflector,* July 7, 1830; reprinted in Francis W. Kirkham, *A New Witness for Christ in America: The Book of Mormon,* 3d ed., 2 vols. (Independence, Mo.: Zion's Printing and Publishing, 1951), 2:50–56. Many of the early newspaper arti-

cles on Mormonism, with some grammar and punctuation changes, can be most conveniently consulted in Kirkham.

6. "Book of Pukei," July 7, 1830.

7. Untitled Editorial, *Palmyra Reflector,* June 30, 1830; reprinted in Kirkham, *New Witness,* 2:53.

8. "The Golden Bible," *Painesville Telegraph,* November 16, 1830; reprinted in Kirkham, *New Witness,* 2:42–43.

9. "The Book of Mormon," *Painesville Telegraph,* November 30, 1830; reprinted in Kirkham, *New Witness,* 2:43.

10. "The Book of Mormon," November 30, 1830.

11. Thomas Campbell to Sidney Rigdon, February 4, 1831, in *Painesville Telegraph,* February 15, 1831; reprinted in Kirkham, *New Witness,* 2:89–94. Milton Backman, an emeritus professor of Church history at Brigham Young University, made photocopies of articles on Mormonism in the *Painesville Telegraph* and other early Ohio newspapers and deposited them in L. Tom Perry Special Collections, Harold B. Lee Library, Brigham Young University.

12. Plain Truth to Mr. Editor, January 1, 1831, in *Palmyra Reflector,* January 6, 1831; reprinted in Kirkham, *New Witness,* 2:64.

13. "Gold Bible," *Palmyra Reflector,* January 6, 1831; reprinted in Kirkham, *New Witness,* 2:64–65.

14. "Gold Bible," January 6, 1831.

15. Alexander Campbell, *Delusions: An Analysis of the Book of Mormon; with an Examination of Its Internal and External Evidences, and a Refutation of Its Pretences to Divine Authority* (Boston: Benjamin H. Greene, 1832), 5–6.

16. "French Prophets," *Painesville Telegraph,* February 15, 1831; reprinted in Kirkham, *New Witness,* 2:60–62.

17. "Gold Bible, No. 2," *Palmyra Reflector,* January 18, 1831; reprinted in Kirkham, *New Witness,* 2:66. See also "Gold Bible, No. 4," *Palmyra Reflector,* February 14, 1831; Campbell to Rigdon, February 4, 1831; and "Gold Bible," *Painesville Telegraph,* February 22, 1831, all reprinted in Kirkham, *New Witness,* 2:70, 93, 95. On Cole as a promulgator of skepticism, see Joseph W. Barnes, "Obediah Dogberry: Rochester Freethinker," *Rochester History* 36 (July 1974): 1–24.

18. "Gold Bible, No. 2," January 18, 1831.

19. "Gold Bible, No. 4," February 14, 1831. See also "Gold Bible, No. 5," *Palmyra Reflector,* February 28, 1831; and "Gold Bible, No. 6," *Palmyra Reflector,* March 19, 1831; reprinted in Kirkham, *New Witness,* 2:73, 76.

20. "Gold Bible, No. 3," *Palmyra Reflector,* February 1, 1831; reprinted in Kirkham, *New Witness,* 2:68. By the same token, Palmyra residents claimed the believers in Mormonism were "generally of the dregs of community, and the most unlettered people that can be found any where." Letter to the Editor, March 12, 1831, in *Painesville Telegraph,* March 22, 1831; reprinted in Kirkham, *New Witness,* 2:98. In Ohio the Mormon missionaries' labors were "principally blest," according to the *Cleveland Herald,* "among the superstitious and ignorant or hypocritical." "'The Golden Bible,'" *Cleveland Herald,* November 28, 1830.

21. "The Book of Mormon," *Painesville Telegraph,* November 30, 1830; reprinted in Kirkham, *New Witness,* 2:43.

22. "The Book of Mormon," *Painesville Telegraph,* December 7, 1830; reprinted in Kirkham, *New Witness,* 2:45.

23. "Mormonism," *Painesville Telegraph,* February 15, 1831; reprinted in Kirkham, *New Witness,* 2:85. Thomas Campbell argued that God provided New Testament missionaries with "such potent and evincive arguments, both prophetic and miraculous, as

no candid inquirer could mistake, without abandoning both his senses and his reason." Campbell to Rigdon, February 4, 1831; compare Campbell, *Delusions*, 15.

The Book of Mormon actually threatened the Bible, unless faith in the Bible could be clearly distinguished from superstitious belief in the Book of Mormon. The Reverend John A. Clark, a local Episcopal priest and acquaintance of Martin Harris, thought this was "one of the most pernicious features of this HISTORICAL ROMANCE,— that it claims for itself an entire equality in point of divine authority with the sacred canon. It is not only calculated to deceive and delude the credulous, and marvel loving, but to strengthen the cause of infidelity." John A. Clark, *Gleanings by the Way* (Philadelphia and New York: W. J. and J. K. Simon and Rover Carter, 1842), 282.

The Book of Mormon eventually spawned a series of volumes dealing with evidences for it, modeled after the apologies for the Bible: Charles Thompson, *Evidences in Proof of the Book of Mormon, being A Divinely Inspired Record, Written by the Forefathers of the Natives Whom We Call Indians* (Batavia, N.Y.: D. D. Waite, 1841); *The External Evidences of the Book of Mormon, Examined* (London: Briscoe, n.d.); J. H. Flanigan, *Mormonism Triumphant!: Truth Vindicated, Lies Refuted, the Devil Mad, and Priestcraft in Danger!!!; being A Reply to Palmer's Internal Evidence against the Book of Mormon* (Liverpool: R. James, 1849); and the culminating work in this genre, B. H. Roberts, *New Witnesses for God*, 3 vols. (Salt Lake City: Deseret News, 1911).

24. William Paley, *The Works of William Paley, D.D.*, 5 vols. (Boston: Joshua Belcher, 1810–12), 2:65–66, 207. This analysis is elaborated more fully in Richard L. Bushman, *Joseph Smith and Skepticism* (Provo, Utah: Brigham Young University Press, 1974), published as chapter 10 below.

25. "Gold Bible, No. 5," February 28, 1831.

26. Campbell, *Delusions*, 15. The story of the First Vision and of the visitation of Moroni as composed in 1838–39 showed more signs of acknowledging the arguments of the rationalists. Joseph presented himself as an innocent boy who met intense persecution and yet clung to his faith because he "had actually seen a light, and in the midst of that light I saw two personages, and they did in reality speak to me." The point was that he had no other reason for believing except the miracles, and he persisted despite the persecution. *History of the Church*, 1:7–8; Bushman, *Joseph Smith and Skepticism*, 7. A visitor to the Whitmers in March 1830 left with the impression that they said, "Twelve apostles were to be appointed, who would soon confirm their mission with miracles." David Marks, *The Life of David Marks, to the 26th Year of His Age* (Limerick, Maine: Morning Star, 1831), 340.

27. Quoted in E. D. Howe, *Mormonism Unvailed; or, A Faithful Account of that Singular Imposition and Delusion, from Its Rise to the Present Time* (Painesville, Ohio: By the author, 1834), 273–74; reprinted in Kirkham, *New Witness*, 1:163; compare Clark, *Gleanings*, 241.

28. "Gold Bible, No. 5," February 28, 1831.

29. "Book of Pukei," June 12, 1830.

30. Letter to the Editor, March 12, 1831.

31. Letter to the Editor, March 12, 1831. The editors of the *Cleveland Herald* (November 25, 1830) and the *Painesville Telegraph* (March 22, 1831) appear to have accepted the idea that the Book of Mormon was "chiefly garbled from the Old and New Testaments." Letter to the Editor, March 12, 1831.

32. Campbell to Rigdon, February 4, 1831.

33. Kirkham, *New Witness*, 2:101. The full citation of Alexander Campbell's pamphlet is in note 14.

34. Campbell, *Delusions*, 11.

35. Ibid., 13.

36. Ibid., 15.
37. Ibid., 13.
38. Ibid., 13, 15.
39. Ibid., 15.
40. Ibid., 11–12.
41. Ibid., 13.
42. Ibid., 7.
43. Ibid., 13.
44. Ibid., 6.
45. Howe, *Mormonism Unvailed,* 278–86.
46. Ibid., 278.
47. Ibid., 100, 289–90. Sidney Rigdon was suspected of complicity in the production of the Book of Mormon by the summer of 1831. James Gordon Bennett, who interviewed people concerning Mormonism in that summer, published this hypothesis in the *New York Morning Courier and Enquirer,* August 31, 1831; and the *Hillsborough* (Ohio) *Gazette* of October 29, 1831, stated that "there is no doubt but the ex-parson from Ohio is the author of the book which was recently printed in Palmyra, and passes for the new Bible." On Bennett, see Leonard J. Arrington, "James Gordon Bennett's 1831 Report on 'The Mormonites,'" *BYU Studies* 10 (spring 1970): 353–64.

I. Woodbridge Riley was the first non-Mormon to publish a refutation of the Spaulding theory; it appeared in his Yale Ph.D. thesis, published as *The Founder of Mormonism: A Psychological Study of Joseph Smith, Jr.* (New York: Dodd, Mead, 1902), 369–95. Further arguments were presented in Fawn M. Brodie, *No Man Knows My History: The Life of Joseph Smith, the Mormon Prophet* (New York: Alfred A. Knopf, 1945), 419–33. The definitive discussion is Lester E. Bush Jr., "The Spalding Theory Then and Now," *Dialogue: A Journal of Mormon Thought* 10 (autumn 1977): 40–69. Spaulding's manuscript was reproduced in Solomon Spaulding, *Manuscript Found: The Complete, Original "Spaulding Manuscript,"* ed. Kent P. Jackson (Provo, Utah: Religious Studies Center, Brigham Young University, 1996). According to Orsamus Turner, the people of Palmyra did not accept the Spaulding theory. Orsamus Turner, *History of the Pioneer Settlement of Phelps and Gorham's Purchase, and Morris' Reserve* (Rochester, N.Y.: William Alling, 1851), 214; compare Clark, *Gleanings,* 240–41, 268.

48. Bush, "Spalding Theory," 55–57.
49. Alexander Campbell himself changed his opinion on the authorship of the Book of Mormon, accepting the Spaulding theory despite the contradictions with his own 1831 analysis. "Mistakes Touching the Book of Mormon," *Millennial Harbinger* 1, 3d series (January 1844): 38; "Millennium," *Millennial Harbinger* 6, 4th series (December 1856): 698.
50. Riley, *The Founder of Mormonism;* Brodie, *No Man Knows,* 419–33.
51. Campbell, *Delusions,* 9. Robert Hullinger has argued that the Book of Mormon was intended to discredit corrupt modern Masonry, but that Joseph Smith drew heavily on Masonic lore and symbols. Robert N. Hullinger, *Mormon Answer to Skepticism: Why Joseph Smith Wrote the Book of Mormon* (St. Louis: Clayton, 1980), 100–119. More recently, Mark Thomas has argued for a "general historical" symbolic connection between Masonry and secret combinations in the Book of Mormon. Thomas, *Digging in Cumorah,* 189–216, quote on 204.
52. William Preston Vaughn, *The Antimasonic Party in the United States, 1826–1843* (Lexington: University Press of Kentucky, 1983), 7–9.
53. Ibid., 28; Ronald P. Formisano and Kathleen Smith Kutolowski, "Antimasonry and Masonry: The Genesis of Protest, 1826–1827," *American Quarterly* 29 (summer 1977): 139–65.

54. Vaughan, *Antimasonic Party*, 54–69, 119–22. See also Paul Goodman, *Towards a Christian Republic: Antimasonry and the Great Transition in New England, 1826–1836* (New York: Oxford University Press, 1988); Charles McCarthy, "The Antimasonic Party: A Study of Political Antimasonry in the United States, 1827–1840," *Annual Report of the American Historical Association for the Year 1902*, 2 vols. (Washington, D.C.: Government Printing Office, 1903), 1:365–574; and Whitney R. Cross, *The Burned-Over District: The Social and Intellectual History of Enthusiastic Religion in Western New York, 1800–1850* (1950; New York: Harper Torchbooks, 1965), 113–25.

William Morgan, an itinerant stonemason and one-time member of the lodge in LeRoy, New York, had joined with others to found a lodge in Batavia, thirty miles southwest of Rochester. The other organizers, apparently doubtful of his character, left his name off the application and went ahead without him. Presumably angered by this rejection, Morgan conspired with a Batavia printer, David Miller, to publish a book exposing Masonic secrets, *Illustrations of Masonry, by One of the Fraternity, Who Has Devoted Thirty Years to the Subject*. Miller was threatened, and an attempt was made to burn his shop. Morgan was arrested on charges of petty theft and jailed in Canandaigua for failure to pay a debt of $3. On September 12, 1826, a group of men came to the jail, paid the debt, and carried Morgan off in a carriage. Later depositions proved that Masons had kidnapped him and driven him with fresh relays of horses across the Canadian border and then back to Fort Niagara. At that point Morgan dropped out of sight forever. Vaughn, *Antimasonic Party*, 2–5; Formisano and Kutolowski, "Antimasonry and Masonry," 146–48.

55. The early Antimasonic documents were compiled in David Bernard, *Light on Masonry: A Collection of All the Most Important Documents on the Subject of Speculative Free Masonry* (Utica, N.Y.: publisher, 1829).

56. Walter Franklin Prince, "Psychological Tests for the Authorship of the Book of Mormon," *American Journal of Psychology* 28 (July 1917): 373–89; "A Footnote: 'Authorship of the Book of Mormon,'" *American Journal of Psychology* 30 (October 1919): 427–28. Another non-Mormon critic was unable to place much credence in Prince's analysis. Theodore Schroeder observed of Prince's tests of Book of Mormon authorship that "to me they seem not at all rigorous nor a valid test of anything, and not even an important contribution to any problem except perhaps to the psychology of Dr. Prince." Theodore Schroeder, "Authorship of the Book of Mormon," *American Journal of Psychology* 30 (January 1919): 67. More recently, psychiatrist Robert D. Anderson has claimed that the Gadianton passages reflect Joseph Smith's "internal moral struggle over hidden corruption" in the U.S. government during the 1820s. Robert D. Anderson, *Inside the Mind of Joseph Smith: Psychobiography and the Book of Mormon* (Salt Lake City: Signature Books, 1999), 188.

57. This point was expanded in Daniel C. Peterson, "The Gadianton Robbers as Guerrilla Warriors," and "Notes on 'Gadianton Masonry,'" in *Warfare in the Book of Mormon*, eds. Stephen D. Ricks and William J. Hamblin (Salt Lake City and Provo: Deseret Book and FARMS, 1990), 146–224.

58. A thorough non-Mormon explication of the Book of Mormon is Thomas F. O'Dea, *The Mormons* (Chicago: University of Chicago Press, 1957), 22–40, followed in a more hostile spirit by Riley, *Founder of Mormonism*, 77–138.

59. William Morgan himself set the pattern for Antimasonic literature in *Illustrations of Masonry, by One of the Fraternity, Who Has Devoted Thirty Years to the Subject*, 3d ed. (New York: Printed for the author, 1827). Twelve editions were brought out in Rochester in 1827. Blake McKelvey, *Rochester: The Water-Power City, 1812–1854* (Cambridge: Harvard University Press, 1945), 154–55. For guides to the literature, see Formisano and Kutolowski, "Antimasonry and Masonry," 140, n. 3, and Milton W.

Hamilton, "Antimasonic Newspapers, 1826–1834," *Papers of the Bibliographical Society of America* 32 (1938): 71–97.

60. See note 47.

61. There are exceptions. Ohio's *Geauga Gazette* quoted Martin Harris saying that the Book of Mormon was "the Anti-masonick Bible." Dan Vogel sees this as evidence that early Mormons more generally read the Book of Mormon as a political commentary against Andrew Jackson and an injunction to flee Jacksonian America for theocracy. Dan Vogel, "Mormonism's 'Anti-Masonick Bible,'" *John Whitmer Historical Association Journal* 9 (1989): 17–30. The *Painesville Telegraph* reported on March 22, 1831, that one Billy Perkins said that Mormonism was the Antimasonic religion "because *all* who have embraced it are antimasons." The editor, himself an Antimason, reminded Perkins that the Mormon bible was printed in a Masonic printing office under a Masonic injunction of secrecy. The exchange probably represented a gambit of the Masonic and Antimasonic parties around Painesville to discredit one another by associating the Mormons with their opponents.

62. Campbell, *Delusions*, 13. For an explication of apparent republicanism in the Book of Mormon, see O'Dea, *The Mormons*, 32–33, 268, nn. 19–21; Kenneth H. Winn, *Exiles in a Land of Liberty: Mormons in America, 1830–1846* (Chapel Hill: University of North Carolina Press, 1989). The incongruities are enlarged upon in Richard L. Bushman, "The Book of Mormon and the American Revolution," *BYU Studies* 17 (autumn 1976): 3–20, published as chapter 5 above.

63. See also Omni 1:12; Mosiah 7:9; 19:26; 23:6.

64. *The Book of Mormon* (1920).

65. The article entitled "The Book of Mormon" appeared in the magazine *New-Yorker* and was reprinted as Josephine, "The Book of Mormon," *Times and Seasons* 2 (February 1, 1841): 305–6, and subsequently in "'One of the Greatest Literary Curiosities of the Day,'" *Dialogue: A Journal of Mormon Thought* 12 (spring 1979): 100–1.

66. Lucy Smith, *Biographical Sketches of Joseph Smith, the Prophet, and His Progenitors for Many Generations* (Liverpool: S. W. Richards, 1853), 152.

67. "Mormonism," February 15, 1831.

68. Quoted in Lucy Smith, *Biographical Sketches*, 186. See also Pratt, *Autobiography*, 59.

69. See, for example, the *Palmyra Register:* "Extract from the Western Gazetteer," January 18, 1818; "American Antiquities," May 26, 1819; "Anecdote of an Indian Chief," June 2, 1819; the *Western Farmer:* "Discoveries on the Canal," September 19, 1821; "Mammoth," July 24, 1822; "American Antiquities," October 30, 1822; "Leo X De," February 19, 1823; and the *Wayne Sentinel:* "Antiquities in Missouri," November 3, 1824; "M. M. Noah's Speech," October 11, 1825.

70. Manchester rental library, accession number 208, in Robert Paul, "Joseph Smith and the Manchester (New York) Library," *BYU Studies* 22 (summer 1982): 350.

71. Robert Silverberg, *Mound Builders of Ancient America: The Archaeology of a Myth* (Greenwich, Conn.: New York Graphic Society, 1968), 83. For sources on the Indians, see Hullinger, *Mormon Answer*, 48–64; and Dan Vogel, *Indian Origins and the Book of Mormon: Religious Solutions from Columbus to Joseph Smith* (Salt Lake City: Signature Books, 1986). 103–44.

72. Silverberg, *Mound Builders*, 82–89.

73. Robert Wauchope, *Lost Tribes and Sunken Continents: Myth and Method in the Study of American Indians* (Chicago: University of Chicago Press, 1962), 97–102. A writer scornful of the idea of a Hebrew connection said the clergy mainly propagated this notion. James Buchanan, *Sketches of the History, Manners, and Customs, of the North American Indians, with a Plan for Their Amelioration*, 2 vols. (New York: William Borradaile, 1824).

74. James Adair, *The History of the American Indians; Particularly Those Nations Adjoining to the Mississippi, East and West Florida, Georgia, South and North Carolina, and Virginia* (London: E. and C. Dilly, 1775). On Adair, see *Dictionary of American Biography*, ed. Allen Johnson and Dumas Malone, 10 vols. (New York: Charles Scribner's Sons, 1964), s.v. "Adair, James."

75. Elias Boudinot, *A Star in the West; or, A Humble Attempt to Discover the Long Lost Ten Tribes of Israel, Preparatory to Their Return to Their Beloved City, Jerusalem* (Trenton, N.J.: D. Fenton, S. Hutchinson, and J. Dunham, 1816). On Boudinot, see Elias Boudinot, *The Life, Public Services, Addresses, and Letters of Elias Boudinot*, ed. J. J. Boudinot (Boston: Houghton, Mifflin, 1896); George Adams Boyd, *Elias Boudinot: Patriot and Statesman, 1740–1821* (Princeton: Princeton University Press, 1952). Boudinot spoke at the City Hotel in Palmyra in 1820. Hullinger, *Mormon Answer*, 58.

76. Ethan Smith, *View of the Hebrews; or, The Tribes of Israel in America*, 2d ed., enl. (1823; Poultney, Vt.: Smith and Shute, 1825), v–viii. The 1825 edition was reproduced with historical introduction in Ethan Smith, *View of the Hebrews: 1825 2nd Edition Complete Text*, ed. Charles D. Tate Jr. (Provo, Utah: Religious Studies Center, Brigham Young University, 1996). On Ethan Smith, see William B. Sprague, *Annals of the American Pulpit*, 9 vols. (New York: R. Couter, 1857–69), 2:296–99.

On popular and scientific theories of Indian origins, see, besides Silverberg, *Mound Builders*, and Wauchope, *Lost Tribes*, Eldridge Huddleston, *Origins of the American Indians: European Concepts, 1492–1729*, Latin American Monographs, No. 11 (Austin: Institute of Latin American Studies, University of Texas, 1967); Peter Toon, ed., *Puritans, the Millennium and the Future of Israel: Puritan Eschatology, 1600 to 1660* (Cambridge, England: James Clarke, 1970), 117–21; Roy Harvey Pearce, *Savagism and Civilization: A Study of the Indian and the American Mind* (Baltimore: Johns Hopkins University Press, 1967); Vogel, *Indian Origins*, 35–52; Justin Winsor, "The Progress of Opinion Respecting the Origin and Antiquity of Man in America," in *Narrative and Critical History of America*, ed. Justin Winsor, 8 vols. (Boston: Houghton, Mifflin, 1884–89), 1:369–412; compare 1:115–16.

77. Josiah Priest, *The Wonders of Nature and Providence, Displayed* (Albany, N.Y.: E. and E. Hosford, 1825), 290–325. On Priest, see Winthrop Hillyer Duncan, "Josiah Priest, Historian of the American Frontier: A Study and Biography," *Proceedings of the American Antiquarian Society* 44 (1934): 45–102.

78. On the comparison of *View of the Hebrews* and the Book of Mormon, see Riley, *Founder of Mormonism*, 126–28; Brodie, *No Man Knows*, 45–49; Mervin B. Hogan, "'A Parallel': A Matter of Chance versus Coincidence," *Rocky Mountain Mason* 4 (January 1956): 17–31; Charles A. Davies, "'View of the Hebrews' and the Book of Mormon," *Saints' Herald* (Independence, Mo.) 109 (August 1, 1962): 9–11; Robert N. Hullinger, "The Lost Tribes of Israel and the Book of Mormon," *Lutheran Quarterly* 22 (August 1970): 319–29; Spencer J. Palmer and William L. Knecht, "View of the Hebrews: Substitute for Inspiration?" *BYU Studies* 5 (winter 1964): 105–13; Roy E. Weldon, "Masonry and Ethan Smith's 'A View of the Hebrews,'" *Saints' Herald* 119 (September 1972): 26–28. The most exhaustive study is David Persuitte, *Joseph Smith and the Origins of The Book of Mormon*, 2d ed. (Jefferson, N.C.: McFarland, 2000).

79. Ethan Smith, *View of the Hebrews*, 70–83, quote on 73.

80. Ibid., 73, 82–83, 172–73.

81. Pratt, *Autobiography*, 38.

82. In his 1816 treatise on the lost tribes, Elias Boudinot commented,

Every serious reader, who takes the divine scriptures for his rule of conduct, must believe that these people of God are yet in being in our world, however unknown at present to the nations.... God has preserved a majority of his people of Israel in some unknown part of the world, for the advancement of his own glory. (Boudinot, *A Star in the West,* 49)

Wherever word of the Book of Mormon spread, people assumed it told of the ten tribes. After visiting the Whitmers in March 1830, David Marks, an itinerant preacher, wrote that the Book of Mormon was "a history of the ten tribes of Israel which were lost." Marks, *Life,* 340. Writing in 1867, Pomeroy Tucker, the Palmyra printer who had met Joseph Smith, said the plates contained a record of "the long-lost tribes of Israel." Pomeroy Tucker, *Origin, Rise and Progress of Mormonism* (New York: D. Appleton, 1867), 29.

83. For an attempt to force dependence of Book of Mormon passages onto *View of the Hebrews,* see Persuitte, *Joseph Smith and the Origins,* 136–230.

84. Quoted in Ethan Smith, *View of the Hebrews,* vi. Smith and Boudinot had exactly the same purpose in mind. Boudinot's view of Israel's future, including the ten tribes, was that "they are to be converted to the faith of Christ, and instructed in their glorious prerogatives, and prepared and assisted to return to their own land and their ancient city, even the city of Zion." "Who knows but God has raised up these United States in these latter days, for the very purpose of accomplishing his will in bringing his beloved people to their own land." Boudinot, *A Star in the West,* 297. Hullinger in *Mormon Answer,* 58, argues that Ethan Smith's primary purpose was to refute skeptics by giving evidence of a second people whom God had preserved through the ages along with the Jews. This viewpoint, in my opinion, underestimates the force of Christian preoccupation with the coming millennium and makes primary what was secondary.

85. On the movement to restore Jews to England, see Peter Toon, "The Question of Jewish Immigration," in Toon, *Puritan Eschatology,* 115–27. On Manasseh ben Israel, see Lynn Glaser, *Indians or Jews? An Introduction to a Reprint of Manasseh ben Israel's The Hope of Israel* (Gilroy, Calif.: Roy V. Boswell, 1973). Increase Mather's sermons on the conversion of the Jews include *The Mystery of Israel's Salvation* (1669), *Strange Doctrine* (1708), *Faith and Fervency* (1710), and *Five Sermons* (1719). In 1621 William Gouge, an influential Presbyterian minister, published a tract by Sir Henry Finch, sergeant at law, called *The Calling of the Jews: A Present to Judah and the Children of Israel that Joyned with Him, and to Joseph (The Valiant Tribe of Ephraim) and All the House of Israel that Joyned with Him.* Peter Toon, "The Latter-day Glory," in Toon, *Puritan Eschatology,* 32.

86. Nahum Sokolow, *History of Zionism, 1600–1918* (New York: Ktav, 1969), 80–82.

87. LeRoy Edwin Froom, *The Prophetic Faith of Our Fathers: The Historical Development of Prophetic Interpretation,* 4 vols. (Washington, D.C.: Review and Herald, 1946–54), 3:239–40.

88. Ernest R. Sandeen, *The Roots of Fundamentalism: British and American Millenarianism, 1800–1930* (Chicago: University of Chicago Press, 1970), 20, 55; Lee M. Friedman, *The American Society for Meliorating the Condition of the Jews, and Joseph S. C. F. Frey, Its Missionary* (Boston: n.p., 1925), 12; Aaron Bancroft, *A Discourse, Delivered before the Worcester Auxiliary Society for Meliorating the Condition of the Jews* (Worcester: William Manning, [1824]); George L. Berlin, "Joseph S. C. F. Frey, the Jews, and Early Nineteenth-Century Millenarianism," *Journal of the Early Republic* 1 (spring 1981): 27–49.

89. Boyd, *Elias Boudinot,* 261–62.

90. Ethan Smith, *View of the Hebrews,* 118. The pamphlet Frey referred to was Charles Crawford, *An Essay on the Propagation of the Gospel; in Which There Are Numerous Facts and Arguments Adduced to Prove That Many of the Indians in America Are Descended from the Ten Tribes,* 2d ed. (1799; Philadelphia: James Humphreys, 1801).

91. Friedman, *American Society,* 7–10. Other Englishmen evinced the same interest. Israel Worsley, *A View of the American Indians . . . Shewing Them to Be the Descendants of the Ten Tribes of Israel* (London: Printed for the author, 1828); Mrs. [Barbara Allan] Simon, *The Ten Tribes of Israel, Historically Identified with the Aborigines of the Western Hemisphere* (London: R. B. Seeley and W. Burnside, 1836). For Frey's writings on Indians as the lost ten tribes, see Berlin, "Joseph S. C. F. Frey," 41–43.

92. Lewis F. Allen, "Founding of the City of Ararat on Grand Island by Mordecai M. Noah," *Publications of the Buffalo Historical Society* 1 (1879): 303–28. For local coverage of Noah, see the *Wayne Sentinel:* "Revival of the Jewish Government," September 27, 1823; "Speech," October 4, 1825; and "M. M. Noah's Speech," October 11, 1825. See also Isaac Goldberg, *Major Noah: American-Jewish Pioneer* (Philadelphia: Jewish Publication Society of America, 1936), 148. A biography of Noah is Jonathan D. Sarna, *Jacksonian Jew: The Two Worlds of Mordecai Noah* (New York: Holmes and Meier, 1981). Noah published his views on Indian origins in M. M. Noah, *Discourse on the Evidences of American Indians Being the Descendants of the Lost Tribes of Israel* (New York: James Van Norden, 1837).

93. Title Page, The Book of Mormon (1830).

94. See also 2 Nephi 6:5; Jacob 5; 3 Nephi 15:15; 16:1–4; 17:4; *Doctrine and Covenants* 35:25; 38:33; 39:11.

95. See also 1 Nephi 13:5–7, 9, 26, 28, 40–41; 14:7, 11; 2 Nephi 10:18–19; 28:6, 14; 3 Nephi 16; 21; 26:20–21; 28:3–4.

96. O'Dea, *The Mormons,* 26.

97. Sandeen, *Roots of Fundamentalism,* 13, 22; Marvin S. Hill, "The Shaping of the Mormon Mind in New England and New York," *BYU Studies* 9 (spring 1969): 353–54. See also *Doctrine and Covenants* 35:7.

98. Lucy Smith, *Biographical Sketches,* 57.

99. George A. Smith, History, cited in Donna Hill, *Joseph Smith, the First Mormon* (Garden City, N.Y.: Doubleday, 1977), 83–84.

100. Lucy Smith to Solomon Mack, January 6, 1831, Church Archives, The Church of Jesus Christ of Latter-day Saints, Salt Lake City.

101. Charles Anthon to Dear Sir [E. D. Howe], February 17, 1834, in Howe, *Mormonism Unvailed,* 271; reprinted in Kirkham, *New Witness,* 1:415.

102. Oliver Cowdery to Joseph Smith, December 28, 1829, Joseph Smith Collection, Church Archives.

103. Larry C. Porter, "A Study of the Origins of the Church of Jesus Christ of Latter-day Saints in the States of New York and Pennsylvania, 1816–1831" (Ph.D. diss., Brigham Young University, 1971), 94–96.

104. Pratt, *Autobiography,* 37.

105. Ibid.

106. Quoted in Porter, "Study of the Origins," 99.

107. Ibid., 207.

108. Quoted in Lucy Smith, *Biographical Sketches,* 166.

109. Lucy Smith, *Biographical Sketches,* 167; *History of the Church,* 1:296–97. For Sidney Rigdon's conversion, see Hill, *Joseph Smith,* 122.

110. Pratt, *Autobiography,* 42.

111. See also *Doctrine and Covenants* 10:45; 19:26; 27:5; 42:12.

112. Grant Underwood, "Book of Mormon Usage in Early LDS Theology," *Dialogue: A Journal of Mormon Thought* 17 (autumn 1984): 35–74.

113. Campbell, *Delusions,* 13.

114. For discussions of the Book of Mormon's appeal, see O'Dea, *The Mormons,* 22–40; Marvin S. Hill, "The Role of Christian Primitivism in the Origin and Development

of the Mormon Kingdom, 1830–1844" (Ph.D. diss., University of Chicago, 1968), 111–20. For the appeal of Mormonism generally, see Leonard J. Arrington and Davis Bitton, *The Mormon Experience: A History of the Latter-day Saints* (New York: Alfred A. Knopf, 1979), 20–43.

115. See Moroni. 10:4.

PART THREE

Joseph Smith and Culture

10

Joseph Smith and Skepticism

When Neal Maxwell was LDS Commissioner of Education, he invited me to speak in a lecture series he was sponsoring on Mormon themes. My lecture was delivered in Provo, Utah, in 1974. By that time, I had left BYU and was teaching at Boston University. I don't recall how he became aware of me or how I got the idea for my subject, but once into the topic, I was entranced. I knew that Joseph walked the boundary between a believing biblical culture and an emerging scientific culture. How the two intersected was unclear until I looked more closely at the extensive apologetic literature in support of the Bible. I sat in the basement of the Harvard Divinity School library examining the piles of books on Christian evidences. From them I not only learned how Joseph's provision of evidence fit into his times, but I saw where B. H. Roberts's A New Witness for God (Salt Lake City: George Q. Cannon and Sons, 1895) came from and, to a certain extent, Hugh Nibley's impulse to prove the Book of Mormon.

Robert Owen, the wealthy Welsh industrialist and reformer, is best remembered in United States history for having invested a fortune in an unsuccessful utopian community at New Harmony, Indiana. In his own time, he was also notable for his religious agnosticism. In the *New-Harmony Gazette*, which he began publishing in 1825, he propagated infidelity along with socialism, and as he stumped the country to spread his ideas, he frequently criticized Christian belief. In New Orleans in 1828 he offered to debate anyone on the proposition that religion was founded on ignorance and was the chief source of human misery. The challenge electrified the audience and subsequently was widely publicized. The person to pick up the gauntlet was Alexander Campbell, the founder and leading spirit of the Disciples of Christ. Campbell and Owen met in a Methodist meetinghouse in Cincinnati in April 1828 and debated for eight days. Campbell's concluding speech took twelve hours. Through all fifteen sessions, the meetinghouse, with seating for a thousand, was filled to capacity. On the last day, Campbell called for a standing vote of those favorable to Christianity and of those opposed. Only three listeners voted against Christianity. Owen, who had been annoyingly vague throughout the debate, fell before the much better prepared Campbell.[1]

That debate opens a window on an interesting aspect of the American religious mentality at the time of the Restoration. The populace of the United States was a believing people. Churches abounded; evangelical revivals were a national institution; for a time after independence, faith in God was a common prerequisite for state office. And yet the United States did not entirely escape the influence of Enlightenment skepticism. The lopsided vote against Owen probably fairly represented the state of unbelief and the overwhelming dominance of Christianity; the packed benches in the Cincinnati meetinghouse also measure the fascination of infidelity. Americans had heard just enough of freethinking arguments to want to hear more, and particularly to hear how Christians answered skeptics.

It was not Alexander Campbell's first encounter with a skeptic nor his last. He had previously crossed swords with a non-Christian contributor to Owen's *New-Harmony Gazette* and later, in 1836, once again took on agnosticism in public debate, this time at Cleveland. Skepticism could not be ignored even in Christian America. Although few in number, the opponents of Christianity were widespread and articulate and carried the authority of some of the great names of the European Enlightenment—Voltaire, Hume, and Thomas Paine. Societies of infidels organized to circulate the best-known works of European skeptics. Even remote areas were penetrated. A freethinking society sprang up in Rochester, New York, around 1800. A clergyman reported that Paine's *Age of Reason,* published in 1794, was within two years "greedily received in Vermont."[2] The most notorious of the native critics of Christianity was Ethan Allen, leader of Vermont's famous Green Mountain Boys, whose *Reason the Only Oracle of Man* appeared in 1784. Allen, a hard-bitten frontiersman, argued that miracles took place only among the "barbarous and ignorant" who were easily "imposed upon." "In those parts of the world where learning and science has prevailed, miracles have ceased."[3] By 1799 it was said of the graduating class at Dartmouth, just a few miles from Sharon, Joseph Smith's birthplace, that only one senior professed Christianity. Skepticism lost ground for a time in the early decades of the nineteenth century and then revived in the 1820s with the founding of Owen's *New-Harmony Gazette.* In the next twenty-five years, about twenty free-thought journals started up. These currents swirled around the Smith family in Vermont and New York, around the first converts to the Church, and had their influence on the early critics of Joseph Smith, among whom was Alexander Campbell.[4]

Skepticism, of course, has had adherents in every period—unbelievers who, in general, have found no grounds for faith or who have condemned God for injustice and suffering and denied his existence. Eighteenth-century skepticism, while encompassing these general impulses, had at its core a distinctive argument. The argument took shape in the early part of the century, when Christianity's most formidable enemy was deism rather than outright atheism. Deists were a theological expression of the new age of science, whose leading practitioner was Sir Isaac Newton. Disregarding Newton's own Christian orthodoxy, deists were deeply impressed by his method and scientific findings. Strictly by observation and reasoning, Newton had discovered fundamental physical laws with immense power in explaining natural phenomena. Deists believed religious principles could be discovered by the same method—without the exercise of faith. From observing the natural order of the world, they deduced the necessity of a divine Creator and the existence of moral principles by which men could achieve happiness. Some accepted the reality of an afterlife. There was very little else. The miracles recorded in scripture seemed an affront to the perfection of God's creations. What need was there for God to tinker with his world once the natural order was established? That criterion brought most distinctive Christian doctrines crashing to the ground—the resurrection, the Atonement, the divine sonship of Jesus. All of these were considered contrary to the natural order, lacking in supporting evidence, and in some instances unreasonable in themselves.

Because deists spoke with authority seemingly borrowed from the most advanced scientific thinking of the time, their criticism troubled Christian intellectuals. They felt compelled to defend the faith in terms deists would accept—that is, with fact and reason alone. On the defensive, Christian apologists felt unable to ground faith on feeling or spiritual experience. They wanted to begin with objective observation and move from there by consistent logic to Christian principles, as scientists moved from observation to physical laws.

Authentication of Biblical Miracles

Miracles seemed to be the answer. A valid miracle would turn the tables on the deists. A miraculous healing was a physical fact and yet, because it occurred outside the natural order of cause and effect, was proof of the supernatural. By an obvious, reasonable step, one could conclude that a worker of miracles exercised divine power. The miracle was a stamp of divine authenticity on his teachings. From being an embarrassment to Christians, miracles, if confirmed, could become the bedrock of their faith. Charles Leslie, the very popular author of *Short and Easy Method with Deists* (1805), told his audience to answer skeptics with Moses and the Red Sea:

> If he brought the children of Israel through the red sea in that miraculous manner, which is related in Exodus, and did such other wonderful things, as are there told of him; it must necessarily follow, that he was sent from GOD; these being the strongest proofs, we can desire, and which every Deist will confess he would acquiesce in, if he saw them with his eyes.[5]

The beauty of Christian teachings, their applicability to human needs, their consistency, all of what were called "internal evidences" gave support to Christian belief, but the conclusive proof was the incontrovertible physical fact of miracles. A demonstration of Moses' miracle at the Red Sea would prove that "he was sent from God."[6] Similarly the miracle of resurrection authenticated Christ's teaching. The entire structure of Christian dogma could be reconstructed again upon a foundation of reason and fact. "Reason alone is appealed to," one apologist asserted at the beginning of his dissertation on Christian evidences, "and no other faith is here necessary but that which arises as the natural and spontaneous fruit of rational conviction."[7] At the end of such a rational investigation, another defender concluded that "we have shown, by sound reasoning and demonstrative proof, that the persons who were the authors of the Old and New Testament dispensations performed miracles, and predicted events, which human sagacity could neither have foreseen, nor conjectured." The consequences of the proof were obvious: "Therefore it has been proved, that the divine attestation was given to them as the servants of the Most High." "It follows as a necessary consequence, that the Bible is a revelation from God."[8]

Authentication of miracles was, of course, no simple matter, and skeptics did nothing to make it easier. Perhaps the most troublesome problem was bogus miracles. Biblical prophets were not the only ones to claim supernatural power. How was a neutral observer to distinguish Moses' powers from those exercised by Egyptian wizards? More telling still for Protestants was how to account for the host of miracles attributed to Roman Catholic saints. These too were palpable experiences of ears, eyes, and touch. A number had multiple witnesses, sometimes thousands of them. David Hume, whose work on miracles was the most powerful of the skeptical attacks, cited the cure of a blind and of a lame man by the Emperor Vespasian, the restoration of a limb in a Spanish church as related by Cardinal de Retz, and the cures performed at the tomb of the Abby Paris in the early eighteenth century.[9] Wherein did these differ from the feeding of Elijah or the New Testament miracles of healing?

Under the prod of skepticism, Christians became highly sensitive to false prophets and miracle workers. Each one was a potential threat to the reasoning on which rational faith was founded. Each one had to be investigated and proved counterfeit to protect the integrity of authentic prophets. Otherwise a David Hume would use the false to cast doubt on the true. Christian apologists perforce took note of historical and contemporaneous prophets and, treating them with contempt, were serious about invalidating their claims. Alexander Campbell, the defender of Christianity, was as obligated to expose Joseph Smith as to refute Robert Owen. From opposite sides, skeptics and pseudoprophets each threatened the rational demonstration of Christian faith.

Against all these counterclaimants, how were biblical miracles to be validated? By the end of the eighteenth century, the argument had been carefully honed and polished and was ready for summary by William Paley, onetime lecturer at Cambridge and archdeacon of Carlisle. Paley confronted the central difficulty directly. His preeminent purpose in *A View of the Evidences of Christianity* (1794) was to examine "the direct historical evidence of Christianity, and wherein it is distinguished from the evidence alleged for other miracles"[10] (fig. 1). The crux of the matter was the credibility of witnesses. Since both true and false miracles were conveyed through the reports of witnesses, Paley's task was to explain why Christian witnesses were to be believed and the others discarded as deceivers or deceived. Paley accumulated a great deal of evidence from sources external to the Bible to show that "many, professing to be original witnesses of the Christian miracles, passed their lives in labours, dangers, and sufferings, voluntarily undergone in attestation of the accounts which they delivered."[11] His first point was that the disciples who witnessed the miracles close-up and had the opportunity to detect fraud would not have suffered so much to spread the teachings of a deceiver. Why lie at such great personal cost? Their lives were proof that they believed they had seen a literal miracle.

Even more significant for his late-eighteenth-century audience, Paley argued that the disciples followed Jesus "solely in consequence of their belief" in miracles.[12] They were initially neutral observers without bias in his favor. There was nothing about his position, no promise of wealth, power, glory, to win them to his cause. They did not initially believe for some extraneous reason and then attest to miracles to confirm their belief. "A young man of mean condition, of a private and simple life, and who had wrought no deliverance for the Jewish nation, was declared to be their Messiah." Without supernatural proofs, that "was too absurd a claim to be either imagined, or attempted, or credited." "When it came to the question, 'Is the carpenter's son of Nazareth the person whom we are to receive and obey?' there was nothing but the miracles attributed to him, by which his pretension could be maintained for a moment." "Miraculous pretentions, and miraculous pretentions alone, were what they had to rely upon." They had no motive to believe except the compelling evidence of their senses that Jesus exercised supernatural power.[13] It was from this argument that apologists came to assert that Christianity was the only religion grounded in reason. The first disciples were driven to believe by the evidence of palpable fact.

Paley also undertook, although with less thoroughness, to prove that witnesses to other similar miracles were not acting solely in consequence of their belief in miracles. Other religious figures had undergone lives of "toil and exertion, of danger and sufferings," but not "*for* a miraculous story." "If

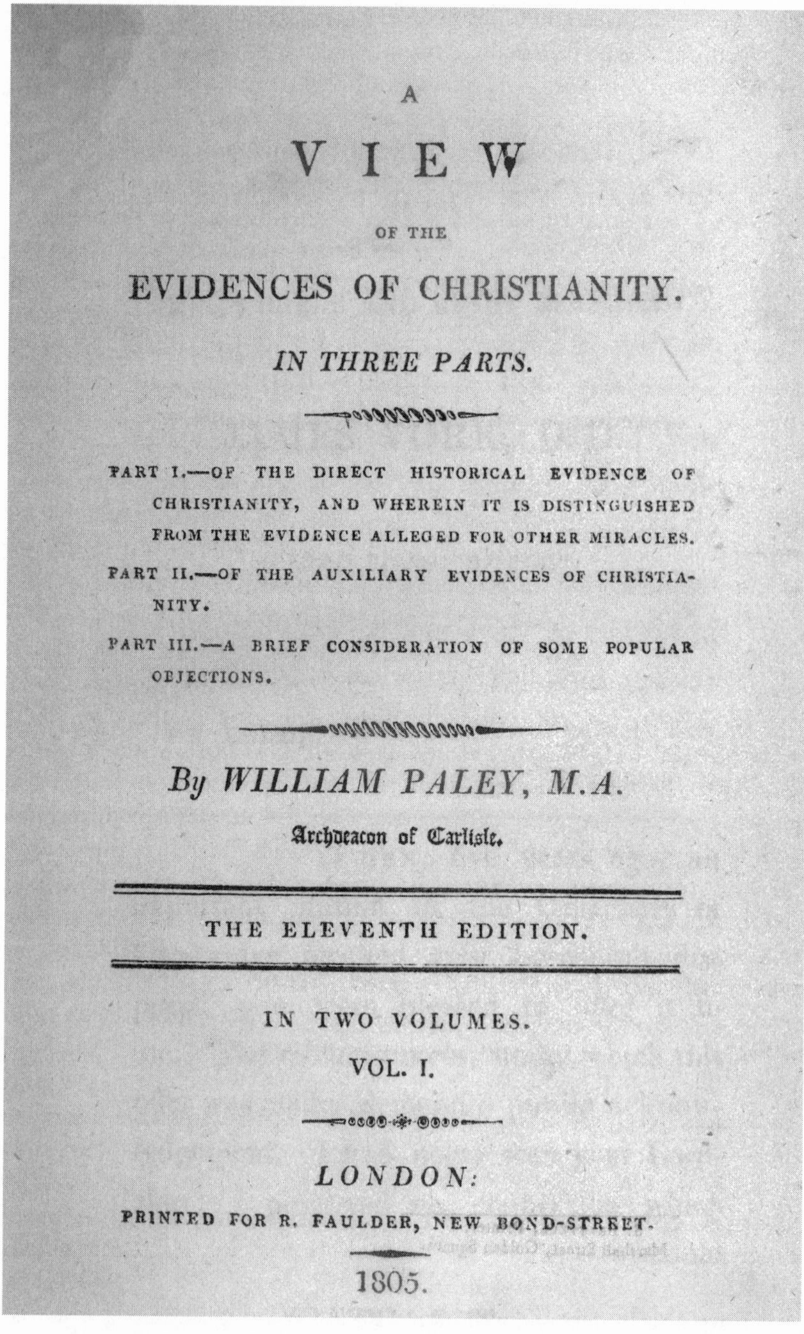

A

VIEW

OF THE

EVIDENCES OF CHRISTIANITY.

IN THREE PARTS.

PART I.—OF THE DIRECT HISTORICAL EVIDENCE OF
CHRISTIANITY, AND WHEREIN IT IS DISTINGUISHED
FROM THE EVIDENCE ALLEGED FOR OTHER MIRACLES.

PART II.—OF THE AUXILIARY EVIDENCES OF CHRISTIA-
NITY.

PART III.—A BRIEF CONSIDERATION OF SOME POPULAR
OBJECTIONS.

By WILLIAM PALEY, M.A.

Archdeacon of Carlisle.

THE ELEVENTH EDITION.

IN TWO VOLUMES.

VOL. I.

LONDON:

PRINTED FOR R. FAULDER, NEW BOND-STREET.

1805.

FIG. 1. First published in London in 1794, William Paley's *A View of the Evidences of Christianity* was a wildly popular work printed in over two dozen editions, including several in Boston and New York.

they had founded their publick ministry upon the allegation of miracles wrought within their own knowledge . . . and if it had appeared, that their conduct really had its origin in these accounts, I should have believed them."[14] But none came up to the standard of apostolic history. Reviewing the cases cited by Hume where miracles were claimed, Paley objected that in none of the three instances did the purported miracle overthrow "established prejudices and persuasions." In none "did the credit make its way, in opposition to authority and power."[15] The supposed miracles merely sustained established institutions and convictions and the predispositions of the witnesses. The lack in general was that in no case did "miraculous evidence lay at the bottom of the argument."[16] Either men taught and suffered but not in support of an allegation of miracles, or belief in the miracle required no suffering. The miracle did not reverse belief or put the believer at odds with his society. The strength of Christianity, on the other hand, as a nineteenth-century American wrote in reviewing Paley's argument, lay in the fact that "Christianity was received at first on the ground of miracles."[17]

Paley's arguments, variously elaborated and organized, appeared in over a score of books on Christian evidences printed in America and Britain in the first half of the nineteenth century. Alexander Campbell would not have had to look far for material in preparation for the Owen debate. The two fat volumes that recorded the debate in print were a compendium of arguments made over and over through the preceding years. All of this impinged on Joseph Smith and the early Church shortly after the publication of the Book of Mormon, when Joseph's claims and a growing number of followers marked him as another competitor of the Christian prophets. As early as October 1829, the *Palmyra Reflector* referred to Joseph as "the Prophet," and the title stuck.[18] The attribution of prophethood boded ill for Joseph and his associates, for the commentators thereby served notice that Joseph Smith was among the bogus miracle workers whose claims might divert allegiance from Christian miracles and whose assertions therefore must be refuted. The task of refutation was assumed by two individuals—Alexander Campbell, who wrote on the Book of Mormon in his own newspaper, the *Millennial Harbinger*, beginning in February 1831, and Obediah Dogberry, the editor of the *Palmyra Reflector*, whose six-part series on Joseph Smith had begun one month earlier.

Efforts to Discredit the Prophet

Writing entirely independently, Campbell and Dogberry both began in the same way. Each put Joseph into a preformed category. Like all nineteenth-century intellectuals who had been exposed to Enlightenment skepticism and the Christian counter-arguments, the two critics were aware of the tradition of false prophets. Both opened their comments with lengthy discourses on religious impostors. In reprinting excerpts from the *Palmyra Reflector*, Fawn Brodie omitted Dogberry's introduction, referring to the narration as a "digression."[19] For her purposes, of course, it was; but for Dogberry and for Campbell, the lists of fraudulent prophets placed and thereby partly explained Joseph Smith. Dogberry's list was quite different in specific content from Campbell's. Dogberry began with "brief notices and sketches of the superstitions of the ancients," alchemy, Mohammad, and legends of hidden treasures, and moved quickly to modern impostures, "the Morristown Ghost, Rogers, Walters, Joanna Southcote, Jemima Wilkinson, &c."[20] Campbell devoted a long page to Jannes and Jambres, the Egyptian magicians who withstood Moses; twenty-four Messiahs who deceived the Jews; ten false Messiahs of the twelfth century; seventeenth-century rumors of a ship arriving in Scotland "with sails and cordage of silk" and mariners who spoke only Hebrew and on the sails a motto, "The Twelve Tribes of Israel"; thence to Munzer, Stubner, and Stork in the Reformation; down to Ann Lee, founder of the Shakers; and one Miss Campbell, who only two years previously had come back from the dead. That the names differed mattered very little. The point was the same: "Every age of the world has produced impostors and delusions."[21] Moreover, every age had its dupes: "The pages of history inform us, that from time immemorable, man has more or less been the dupe of superstitious error and imposition." "Where ignorance is found to prevail, superstition and bigotry will abound."[22] Joanna Southcote, the false prophetess, had recently attracted a large following in London.

> If an imposture, like the one we have so briefly noticed, could spring up in the great metropolis of England, and spread over a considerable portion of that kingdom, it is not surprising that one equally absurd, should have its origin in this neighborhood, where its dupes . . . ever will be numerous.[23]

The comparison much simplified the work of refutation, for association with the proven deceptions of Southcote, the false Messiahs, and the Egyptian magicians discredited Joseph Smith before a single fact about him was known. He was merely one more among the vast company of impostors whose purported miracles were no evidence for divine authority, unlike the miracles on which Christianity was based.

Having classified Joseph Smith with the impostors, the critics had available to them ready-made arguments. They could follow the patterns that Paley and the other apologists had established for distinguishing false prophets from the true. The subtitle of Campbell's analysis of the Book of Mormon was *An Examination of Its Internal and External Evidences, and a Refutation of Its Pretences to Divine Authority*, and his work followed the standard categories of Christian apologetics. Lacking details of any claims to miracles, Campbell, writing from Bethany, Virginia, could only briefly treat the "External Evidences," the most important category. Perforce he devoted the bulk of his observations to the "Internal Evidences," the more vague and miscellaneous half of Christian apologetics. Dogberry in Palmyra could presumably collect information firsthand and deal directly with Joseph's claims to miracles. The point he had to make in accord with the established canons of Christian evidences was that Joseph had not begun his prophetic career with a miracle. He was not a dispassionate observer who was compelled to believe by sensory evidence. Miracles were not, as for Paley, "at the bottom of the argument."

Dogberry had much more to say about Joseph than that, but he did make the same point, leading up to it with a similar observation about Mohammad:

> Mohamet had a regular plan from the beginning; in the commencement of his imposture, he professed an intimate connexion with the angel Gabriel, and was afterwards allowed, as he declares, numerous conferences with God himself. He was too cunning to attempt many miracles before his followers, and even the story of the tame pigeon, who had been taught to light upon the shoulder of the prophet, and eat millet from his ear, is denied by many of the Arabian historians.
>
> It is well known that Joe Smith never pretended to have any communion with angels, until a long period after the *pretended* finding of his book, and that the juggling of himself or father, went no further than the pretended faculty of seeing wonders in a "peep stone," and the occasional interview with the spirit, supposed to have the custody of hidden treasures.[24]

The way of most impostors is that they lay their cunning plans and then claim miracles to hoodwink their followers. Such was the sequence in Mohammad's life. He had a regular plan and *afterward* reported conferences with God. The faith of his followers was equally inconsequential, for he was not so bold as to attempt miracles before witnesses. Even the one claimed for him was denied by some Arabians. Their claims could be dismissed because neither Mohammad nor his followers began with a miracle. Having made the point for Mohammad, Dogberry jumped at once to Joseph Smith without intervening transition, since the point to be made was the same. Similarly, "Joe Smith never pretended to have any communion with angels" until long after pretending to find the book. There were admittedly supernatural communications earlier, but Dogberry chose to describe these as "the occasional interview with the spirit," meaning the spirit standing guard over the treasure Joseph sought. Dogberry's main argument was that Joseph Smith was at the outset a mere money digger who propagated and perhaps believed the superstitions associated with hidden treasures. "It will be borne in mind that no *divine* interposition had been *dreamed* of at the period."[25] Nothing like a Christian miracle or heavenly vision started Joseph on his religious career. He had pretensions only to vulgar treasure hunting until well after finding the book. Indeed, Dogberry said it appeared "quite certain that the prophet himself never made any serious pretentions to religion until his late pretended revelation."[26] Cast in that mold, Dogberry's Joseph, by the standards of Christian apologetics, was no more a prophet nor even a pretender to prophethood than Mohammad. A miracle had initiated neither career.

The Prophet's Response to His Critics

What did Joseph say in reply to his critics? We know his answer to the money-digging charges, that what he had done was in another man's employ and not at his own instigation. What about miracles? Was there any attempt to meet the skeptics' demand for proof, to claim he had been a miracle worker from the beginning? It would have been difficult to remain oblivious to the debates over Christianity. They were in the air, in the Vermont and New York air as everywhere else. The "infidel" was a stock character in vernacular sociology. Moreover, the request for evidence was brought close to home through Martin Harris and Oliver Cowdery, both rationalists of a sort. Why would Martin carry the transcribed characters all the way to New York City, if not in pursuit of some "external" proof? Judging from one of the revelations, Oliver Cowdery too seems to have desired a "witness" in the form of at least a small miracle. The desire seems to have been general. In July 1830 the Lord had to admonish the Church to "require not miracles" (D&C 24:13). A year later another rebuke: "Verily, I say unto you, there are those among you who seek signs, and there have been such even from the beginning" (D&C 63:8). The longing was there for concrete evidence.[27]

And why not factual evidence of divine authenticity for a scientific age? The returns, as the spiritualists were later to show, could be high. Some of the recipients of spiritual messages several years later appeared to fulfill the requirement for a neutral observer converted by a miracle. The Fox sisters were mere children, twelve and thirteen, when they first heard the rappings in the Hydesville, New York, farmhouse in 1847. Developing a system for asking questions and getting answers, they made some startling predictions. As the phenomenon spread, others performed feats hard to explain without admitting supernatural intervention. Spiritualists subjected themselves to scientific scrutiny, and among the frauds were a number whose performances could not be dismissed. As the evidence accumulated, doubters became converts. Robert Dale Owen, son of the communitarian reformer and editor of his father's freethinking newspaper in its virulent skeptical stage, was exposed to spiritualism in 1856 and converted. In 1860 Owen published *Footfalls on the Boundary of Another World*, explaining how a skeptic discovered spiritualism and was won over to belief.[28]

Conversions of that sort seemed to be within the grasp of the restored Church. The very idea of a restoration implied the return of miracles. The Book of Mormon taught that "the day of miracles" would not cease so long as men had faith (Moro. 7:35–37). The revelations to Joseph boldly promised not just miracles but "signs" to believers (D&C 84:65–72). The miracles occurred, too—among them the combined viewing of the plates by three men at the hands of an angel. Why not make something of this "proof" for the benefit of honest skeptics? Was it not consistent for the Lord, after promising the new Church to "reason with you, and speak unto you and prophesy, as . . . in days of old" (D&C 45:15), to satisfy the hungers of rational men deprived of spiritual nourishment by the insistent questions of their time?

It was not to be. Indeed, the revelations quite specifically rejected the demands of the Christian rationalists. "Require not miracles," the Church was told early on (D&C 24:13). "He that seeketh signs shall see signs, but not unto salvation" (D&C 63:7). Signs in the Book of Mormon were a condemnation for those who refused to believe. Among believers, signs were a reward and blessing of faith: "Behold, faith cometh not by signs, but signs follow those that believe. . . . Wherefore, I, the Lord, am not pleased with those among you who have sought after signs and wonders for faith, and not for the good of men unto my glory" (D&C 63:8, 12). Miracles were to bless the faithful, not to convert doubters (D&C 63:9–10). Then, as now, the true principle is that faith precedes the miracle.

All this was incomprehensible to Alexander Campbell. Near the end of his analysis of the Book of Mormon, he entered into an imaginary dialogue with the followers of Joseph Smith. In response to the question of how he was to know their witness was true, they say, "Ask God in faith"—a ridiculous contradiction. For Campbell that meant "*I must believe it first, and then ask God if it be true!*" A reversal of the order Christian rationalists expected: the miracles should come first, then the faith. Campbell persisted in his demand for a sign. They claim to be true believers. "Have they wrought any miracles?" Have they cut off an arm and restored it? Joseph, as a true prophet, should have predicted future events. "Smith has failed in every instance to verify one of *his own* sayings."[29] Without evidence of a miracle to prove they came with power, Campbell readily dismissed the Mormonites, who perversely insisted that faith come first.

What of the testimony of the Three Witnesses? There was sensory evidence of a miraculous occurrence. Could Campbell dismiss their statement? He could and did, partly by sarcastically calling them "disinterested retailers" of the book, implying their support was about as weighty as testimonials in patent medicine advertisements. His more substantial objection, although briefly made, was that the testimony of the witnesses did not enlarge upon the miraculous part of the event. They did not witness a real miracle. The witnesses stated they knew the Book of Mormon was true because the voice of God had testified to them. Campbell's question: "I would ask them how they knew that it was God's voice which they heard?"[30] What was miraculous about a voice in the forest? Where was the parting of the sea, the instantaneous healing, the raising of the dead to prove the voice divine? It may have been a miracle when "an angel of God came down from heaven" to show the plates, but the witnesses made nothing of the supernatural aspect of the occurrence.[31] They seemed much more concerned to report that they had seen the plates and that they felt under an obligation to obey the command of God to testify of the truth of the Book of Mormon. The miracle of an angelic appearance was not the heart of the matter. Given his expectations for miraculous proof, Alexander Campbell was not impressed enough to attempt serious refutation.

Only once, to my knowledge, did Joseph Smith go even partway toward meeting the rationalist demand for evidence. In the 1839 account of his First Vision, Joseph cast the story in a form that met Paley's standards for authentic miracles. There were, of course, no witnesses beyond himself, but Joseph did meet the requirement of a neutral observer whose call had begun with a miracle. He had not expected a divine visitation. He was merely a puzzled boy asking for help. When he innocently reported what had occurred in the grove, he met nothing but scorn. Yet he could not back down on the story, for he knew it was true: "I had actually seen a light, and in the midst of that light I saw two Personages, and they did in reality speak to me; and though I was hated and persecuted for saying that I had seen a vision, yet it was true" (JS–H 1:25). The memory of the sensory evidence, what he had seen and heard, bound him to his testimony through all the persecution that followed. Whether or not Joseph understood the intricacies of the rationalist argument, all the components of a valid witness were there: the neutral observer, the supernatural event, the commitment to the miraculous story in spite of persecution and personal loss. As Joseph narrated the events, he suffered for a miraculous story just like Paley's early Christians. The subsequent description of Moroni's visit heightened the supernatural aspects of the event with the scrupulous attention to details: feet off the floor, the increasing light, the sudden appearance of the angel, the whiteness of the robe, the opening conduit through which Moroni ascended. In contrast to the Three Witnesses, Joseph left no question about his having experienced a bona fide miracle.

Although Joseph was an astute observer, this seems to be the only report designed to meet the needs of Christian rationalists. The likes of Alexander Campbell apparently did not loom large in his consciousness. An early revelation promising miracles charged the Saints not to "boast themselves of these things, neither speak them before the world; for these things are given unto you for your profit and for salvation" (D&C 84:73), not to convert unbelievers. Joseph followed the admonition and said little. Even before the Church's organization, he learned that "if they will not believe my words, they would not believe you, my servant Joseph, if it were possible that you should show them all these things which I have committed unto you" (D&C 5:7). Perhaps with that in mind, Joseph made no serious effort to fill the categories of internal and external evidence required by the rationalists, nor, with this one exception, to present the miraculous events of his life as proof.

Modern Answers to Rationalism and Skepticism

Since Joseph Smith's time, other Latter-day Saints have had greater regard for rationalists and skeptics. The most distinctly rationalist treatise produced by a Latter-day Saint is B. H. Roberts's *A New Witness for God*.[32] Its organization follows the classic lines, internal evidences and external evidences, with large sections under external evidences devoted to miracles and prophecy. The modern effort to demonstrate the historical authenticity of the Book of Mormon, though less bound to the nineteenth-century structure, pursues the same line of reasoning. If historically authentic, the Book of Mormon must have been received miraculously, and the miracle authenticates Joseph's prophethood. The point now, as in the early nineteenth century, is to show there is no acceptable explanation for an event but divine power and then to argue that the beneficiary of that power, in our case Joseph Smith, is thereby certified as a divine spokesman.

The work of our apologists certainly has had a beneficial influence. Hugh Nibley's *Lehi in the Desert* sustained my faith at a critical moment.[33] Latter-day Saint scholars who have subjected the Book of Mormon to rational tests have been greatly satisfied with the results. Close examination lays bare the complexity and intricacy of the narrative, the unexpected consistencies, and the clear marks of antiquity. Although the Foundation for Ancient Research and Mormon Studies (FARMS), the organization most devoted to this research, has now been absorbed by Brigham Young University, the Church puts little emphasis on this form of persuasion in its missionary program. Other methods seem much more fruitful. It seems to be true in the largest sense that "if they will not believe my words, they would not believe you, my servant Joseph, if it were possible that you should show them all these things which I have committed unto you" (D&C 5:7).

The way of the Lord is testimony, not miracles. Miraculous events sometimes enter in, but not essentially. At the center of testimony is the experience of God's power and truth. Through many years we have learned as a people that such knowledge is not acquired through the senses from events outside ourselves. Unlike the men of the Enlightenment, who valued objective sensory information, recorded in the ideal case by a machine to eliminate personal bias, Latter-day Saints depend on personal testimonies, specific to each individual. We convert people by describing what we know personally, what we have experienced spiritually ourselves, as the power of God and the truths of the gospel have intertwined with our lives. The power of the Church comes not from a single incontrovertible miraculous event, such as the parting of the sea or the raising of the dead, which compels all to believe. The power lies in thousands of wholly subjective experiences, however subject to flaws and distortions, wherein God has been known by one person.

The Three Witnesses seem actually to have been bearing this kind of testimony rather than serving as witnesses to a miraculous occurrence in nature. It was not the miracle of a voice coming out of nowhere in the forest that told them God was speaking. They sensed the power of the voice in their spirits, not in their ears. The testimony of the Twelve Apostles as witnesses to the Doctrine and Covenants is much closer to the testimony of the Three Witnesses than the external circumstances lead us to believe. The Twelve testified that "the Lord has borne record to our souls, through the Holy Ghost shed forth upon us, that these commandments were given by inspiration of God, and are profitable for all men and are verily true" (D&C, "Explanatory Introduction"). The voice heard by the three bore record to their souls, too, or they would have had no grounds for testimony.

The Latter-day Saint answer to skepticism is not conventional evidence. Alma's declaration to Korihor, the archetypal skeptic, is our response still: "Will ye say, Show unto me a sign, when ye have the testimony of all these thy brethren, and also all the holy prophets?" (Alma 30:44). We ask that skeptics listen to the testimonies of believers who trust God because they have experienced his power and truth. Not only the Olympian testimonies of the prophets who, like Joseph, can say "that He lives! For we saw him, even on the right hand of God; and we heard the voice bearing record that he is the Only Begotten of the Father" (D&C 76:22–23)—not only these few, but "all these thy brethren," today numbering in the hundreds of thousands, also know the truth because of the record borne to their souls. This is our evidence, your testimony and mine, our children's and our friends'. Among those who can so testify and who seek thereby to bring faith to the unbelieving, I am grateful to be one, in the name of Jesus Christ. Amen.

NOTES

1. Albert Post, *Popular Freethought in America, 1825–1850* (New York: Columbia University Press, 1943), 131–37.

2. Ibid., 23–24, 36, 136.

3. Ethan Allen, *Reason the Only Oracle of Man; or a Compenduous* [sic] *System of Natural Religion* (Bennington, Vt.: Haswell and Russell, 1784), 265.

4. Post, *Popular Freethought*, 21, 34.

5. Charles Leslie, *A Short and Easy Method with Deists, wherein the Certainty of the Christian Religion is Demonstrated by Infallible Proof from Four Rules, in a Letter to a Friend* (1698; Cambridge, Mass.: William Hilliard, 1805), 12.

6. Ibid., 12.

7. Alexander Keith, *Evidence of the Truth of the Christian Religion Derived from the Literal Fulfillment of Prophecy; Particularly as Illustrated by the History of the Jews, and by the Discovery of Recent Travellers* (New York: Harper and Brothers, 1836), 21.

8. James Smith, *The Christian's Defence, Containing a Fair Statement, and Impartial Examination of the Leading Objections Urged by Infidels Against the Antiquity, Genuineness, Credibility and Inspiration of the Holy Scriptures* (Cincinnati: J. A. James, 1843), 358.

9. David Hume, *Philosophical Essays Concerning Human Understanding* (London: A. Millar, 1748), 192–95.

10. William Paley, *A View of the Evidences of Christianity*, vol. 2 in *The Works of William Paley, D.D.*, 5 vols. (Boston: Joshua Belcher, 1810), title page.

11. Ibid., v.

12. Ibid., 63.

13. Ibid., 65–66.

14. Ibid., 180.

15. Ibid., 207.

16. Ibid., 66.

17. William E. Channing, *A Discourse on the Evidences of Revealed Religion*, 3d ed. (Boston: Isaac R. Butts, 1826), 30.

18. "Selected Items," *Palmyra Reflector*, October 7, 1829; reprinted in Francis W. Kirkham, *A New Witness for Christ in America*, 2 vols., 3d ed., enl. (Independence, Mo.: Zion's Printing and Publishing, 1951), 1:269; cf. 1:27.

19. Fawn M. Brodie, *No Man Knows My History: The Life of Joseph Smith, the Mormon Prophet* (New York: Alfred A. Knopf, 1945), 407.

20. "Gold Bible," *Palmyra Reflector*, January 6, 1831; reprinted in Kirkham, *New Witness*, 1:284.

21. Alexander Campbell, *Delusions: An Analysis of the Book of Mormon, With an Examination of Its Internal and External Evidences, and a Refutation of Its Pretences to Divine Authority* (Boston: Benjamin H. Greene, 1832), 5–6; reprinted from Alexander Campbell, "Delusions," *Millennial Harbinger* 2 (February 1831): 85–96.

22. "Gold Bible, No. 2," *Palmyra Reflector*, January 18, 1831; reprinted in Kirkham, *New Witness*, 1:285.

23. "Gold Bible, No. 4," *Palmyra Reflector*, February 14, 1831; reprinted in Kirkham, *New Witness*, 1:289.

24. "Gold Bible, No. 5," *Palmyra Reflector*, February 28, 1831; reprinted in Kirkham, *New Witness*, 1:291.

25. "Gold Bible, No. 4," February 14, 1831.

26. "Gold Bible, No. 3," *Palmyra Reflector*, February 1, 1831; reprinted in Kirkham, *New Witness*, 1:287–88.

27. See also Doctrine and Covenants 5:1, 23; 6:17, 22, 24.

28. Sydney E. Ahlstrom, *A Religious History of the American People* (New Haven: Yale University Press, 1972), 488–89.

29. Campbell, *Delusions*, 15.

30. Ibid., 15.

31. The quotation comes from "The Testimony of Three Witnesses," Book of Mormon.

32. B. H. Roberts, *A New Witness for God* (Salt Lake City: George Q. Cannon and Sons, 1895).

33. For more on this incident, see the essay "My Belief," chapter 2 above.

11

Joseph Smith in the Current Age

This essay was written as a lunch talk for a conference on Joseph Smith sponsored by BYU's College of Religious Education. The occasion was the dedication of the Joseph Smith Memorial Building at BYU in 1991. LDS apostle Gordon B. Hinckley gave a marvelous opening address on his feelings about Joseph, far more to the point than my rather acerbic speech, which was very much a response to events of the past few years, especially the fall of communism in the Soviet Union. My talk reflects my sense that we needed a critique of corporate capitalism in a world where it no longer had natural enemies. I was hoping that Mormonism might mount that criticism and make a small contribution to upholding humane society in a world increasingly devoted to profit. The same talk given a decade later would require a new set of arguments, perhaps ones related to conflicts between civilizations and world religions.

What is the place of Joseph Smith's teachings in our time? What do his writings have to say in a world so different from the one in which he himself lived? If Joseph Smith were alive today, he would be 186 years old.[1] Most of his writings have been in circulation for over 150 years. During that century and a half, vast changes in government, the economy, philosophical outlook, and popular values have transformed society. After all this, what do Joseph Smith's teachings have to say about the problems of late-twentieth-century society? We do not expect his writings to illuminate all of the issues in our daily newspapers, much less the multitude of questions that accumulate from decade to decade in our legislatures, in the press, and in our lives. But we are interested in knowing what issues Joseph's teachings do address and what help he can give us with the underlying problems of the current age.

In terms of influence on human lives, there is no question that Joseph's teachings are still important, especially when compared to the ideas of his own contemporaries. Few Americans of the first half of the nineteenth century have had greater influence on the conduct of life or the organization of human affairs than Joseph Smith. Ralph Waldo Emerson is widely read and admired, but not many people govern their lives by his mysterious epigrams. Thoreau's principle of civil disobedience has been practiced around the globe, but comparatively few read his writings to learn how to live.

Andrew Jackson is acknowledged to have been a great president, but his political ideas are only vaguely applicable today. Among lesser-known figures of great influence in Joseph Smith's time—Horace Bushnell, Charles Grandison Finney, Harriet Beecher Stowe, William Emery Channing—none has reached so deep into individual character and none has inspired an organization comparable to the church Joseph Smith founded. The range of Joseph Smith's influence may be narrow—seven million people is a tiny fraction of the world's population—but among his followers, it is profound.

The durability of Joseph Smith's teaching is remarkable in light of the changes that have altered the world since he organized the Church of Jesus Christ of Latter-day Saints. In 1830 people crossed the Atlantic by the same means as Nephi and Lehi—wind and sail. Messages were hand carried from place to place. There were no railroads to speak of in 1830; canal boats were the great transportation innovation of the time. More than seventy percent of the population in the United States still lived in rural areas, and well over half were engaged in farming. Before 1844 only a small number of Latter-day Saint converts had gone to college; fewer still had graduated; and that was true of most Americans. Joseph's teachings have maintained their influence through a century and a half of the most far-reaching change to have occurred at any time in history.

But apart from the Church, where Joseph Smith's influence is concentrated, what do his writings have to say to a time so vastly different from his own? What is the relevance of his teachings in the late twentieth century in view of the transformation in human life since the Prophet organized the Church in 1830? I will focus more on the public realm than on private life, although it must never be forgotten that individual salvation lies at the heart of the gospel and will always be of highest significance. I emphasize the public side because Joseph Smith's writings are not restricted to the private sphere. His teachings and his life have implications for culture and society as a whole. The Book of Mormon prophets, whose writings Joseph translated, were deeply concerned about public morality, the rise and fall of peoples, and the ultimate conclusion of human affairs. Not long after the organization of the Church, the revelations to Joseph began to sketch in a new economic and social order, summed up in the word *Zion*. By the end of his life, Joseph Smith had built cities, planned a university, and run for president of the United States. This was a man whose thinking compassed the whole of society and culture. He envisioned the work of the Kingdom as transforming public as well as private life. With this in mind, we have ample reason to consider the implications of Joseph's thought for the public realm in the current age. In particular, what now is the significance of three major principles of Joseph's teachings: revelation, the Kingdom, and Zion?

Revelation

Of these principles, revelation is the most disputed and perhaps the most important. A casual conversation reminded me recently of the difficulty of accepting revelation. Last summer the time came to have my picture taken again, and we asked a photographer-friend to come to the house. After the sitting, while talking casually, she asked which is more important to Mormons, their way of life or their beliefs. "The way of life is wonderful," she went on to say, "but the beliefs, you know, are a little hard to swallow." I knew she was thinking of the revelations—the visit of Moroni, the miraculous translation, the claim to speak for God in the Doctrine and Covenants, more angels, more revelations, down to the end of Joseph Smith's life. How can a rational, educated person in the late twentieth century accept all of what an undergraduate teacher of mine at Harvard delicately termed "garbage"? People have trouble seeing that our way of life is founded on our beliefs.

The revelations to Joseph Smith were hard to take in his own time. Ministers scoffed at his report of the First Vision. The very idea of the Book of Mormon made the Palmyra townspeople furious before they had read a word of it. Joseph Smith was ridiculed throughout his life for claiming he communicated with God, even by those who believed in God and acknowledged the occurrence of revelation in the Bible.

Today the revelations are even more difficult to believe than they were in the past. The official scientific culture of our time has largely discredited the divinity of the Bible and is agnostic on the existence of God. One of the great transformations since 1830 is the enshrinement of science as the dominant culture of the age. Science was well launched by 1830, and since then its influence has enlarged immensely, especially among the educated populace. Science has become the court of last resort in determining what is true. Unless something can be proven scientifically, its validity must remain in question. Although private individuals and even large organizations maintain belief in God, only those ideas with scientific validation receive general acknowledgment. By science I mean not only the physical sciences, but also those forms of scholarship that employ evidence, appeal to reason, and leave the determination of truth to communities of reasonable men and women. In educated circles where the power of science is generally acknowledged, the validity of revelation is commonly doubted. Many educated people consider revelation an imagined fabrication, in a class with witchcraft, magic, and astrology. My photographer-friend's husband is a physicist; from her point of view, Joseph Smith's revelations were outlandish.

Science is not the whole story in our culture, however. While dominant in the official culture that governs awards of government grants, for example, agnosticism on the question of revelation does not reign everywhere. In our popular culture, we see many signs of a deep yearning for contact with a higher sphere. The desire for supernatural communication shows up in science fiction, the popularity of astrological charts, the stories of life after death, and the movies about departed spirits. Think of the popularity of *E.T., Close Encounters of the Third Kind,* or *Star Wars.* In all of these movies, the existence of powers outside our scientifically known world lies at the center of the plot. How to reach these supernatural intelligences, how to cultivate them, how to bring them into our lives are the questions the stories ask. "May the Force be with you," Luke Skywalker is told in *Star Wars.* Latter-day Saints equate Force with Holy Ghost and consider it a religious achievement when Luke does trust the Force. But does not everyone in the movie audience feel the same? Does not everyone want Luke to trust the Force? For a minute or two, the whole audience believes that supernatural power can expand human intelligence, and that all should trust the Force. At that point in the story, they believe in listening to the Spirit.

Everywhere in our culture, we see signs of this yearning for contact with invisible powers beyond ordinary life, contact that science can neither satisfy nor justify. Occasionally scientists working on the origins of the universe or at some other boundary of knowledge offer a glimpse of something deeper and more wonderful than swirling, cold power. We wait eagerly for them to tell us what it is, but in vain. We want to know: Is there a higher power? Is it benevolent? Will it speak to us? But the questions coming from our popular culture are never answered by scientific culture.

All of us, including the believers in Joseph Smith, stand in the middle of this ambiguity. What are we to do? Our calling as believers, I think, is to affirm the reality of revelation. We need to give encouragement to those who yearn for communication from heaven but who are discouraged by the prevailing scientism. We must speak out because we are better prepared than most religions to offer that assurance. Last summer, along with three other Latter-day Saint scholars, I attended a conference at Pepperdine University on restoration religions. Disciples of Christ, Church of Christ, Pentecostal, and Amish, as well as the Latter-day Saints, were among the churches under discussion, and members of other denominations were in the audience. After we had made our presentations, someone asked how Latter-day Saints know Joseph Smith's revelations were from God. In reply I asked the audience of about 150 people, all of them religious, how many used the phrase "Listen to the Spirit." Some replied that their churches discouraged listening to the Spirit; others said they did recall hearing those words from time to time.

The lukewarm response surprised me. It made me realize how much more Latter-day Saints make of personal revelation than most other Christians. From an early age, we are told to listen to the Spirit. When we are in doubt about our lives—what course to take, what we believe, what dangers threaten us—we consult the Spirit. Long before children understand the intricacies of doctrine, they are told to listen to Heavenly Father whispering to them. We call business executives, scientists, doctors, builders, schoolteachers to serve as stake presidents and bishops with virtually no training and tell them to depend on the Spirit to solve the thorny problems that they will assuredly confront. Moreover, we assume that if every Saint calls upon God for revelation, all these individual inspirations will sustain the teachings of the General Authorities—and more often than not, the two do coincide. The discipline of spiritual listening lies at the heart of the Church's organization and teaching. We see it working every day of our lives.

Strengthened by this powerful tradition, we can assure people that God will hear them, that he loves them, and most important of all, that he will speak to them. Joseph Smith once said that what distinguished the Latter-day Saints was the Holy Ghost.[2] Possessors of that gift in a world uncertain about revelation have a responsibility. Latter-day Saints must assure people that God will speak to them through his Holy Spirit. The very uncertainty about revelation caused by the limitations of our scientific culture requires us to take a stand on behalf of this central teaching of the Prophet.

The Kingdom

A second prominent theme in Joseph Smith's teachings is the organization of the Kingdom, an idea as contested as revelation. In Joseph Smith's time, Christians largely agreed that believing people should be organized into churches. A great deal of energy went into forming little congregations along the frontier, constructing church buildings, and training ministers. Joseph was among the greatest of the organizers, a genius at developing ways to mobilize people for godly purposes. By revelation he established orders of the priesthood, organized stakes, set up conferences, formed the Relief Society, sent out missionaries, designed cities, outlined a new economic system, all as part of building the Kingdom. That impetus did not slow after his death. Brigham Young went on to develop the ward organization, establish auxiliaries, build and staff temples, found schools, settle new communities, and organize united orders. The Kingdom did not dwell only in the hearts of individuals. The Kingdom consisted of elaborate institutions for accomplishing God's work.

Latter-day Saints take pride in the effectiveness of this organization and the blessings it brings to many lives. At the same time, we know that organized religion has gotten a bad name. Organized religion has come to mean large bureaucratic structures, high costs, and political machinations that appear to dampen the religious spirit rather than enhance it. Everywhere we see Christians breaking away from churches to worship in their own homes, with family and neighborhood groups replacing ministers and churches. Ministers make jokes about the very organizations of which they are a part because they understand their listeners' skepticism. A few Sundays ago, I attended a Catholic service in downtown Philadelphia and heard the parish priest's powerful Christian sermon. To my surprise, he spoke openly of the dysfunctions of the Catholic Church. He got a hearty laugh when he referred to the misuse of money by a Catholic fund-raising group in New York. By poking fun, he appeared to join with his parishioners in acknowledging the failings of the institutional church.

More than a little of that spirit has infected the Latter-day Saints. We sometimes hear discontented young people say they believe the gospel while having trouble with the Church. The prevalence of this idea led Eugene England to give a sermon on why the Church is as true as the gospel.[3] To a degree, the young people may not be entirely wrong. Perhaps we have let our enthusiasm with organization carry us too far. In recent years, we have lightened the meeting schedule and simplified the organization in an effort to focus attention on family religion and personal worship.

But while making commonsense changes, we should not lose sight of the Kingdom principle in Joseph's teachings. In all he did was the implicit conviction that we must work together as a united body of believers to carry forward God's work. I believe the principle of the Kingdom is more essential now than ever because of one of the most significant developments in our society since 1830. I refer to the emergence of corporations.

Only a small number of corporations existed in Joseph Smith's time. The organization of human affairs was far simpler than it is today. The bulk of the population lived and worked on family farms. Virtually everyone's productive life coincided with the family organization and went no further. The corporate bodies that did exist were relatively simple banks and canal companies. The federal government occupied a small number of offices in Washington with employees numbered in the hundreds rather than the hundreds of thousands as today.

Since that time, huge corporate organizations have been formed, extending across the continent and around the globe. I am not only thinking of mammoth business corporations, such as Exxon or DuPont, with offices and factories in every corner of the earth. Now virtually all work is corporate. Museums and universities are organized as not-for-profit corporations. So are charities, symphony orchestras and opera companies, historical societies and labor unions. It is a rare working individual who is not part of a corporation, whether for profit or not. Mothers are the largest body of working people who function outside a corporation, making them particularly helpful in identifying the failings and dangers of corporate work.

The power of these corporations is immense, not only in organizing the economy but in organizing our inward lives. Corporations focus vast amounts of energy and will to accomplish the corporate purpose. My New York office overlooks another large office across Amsterdam Avenue. Through the windows in that office, I can see people sitting at their desks, moving about with papers in their hands, consulting around a table, talking on the telephone. All those people devote their powers of mind and character to the achievement of corporate ends. The corporation not only gives them a purpose for working, but offers them wages, advancement, recognition, and power. To be recognized by the corporation brings to focus the approbation of the thousands of people who work there. In some cases that approbation can be followed with admiration, power, and wealth. Some of life's greatest thrills are advancement in the corporate organization. The corporations dangle golden ladders to the earth and invite us to climb them. They are the great and spacious building of Lehi's dream.

These corporations rarely point fingers of scorn at the humble Saints as in Lehi's vision, but implicitly they do deprecate religion. One of my sons recently joined a banking firm in New York City, and over the past six months he has often put in work weeks of sixty to seventy hours. The corporation confidently demands that commitment from its recruits because its purpose is considered to be so transcendently important. The bank tells its young bankers in training that if family is more important, if seventy hours away from wife and children is too much, then the golden ladder will be gone. The rejects must wander on the misty plain. And so the corporation harnesses our energies and ambitions, consumes our time, and implicitly tells us that nothing, including our religion, is as important. Anyone who chooses other values, having failed the corporation in its designated purpose, will suffer rejection and see the finger of scorn.

President David O. McKay warned us of these potent corporate forces when he proposed that no success in life compensates for failure in the home.[4] But how can we break the grip of the corporation on our hearts? How can we overcome its hold on our competitive urges, our longing for recognition, our need for security and identity—all satisfied by the corporation?

Surely one answer must be to focus human energy and desire on the purposes of our religion just as the corporation focuses desire on its purposes. We need a corporate defense against the onslaught of secular corporatism, and we offer that defense through our organization into a Kingdom.

Latter-day Saints often bear testimony to the strength received from church attendance. As Saints, we know that we need each other to keep our lives properly oriented. After hearing an effective sermon or testimony, we fervently resolve to live more purely and to devote our lives wholly to God's purposes. In our best meetings, we know that our families are more important than promotions, that teaching the gospel has greater rewards than recognition at the office. Living the gospel seems easy and natural at church.

The impetus to live righteously is all the stronger when we receive a church calling. One of the miracles of our lives is the dedication of bishops, Relief Society presidents, and countless other officers in wards and stakes around the globe. We sometimes forget to marvel that so many ordinary people devote themselves to selfless work for the well-being of others. Tens of thousands of them serve in their offices and through their service are refined by the pure love of Christ. The Kingdom organizes us for this work and so blesses our lives by focusing our desires on eternal purposes.

Our callings and our common worship are to a degree an antidote to the seductive powers of the corporation. Not that the evil we face is intentionally malicious. Corporations accomplish noble purposes. Corporations are largely responsible for the massive wealth that our society produces. Corporations in the form of universities and schools educate our children. The institutions that govern and defend us function as corporations. Many of us are employed by corporations and cannot otherwise find work fitted for our skills and abilities. But we must recognize the corporation's insidious power to alienate our affections from the persons and causes we love. To resist the siren call, we must continually review our deepest values and confirm our truest identity as followers of Christ, and that can best be done in common worship. I believe that only in our own form of corporate organization, the Kingdom of God, will we find the strength and wisdom in this corporate age to live as we believe.

Zion

Finally, I come to Zion and its place in Joseph Smith's depiction of world history. Joseph Smith's first published work, the Book of Mormon, is set on a large historical stage. The story reaches far back in time and extends forward to the final end in the future. Underlying everything Joseph taught was a sense of events moving toward culmination at the Second Coming of Christ, followed by the millennial reign, and then the final transformation of the earth. In Joseph's writings, peoples receive dispensations of power and truth, they rise and fall away, and ultimately they come together when the Savior returns. The Latter-day Saints, the people of Joseph Smith's dispensation, are to prepare the earth for Christ's appearance, when the hopes of the prophets will finally be fulfilled. The perfect society we seek to create we call Zion.

Are these teachings about history helpful in understanding our position in the world today? Latter-day Saints have always wondered how the prophecies of the last days coincide with actual historical developments. What is the evil power seen both in the book of Revelation and in Nephi's vision of the future? How is God working in the nations of the earth to bring about his purposes? Outside of the Church itself, where are the forces of good with which we should ally? These questions have always been asked and never precisely answered.

We still cannot tell exactly how God's providential purposes are being worked out in the events going on around us. We are conscious of deep change in the world but can only speculate on how the new configuration of forces brings us closer to the last day. The best we can do is hold to the teachings of the Prophet and his successors, to be sure that we do our parts in advancing providential history—even when the hand of God can only be vaguely discerned.

What is happening right now that may play into the divine plan of history? One answer has been given by the State Department official Francis Fukuyama in an article (and more recently a book) called "The End of History?"[5] By "the end of history," Fukuyama meant that the great ideological struggle that structured history in the twentieth century has been resolved by the demise of communism. Events and changes will continue to occur but without their former significance. Latter-day Saints may be able to understand Fukuyama's idea better than most. In a sense, his conception of the end of history is comparable to the Latter-day Saint idea of the Millennium, when Satan will be bound. Significant events will happen in the Millennium, but the great conflict between good and evil will cease. History without an evil antagonist will be different.

For nearly a century, the rivalry between two great ideological systems has given significance to many events. Small happenings in obscure countries have taken on importance because of their relationship to the titanic struggle between democracy and communism. Now that this struggle has died away, world events have less ideological significance. In that sense, history has ended.

However we judge Fukuyama's argument, he causes us to realize that the polarity of capitalism and communism has deeply structured our thinking about politics and world history. For years we have spoken of creeping socialism, as if the crucial path for American politics ran between free enterprise and socialism. Our progress or decline was measured by our position on that one road. With the collapse of communism in Eastern Europe and the Soviet Union, one pole has dissolved. No viable alternative to free-enterprise capitalism remains, compelling us to change the way we think about our nation and the world.

As we now view world development, the primary question is how and when democracy and capitalism will take over. Communism is no longer thought of as a serious alternative for social and political organization. We only wonder when the old regimes will fall and when capitalism and democracy will rise. Their eventual triumph seems inevitable.

Do Latter-day Saints see in this reorientation of world politics a prelude to a new and better world, one leading to Christ's millennial reign? We certainly rejoice with all the peoples who have been liberated from communism's oppressive yoke. We rejoice for their freedom and for the promise of improved living conditions that free enterprise offers. But would a world dominated by capitalism be nearly synonymous with Zion? Would it be the world that Joseph Smith foresaw and prophesied of when he spoke of the last days?

The demise of communism has freed us to look more candidly at a capitalist social order. In the preceding half century, criticism of capitalism was often misconstrued as sympathy for communism. During that time, we Latter-day Saints took great pains to differentiate the law of consecration and the United Order from communism because we knew their fundamental principles were so deeply antagonistic.[6] We wanted to be clear that our sympathies lay with the forces of freedom, not authoritarian rule. With the collapse of communism and the possibility of that misunderstanding out of the way, we can now ask what we would think of a world under the sway of capitalism, since the way seems clear for that very expansion to occur.

Reflecting on our new situation, we realize that the triumph of capitalism would not make us happy, although it might make us rich. We know the benefits of capitalism and have battled on its behalf for half a century. But that does not diminish the fact that, as a cultural and economic system, capitalism is amoral. It cannot differentiate the sale of cars from the sale of pornography; all that matters under capitalism is the production of goods for which there is a demand. The effect of the goods on the well-being of the purchasers is never taken into account.

Capitalism is merciless in its treatment of people. It trims waste from the productive process whether the unneeded parts are human or mechanical. Outmoded or unnecessary workers, as with outmoded machinery, get discarded. The immense success of free-enterprise competition in producing the best goods at the lowest price depends on this harsh treatment of inefficient workers, whether they be vice presidents or laborers on the line. In its pure form, capitalism is concerned about the welfare of its workers only insofar as they contribute to productivity. The workers' personal needs and circumstances are irrelevant. On the question of God, capitalism is absolutely neutral; nothing religious operates in the capitalist system to moderate its cruelty.

Is this the kind of world Joseph Smith prophesied for the end of history? I think not; nor is it what men and women of good will generally desire. People have always brought other values to capitalism, softening its excesses, and unrestrained capitalism is desirable no more now than ever. We can be sure that many forces will work to modify and humanize free enterprise, but among these counterforces should be Joseph Smith's teachings about Zion.

Zion was firmly rooted in freedom and individual initiative, but not in selfishness. Joseph Smith envisioned stewardship to be at the heart of the new order. In Joseph's Zion, men and women did not receive wealth or authority for their own gain and glory. The Lord granted them stewardships for the good of others—their families first, and then the larger community. A steward's chief responsibility was to bless others. That sense of working for the good of all underlies the description of Book of Mormon society after Christ's visit. "They had all things common among them; therefore there were not rich and poor, bond and free, but they were all made free, and partakers of the heavenly gift" (4 Ne. 1:3). The clash of social classes disappears when the common good governs.

Adapting this principle to modern times, managers of large enterprises should think of their stewardships not as occasions for self-fulfillment but as opportunities to provide productive work to people in need of employment. Laborers in industry should work hard for the common good and not be concerned solely for enlarging their paychecks. Stewards think of their wealth and position as the means to bless others, not to aggrandize themselves.

The principle applies to every form of work—in industry, education, or the arts. In all work, the motive should be to benefit humanity, not to seek glory or advancement for oneself. Stewardship applies to every form of power, including the power of government. We yearn for leaders who are dedicated to the public good, leaders who do not wish to perpetuate themselves in office for their own honor and satisfaction but who seek the advancement of the people and relinquish power when others are more qualified to govern. Sincerely applied, stewardship would transform politics and work and would make capitalism and democracy humane as well as fruitful.[7]

Conclusion

Will the teachings of Joseph Smith be relevant to world developments in the coming years? I believe they will. I do not think we Latter-day Saints should set up our beliefs in outright opposition to the reigning ideological forces. We do not wish to make Zion the antagonist of capitalism as communism once was. We know the benefits of free enterprise and democracy and embrace both. But if we remain loyal to the teachings of Joseph Smith, we will constantly modify our involvement by heeding other principles that compel us to treat our brothers and sisters as ourselves and to use our powers as stewards to bless those around us.

Joseph Smith's teachings have survived a century and a half of historical change. In many respects, they are more relevant now than ever. The world hungers to hear from God, and we teach people to listen to his voice. We need strength to resist the seductive powers of the corporation, and the Church strengthens us. We want to refine free enterprise and democracy, and the principle of stewardship suggests the way.

As private individuals, we will continue our struggles to obey the commandments and heed the Spirit. Most of the time our personal salvation and the well-being of our families and wards will occupy us. But in living as Latter-day Saints, followers of Joseph Smith, we may also, by small strokes, be directing the course of world history toward the promised end that God revealed to the Prophet.

NOTES

1. This essay was written in 1991.

2. Joseph Smith Jr., *History of the Church of Jesus Christ of Latter-day Saints*, ed. B. H. Roberts, 2d ed., rev., 7 vols. (Salt Lake City: Deseret Book, 1974), 4:42.

3. Eugene England, *Why the Church Is as True as the Gospel* (Salt Lake City: Bookcraft, 1986).

4. David O. McKay, "What a Person Does Practically Believe, Determines His Character," *Improvement Era* 67 (June 1964): 445.

5. Francis Fukuyama, "The End of History?" *National Interest*, no. 16 (summer 1989): 3–16; and *The End of History and the Last Man* (New York: Free Press, 1992).

6. See, for example, J. Reuben Clark Jr., "Private Ownership Under the United Order, and the Guarantees of the Constitution," *Improvement Era* 45 (November 1942): 688–89, 752–54; Marion G. Romney, *Look to God and Live: Discourses of Marion G. Romney*, ed. George J. Romney (Salt Lake City: Deseret Book, 1971), 215–29.

7. On the historical background of Zion, see Leonard J. Arrington, Feramorz Y. Fox, and Dean L. May, *Building the City of God: Community and Cooperation Among the Mormons* (Salt Lake City: Deseret Book, 1976). For the future of the Zion idea, see James W. Lucas and Warner P. Woodworth, *Working Toward Zion: Principles of the United Order for the Modern World* (Salt Lake City: Aspen Books, 1996).

12

Making Space for the Mormons

I wrote this essay while at the Huntington Library on a research fellowship as I was just beginning work on a full-length cultural biography of Joseph Smith. I wanted to live up to the honor of being the first after Leonard Arrington to give the annual Leonard J. Arrington Mormon History Lecture, a series sponsored by Utah State University. I delivered the lecture in Logan, Utah, in October 1996. The idea of space as a method of cultural analysis was in the air then, and it seemed fitting to apply it to early Mormonism. The preparation helped me to understand the centrality of Zion as a physical space in Joseph Smith's thinking.

With reasonable success, I gave versions of the same lecture at Columbia University and the University of Chicago. In repeating the lecture after the Logan talk, I found that Mormons were less interested in the presentation than general audiences. The city of Zion was too familiar, and the Chicago comparisons were less than exciting. Non-Mormons, on the other hand, were intrigued by the existence of an alternative to dominant American commercial values.

The organizers of this event are to be commended for initiating a lecture series named for Leonard Arrington, and I truly hope I can do justice to the occasion. I am tempted to devote the time to Leonard himself, for though his immense talents are widely appreciated, we always feel they are not appreciated enough.

I met Leonard in 1960 when I took my first job at BYU as a new Ph.D. To my surprise one day in the fall, an envelope from Utah State appeared in the mail, and in it was a letter from Leonard welcoming me to the community of scholars in Utah. How did he know about me and why had he written from Logan to Provo? I realized eventually that he took responsibility for the entire enterprise of Mormon and Great Basin history and wanted to encourage me in the good work.

A little over a decade later he came into our lives again when he got wind of a group of Boston women's plans to write a history of women in the Church. He was there immediately with encouragement, interest, and a little subsidy to help publish *Mormon Sisters.*[1] He won the hearts of those women, and made Claudia Bushman, the ringleader and my wife, his friend for life.

Leonard drew me into Mormon studies by proposing that I write the first volume of the projected sixteen-volume history of the Church. I had

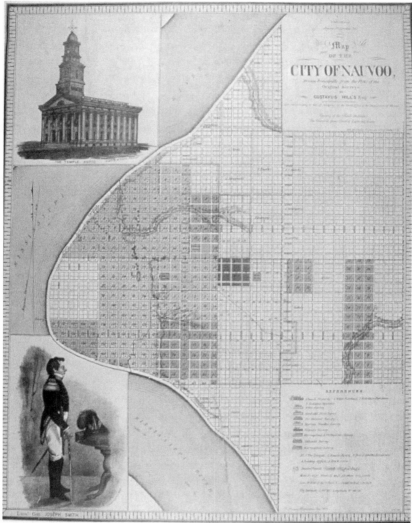

FIG. 1. Map of the City of Nauvoo (1842). Drafted by Gustavus Hill.

planned for years to work on Joseph Smith but kept putting it off in favor of other projects. Leonard persuaded me to take on the assignment and made it easy to work from Boston by sending photocopies of key documents. Later he edited and defended the work, and I dedicated *Joseph Smith and the Beginnings of Mormonism* to Leonard because it is his book as well as mine.[2] Scores of authors could tell similar stories, and scores of books would not have been written without him. He is truly the patriarch of Mormon studies in our generation.

Now I am returning to Joseph Smith at the suggestion of Ron Esplin, Leonard's successor as director of the Joseph Fielding Smith Institute for Latter-day Saint History. The Smith Institute's staff saw the need for a biography that would both develop Joseph Smith's religious thought and give more credence to his spiritual influence on his followers, and they asked me to take on the assignment.

Although I am just starting the research and have little to report so far, I want to give you an idea of my general perspective. I am writing a cultural biography of Joseph Smith that will be akin to the studies of literary scholars who situate their texts in the culture of a period. A cultural biography makes a greater effort than usual to relate the subject's thought to the thinking in his larger environment. I would like to know where Joseph stood in relation to contemporary theologians, reformers, and preachers. How do his ideas of Israel, priesthood, Zion, temples, riches, history, and so forth compare to the ideas of his time?

This approach may seem out of place for a believing Latter-day Saint like myself, because it sounds like the method of historicist scholars who want to explain away Joseph Smith's revelations. People like John Brooke or Fawn Brodie search contemporary sources for references to Melchizedek or baptism for the dead or eternal marriage or Enoch to show that Joseph got his ideas from his environment and that Mormonism came about through natural historical processes rather than by divine intervention as Mormons believe.

My method is similar, but my purposes are different. I want to reconstruct the world around Joseph Smith just as the historicists do, but in order to understand him, not to find historical sources for the revelations. How are we to see and appreciate this many-faceted man without putting him in context? We define ourselves by comparison to others who are the same or different, and people from the past are understood in the same way. On the principle that a fish is the last one to discover water, I think Mormons themselves will not accurately perceive Joseph Smith until he is situated in his culture.

As an example of what I mean, I want to talk tonight about space—Joseph Smith's conception of space in comparison to the spatial constructions of his contemporaries. I do not mean the outer space of astronauts or the inner space of meditation; I am talking about the space in which we see and work, build, and travel—in short, geography.

Maps and Power

We sometimes think of space as simply there, a fixed uniformity for everyone. But on second thought we know that we all shape the spaces we inhabit. Claudia and I recently moved to Pasadena, and at first everything was a confusing, undifferentiated mass of buildings, streets, and shops. Then gradually places began to stand out on the landscape—the bank, grocery store, church, copy shop, a museum or two—and having located them, we lined out the best routes to each one. Now we have personal maps of Pasadena in our minds that suit the needs of our everyday routines.

Every map works much like our mental maps of Pasadena. We sometimes think a map depicts the simple truth about space; it simply tells us what is there. Actually maps work only by suppressing the truth. Each map constructs a specialized and limited picture of space. A map of the United States that told everything about the country would be useless, for it would be the United States itself. Maps have to exclude information, huge amounts of it, to be workable at all, whether the map is of Utah, Logan, this room, or this podium. In making a map, most of what is known about each of these spaces must be left out.

This reduction of spatial reality to a limited number of lines is an act of power. Someone has to decide what matters and eliminate everything else, thereby reshaping reality. In the old days, as the English geographer J. B. Harley has written, mapmaking was the "science of princes." They drew lines to trace in their kingdoms and to give an air of reality to their territorial claims. *King Lear* opens with a map scene and the plot grows out of the divisions Lear makes in the kingdom. More recently, as Harley points out, maps have been the "weapons of imperialism" as much as guns or warships. "Maps were used to legitimise the reality of conquest and empire."[3] Many of us remember maps with the British possessions in pink, confirming the claim that the sun never sets on the British empire. The designation of Greenwich, England, as the meridian for time zones around the earth intimated this one nation's control over the whole earth.

In modern times, maps reflect another kind of power: cultural power. We enter our social values onto maps. In the familiar case of the road map, we designate urban places and the routes that enable us to speed between them—leaving off trees, mountains, ethnicity, architecture, soil types, and innumerable other matters in our preoccupation with movement between cities. Other maps record other values, and were we to bring together all the maps, we would have a map not just of space but of all contemporary culture. Maps and culture continually interact, the maps directing and controlling thought on the one hand, and reflecting and expressing values on the other.

Joseph Smith and Mormon Space

We should not be surprised, therefore, when the Mormons' adoption of new religious values led almost immediately to new kinds of space. Joseph Smith was one of those revolutionary figures whose creative energies generated original spatial configurations in the form of maps, cities, and buildings. Although Joseph mainly addressed the spiritual condition of humanity, his doctrines transformed physical space for his followers. Considering his later legacy in Utah, he may have made a more indelible mark on the American landscape than any single figure in United States history.

One of his most powerful acts was to configure a map that governed the movement of tens of thousands of people through the entire second half of the nineteenth century. Were we to map Mormon space in the 1850s, it would begin with wispy little lines originating in Scandinavian villages and the side streets of English industrial towns, and these thin lines would converge and grow darker as they approached port cities on the continent and in Britain. Then the map would show even darker sea routes from the ports to New Orleans, and then up the river to a jumping-off place where all the lines come together in a wide, dark path across the prairies and through the mountains to Salt Lake City. Then the lines would thin down again and spray like a starburst out to many sites in the Great Basin. This map was drawn after Joseph Smith died, but it was very much his creation; and during his life, similar maps laid out the routes of Mormon converts to Nauvoo and the other gathering sites.

Joseph Smith turned space into a funnel that collected people from all over the world and drew them like gravity to a central point. At that center, he formed another kind of space, a city. He held the belief, rare for one who had grown up in villages, that everyone, including farmers, should live in a city—but an urban place of an unusual kind. In 1833 he and his counselor Frederick G. Williams sent a plat for the "City of Zion" to the Saints in Jackson County, Missouri (fig. 2). Soon after, as historian Mark Hamilton discovered some years ago, they followed up with a second plat that simplified the first and enlarged it to hold more blocks. The original plat had a central square for the bishop that was eliminated in the revised plat, but both plats showed two central squares—fifteen acres on the original, ten acres on the revised—with twelve temples on each one. These structures served as the "public buildings," as the instructions on the margins called them, for the one-and-a-half-square-mile town. The temples were to serve as schools and houses of worship, and not just places for religious worship

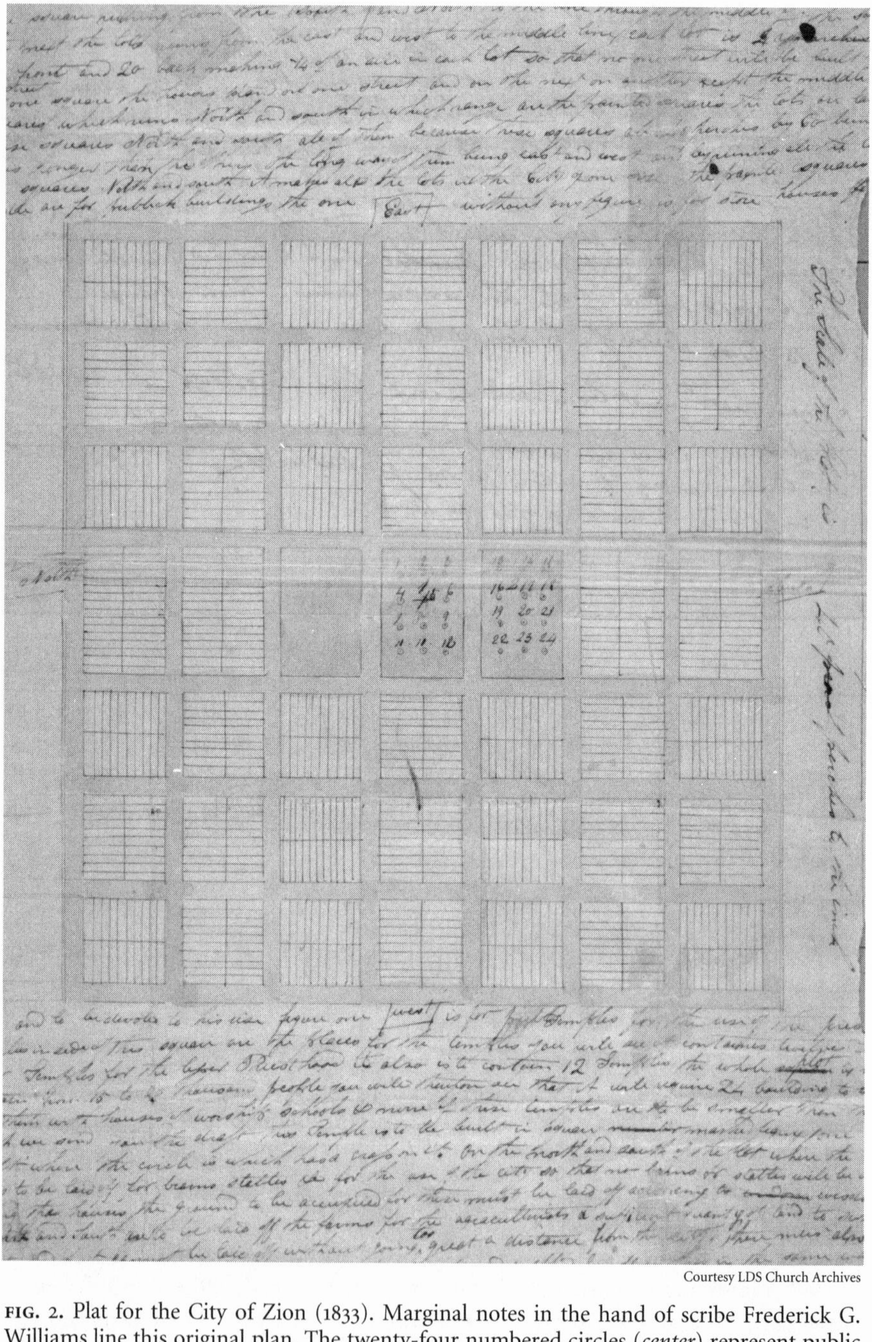

FIG. 2. Plat for the City of Zion (1833). Marginal notes in the hand of scribe Frederick G. Williams line this original plan. The twenty-four numbered circles (*center*) represent public buildings Joseph Smith called "temples," all of which had elaborate names that included various orders of the priesthood. The empty block left of center was to be a bishop's storehouse. A revised plat, enlarging the city, was drawn by Williams soon after the original was produced.

like Mormon temples today. On the surrounding blocks that made up the bulk of the city, each family's brick or stone house stood on a half acre of land with a grove in front—planted according to individual taste, the instructions said—and gardens in back. Barns and stables lay outside the city where the farmland began. Farmers would live in the city and go out each day to work. All together the revised plat contained 2,600 lots, and the instructions in the margins set the population at fifteen to twenty thousand. When the population reached that number, the plat instructed, "Lay off another in the same way, and so fill up the world in the last days."[4]

Mormon space, then, consisted of these two elements: first, the convert population streaming along the lines of gathering from all over the globe, and second, the central city of Zion where the Saints settled or were distributed to similar cities plotted on the broader Zion landscape.

Zion and American City Planning

In preparing a plat for the city of Zion, Joseph made a modest entry into a grand tradition, the planning and building of cities. He joined an enterprise that, like mapmaking, had been the work of princes throughout the ages. To found a city was one of the magnificent gestures of a king. When Peter the Great wanted to bring European refinement to Russia, he founded St. Petersburg in 1703, and Catherine II made it a great capital. All the European Renaissance princes looked after their cities, straightening the streets and laying out grand vistas pointing toward imposing monuments. The burning of London gave Charles II an opportunity to redo his capital city, under the direction of Christopher Wren, with those characteristic baroque streets striking through the blocks toward central monuments. When the United States laid out its capital city, Charles L'Enfant, a French engineer who had volunteered for the American revolutionary army, introduced baroque design into the United States.[5]

In Europe the opportunities to found entirely new cities came only rarely, and even major remodeling (like London's) required that part of the old city be destroyed. America was different. Because of its abundant open space, city building was almost an everyday affair as immigrants poured across the Atlantic and new towns sprang up everywhere. In the seventeenth century, little heed was paid to design principles; Boston streets, for example, grew organically, conforming to the natural flow of topography and making no attempt at squaring the blocks. But by the time William Penn laid out Philadelphia in 1682, conscientious planning had become the norm. By Joseph Smith's day, virtually every land speculator included town sites in his scheme, each with a plat put down on paper to convince prospective buyers of the city's reality, even when it was only an imagined hope. Joseph's city of Zion was one flake in a blizzard of town plans in nineteenth-century America.

Joseph's ideas are sometimes said to have come from his native New England. His city does resemble the towns of Massachusetts and Connecticut more than the fabulous New Jerusalem in the Book of Revelation with its twelve pearly gates, walls of jasper, and streets of gold (Rev. 21:10–21). Joseph toned down the extravagant decorations of the scriptural city to make the city of Zion into a farming community like the towns he knew in Vermont. In the 1830s, during the same decade when Joseph was establishing Zion, John Warner Barber, a Connecticut-born wood engraver and author, sketched some 320 New England towns and published his engravings with short histories of each town in his *Historical Collections* (fig. 3).[6] Taken together, Barber's villages, following one after another through the pages of his book, appear very much like Joseph's Zion, filled up with cities like the one Joseph and Frederick G. Williams plotted for the Jackson County Saints in 1833.

But the New England comparison can be carried only so far. Joseph's city of Zion is not a replica of a New England village transported to the frontier. Zion was a city, not a village or even a town. In 1830 the largest city in the West, St. Louis, had only ten thousand inhabitants, compared to Zion's projected fifteen to twenty thousand. Only seven cities in the entire United States in 1830 had more than twenty-five thousand inhabitants. Joseph's city was larger than any city he had ever seen, save Cincinnati, which he visited on his way to Missouri in 1831 and which had about

Courtesy LDS Church Archives

FIG. 3. Town Center, Dedham, Massachusetts. This view of a typical New England town shows public buildings, such as courthouse and churches, at the center. Engraved by E. L. Barber, New Haven, Connecticut, based on sketches by J. W. Barber. John Warner Barber, *Historical Collections* (Worcester: Dorr, Howland, 1840), 454.

twenty-nine thousand inhabitants (fig. 4).[7] Moreover, the city of Zion resembled Philadelphia in format more than a New England village. Philadelphia, like the city of Zion, had straight streets, square blocks, and a square placed precisely in the center of the grid where the public buildings were to stand (fig. 5). In the 1820s and 1830s, New England towns were just beginning to develop small village greens, and they usually knew little of straight streets. Much more in the city mode, Zion resembled Washington, D.C. (fig. 6). Jefferson thought the federal capital would fit into 1,500 acres, about the same size as Zion, and had asked for 100-foot-wide streets, grand boulevards by standards of the time, comparable to Joseph's 132-foot-wide streets. (In the revised plat, Joseph narrowed most streets to 82 $^1/_2$ feet, but so did L'Enfant, reducing Washington's to 80-foot widths.)[8] We have no idea of the origins of Joseph's spacious conceptions, but they certainly do not conform to the New England town model.[9]

The city of Zion, moreover, was situated differently in its worldwide geography. New England towns existed more or less on a level plane, with Boston and a few other commercial centers elevated above the rest. The city of Zion stood at the center of a global vortex; all converts were to turn their faces to Zion. It was a place of refuge in the apocalyptic destructions that were to precede the coming of Christ. The revelations called Zion the "center place," the point where all the Saints were to gather (D&C 45:66; 57:1–3). New England towns were dotted more or less evenly across the landscape; Zion was the point toward which all the gathering routes converged.

Temple as Primal Architectural Space

In another departure from New England conventions, Joseph added a third dimension to the two-part Mormon geography of gathering and city: architectural space. At the center of the city, on two central squares, would rise twenty-four temples, quite unlike anything in New England towns, even if we take into account the village greens with their churches, banks, and schools. A few lines on the plat descriptions do make the temples sound like the civic structures planned for Philadelphia's public square. The lines read, "The painted squares in the middle are for public buildings" and go on to explain, "It will require twenty-four buildings to supply them with houses of worship, schools, etc." Those are the words of conventional town planning, but in the next paragraph, the titles for the temples shoot off into the heavens. Each temple is numbered on the plat and a title assigned to each group of three: "Numbers 10, 11, 12, are to be called House of the Lord, for the Presidency of the High and Most Holy Priesthood, after the order of Melchizedek, which was after the order of the Son of God, upon Mount Zion, City of the New Jerusalem." Each trio had similarly elaborate names: "Numbers 19, 20, 21, House of the Lord, the Law of the

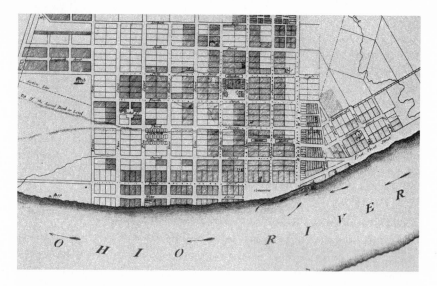

FIG. 4. Plan for Cincinnati, Ohio (1815). School, church, and market converged at Cincinnati's town center. Below the shops designated "Market" are the Lancaster Seminary and the Presbyterian church. John W. Reps, *The Making of Urban America: A History of City Planning in the United States* (Princeton: Princeton University Press, 1965), 226.

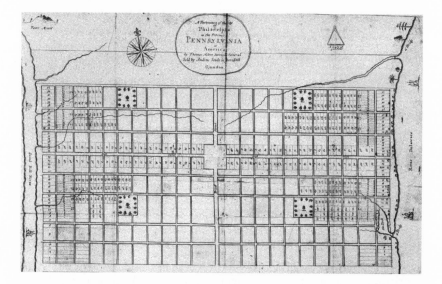

FIG. 5. Plan for Philadelphia, Pennsylvania (1682). Thomas Holme, surveyor-general for William Penn's new colony, laid out perpendicular steets and a ten-acre public square (*center*) he said was for schools, markets, churches, and government houses. John W. Reps, *The Making of Urban America: A History of City Planning in the United States* (Princeton: Princeton University Press, 1965), 161–62.

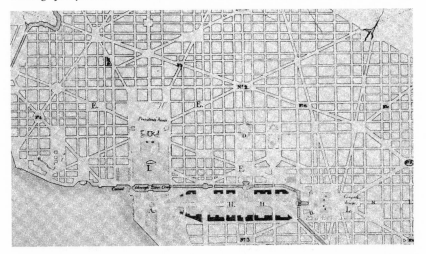

FIG. 6. Plan for Washington, D.C. (1791). Pierre Charles L'Enfant's plan had wide streets converging on the White House and Capitol buildings. The dark lines extending from the Capitol were to be public gardens bordering an avenue four hundred feet wide and nearly a mile long—the present-day Mall. John W. Reps, *The Making of Urban America: A History of City Planning in the United States* (Princeton: Princeton University Press, 1965), 251.

Kingdom of Heaven, and Messenger to the People; for the Highest Priesthood after the Order of Aaron." All eight titles are couched in an extravagant language that suggests exotic functions not to be imagined in New England or Philadelphia public buildings.[10]

This third spatial dimension, temples, appeared on Mormon maps from the beginning, even when the uses of the temples were largely unknown. The only known purpose for the temple in Independence, when it was designated in an 1831 revelation, was to be a place for the return of Jesus. The lack of known functions for the temples implies that the space was to be created first and its uses derived afterward. The purposes of the twenty-four temples on the Jackson County plat never got beyond the vague hints in the descriptions. In Kirtland, the revelations called for two buildings: one a temple for the "work of the presidency" and the other a twin of the first on an adjoining lot for printing and translating—a structure that was never built (see D&C 94). As it worked out in the cities Joseph did build, the functions of the twenty-four temples were boiled down to fit into one building that served a variety of purposes (fig. 7).

Little by little, this single temple's place in Mormon space was clarified. In a revelation in Jackson County in 1831, the site of the temple in Independence was called the "center place," and a year later another revelation said, "The city New Jerusalem shall be built by the gathering of the saints, beginning at this place, even the place of the temple" (D&C 57:3; 84:4). The city

was the center of gathering, and the temple was the beginning of the city—
the center of the center—thus connecting the temple to the whole world.[11]
Gradually between 1831 and 1835, the dynamic of this spatial formation
took shape. Converts from all over the earth were to collect in the central
city to be "endowed with power" and then go back into the wide world to
teach the gospel (D&C 38:32–33, 38; 39:15; 43:16; 95:8; 105:11–12). The temple,
the city, and the gathering formed a pattern of movement and preparation
in a distinctive Mormon geography.[12]

It is difficult to grasp exactly what the endowment of power in the
temple entailed. Partly it was a pentecostal experience of spiritual illumina-
tion, visions, and even a view of God's face. "Let thy house be filled, as with
a rushing mighty wind, with thy glory," Joseph prayed at Kirtland (D&C
109:37). Partly the endowment involved learning through rituals and ordinances, such as the washing of feet, and through study of the "best books"

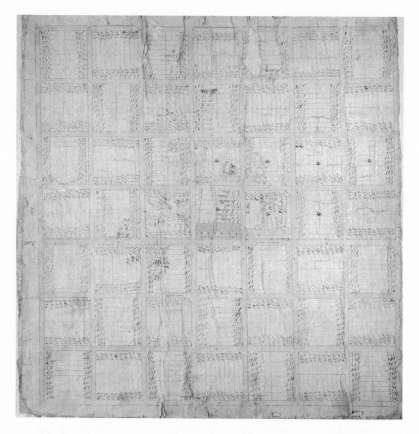

FIG. 7. Plat for Kirtland, Ohio (1833). A single city block holds temples at the center of
this plan for Kirtland. Unlike the plat for the city of Zion, all streets on the Kirtland plat
are the same width.

(D&C 88:118). Partly it was purification to rid the people of every sin. "Sanctify yourselves that your minds become single to God, and the days will come that you shall see him" (D&C 88:68).

The combination of holy experience, knowledge, and righteousness was to empower the recipients spiritually, enabling them to preach more convincingly. Having been strengthened and instructed, they were to go out into the world and harvest more souls.[13] In the dedicatory prayer in the Kirtland temple, Joseph asked that "thy servants may go forth from this house armed with thy power" and "from this place . . . bear exceedingly great and glorious tidings, in truth, unto the ends of the earth" (D&C 109:22–23). The whole scheme divided space in two, with Zion and the temple at the center emanating spiritual power, and a Babylon-like world outside, where people were to be converted and brought to Zion, the missionaries going out and the converts coming in.[14]

Joseph spoke of this combination of tasks, spaces, and movements as "the work."[15] As he realized almost immediately after the Church's organization, the work required the three-part combination of temple, city, and gathering; and wherever circumstances led him, he strove with all his might to bring those spaces into existence. However impoverished and despairing the Saints were after moving to a new place, he began at once to reignite the work and construct these spaces. A simple temple was planned for Jackson County before the Saints were expelled in 1833. Though only a shed-like structure with a plain facade, the Independence temple had two assembly rooms and double altars like the later Kirtland temple. Then, while the Saints in Jackson County were still putting down their roots, Joseph made plans for Kirtland. Though the Saints owned very little land and were relative newcomers, he mapped a plat for Kirtland on the model of the city of Zion. A revelation in May 1833 referred to Kirtland as "the city of the stake of Zion," and at the center was to be a house of the Lord just as in Independence (D&C 94:1). After being driven out of Kirtland, Joseph repeated this process at Far West, again planning for a temple and mapping a city plat, this time with one center square, but with the same 132-foot-wide main streets and 82 ½-foot-wide side streets.[16] At Nauvoo the temple was again the leading feature on the plat of the city prepared by Gustavus Hill. After Joseph's death, Brigham Young replicated the pattern in Utah. By this time, the basic model was ingrained in Mormon practice. In five locations from Jackson County to Salt Lake City, the Saints reconstructed the gathering-city-temple model of space that was mapped within a year after the organization of the Church.[17]

Joseph built temples to the neglect of far more sensible chapels and meetinghouses. As the Church grew in Kirtland, the brethren suggested that they enlarge their meetinghouse like the other denominations in town. Joseph would have none of it, even with converts arriving by the hundreds. He proposed a building that would be huge for the time: 65 by 65 feet wide and two stories high, with a 120-foot bell tower entirely out of scale for the little village even now.[18] Later, in Nauvoo, the same vision possessed him. He could not even be bothered to find suitable places for the Saints to meet on Sundays. They collected in houses, back rooms of stores and printing offices, and, in good weather, out of doors; they never did build a proper chapel, even when the Mormon population surged to over ten thousand. The building effort all went into a temple that stretched their resources to the limits, as if the temple was a vital part of the work and chapels and Sunday meetings were incidental.[19]

The temple was early Mormonism's primal architectural space just as the city was its living space and the gathering routes from the mission fields were its world geography. Joseph's temples, like temples throughout history, focused sacred power at a single spot. Temples are traditionally the places where heaven touches the earth; in them the true nature of the cosmos and the individual person is laid down in ritual and architecture. "The temple is the reduced plan of the cosmos," the temple scholar John Lundquist has written, "and as such must be an accurate representation of the heavenly prototype."[20] Temples are similarly models for the body, which is sometimes called a temple.[21] People enter temples to divine the meaning of existence and to put themselves in touch with the holy.[22] Joseph Smith's temples, located in the center (or in the case of Nauvoo, at the high point) of a central city, sacralized the landscape. At Kirtland, Joseph prayed that God's "holy presence may be continually in this house" (D&C 110:12–13). Instead of all spaces having an equal amount of divine presence, in this one space, the temple, God was present in greater intensity, sharply focusing Mormon religious space.

The Mormons' sacred geography had no equivalent elsewhere in the United States.[23] Americans scattered their church buildings, putting up two or three in a single little town. Evangelical Christians would say God was diffused even more widely, into the hearts of all believers. No one place or building could lay special claim to God's presence. The American religious landscape was flat, with no foci, no peaks, no vortexes; divinity was spread democratically through religious space just as political rights were distributed through civic space.

The closest most Americans came to focused holiness was in the presence of sublime nature. Many visitors felt exalted as they stood before Niagara Falls or looked from a high promontory at the great bend in the Connecticut River. "If, in th' immensity of space," an observer at Niagara wrote, "God makes one spot his special dwelling-place, / That spot is this."[24] But sublime nature was not like Mormon space either, for the most inspiring scenes lay outside of settled society, beyond the margins of everyday life, while the Mormon temple stood at the center of the city, where daily life circulated around it.

Nauvoo and Chicago

Was there anything like the temple and the city of Zion in the contemporary United States? More like Mormon geography than any other religious configuration was the space that formed around Nauvoo's neighbor two hundred miles to the east, Chicago. Chicago came into its own within a few years of Nauvoo's founding and, though raised on entirely different principles, had a parallel spatial structure based on the powerful attraction of its markets. The signs of its future greatness were recognized soon after the United States received title to Chicago from the Indians in 1833. The continental divide, between Lake Michigan and the Atlantic Ocean on one side and the Mississippi and the Gulf of Mexico on the other, lay just a few miles southwest of Chicago and only about fifteen feet above the level of the lake. A swampy patch of ground covered the divide, and in high water season, a canoe could traverse it without portaging, making it possible theoretically to canoe from the Gulf of St. Lawrence through the lakes, up the Chicago River and across the portage to the Illinois and Mississippi Rivers and finally down to New Orleans, all without leaving the water. Developers immediately saw that a relatively short canal could connect Chicago on Lake Michigan to the tributaries of the Mississippi, putting the Great Lakes in touch with the Gulf of Mexico.[25]

For four years after the Indian treaty in 1833, the city boomed. Population leaped from four hundred to four thousand, and land prices rose proportionately. Plans were laid out for a canal and a railroad, and the city was on its way. Then the nationwide Panic of 1837 stopped development in its tracks, and for the next seven years, while Nauvoo was growing, Chicago stood still. Only when the Saints were about to leave Illinois for the West did confidence return to Chicago. In 1848 the canal and the first stretch of railroad were completed, and the city began the sustained growth that made it the second largest in the nation by the end of the century.[26] At its peak population in 1846, Nauvoo may have been about as large as Chicago.

Chicago resembled Nauvoo in standing at the center of a vortex of converging forces. But in Chicago the magnet was the market rather than the temple (fig. 8). William Cronon's magnificent study of the Chicago hinterland, *Nature's Metropolis,* describes the Chicago market's organizing influence on forests and prairies hundreds of miles away from the city. "Those who sought to explain its unmatched expansion," he writes, "often saw it as being compelled by deep forces within nature itself, gathering the resources and energies of the Great West—the region stretching from the

Appalachians and the Great Lakes to the Rockies and the Pacific—and concentrating them in a single favored spot at the southwestern corner of Lake Michigan."[27] Lumbermen felled trees in remote forests, herded them downstream to the lake, where boards were sawn, and sent the finished products on to the city, where they were sold to house builders who furiously constructed dwellings for the mushrooming population. Cattlemen started their drives on distant prairies, headed the animals to the railheads, and put them into cars for slaughter at the Chicago market. Farmers plowed, planted, and harvested their grain, had it graded, and shipped it to Chicago to get the best price. For hundreds of miles in every direction, the Chicago market mobilized the energies, schemes, and hopes of virtually the entire countryside. If the people themselves did not come, the products of their work converged on Chicago, just as Mormon converts gathered to Nauvoo.

The shape of space was the same for the two cities—an expansive funnel collecting for a central city where energy was focused in a single institution. But the underlying principles were entirely different. The magnet for one was the market; for the other, the temple. Chicago's central principle was wealth; Nauvoo's, spiritual empowerment. Chicago's work was to collect products, bring them to market, and exchange them for money to purchase manufactured goods coming from the east by ship and rail.[28] Nauvoo's work was to collect converts, bring them to Nauvoo for instruction, fill them with divine intelligence, and prepare them for life in the city of Zion.[29]

Market and Temple Societies

With these two systems standing side by side, the natural question to ask is how the principles of market and temple affected the two societies.[30] The name Joseph gave to his city, Nauvoo, seems like a start on an answer, especially when we remember that the previous owners called the site Commerce. The earlier name expressed the hope that the flat pushing out into the Mississippi River had commercial possibilities. The rapids just below the city blocked downstream river traffic, making Commerce a natural terminus of shipping from further upstream. As early as 1830, a petition to Congress had requested federal aid to dig a canal to help realize the commercial potential. The drop in the river at Commerce also inspired hope that the Mississippi's vast energy could be harnessed for manufacturing, which, combined with the canal, promised a great future for the site.[31]

Joseph Smith did not squelch these dreams nor attack the mercantile capitalists who conceived them. The plan for Nauvoo showed a canal running across the peninsula down the main street just like the previous owners' plans for the city. John C. Bennett proposed a wing dam in the Mississippi to trap water for industrial use. Joseph did nothing to discourage these plans and even gave them his blessing.[32] His letters to Britain, where the

FIG. 8. The Great Hall of the Board of Trade, Chicago, Illinois.

Quorum of the Twelve was managing the missionary work, urged them to convert capitalists and send them to Nauvoo to develop manufactures. Joseph rather enthusiastically supported commerce.

And yet he changed the city's name from Commerce to Nauvoo, a Hebrew word signifying beauty and repose, as if he had something else in mind.[33] The change did not exactly signify opposition to commercial capitalism, only a desire to harness it to his own ends. His invitation to capitalists said nothing of profits or great wealth, and in fact he invited them to Nauvoo during a depression, a poor time to begin a new venture. Nauvoo had its great spurt in population in the middle of the slow economic times that put Chicago's growth on hold because people were reluctant to invest. Nauvoo's growth was not dependent on people making a lot of money as Chicago's was; other forces drove Joseph's city. The Prophet wanted the capitalists for one reason—to give work to the poor. In "A Proclamation of the First Presidency of the Church to the Saints Scattered Abroad," he urged all "who have been blessed of heaven with the possession of this world's goods" to "establish and build up manufactures in the city" in order to "strengthen our hands, and assist in promoting the happiness of the Saints."[34] Joseph's eyes were on the people moving along the gathering routes and on the thousands already in Nauvoo. They needed jobs, and the capitalists could provide them. Capitalism was welcome in Nauvoo, but on Joseph's terms to advance "the work."

In Chicago, the commanding purpose was wealth. Even the streets had a different look. By the late 1840s, Chicago had three hundred dry goods shops and grocers, doing a million dollars' worth of business a year, not counting hundreds of artisan shops where craftsmen plied their trades. Nauvoo had only a few general stores and a handful of artisan shops.[35] Wagonloads of outlying farmers did not converge on Nauvoo, as they did on Chicago, to sell the products of a year's labor. In Chicago a farmer saw in one day 1,200 wagons full of wheat, harvested to exchange for clothes and tools.[36] In Nauvoo, trade was between the city's own residents and settlers from the immediate vicinity. If Nauvoo's reach for converts was worldwide, its commercial reach went only a few miles into the countryside.

Less tangible differences in the two cities are more difficult to measure. How did the temple, on the highest spot in Nauvoo, make life different from Chicago, where the Board of Trade with its cavernous hall echoing the shouts of the traders focused activity (fig. 9)? What ideas of manhood and womanhood prevailed when divine intelligence was valued more than wealth? We must assume power went to people of a different sort. For its first mayor, Chicago elected William B. Ogden, born the same year as Joseph Smith and the epitome of the best commercial values. He was attracted to Chicago by real estate speculation, made a fortune in land and railroads, and had enough surplus capital to give Cyrus McCormick, inventor of the grain reaper, his start. Ogden exemplified the successful man of business and civic leadership. He was the first president of the Union Pacific Railroad, president of Rush Medical College, and president of the University of Chicago Board of Trustees. Ogden was Chicago's leading citizen and the embodiment of a business society's finest qualities.

The mayor of Nauvoo tried to sell real estate in his city but kept making mistakes. At one point, he declared bankruptcy, and he died with little property.[37] Without wealth or business success to his credit, Joseph Smith was given all the highest posts in the city and received its nomination for U.S. president—and why? Because in the minds of the converts, he opened a conduit to heaven. He promised glories in the hereafter and divine authority to seal marriages and baptize for the dead. He spoke of gods and of ruling other worlds. Joseph Smith could come to power only in a society where divine intelligence and spiritual power outranked wealth and business acumen on the scale of values.

Courtesy LDS Church Archives

FIG. 9. Nauvoo Temple, Nauvoo, Illinois (ca. 1846). The temple, built on bluffs overlooking the Mississippi River, oriented Mormon spiritual and temporal interests.

Mormon Space Over Time

The Marxists tell us that in a market society people turn themselves into commodities. We package ourselves, sell ourselves, and value people for their worth in the market of social exchange—that is, by status or position. We become in our essence what we are in our work—a professor, a stockbroker, a secretary, a car mechanic. The market invades our imaginations and takes over our ways of thinking about all of life. How would people in a temple society conceive of themselves and other people? What would be the metaphors to govern self-understanding in Zion? These questions must be asked of nineteenth-century Mormon space, even if the answers are unclear.[38]

Thinking in this vein, I came across a passage in Plato's *Republic* where Socrates and Glaucon describe an ideal man of understanding who refuses to pursue power or wealth like most men of his time. The questioner asks how the man can go on living in the city when doing so goes against common sense. The answer is that he does not live in an earthly city but in an ideal city, for only there can he be his best person. "In heaven," Socrates says, "there is laid up a pattern of it, methinks, which he who desires may behold, and beholding, may set his own house in order. But whether such an one exists, or ever will exist in fact, is no matter; for he will live after the manner of that city, having nothing to do with any other."[39] Elsewhere, in his *Laws*, Plato argues that priorities must be changed for human life to flourish. "There are in all three things about which every man has an interest; and the interest about money, when rightly regarded, is the third and lowest of them: midway comes the interest of the body; and, first of all, that of the soul; and the state which we are describing will have been rightly constituted if it ordains honours according to this scale."[40] Joseph Smith, knowing nothing of this philosophical tradition, tried to build the heavenly city on earth and to put the cause of the soul first.

Nauvoo did not long survive Joseph Smith. Just as Chicago was taking off, Nauvoo was obliterated. Within two years after Joseph's death, a majority of Mormon residents were straggling westward across the Iowa prairie, and the city was left empty. Two years later, an arsonist burned the temple. Thereafter, Nauvoo fell into a deep sleep from which it awakened in the twentieth century as a historical shrine.

But the destruction of the physical city did not erase Joseph Smith's map from Mormon minds. "The work" began again the moment the Saints reached the Salt Lake Valley. The city of Zion rose at the foot of the Wasatch mountains, and Brigham Young filled up the world with smaller satellite cities. Until the end of the century, the Mormon vortex gathered people with ever-increasing force. And at the center of Salt Lake, the temple anchored the whole system, as it had done in previous Zions.

While the work went on as before, Mormon space also evolved during its Utah years. Long before the Salt Lake temple's completion, it had numerous competitors in the realm of sacred space. In Utah, Mormons for the first time constructed chapels for worship and activity, creating hundreds of little epicenters of religious life. The diffusion of church buildings necessarily flattened the religious landscape, making Mormon space more like Protestant space. In the twentieth century, chapel and temple building has accelerated wherever the Saints reside, while the voice and face of the Church president, relayed via satellite, are heard and seen on every continent. In modern Mormon space, one temple and one city do not focus a global geography as they once did; Salt Lake City is head-quarters rather than the central place. The reversal of the gathering doc-trine, coupled with this multiplication of temples and chapels, means that Mormon space is no longer a funnel with light from a single center. Mis-sionaries gather converts into thousands of wards and stakes found almost everywhere.[41]

These changes may appear to support the common reading of Mor-mon history as a twentieth-century apostasy from a nineteenth-century visionary culture, a decline like the better-known decline of Puritanism in colonial America. I am not persuaded by that understanding of Mormon history, nor do I believe that Joseph Smith would have regretted the spread of temples and chapels around the globe. He himself hinted that there would be temples in other places. He did not think of the temple, as the ancient Jews did, as a singular location. If Joseph Smith was nothing else, he was expansive, and he saw virtually unlimited possibilities for the work he began. The global ambitions of Mormonism today would have pleased him.

But if *apostasy* is not the right word, then *change* certainly is. For Mor-monism's spatial configuration has evolved over a century and a half. In the early Church, Joseph believed that the work required converts to gather, and so he pulled them out of the world into a city where divine intelligence would illuminate their lives and make them into Saints. He built his cities more or less without heed to the commercial forces organizing national space in nineteenth-century America. He gathered people with promises of a spiritual endowment, not wealth. The converts who came to Nauvoo from many backgrounds, Joseph said, all "feel a great attachment to the cause of truth." If they would hold on and live right, he predicted, "the intelligence of heaven will be communicated to them, and they will, even-tually, see eye to eye, and rejoice in the full fruition of that glory which is reserved for the righteous."[42] That he attracted so many to his peculiar reli-gious enterprise in a period when the market was riding high is a tribute to the force of his remarkable vision.

NOTES

1. Claudia L. Bushman, ed., *Mormon Sisters: Women in Early Utah* (Cambridge, Mass.: Emmeline, 1976).

2. Richard L. Bushman, *Joseph Smith and the Beginnings of Mormonism* (Urbana: University of Illinois Press, 1984).

3. J. B. Harley, "Maps, Knowledge, and Power," in Denis Cosgrove and Stephen Daniels, *The Iconography of Landscape: Essays on the Symbolic Representation, Design and Use of Past Environments,* Cambridge Studies in Historical Geography, vol. 9 (Cambridge: Cambridge University Press, 1988), 281–82, 302.

4. C. Mark Hamilton, *Nineteenth-Century Mormon Architecture and City Planning* (New York: Oxford University Press, 1995), 15–18, 33–34.

5. John W. Reps, *The Making of Urban America: A History of City Planning in the United States* (Princeton: Princeton University Press, 1965), 15–16, 19, 24.

6. John Warner Barber, *Historical Collections, Being a General Collection of Interesting Facts, Traditions, Biographical Sketches, Anecdotes, etc., Relating to the History and Antiquities of Every Town in Massachusetts, with Geographical Descriptions, Illustrated by 200 Engravings* (Worcester: Dorr, Howland, 1840).

7. Warren S. Thompson and P. K. Whelpton, *Population Trends in the United States* (New York: McGraw-Hill, 1933), 26; *U.S. Census* (1830). According to Thompson and Whelpton, there were fifty-eight towns with populations between 2,500 and 10,000, and sixteen with populations between 10,000 and 25,000. The population projection for the city of Zion put it in the top quarter of all American cities in 1830. Only one city, New York, had over 100,000 people at that time.

8. Reps, *Making of Urban America,* 243, 245, 250. Joseph's four main boulevards remained a generous 132 feet wide.

9. Thomas Graves, the surveyor and engineer for the Massachusetts Bay Company in 1629, favored square towns with a meetinghouse at the center, but with farmers on forty-acre farm lots and fewer than 150 families per town, compared to the city of Zion's 2,600 house lots. Sylvia Doughty Fries, *The Urban Idea in Colonial America* (Philadelphia: Temple University Press, 1977), 48–49. Fries argues that Puritans were wary of urban concentrations and wanted to plant small country towns. James Machor resists Fries's anti-urban emphasis and sees the Puritans configuring an urban-pastoral landscape where town and country blend and people enjoy the virtues of both. James L. Machor, *Pastoral Cities: Urban Ideals and the Symbolic Landscape of America* (Madison: University of Wisconsin Press, 1987), 47–70.

John Reps, the leading student of town planning in the United States, links Joseph Smith's square cities and farms outside the city boundaries to the biblical cities described in Numbers 35:1–5 and Ezekiel 42, 45, and 48. Reps, *Making of Urban America,* 472. For analysis of Puritan adaptations of the biblical cities, see Fries, *Urban Idea in Colonial America,* 64–66.

10. I read into these incongruent descriptions the divergent minds of Joseph Smith and Frederick Williams. Joseph calls for twenty-four temples and Frederick asks, "What for?" They are public buildings, Williams concludes, and Joseph lets it pass, for they were that, though their potential uses were far more elegant than Joseph could then explain or perhaps even understood himself.

11. A Latter-day Saint convert in Nauvoo understood that the Saints gathered for safety's sake in the first place, and then "that they may build a sanctuary to the name of the Most High . . . and attend to such ordinances and receive such blessings as they could not while scattered upon the face of the whole earth." Francis Moon, quoted in

Robert Bruce Flanders, *Nauvoo: Kingdom on the Mississippi* (Urbana: University of Illinois Press, 1965), 69–70.

12. The reason for gathering was partly to build the city and the temple. As Joseph Smith explained,

> He that believeth shall not make haste, but let all the Saints who desire to keep the commandments of heaven and work righteousness, come to the place of gathering as soon as circumstances will permit. It is by united efforts that great things are accomplished, and while the Saints are scattered to the four winds, they cannot be united in action, if they are in spirit; they cannot all build at one city, or lift at one stone of the great Temple, though their hearts may all desire the same thing. (Joseph Smith Jr., *History of the Church of Jesus Christ of Latter-day Saints,* ed. B. H. Roberts, 2d ed., rev., 7 vols. [Salt Lake City: Deseret Book, 1971], 4:450 [hereafter cited as *History of the Church*])

13. The meaning of the endowment of power seems especially to be the burden of *Doctrine and Covenants* 88, though many passages in the revelations speak to the same end. The dedicatory prayer at the Kirtland temple summed up much of Joseph's vision of a Zion people.

14. In "An Epistle of the Twelve Apostles to the Saints Scattered Abroad in England, Scotland, Ireland, Wales, the Isle of Man, and the Eastern Continent," dated November 15, 1841, Joseph Smith declared:

> The first great object before us, and the Saints generally, is to help forward the completion of the Temple and the Nauvoo House— buildings which are now in progress according to the revelations, and which must be completed to secure the salvation of the Church in the last days; for God requires of His Saints to build Him a house wherein His servants may be instructed, and endowed with power from on high, to prepare them to go forth among the nations, and proclaim the fullness of the Gospel for the last time, and bind up the law, and seal up the testimony, leaving this generation without excuse, and the earth prepared for the judgments which will follow. In this house all the ordinances will be made manifest, and many things will be shown forth, which have been hid from generation to generation. (*History of the Church,* 4:449)

The center-periphery division shows up in writings to "the Saints scattered abroad," and in the verb "go forth," commonly used for missionaries sent from Zion into the world. Zion was home, peace, and truth; the world was darkness, struggle, and danger.

15. The revelations used the word *work* to describe the program of the Church well before the program's scope was fully understood. See, for example, *Doctrine and Covenants* 4:3; 11:1, 9; 12:1; 14:1; 52:11. The "work" was seen in its full dimensions in the passages surrounding *Doctrine and Covenants* 88:73. In January 1841, "A Proclamation of the First Presidency of the Church to the Saints Scattered Abroad" summed up "the work" in one sentence:

> The Temple of the Lord is in process of erection here, where the Saints will come to worship the God of their fathers, according to the order of His house and the powers of the Holy Priesthood, and

will be so constructed as to enable all the functions of the Priest-
hood to be duly exercised, and where instructions from the Most
High will be received, and from this place go forth to distant lands.
(*History of the Church*, 4:269)

16. Reps, *Making of Urban America*, 468–69.

17. For temple architecture, see Laurel B. Andrew, *The Early Temples of the
Mormons: The Architecture of the Millennial Kingdom in the American West* (Albany:
State University of New York Press, 1978); for the town plats, see Hamilton, *Nineteenth-
Century Mormon Architecture*, 33–37, 39.

18. On the architecture and design of the Kirtland Temple, see Elwin C. Robison,
*The First Mormon Temple: Design, Construction, and Historic Context of the Kirtland
Temple* (Provo: Brigham Young University Press, 1997).

19. On the absence of Mormon meetinghouses and the comparison to other
denominations, see Milton V. Backman Jr., *The Heavens Resound: A History of the
Latter-day Saints in Ohio, 1830–1838* (Salt Lake City: Deseret Book, 1983), 38–39, 275–76;
and Andrew, *Early Temples*, 59.

20. John M. Lundquist, *The Temple: Meeting Place of Heaven and Earth* (London:
Thames and Hudson, 1993), 12.

21. On the homologies of temple, home, body, and heart, see Gerardus van der
Leeuw, *Religion in Essence and Manifestation*, trans. J. E. Turner (1933; Princeton:
Princeton University Press, 1986); and David Chidester and Edward T. Linenthal, eds.,
American Sacred Space (Bloomington: Indiana University Press, 1995), 7.

22. The orienting function of sacred space is well described in a study of American
sacred space.

> In its material production and practical reproduction, sacred space
> anchors a worldview in the world. As the anthropologist Robert
> Redfield suggested, a worldview is comprised of at least two
> dimensions: classification of persons, and orientation in space and
> time. Sacred space is a means for grounding classifications and ori-
> entations in reality, giving particular force to the meaningful focus
> gained through these aspects of a worldview. Sacred places focus
> more general orientations in space and time that distinguish center
> from periphery, inside from outside, up from down, and a recol-
> lected past from a meaningful present or an anticipated future.
> (Chidester and Linenthal, *American Sacred Space*, 12)

Joseph Fielding, an English convert who first saw the site of the Nauvoo temple in
1841, spoke of the temple as an earthly prototype of heaven:

> It would be vain to attempt to describe my feelings on beholding
> this interesting sight; but if you have the same faith as myself in the
> great work of God, and consider that the things on earth are pat-
> terns of things in heaven, at the same time look back on the form of
> the temple and font, you may judge of my feelings. Many have been
> baptized therein for their deceased relatives, and also for the healing
> of their own afflicted bodies. (Quoted in Flanders, *Nauvoo*, 87–88)

23. For a useful overview of the literature and relevant theory on sacred space in
the United States, see Chidester and Linenthal, *American Sacred Space*, 1–42.

24. Quoted in Patrick McGreevy, "Niagara as Jerusalem," *Landscape* 28 (1985): 29.
For the designations of sacred sites in America, see Edward Tabor Linenthal, *Sacred*

Ground: Americans and Their Battlefields (Urbana: University of Illinois Press, 1991);
and John E. Sears, *Sacred Places: American Tourist Attractions in the Nineteenth Century*
(New York: Oxford University Press, 1989).

25. William Cronon, *Nature's Metropolis: Chicago and the Great West* (New York:
W. W. Norton, 1991), 24–25, 31–33.

26. Cronon, *Nature's Metropolis*, 29–30, 64–93.

27. Ibid., 9.

28. Cronon spelled this out:

> Although no booster would have put it quite so bluntly, the center
> of metropolitan empire—and of Turner's frontier—was the mar-
> ketplace of modern capitalism. When Turner spoke of the frontier
> as "the outer edge of the wave," what he unintentionally described
> was not some implicitly racist "meeting point between savagery
> and civilization" but the ongoing extension of market relations
> into the ways human beings used the land—and each other—in
> the Great West. (Ibid., 52–53)

29. There seems to be general agreement among historians about the religious
motivation behind the nineteenth-century Mormon gathering. As Arrington and Bitton put it:

> One must remember that in many ways Mormonism was the least
> attractive of the several available means of emigration to a new
> country. Demanding of the emigrant strict obedience and contin-
> uing economic sacrifice, it offered in return a home in one of the
> least inviting regions of the hemisphere. Clearly the Mormon reli-
> gion itself, if not the sole factor behind the emigration, was the key
> to the process. (Leonard J. Arrington and Davis Bitton, *The Mor-
> mon Experience: A History of the Latter-day Saints* [New York:
> Alfred A. Knopf, 1979], 129)

Laurel Andrew recognized the absence of economic attraction in Nauvoo:

> Nauvoo, whose sole basis for existence was religious, was an artifi-
> cial creation with no foundation in commerce or manufacturing;
> moreover an unusual number of its members could not contribute
> capital or skills. . . . Its return to somnolence after the Mormon
> exodus is indicative of the limited possibilities which this location
> offered. (Andrew, *Early Temples*, 56–57)

30. The theoretical explanations for Chicago, advanced by nineteenth-century
theorists of city growth, emphasized commerce as the governing principle. Cronon,
Nature's Metropolis, 34–43, 53–54.

31. Flanders, *Nauvoo*, 40.

32. On Nauvoo's commercial possibilities, see ibid., 40, 43, 150–51, 153.

33. Ibid., 41; *History of the Church*, 4:121.

34. *History of the Church*, 4:268–69.

35. Cronon, *Nature's Metropolis*, 60; Flanders, *Nauvoo*, 153–54.

36. Cronon, *Nature's Metropolis*, 59–60.

37. For the bankruptcy case and the land business in Nauvoo, see Flanders, *Nauvoo*,
115–43, 168–69.

38. Along with the market, democratic politics is the other source of ruling
metaphors in modern American society. In one we buy and sell; in the other we vote as

deliberative and equal citizens. In a temple society, people come into God's presence to be spiritually empowered.

39. *The Dialogues of Plato*, trans. B. Jowett, 2 vols. (1892; New York: Random House, 1937), 1:851.

40. Ibid., 2:509–10.

41. On the termination of gathering, see Arrington and Bitton, *Mormon Experience*, 140.

42. *History of the Church*, 4:272–73.

13

The Visionary World of Joseph Smith

Cultural historians use the word situate *to describe the process of relating a person or an idea to the surrounding culture. How did an idea resemble or differ from other cultural formations? How did it function? How did it develop? To situate an idea does not imply identifying its source but merely establishing a relationship.*

This was the task that fell on me in writing a cultural biography of Joseph Smith. I had to situate him in early-nineteenth-century American culture, not to discover the sources of his ideas but to describe his place in his time. Soon after I started, I began looking into the foremost words or principles in Joseph Smith's life. Vision *was one of these. I knew that the Transcendentalists sought for visions, and other Christians sometimes experienced revelation, but not until I investigated the subject did I discover how widespread visions were in early America. I thought of this essay as an interim report on what I found.*

Latter-day Saints may be perplexed by the reports of so many visions in Joseph Smith's time. We tend to think of the First Vision as unique. The natural Latter-day Saint response is to ask, Were the other visions valid? In this essay, I recommend a certain humility in judging the ways of God with mankind. Latter-day Saints must leave open the possibility of others besides Joseph Smith hearing from the heavens.

In the fall of 1829, when the first proofs of the Book of Mormon were coming off E. B. Grandin's press in Palmyra, Solomon Chamberlin, a restless religious spirit who lived twenty miles to the east, broke a journey to Upper Canada, stopping not far from the residence of Joseph Smith Sr. Born in Canaan, Connecticut, in 1788, Chamberlin had joined the Methodist Episcopals at age nineteen, moved on to the Reformed Methodist Church about seven years later, and then tried life on a communal farm where property was held in common, following the New Testament pattern.

Dissatisfied with the religions he had tried, Chamberlin prayed for further guidance, and in 1816, according to his account, "the Lord revealed to me in a vision of the night an angel,"[1] whom Chamberlin asked about the right way. The angel told him that the churches were corrupt and that God would soon raise up an apostolic church. Chamberlin printed up an account of his visions and was still distributing them and looking for the apostolic church when he stopped in Palmyra.[2]

In "A Short Sketch of the Life of Solomon Chamberlain," written at Beaver, Utah, when Chamberlin was nearly seventy, he said, "When the boat came to Palmyra, I felt as if some genii or good Spirit told me to leave the boat." Guided by his inspiration, Chamberlin walked south from the town center and heard about the "gold bible" at the house where he spent the night. The next day, he made his way to the place where Joseph Smith Sr. was living.

> [I] found Hyrum [Smith] walking the floor, As I entered the door, I said, peace be to this house. He looked at me as one astonished, and said, I hope it will be peace, I then said, Is there any one here that believes in visions or revelations he said Yes, we are a visionary house. I said, Then I will give you one of my pamphlets, which was visionary, and of my own experience. They then called the people together, which consisted of five or six men who were out at the door. Father Smith was one and some of the Whitmer's. They then sat down and read my pamphlet. Hyrum read first, but was so affected he could not read it. He then gave it to a man, which I learned was Christian Whitmer, he finished reading it. I then opened my mouth and began to preach to them, in the words that the angel had made known to me in the vision, that all Churches and Denominations on the earth had become corrupt, and no Church of God on the earth but that he would shortly rise up a Church, that would never be confounded nor brought down and be like unto the Apostolic Church. They wondered greatly who had been telling me these things, for said they we have the same things wrote down in our house, taken from the Gold record, that you are preaching to us. I said, the Lord told me these things a number of years ago, I then said, If you are a visionary house, I wish you would make known some of your discoveries, for I think I can bear them.

After hearing the Smiths' story, Chamberlin was convinced that this was the work he was looking for. The Smiths gave him sixty-four pages of Book of Mormon proofs, and he set off again for Canada, this time as a missionary for the gold bible. Chamberlin was later baptized by Joseph Smith and, in 1862, died in Washington County, Utah.[3]

Chamberlin's story captures the attention of anyone interested in the cultural history of Joseph Smith's time. One reason is that Solomon and Hyrum, though complete strangers when they met in 1829, recognized each other as kindred spirits. When Solomon asked Hyrum if he believed in visions or revelations, Hyrum answered, "Yes, we are a visionary house." Apparently Hyrum saw in Chamberlin's pamphlet the same message that he and the others had learned from Joseph's experiences and from the Book of Mormon. At least as Solomon told the story—and John Taylor later copied the whole account into his Nauvoo journal—Joseph Smith and Solomon Chamberlin had received similar instructions from heaven.[4]

Chamberlin's story of meeting the Smiths, although involving only himself and a half dozen others, had wider implications. Chamberlin's and Hyrum's mutual understanding of the word *visionary* implies a general category of people who were known to believe in visions. For the recognition to occur, visionary houses and visionary persons must have been a well-known type. Solomon and Hyrum shared membership in a class of people who believed that the heavens sometimes opened to human view.

Evidence of this early-nineteenth-century visionary culture can be found in today's computer culture with a few clicks of a mouse. The heading "visions" turns up a dozen titles in a standard research library's catalog, and a little more searching produces more. I have found thirty-two pamphlets that relate visionary experiences published in the United States between 1783 and 1815, all but seven about visions experienced after 1776 (see pp. 211–13 below).

Still more visions are embedded in religious autobiographies of the period. The famed revivalist Charles Grandison Finney, for example, who was living in Adams, New York, in 1821, stole into the woods to pray privately for forgiveness and afterward in his law office had a vision of the Savior. "It seemed as if I met the Lord Jesus Christ face to face," he wrote in his autobiography. Later in life, he decided the vision was "a mental state," but at the time, he said, "It seemed to me that I saw him as I would see any other man. It seemed to me a reality, that he stood before me, and I fell down at his feet and poured out my soul to him."[5] Finney was not alone in thinking he had seen a heavenly being; many others, some on their way to careers as preachers and reformers like Finney, had such stories to tell.[6] With additional effort, more visionary pamphlets of the type studied here would doubtless be uncovered.[7]

The interest in visionary writings goes back in Anglo-American culture to a time when even the most educated segments of the population thought that supernatural wonders appeared in the heavens, and visions of angels and devils were open even to simple peasants.[8] Then as the Enlightenment developed momentum in the early eighteenth century, writers at the upper levels of society cast doubt on all the wonders of late Renaissance culture—magic, dreams, and visions—labeling them all superstition. Belief in supernatural miracles of any kind was left for credulous and ignorant common people. A 1793 parody of the visionary accounts offered the common elitist judgment that "a great part of mankind, in every age, are pleased with the marvellous. Stories of witchcraft, fairies, hobgobblins, revelations, visions, and trances always excitce [*sic*] the attention of the superstitious, gain belief, and afford them unspeakable pleasure." In the parodist's story, a visionary is caught in many foolish mistakes by "a man of discernment and knowledge," implying that discerning people would never believe such reports.[9] In that rationalist atmosphere, an educated man like Finney could not believe even his own visionary experience and, to protect his credibility, had to call it "a mental state."

But the Enlightenment could not dam all the currents of belief flowing from the seventeenth into the nineteenth century. An 1814 pamphlet published in Philadelphia went back to an earlier period for instances of divine occurrences, joining an older age to modern times. *Some Extraordinary Instances of Divine Guidance and Protection and Awful Warnings of a Just Retribution through Dreams and Visions* was a 108-page miscellany of various uncanny happenings and brushes with the supernatural collected from many times and places going back several centuries. Interspersed with a tale of Thomas Cranmer in the reign of Queen Mary Tudor was a 1798 "Account of a Trance or Vision of Sarah Alley, of Beekman Town, Dutchess County, State of New-York."[10] In the editor's eyes, the older world of wonders was as relevant in 1814 as the most recent vision, perhaps proving the parodist was right in thinking that the marvelous brought together people from every age.

Besides reprinting stories from centuries earlier, the visionary pamphlets mingled people of different nations and social classes. Experiences in England and Canada were on a par with those from the United States; only three of the thirty-two pamphlets in the sample directed their messages to America as a nation.[11] Gender and social class figured scarcely at all in the accounts. In a time when a female preacher would have been an oddity, women commonly had visions. Over a third of the accounts concerned female visionaries, and their stories gained hearers as readily as the men's. The pamphlets were virtually oblivious to social class. The stories that were carried over from England were somewhat more likely to speak of wealth and poverty; one of the American tales spoke of the subject's trouble in finding employment, and another told of a prostitute's repentance.[12] Otherwise, the stories, especially the American ones, were socially neutral. The wealth, the social position, the economic aspirations of the visionaries were nearly invisible. The classifications that mattered were religious: wickedness and righteousness, belief and disbelief, conversion or preconversion, illness and health. The stories united all kinds of people in a visionary culture.

Common religious themes, more than the visionaries' social position or national outlook, give the stories their characteristic flavor. Ten of the thirty-two pamphlets delivered apocalyptic warnings of impending judgments, usually without specifying the exact nature of the danger save that a conclusive change was near.[13] *A Dream, or Vision, by Samuel Ingalls, of Dunham, in the Province of Lower Canada, on the Night of Sept. 2, 1809* was typical of the apocalyptic visions. Standing on the bank of the White River in Vermont in 1809, a mile upstream from the Connecticut River and so within a few miles of the farm where Joseph Smith was born, Ingalls heard a rushing noise in the air; and instantly casting my eyes upward, there appeared to my view three carriages of polished gold, (in the form of the top of a chaise without wheels) passing through the air in a direct line abreast, and steering toward the South.

One carriage contained three women, the second three men, and the third "three Angels as I supposed by their having wings suspended from their shoulders." The angels sang a hymn from which Ingalls recalled one line: "Prepare to give me room, ye nations, I am coming!"[14]

Ingalls saw the angels descend over the town of Hartford on the west bank of the Connecticut River, where they paused to talk. They condemned to immediate destruction a "wicked club, who are laying plots to deceive the nations" and announced that God would spare the world for 140 years. Then they disappeared, and Ingalls's vision ended.[15] The author drew no moral, claimed no authority for himself, issued no explicit warning. For an apocalyptic people, the message was clear: Evil was abroad in the land, God surveyed it all, and the end was near.

Another apocalyptic visionary, Caleb Pool of Gloucester, Massachusetts, who published *News from Heaven* in 1805, opened his account by reporting that "God has been speaking by signs, by wonders and visions, to me for many years." In the first of his visions, he saw in a dream "two fierce bulls coming very fast in pursuit of me, roaring, and their tongues lolling out of their mouths." Provided with "the sword of the Spirit," he thrust it into the head of one and into the side of the other, causing them to flee. Pool's inspiration told him one bull was the devil and the other the evil spirit of the adversary "infused into men, raging wonderfully against the gospel." The bulls raged because their time was short: "God will convince them that are striving against his Holy Spirit in a few years, perhaps in two or three," and "they shall bow the knee to King Jesus." After other dreams and visions, Pool asked for an audience with his local parish congregation following their meeting and told them, "I come, to let you know that God is angry with you." He reported his dreams and visions "and with a loud voice called upon them to repent and turn unto the Lord." Meeting only disbelief, Pool predicted an imminent earthquake, which struck an hour later. The church people's disregard did not discourage Pool. He went on receiving visions, being healed by Jesus personally in one of them, and concluded his pamphlet by expressing the hope that it would "be a mean[s] of opening the eyes of blind sinners, and shewing to many the error of their ways."[16]

The attitude of warning characterizes virtually all of the pamphlets, save for a few that seem merely agog at the fabulous marvels reported.[17] The apocalyptic visions were embedded in the familiar biblical story of the coming end of the world and the judgment awaiting unrepentant sinners.

A second category of visionary stories, the heavenly journey visions, comprising another nine of the thirty-two pamphlets, send a warning to readers based on the promise of heaven and the threat of hell.[18] In their journeys into the afterlife, these visionaries saw actual acquaintances either in bliss or suffering and brought the news back to their earthly acquaintances. Often an angel or guide accompanied the visionaries as they were lifted from the earth and entered heaven. Commonly, Satan raged at them as they proceeded on their heavenly journey, but the traveler passed by unharmed just beyond the devil's reach. The obvious message to readers is to stay out of Satan's grasp.

One author of a heavenly journey pamphlet, Sarah Alley of Beekman Town, New York, a twenty-year-old single woman, fell into a swoon for four or five hours while sitting by the fire in her father's house and was transported to the world beyond. Accompanied by an angel, she came first to a burning lake where an "abundance of people who appeared to be in the utmost anxiety, distress, and unutterable misery" sat one above the other, "the flames of fire passing up between them." A great devil tried to lay hold on her but was tethered by a chain. A man she knew well urged her "to go and warn his family and friends to do better than he had done" before it was too late. Her guide then conducted her to a place of happiness "where I saw Christ and the holy angels around him, and abundance of people clothed in white robes," though she could not recognize any of them.

Returning to consciousness and finding several people around her, Alley "pressingly advised them to take warning by her." Then she fainted again, and her guide took her directly to heaven, where this time she did recognize many of the inhabitants:

> They appeared to be sitting, and in a situation of perfect peace and happiness, God sitting above them, and my guide telling me which he was, though he did not converse with me. I also saw Christ, who seemed a little before the rest, of whom I begged entrance into that peaceful situation.

Christ said no; she must return and warn people, a charge repeated by a person she knew well who "pressingly desired me to warn his friends and relations to change their way of walking." After more such admonitions, "they seemingly all joyfully bid me farewell, and my guide conducted me back to my body."[19]

Sarah Alley's experience, like that of all the apocalyptic and heavenly journey visionaries, changed her into a witness. While intensely personal, often involving the visionary's own conversion, a revelation of heaven carried a responsibility to tell everyone. Sarah Alley was admonished over and over to warn her friends; Caleb Pool called a meeting of church people to hear his story. All of the accounts in the sample were published, just as Solomon Chamberlin had his account of his vision printed for distribution.

While private and personal, the vision was for the public. The experience set up an obligation to tell and warn the world, forcing the visionaries to make connections outside of their personal spheres.

The impulse to speak ultimately created or, perhaps more accurately, perpetuated visionary culture. To make the voice of warning heard, visionaries, or sometimes their friends, called printers to their aid. The published narratives linked the visionaries to many others—the circle of friends who helped with the printing, a band of small-town printers who knew the market, and a wider audience who read the accounts with varying degrees of belief and skepticism. This conglomerate of visionaries, friends, printers, and readers made up the visionary culture that enabled Solomon Chamberlin and Hyrum Smith to recognize their spiritual kinship.[20]

Solomon Chamberlin's attraction to the Smiths is easy to understand. Not only was Joseph Jr. a visionary, but his father was also. Furthermore, Joseph Sr.'s dreams were similar to some of the visions in the pamphlets. Recorded by Lucy Smith in her *Biographical Sketches of Joseph Smith the Prophet,* Joseph Smith Sr.'s dreams sound like the visions of Caleb Pool. Joseph Sr. saw wild beasts, desolate landscapes, ominous buildings, and antagonistic crowds, all symbolizing the spiritual condition of the world.[21] These scenes would not have surprised readers of visionary pamphlets. Running through Joseph Sr.'s dreams was the familiar sense of moral decay and danger and the implied warning to turn to God now.

We are most interested, however, in Joseph Smith Jr.'s place in the visionary culture. How did his revelations compare to the stories in the pamphlets? Of all the pamphlets, the one most like any of Joseph's revelations was *The Religious Experience of Norris Stearns, Written by Divine Command, Shewing the Marvellous Dealings of God to His Soul, and the Miraculous Manner in Which He Was Delivered from the Jaws of Death and Hell; and His Soul Set at Liberty,—Likewise His Appointment to the Ministry; and Commision from on High, to Preach the Gospel to Every Creature,* published in 1815. In its entirety, Stearns's narrative is a shapeless, picaresque story of a marginal young man's wanderings about New England and New York, punctuated by occasional visions and premonitions. Though Stearns's life was quite different from Joseph's, here and there Stearns's account strikes a familiar note, as in a few sentences in the preface.

> The public are here presented with a book written by an illiterate youth, who has been highly favoured of God, and shown many things, which he is now commanded to write. He earnestly solicits the candid attention of every reader, that it may not stand (as the useless Parenthesis) among the other books of the world; for it is written in obedience to the Divine Command, *as a Testimony* to show his Calling. Care has been taken, that nothing should be written, but by the immediate command of the Lord; whose *Servant* and *Prophet* I am.[22]

The religious predicament of the Smith family is also echoed in Stearns's description of his father's faith:

> My Father was once a praying man, and belonged to the Baptist Church in Leyden; but not having faith in ceremonial ordinances, and dead forms of religion, he withdrew from their meetings, and was soon given up to the buffetings of Satan, that his soul might be saved in the day of our Lord Jesus.[23]

Most of the story sounds nothing like Joseph Smith's, but one striking passage resonates with the 1839 account of the First Vision. Stearns had a vision early in his life, when he was still laboring through heavy doubts about religion:

> At length, as I lay apparently upon the brink of eternal woe, seeing nothing but death before me, suddenly there came a sweet flow of the love of God to my soul, which gradually increased. At the same time, there appeared a small gleam of light in the room, above the brightness of the sun, then at his meridian, which grew brighter and brighter: As this light and love increased, my sins began to separate, and the Mountain removed towards the east. At length, being in an ecstacy of joy, I turned to the other side of the bed, (whether in the body or out I cannot tell, God knoweth) there I saw two spirits, which I knew at the first sight. But if I had the tongue of an Angel I could not describe their glory, for they brought the joys of heaven with them. One was God, my Maker, almost in bodily shape like a man. His face was, as it were a flame of Fire, and his body, as it had been a Pillar and a Cloud. In looking steadfastly to discern features, I could see none, but a small glimpse would appear in some other place. Below him stood Jesus Christ my Redeemer, in perfect shape like a man—His face was not ablaze, but had the countenance of fire, being bright and shining. His Father's will appeared to be his! All was condescension, peace, and love!![24]

Nothing after these passages parallels Joseph Smith's experience. Stearns was actually beset by skepticism and was driven to believe in the divine by visions whose reality he initially doubted. After the vision related here, he wandered aimlessly from one job to another, dabbling in preaching, seeking a vocation, and forever stumbling up against the supernatural. He broke off the pamphlet in the middle, before his life's work was resolved and even before his own beliefs were crystallized.

What are we to make of Stearns's account? Although his life never came into focus and his visions went nowhere, we still are interested in his relationship to the Restoration and Joseph Smith. Were Stearns's visions a premonition of what was to come or in some way a preparation for a later revelation of God? Chamberlin's visions readied him to believe visions and to accept the Book of Mormon without the doubts that impeded most Americans. Did the visionary culture open the minds of others? Can we imagine little gleams of light breaking through the clouds everywhere, as a preliminary to the fullness of the Restoration? Or were the visions mere delusions, manufactured by the visionaries' own feverish imaginations or by Satan?

Unfortunately, we have no way to judge the authenticity of these visionary accounts: Some present fabulous, cumbersome stories that sound like the fantasies of troubled souls, straining one's credulity. Others, like the heavenly journey of Sarah Alley, may have sobered readers and turned them to God. Why not concede to Alley a measure of divine inspiration?

Inspired or not, Stearns's pamphlet and the writings of the other vernacular visionaries dispel the idea that revelations were unknown until the First Vision opened the heavens in 1820. In the experience of the visionary writers, the heavens were anything but sealed, for the writers saw angels, bizarre beasts, and sacred mountains or looked into heaven and hell and saw and heard Christ and the devil. We can imagine this flow of religious stories trickling through rural villages and possibly washing over the Smiths. It is unlikely that we will ever know if any single pamphlet save Chamberlin's reached them, and we cannot conclude that the similarities of tone and style mean that Joseph imitated Norris Stearns or anyone else. What the resemblances between the 1839 account of the First Vision and a few passages in Stearns's narrative do demonstrate, in my opinion, is that Joseph did not have to invent a literary voice for himself any more than he had to invent the English language. When he was searching for the right tone for his story, one was readily available. Precedents existed for a young boy offering a simple account of his experience. The visionaries did not argue for the reality of their visions, apparently not troubling themselves with the questions of skeptics. The writers simply stated the facts of their visions, as if awed and impressed themselves by what transpired. That voice suited Joseph perfectly, and he adopted it as his own with immense success in his simple narrative of innocence overtaken by divinity.

The stylistic similarities only highlight, however, the differences between Joseph and the host of now forgotten visionaries. Putting him alongside Norris Stearns forces on us the question of why their lives took such divergent paths. Stearns proclaimed himself a prophet, but he did not go on to organize a church. His writings did not become scripture or attract believers. Nor did the writings of any of the other thirty-one pamphleteers. People did not flock to hear the visionaries' teachings or pull up roots to gather with fellow believers. Followers of Joseph Smith did all of these things and more. They reoriented their entire lives to comply with his revelations. The differences are so great that we can scarcely even say Joseph was the most successful of the visionaries; taking his life as a whole, we must conclude that he was of another species.

Focusing on the differences rather than the similarities, we see the limited force of the visionary writings. The narratives of dreams and miraculous appearances did not imply the construction of any institutional forms; they did not propose doctrine; they did not proclaim commandments. They were apocalyptic warnings, visions of worldly wickedness and onrushing doom. In a sense, they were titillations of the religious sensibilities that imposed no obligations beyond a general revulsion against sin and responsiveness to divine purpose. The visionary writings were a later version of the Puritan preoccupation with wonders. They inspired awe at the presence of invisible powers made visible but were an occasion to marvel rather than to act.

Joseph Smith's revelations, by contrast, radically redirected people's lives. His writings became authoritative statements of doctrine and the divine will. They implied an ecclesiastical polity and a reorganization of society. Out of a few verses in the Doctrine and Covenants, a new economic order emerged. Moved by the revelations, people went on missions to distant places, migrated to Missouri, paid tithing, underwent life-threatening persecutions, built cities. The revelations formed a new society created in the name of God. Joseph's words were read as divine commandments with immediate implications for the conduct of life.

The contrast with other visionary writings compels us to ask how Joseph Smith turned into a prophet who led a movement. What path took him away from the visionaries who wrote a pamphlet or two, issued warnings to their neighbors, and then disappeared into obscurity? If the similarities gave Solomon and Hyrum instant recognition of one another, how did Joseph Smith separate himself from the visionary culture and become the prophet to a people?[25]

Perhaps the most important difference between Joseph and the visionaries was the way Joseph first presented himself to the world. In the early years, the key formal statements, the ones recorded as revelations in the Doctrine and Covenants, played down visionary experiences. One might expect Joseph Smith to preface the Doctrine and Covenants with the story of the First Vision, as Mormon missionaries later handed out the pamphlet *Joseph Smith's Own Story* to prospective converts. But judging from the written record, the First Vision story was little known in the early years.

For twenty years after the vision occurred, Joseph Smith published nothing about the vision of the Father and the Son to link him to the other visionaries. By his own account, after he returned from the grove he did not tell his own mother about the vision. He related the experience to a local clergyman, whose negative response must have discouraged further retellings.

The vision gets an oblique reference in section 20 (1830) as a time when "it was truly manifested unto this first elder that he had received a remission of his sins," without so much as mentioning the appearance of the Father and the Son (D&C 20:5).[26] The account of the vision at the beginning of

Joseph Smith's 1832 history again emphasized forgiveness of sins and played down the details of what he saw, saying only that "I saw the Lord and he spake unto me."[27] Even that spare account was not published, and the whole story made so little impact that for years some scholars believed no narration of the First Vision existed until his 1839 history.[28] Rather than cultivating the kinship with Solomon Chamberlin's culture, Joseph seems to have made little of the revelation that connected him most strongly to the visionaries of his time.

He was less reticent about the visit of Moroni—a visionary story, albeit one without parallel among the visionary accounts. Still, he held back information about Moroni, too. Although Joseph told family and friends about the angel's appearance, the preface to the first edition of the Book of Mormon says nothing about the angel, only that "the plates of which hath been spoken, were found in the township of Manchester, Ontario county, New-York."[29] If he had been playing to the visionary culture, the visit of an angel would have received top billing. When questioned about the discovery of the plates, Joseph Smith at first was reluctant to elaborate, saying it was not expedient for people to know more.[30] Only later did he choose to include it as a standard part of the story he told about the Church's origins.

By the same token, descriptions of the angelic visitations of John the Baptist and Peter, James, and John were not included in the 1833 Book of Commandments. The 1835 edition of the Doctrine and Covenants made references to the angelic visitations that were only slightly more descriptive than the mention of the First Vision in section 20.[31] The current section 13, which records John the Baptist's words, did not appear in either of the early compilations; Joseph apparently had said little about John the Baptist's bestowal of the Aaronic Priesthood[32] until Oliver Cowdery gave an account of it in an 1834 letter published in the *Messenger and Advocate*. Oliver went into raptures about the experience: "What Joy! what wonder! what amazement!"[33] When Joseph finally wrote about the event in 1839, he was much more low-key, avoiding the sensational: "A Messenger from heaven, descended in a cloud of light, and having laid his hands upon us, he ordained us."[34] Joseph never gave a detailed written description of the visit of Peter, James, and John; he simply mentioned that it happened (D&C 27:12; 128:20). He was closemouthed enough that we have trouble now knowing exactly when it occurred.[35]

Joseph himself never made reference to other visionaries, and we cannot tell for sure if he consciously distanced himself; but when compiling revelations for publication in these early years, he did omit almost every account that might connect him to the visionaries of his time. The revelations he published struck another note entirely. The opening line of Doctrine and Covenants 20, a primary defining document in the 1835 compilation of revelations, sounds a theme unheard in any of the visionary reports: "The rise of the Church of Christ in these last days . . . it being regularly organized and established agreeable to the laws of our country, by the will and commandments of God." None of the visionaries spoke of the rise of a church. Mostly these people stood along the margins of conventional church life, skirting it, sometimes resisting it, usually disregarding it altogether.[36] By publishing a pamphlet rather than seeking a place in the pulpit or space in the denominational newspapers, the visionaries circumvented the institutional. Caleb Pool knew he could not speak to the congregation during services and asked to be heard after the meeting. The visionaries turned to the printers to get the warning message out, rather than to the clergy. Sarah Alley fulfilled her obligation by speaking to her immediate friends and then writing up her account for publication. The visionaries related to the whole world through the press rather than to a congregation through a church.

After the publication of the Book of Mormon, Joseph Smith immediately organized a church. Rather than dissipating his religious energies in messages published to the world at large, he focused on the formation of an institution. The early revelations to his father and his brother, to Joseph Knight Sr., and to the Whitmers, stressed the theme that "a great and marvelous work is about to come forth among the children of men." He told them to preach repentance, to "establish the cause of Zion," and to ready themselves to reap the harvest of souls (D&C 11:1, 6; compare sections 4, 12, 14–16). Instead of impressing his followers with the miraculous visions he had seen, he recruited them to carry the gospel to the world. "Say nothing but repentance unto this generation," Hyrum was told (D&C 11:9).

Speaking in that voice, Joseph Smith set himself apart from the visionary culture of Solomon Chamberlin and Norris Stearns. He did not repudiate that culture, but he took another path. To be sure, the similarities that did exist likely worked in Joseph's favor. One can imagine a warm reception for the Mormon message among people who believed that the heavens were not sealed. After asking the Smiths to tell their visions, Solomon Chamberlin assured them, "I can bear them,"[37] implying that some Christians might balk at renewed revelation, while he was sympathetic. A population ready to bear such news would be of great help to the infant church.[38]

Also embedded in Joseph's works are the two narratives that ran through the visionary reports—the coming judgments on the earth and the punishment and rewards of the life to come. The first narrative foresaw the return of Christ; the second told of the soul's journey from earth life through death to the hereafter. Both stories had as much meaning for the Saints as for the visionaries. The preface to the Doctrine and Covenants was a "voice of warning" to all people prior to the Second Coming, and the vision of the three degrees of glory held out promises of glory in the afterlife.

But in Joseph's teachings, another narrative stood out above either of these—the building of Zion in the last days. Unlike the pamphlet visionaries, Joseph harnessed the energy of his visions to the cause of the Church.[39] His followers loved the stories of visions and made more of supernatural occurrences in their tales of Joseph than he did himself. Not wanting to suppress the visionary entirely, Joseph did relate the details of the First Vision and the coming of Moroni—after the Church was firmly established.[40] Having put Zion first, Joseph inspired his followers to preach the gospel in all the world, to gather from the four quarters of the earth, and to build cities and temples. Going beyond the simple warnings of the visionary pamphlets, Joseph's revelations became the founding stories of a new religious movement.[41]

Joseph Smith's experiences can be compared to reports from the visionaries of his time, just as he can be linked to other nineteenth-century cultures—universalism, rational skepticism, republicanism, progress, revivalism, magic, communitarianism, health reform, restorationism, Zionism, and a host of others. But no one of these cultures, or even all of them added together, encompasses the whole of his thought. Joseph went beyond them all and produced a culture and society that the visionaries around him could not even imagine. Visions and revelations lay at the core of the Restoration, but the doctrinal and institutional outworks extended well beyond the limits of Solomon Chamberlin's visionary culture.

LIST OF PAMPHLETS

Adams, Ebenezer. *A True and Wonderful Relation, of the Appearance of Three Angels, (Cloathed in White Raiment) to a Young Man in Medford, near Boston, in New-England, on the 4th of February 1761, at Night.* Boston: Green and Russell, [1761?].

Alley, Sarah. "Account of a Trance or Vision of Sarah Alley, of Beekman Town, Dutchess County, State of New-York." In *Some Extraordinary Instances of Divine Guidance and Protection and Awful Warnings of a Just Retribution through Dreams and Visions.* Philadelphia: Joseph Rakestraw, 1814.

Anonimus's Travels throu' Europe and America, and Some Visions of Many Heavenly Mansions in the House of God, John XIV, 13. Ephrata, *1793.*

Ashburn, Rebecca. *Three Remarkable Dreams in Succession, on Thursday Night, April 15th, Friday Night, April 16th, and Saturday Night, April 17th, 1802.* [Philadelphia?]: n.p., 1802.

De Benneville, George. *A True and Remarkable Account of the Life and Trances of Dr. George De Benneville.* Norristown: David Sower, 1800.

Chamberlain, Thomas. *America's Timely Remembrancer; or, the Minister Preaching His Own Funeral Sermon; Being a Warning from Heaven to All Vile Sinners on Earth.* Frederick-Town: M. Bartgis, 1794.

Chamberlin, Solomon. *A Sketch of the Experience of Solomon Chamberlin, to Which Is Added a Remarkable Revelation, or Trance of His Father-in-Law Philip Haskins.* Lyons, N.Y.: n.p., 1829.

Child, Isaac. *The Vision of Isaac Child, Which He Saw concerning the Land of His Nativity.* Philadelphia: H. Bickley, 1814.

Churchill, Mehetable. *A Remarkable Instance of the Interposition of the Spirit of Grace, to Save from Death a Guilty Sinner.* [Springfield, N.H.?]: Joseph Warriner, 1783.

Cish, Jane. *The Vision and Wonderful Experience of Jane Cish, Shewing How She Was Converted, and How She Fell into a Trance on the Third of May, 1780, and Saw Heaven and Hell, with Many Other Strange Things.* Philadelphia: n.p., 1798.

[Clarke, Samuel.] *The Strange and Wonderful Swansey Vision.* Boston: n.p., [178–?].

Culver, Nathan. *A Very Remarkable Account of the Vision of Nathan Culver . . . to Which is Added, an Extraordinary Vision, Seen by a Gentleman of Philadelphia.* 5th ed. Portsmouth: Oracle Office, 1796.

The Glory of the Heavenly City, and Blessedness of Departed Saints: Graciously Manifested in a Vision to a Young Lady of Bristol; on the Tenth of October 1781: As Related by Herself. Albany: Barber and Southwick for Thomas Spencer, 1793.

Goodwin, Hezekiah. *A Vision.* N.p., 1802.

Havens, Nicodemus. *Wonderful Vision of Nicodemus Havens, of the City of New York, Cordwainer, Wherein He Was Presented with a View of the Situation of the World, after the Dreadful Fourth of June, 1812 and Shewing What Part of New York Is to Be Destroyed.* Boston: Coverly Jr., 1812.

Ingalls, Samuel. *A Dream, or Vision, by Samuel Ingalls, of Dunham, in the Province of Lower Canada, on the Night of Sept. 2, 1809.* [Windsor, Vt.?]: n.p., [1810?].

[Knowles, Mary (Morris).] *A Brief Account of the Vision and Death of the Late Lord Lyttleton.* Stanford, [N.Y.]: Daniel Lawrence, 1804.

Lee, Richard. *The Melancholy End of Ungrateful Children.* Rutland, Vt.: By the author, 1795.

M'Gowan, John. *Death, a Vision: or, the Solemn Departure of Saints and Sinners, Represented under the Similitude of a Dream. From the 6th London edition.* Harrisburgh, Pa.: John Wyeth, 1796.

Mills, John. *The Vision of John Mills, in Bedford County, at Virginia, in the Year 1785.* N.p., [1785?].

[Phillips, Ann.] *A Vision of Heaven and Hell.* Barnard, Vt.: Joseph Dix, [1812].

Pool, Caleb. *News from Heaven, by Visions, Communicated Miraculously to, and Explained by, Caleb Pool, of Gloucester.* Salem: By the author, 1805.

Ripley, Dorothy. *The Extraordinary Conversion, and Religious Experience of Dorothy Ripley, with Her First Voyage and Travels in America.* New York: G. and R. Waite, 1810.

Say, Benjamin. *A Short Compilation of the Extraordinary Life and Writings of Thomas Say; in Which Is Faithfully Copied, from the Original Manuscript, the Uncommon Vision, Which He Had When a Young Man.* Philadelphia: Budd and Bartram, 1796.

Stearns, Norris. *The Religious Experience of Norris Stearns, Written by Divine Command, Shewing the Marvellous Dealings of God to His Soul, and the Miraculous Manner in Which He Was Delivered from the Jaws of Death and Hell; and His Soul Set at Liberty,—Likewise His Appointment to the Ministry; and Commission from on High, to Preach the Gospel to Every Creature.* Greenfield, [Mass.]: By the author, 1815.

Thomas, Eliza. *A Vision; Tending to Edify, Astonish, and Instruct; Experienced by Miss Eliza Thomas.* [Stoningtonport]: n.p., 1800.

A True Narrative of a Most Stupendous Trance and Vision, Which Happened at Sharon, in Connecticut. in January, 1789. N.p., 1793.

[Walker, Timothy P.] *The Flaming Sword, or a Sign from Heaven Being a Remarkable Phenomenon, Seen in the State of Vermont.* Exeter, [N.H.]: J. Richardson, 1814.

A Warning to Disobedient Youth: Being a Relation concerning a Certain Henry Webb. Carlisle: James Kiteley, 1788.

Willey, Chloe. *A Short Account of the Life and Remarkable View of Mrs. Chloe Willey, of Goshen, N.H., Written by Herself.* New York: John C. Totton, 1810.

A Wonderful Account of a Little Girl of Nine Years Old, Who Lives in the Town of Jericho, in the State of Vermont; by the Name of Hannah Coy. [Windsor, Vt.]: n.p., 1800. Published with *An Account of the Vision or Trance of a Young Woman, Who Lives on the West Side of Lake Champlain, in the State of New-York, in the Town Called Pleasant Valley.* [Windsor, Vt.]: n.p., 1800.

Wood, Abraham. *A Remarkable Prophecy of Abraham Wood, Who Was Born Dumb and Blind, and It Pleased the Lord to Unloose His Tongue and Open His Eyes, to Declare the Truth unto the World at Twenty-Three Years of Age. Published for the Benefit of God's Children.* Lancaster, [Pa.]: n.p., 1811.

NOTES

1. Dean C. Jessee, ed., "The John Taylor Nauvoo Journal, January 1845– September 1845," *BYU Studies* 23, no. 3 (1983): 45.

2. For Chamberlin's life, see David F. Boone, "Prepared for the Restoration: Spiritual Manifestations Foreshadowed the Return of the Gospel to the Earth," *Ensign* 14 (December 1984): 17–21. Chamberlin's 1828 pamphlet partially supports his later account of his vision. He describes his discovery of apostasy in 1816 and his search for God's "true church and people," but another vision that year led him to the Reformed Methodists, among whom he found "Gods dear children." The pamphlet does not mention a search for an apostolic church. A recently discovered copy of Chamberlin's tract, *A Sketch of the Experience of Solomon Chamberlin, to Which Is Added a Remarkable Revelation, or Trance of His Father-in-Law Philip Haskins* (Lyons, N.Y.: n.p., 1829), is now on deposit in L. Tom Perry Special Collections, Harold B. Lee Library, Brigham Young University, Provo, Utah, and was published with an introduction in Larry C. Porter, "Solomon Chamberlin's Missing Pamphlet: Dreams, Visions, and Angelic Ministrants," *BYU Studies* 37, no. 2 (1997–98): 113–40. Solomon wrote his name "Chamberlin"; family members later changed the name to "Chamberlain." See also "Remarkable Vision and Revelation: as Seen and Received by Asa Wild, of Amsterdam, N.Y.," reprinted from the *Amsterdam, N.Y., Mohawk Herald,* October 1, 1823, in the *Palmyra, N.Y., Wayne Sentinel,* October 22, 1823. Wild's account was published with commentary in Elden J. Watson, "The 'Prognostication' of Asa Wild," *BYU Studies* 37, no. 3 (1997–98): 223–30.

3. Larry C. Porter, "Solomon Chamberlain—Early Missionary," *BYU Studies* 12, no. 3 (1972): 314–18.

4. Jessee, "John Taylor Nauvoo Journal," 44–46.

5. Charles G. Finney, *Memoirs of Rev. Charles G. Finney. Written by Himself* (New York: A. S. Barnes, 1876), 19–20. Finney later appealed to what he called the "affirmation of reason." See Noel B. Reynolds, review, *BYU Studies* 32, no. 1–2 (1992): 292.

6. For citations to visionary experiences, see John L. Brooke, *The Refiner's Fire: The Making of Mormon Cosmology, 1644-1844* (Cambridge: Cambridge University Press, 1994), 41–42, 63, 126–27; and Stephen A. Marini, *Radical Sects of Revolutionary New England* (Cambridge: Harvard University Press, 1982), 72–75.

7. For two visionaries closer to Joseph Smith's time and place, see Richard L. Bushman, *Joseph Smith and the Beginnings of Mormonism* (Urbana: University of Illinois Press, 1984), 58. See the additional references in Neal E. Lambert and Richard H. Cracroft, "Literary Form and Historical Understanding: Joseph Smith's First Vision," *Journal of Mormon History* 7 (1980): 34–35. Professor Herbert Sloan of Barnard College has drawn my attention to a pamphlet beyond the time boundaries of the sample: *Remarkable Visionary Dreams, of a Mulatto Boy, in Northfield, Mass. by the Name of Frederic W. Swan, Aged Thirteen Years: Together with a Sketch of His Life, Sickness, Conversion, and Triumphant Death* ([Chesterfield, N.H.]: Joseph Merriam, 1822). Swan's dreams fell into conventional patterns, including a heavenly journey, as analyzed in this paper.

8. David D. Hall, *Worlds of Wonder, Days of Judgment: Popular Religious Belief in Early New England* (New York: Alfred A. Knopf, 1989), 71–116.

9. *A True Narrative of a Most Stupendous Trance and Vision, Which Happened at Sharon, in Connecticut. in January,* 1789 (n.p., 1793), 3, 11.

10. *Some Extraordinary Instances of Divine Guidance and Protection: And Awful Warnings of a Just Retribution through Dreams and Visions* (Philadelphia: Joseph Rakestraw, 1814), 13, 50–55.

11. Nicodemus Havens and Abraham Wood pamphlets are cited in full in the list of pamphlets at the end of this essay; see pp. 211–13. Hereafter, author's names without citation refer to this list.

12. Norris Stearns and Mehetable Churchill.

13. The ten apocalyptic pamphlets include those by Ebenezer Adams, Isaac Child, Samuel Clarke, Nicodemus Havens, Samuel Ingalls, Ann Phillips, Caleb Pool, Norris Stearns, Timothy Walker, and Abraham Wood.

14. Samuel Ingalls.

15. Ibid.

16. Caleb Pool, 3–4, 9–10, 31.

17. Rebecca Ashburn, Norris Stearns, and Benjamin Say.

18. The heavenly journey pamphlets, cited in full in the list of pamphlets, include Sarah Alley, *Anonimus's Travels,* Nathan Culver, *The Glory of the Heavenly City,* John Mills, *A True Narrative, A Warning to Disobedient Youth,* Chloe Willey, and *A Wonderful Account.*

19. Sarah Alley, 50–55.

20. The visionaries who published their dreams and visions in pamphlets are only part of the larger visionary world of that era. A computer catalog brings up a half dozen books on visionary poetry, much of which was written in the late eighteenth and early nineteenth centuries. These books are a reminder that within the span of Joseph's life, the idea of divine revelation fascinated all segments of the cultural spectrum. The interest was nearly as common among the educated classes as among the uneducated. William Blake—learned, sophisticated, and acclaimed—reported daily visions and wrote poems that were close to automatic writing. Poets from Shelley to the American John Trumbull used visions as frames for their poems. Emerson admonished the graduating class at Harvard Divinity School in 1837 to dream dreams and see visions. Where Joseph fit into this broader picture is a question that also deserves attention. See, for example, Judith Weissman, *Of Two Minds: Poets Who Hear Voices* (Hanover, N.H.: University Press of New England, 1993); and Andrew J. Welburn, *The Truth of Imagination: An Introduction to Visionary Poetry* (London: Macmillan, 1989).

21. Lucy Mack Smith, *Biographical Sketches of Joseph Smith the Prophet and His Progenitors for Many Generations* (1853; reprint, Orem, Utah: Grandin, 1995), 57–59, 70–72.

22. Norris Stearns, preface; italics in original.

23. Ibid., 5.

24. Ibid., 12. God or Christ or both appear in visions in ten of the pamphlets: Sarah Alley, George De Benneville, Nathan Culver, *Glory of the Heavenly City,* John M'Gowan, Caleb Pool, Dorothy Ripley, Norris Stearns, *A Warning to Disobedient Youth,* and *A Wonderful Account.* Many of the appearances occur in the heavenly journey stories where the visionary sees God or Christ in a celestial setting.

25. The question is addressed from a literary perspective in Lambert and Cracroft, "Literary Form and Historical Understanding," 31–42.

26. In the 1835 edition of the Doctrine and Covenants, what appears as section 20 in the present edition was prominently located immediately after the revealed preface, appearing as section 2. *Doctrine and Covenants of the Church of the Latter Day Saints* (Kirtland: F. G. Williams, 1835).

27. Dean C. Jessee, "The Early Accounts of Joseph Smith's First Vision," *BYU Studies* 9, no. 3 (1969): 280.

28. Fawn Brodie, *No Man Knows My History: The Life of Joseph Smith, the Mormon Prophet,* 2d ed., rev. (New York: Alfred A. Knopf, 1979), 21–25; James B. Allen, "The Significance of Joseph Smith's 'First Vision' in Mormon Thought," *Dialogue: A Journal of Mormon Thought* 1 (autumn 1966): 28–45; James B. Allen, "Emergence of a Fundamental: The Expanding Role of Joseph Smith's First Vision in Mormon Religious Thought," *Journal of Mormon History* 7 (1980): 43–61; and Milton V. Backman Jr., *Joseph Smith's First Vision: Confirming Evidences and Contemporary Accounts,* 2d ed., rev. and enl. (Salt

Lake City: Bookcraft, 1980). Joseph's 1838 history was published beginning in the *Times and Seasons* in 1842.

29. *The Book of Mormon* (Palmyra: E. B. Grandin, 1830), preface, reprinted in Wilford C. Wood, *Joseph Smith Begins His Work* (n.p.: Deseret News Press, 1958), unpaged.

30. "The Conference Minutes, and Record Book, of Christ's Church of Latter Day Saints," October 25, 1831, cited in Donald Q. Cannon and Lyndon W. Cook, eds., *Far West Record: Minutes of the Church of Jesus Christ of Latter-day Saints, 1830–1844* (Salt Lake City: Deseret Book, 1983), 23.

31. *Doctrine and Covenants of the Church of the Latter Day Saints*, 180 (now Doctrine and Covenants 27:7–8, 12).

32. See Brian Q. Cannon and BYU Studies Staff, "Priesthood Restoration Documents," *BYU Studies* 35, no. 4 (1995–96): 175–77.

33. Oliver Cowdery to W. W. Phelps, September 7, 1834, Norton, Ohio, in *Messenger and Advocate* 1 (October 1834): 14–16, quoted in Dean C. Jessee, ed., *The Papers of Joseph Smith*, 2 vols. (Salt Lake City: Deseret Book, 1989), 1:31.

34. Jessee, *Papers of Joseph Smith*, 1:290; see also 1:238.

35. Stories of priesthood restoration may have circulated unofficially, judging from Ohio newspaper reports on Mormon claims to authority. *Painesville Telegraph,* November 16 and December 7, 1830. The "Visions of Moses" given in June 1830 carried the instruction to "show them not unto any except them that believe" (Moses 1:42) and had little circulation for many years. See also Cannon and BYU Studies, "Priesthood Restoration Documents," 162–207, especially 177, no. 7; and Jessee, *Papers of Joseph Smith*, 1:238–39.

36. Only three of the visionaries in the sample are explicitly favorable to or at ease with a church or minister: Rebecca Ashburn, Thomas Chamberlain, and *A Wonderful Account*.

37. Porter, "Solomon Chamberlain—Early Missionary," 317.

38. Visionaries were probably bound to one another by their willingness to suspend disbelief, for they had in common the opposition of a doubting world. On the one hand, visionaries suffered from the attacks of skeptics spawned by the Enlightenment who were questioning all the Christian revelations, and, on the other, by preachers in most of the mainstream denominations who were embarrassed by any manifestation of enthusiasm. A writer in the *Connecticut Evangelical Magazine* in 1805 wrote that no person should "publish to the world the discoveries of heaven or hell which he supposes he has had in a dream, or trance, or vision." Cited in Bushman, *Joseph Smith*, 59.

39. After Joseph's time, Ellen G. White similarly combined visions with church building, as did the Methodists earlier. See Jonathan M. Butler, "The Making of a New Order: Millerism and the Origins of Seventh-day Adventism," in Ronald L. Numbers and Jonathan M. Butler, eds., *The Disappointed: Millerism and Millenarianism in the Nineteenth Century* (Bloomington: Indiana University Press, 1987), 202–5; and John H. Wigger, "Taking Heaven by Storm: Enthusiasm and Early American Methodism, 1770–1820," *Journal of the Early Republic* 14 (summer 1994): 167–94.

40. Doctrine and Covenants 128:21 refers to visitations that were never reported to the church. In May 1843, Joseph said, "I could explain a hundred fold more than I ever have of the glories of the kingdoms manifested to me in the vision, were I permitted, and were the people prepared to receive them." Joseph Smith Jr., *History of the Church of Jesus Christ of Latter-day Saints*, ed. B. H. Roberts, 2d ed., rev., 7 vols. (Salt Lake City: Deseret Book, 1971), 5:402.

41. This last point is the argument of Lambert and Cracroft, "Literary Form and Historical Understanding," 39–42.

14

Was Joseph Smith a Gentleman?
The Standard for Refinement in Utah

When Ron Walker, a Brigham Young University faculty member, asked me to contribute to the 1998 Smith Institute symposium on everyday life in nineteenth-century Utah, I said I could talk only on Joseph Smith. My grasp of LDS history after 1844 tails off sharply, and I have nothing to say on any Utah history subject. When he persisted, I got around the problem by proposing a question about Joseph Smith's values as a foundation for later Utah culture.

The essay has a slightly iconoclastic undertone, the icon at risk being nineteenth-century Utah gentility. I question whether Joseph put as much emphasis on polish and style as later proponents of gentility in the West. In answering "no" to the question of the title, I knew I subverted a fundamental myth about the early Utah immigrants, a myth lived out by my own grandmother. While honoring her and all the other practitioners of genteel living, I say that refinement was not basic to the Prophet. My book on American gentility, The Refinement of America: Persons, Houses, Cities *(New York: Alfred A. Knopf, 1992), published just before the symposium, manifests a similar ambivalence. Throughout the whole book, I never decide if gentility was high-minded or superficial. In this essay, I avoid burdening the Prophet with this rather skin-deep ideal of human conduct.*

Frances Trollope, mother of the novelist Anthony Trollope, came to America in 1827 with her husband, a failed barrister and farmer, to open a fancy-goods shop in Cincinnati. While her husband kept shop, Frances traveled about the country, observing the American scene. After still another business failure, the Trollopes returned to England, and in 1836 Frances Trollope published *The Domestic Manners of the Americans.* Although it was an immediate hit in England and was subsequently translated into French and Spanish, the book infuriated readers in the United States. Everywhere Mrs. Trollope looked, she had found vulgarity, which she depicted in broad, humorous strokes. On the steamboat that carried the Trollopes up the Mississippi from New Orleans, the respectable passengers dined together in what was called "the gentleman's cabin," a compartment "handsomely fitted up, and the latter well carpeted," she said, "but oh! that carpet! I will not, I may not describe its condition. . . . I hardly know any annoyance so deeply repugnant to English feelings, as the incessant, remorseless spitting of Americans." Her feelings were equally riled by the table manners of the so-called gentlemen, who included among their number a judge and men with the titles of general, colonel, and major.

> The total want of all the usual courtesies of the table, the voracious rapidity with which the viands were seized and devoured, the strange uncouth phrases and pronunciation; the loathsome spitting, from the contamination of which it was absolutely impossible to protect our dresses; the frightful manner of feeding with their knives, till the whole blade seemed to enter into the mouth; and the still more frightful manner of cleaning the teeth afterwards with a pocket knife, soon forced us to feel that . . . the dinner hour was to be any thing rather than an hour of enjoyment.

Ordinary people appeared still more degraded to her eyes: "All the little towns and villages" seen from the deck of the steamboat were "wretched-looking in the extreme. . . . I never witnessed human nature reduced so low, as it appeared in the wood-cutters' huts on the unwholesome banks of the Mississippi." She was surprised to find that the mayor of Memphis was "a pleasing gentleman-like man"; to her he seemed "strangely misplaced in a little town on the Mississippi."[1]

Trollope wrote with an ideological grudge. She candidly announced in the preface that in describing "the daily aspect of ordinary life, she has endeavoured to shew how greatly the advantage is on the side of those who are governed by the few, instead of the many." In other words, aristocratic England had it all over democratic America. She wanted her countrymen to see "the jarring tumult and universal degradation which invariably follow the wild scheme of placing all the power of the state in the hands of the populace."[2] But if ideology gave a special edge to her writing, her standard for measuring democratic degradation was by no means unique. Travelers from France and Spain, from New England, Philadelphia, and New York— virtually everyone who ventured into the western portions of the country—asked Trollope's question: how civilized were the inhabitants of the new regions? Though the answers varied, the question was the same. Where did the manners of the people put them on the scale of civilization? Were they ladies and gentlemen or barbarians?

The West came under particular scrutiny because of the common belief that civilization fell away as one ventured farther into the wilderness, the home of the savage tribes. Easterners feared that civilized manners were stripped from migrants to the unsettled frontier, reducing them slowly but surely to barbarism. In other words, history reversed itself as people migrated west; they returned to the primitive condition of humanity before civilization had developed. Horace Bushnell, the illustrious Congregational preacher and theologian in Hartford, Connecticut, delivered a despairing sermon on the West entitled "Barbarism the First Danger."[3]

Sermons like Bushnell's made clear that the measurement of civilization in the West was of more than academic interest. In a democratic
nation where power is in the hands of the populace, the western states were
in danger of coming under the control of barbarians who would not only
govern their own regions but send representatives to the Congress of the
United States. Reports that guests at Andrew Jackson's 1829 inaugural
stood in muddy boots on damask chairs and generally trashed the White
House sent terror through the civilized East. Jackson seemed to head the
vanguard of western barbarians taking power in the nation's capital. Josiah
Quincy, the Bostonian who later visited Nauvoo, said of General Jackson's
administration that it "swept away much of the graceful etiquette which
was characteristic of the society as I saw it." In the face of the onslaught,
"social barriers" were demolished "by the unrefined and coarse."[4]

The question of refinement cut even more deeply in Utah in the early
days when the governance of the territory was at issue. The Latter-day
Saints worked with a double handicap in striving to win respect from eastern travelers: in addition to the usual doubts about civilization in the West,
the visitors were skeptical about Mormon religious fanaticism. Travelers
came expecting that the poor credulous fools who submitted to the rule of
Brigham Young would lack education, manners, taste, and intelligence—in
short, would be as degraded as the woodcutters Trollope sighted along the
banks of the Mississippi. The Saints for their part had a lot at stake in proving the travelers wrong. If they could not persuade visitors of their religious
beliefs, the Mormons at least wanted to demonstrate their refinement.
Besides respect from eastern cultural centers, control over their government
hung in the balance. William Warner Major's fanciful portrait of Brigham
Young sitting amid columns and elegant furnishings, every inch the polished gentleman, epitomized the campaign to demonstrate Mormon refinement (fig. 1).

This cultural struggle affected the way early Utahns presented themselves to the world and the way history has been written ever since. From
the mid-nineteenth century on, Mormons in telling their story have
emphasized cultural respectability. The history of "refinement in the
wilderness," as this narrative might be called, has appeared in formal histories and been elaborated in Mormon folktales. The history succeeds
because it does rest on a factual base. Like the "suffering pioneer" narrative
of Utah history, real stories can be told in support of this point of view. We
have accounts of pioneers eating crickets and of water dripping from sod
roofs to prove the pioneers really did suffer. We also have records of barrels
of fine china being carried across the plains to show that the Mormon settlers brought civilization to barren Utah. The Daughters of Utah Pioneers
museum is an impressive monument to this history—the story of a refined

and enlightened people driven to the West, where they reestablished civilization in the desert.

Although the story of Utah refinement is myth in the good sense of being an overarching story that grew from people's view of the world as well as from the reality of their lives, it is a myth with truth to it. My own grandmother, largely a twentieth-century person to be sure, started life sewing overalls in a ZCMI factory, and yet on her husband's salary as a shoe salesman, she turned her house on the lower avenues in Salt Lake City into a tiny palace of taste and homemade beauty. She not only believed the civilization-in-the-wilderness myth, she lived by it, changing the material conditions of her life to conform to the story.

This mingling of myth and reality means that historians should not disregard these traditional narratives and try to replace them with their own versions of the "truth" based on supposedly hardheaded research. We do not want to demolish a narrative that has proven so fruitful, but rather to test its limitations and develop its analytical power. We can usefully ask, for example, how civilization-in-the-wilderness history accounts for the large portion of the population that did not live by this myth so far as we can see. George Anderson's photos, while documenting much refinement, also inform us that gentility did not prevail everywhere in Utah, even by the 1890s. People lived in shacks as well as mansions, and we can imagine that still more shabbily dressed people lived in crude cabins in rough and tough areas of the state where Anderson never ventured.

In the unadulterated refinement-in-the-wilderness narrative, these rough Utahns are often looked on as unfinished Latter-day Saints on whom the gospel had not yet worked its refining influence. In time, the uplifting spirit of the Mormon religion, plus a little prosperity, would civilize crude farmers and turn their cabins into comfortable and refined houses. Refinement, in other words, was thought to be the natural destiny of good Mormons, an integral part of Latter-day Saint culture. Besides entering into Utah through middle-class American culture, refinement came to Utah through Mormon religious beliefs. In this view, "everything virtuous, lovely, or of good report, or praiseworthy" in the thirteenth article of faith must refer to good manners, decorated houses, well-kept gardens, and handsome clothes—the marks of refinement. The improvement of domestic manners and beautification of houses and yards was an aspect of personal salvation, as I think my grandmother surely believed, so that every good Mormon was on the way to becoming genteel.

If refinement was part of the religion, the foundations would have been laid down by Joseph Smith in Kirtland and Nauvoo, where Mormon culture was born. In those places, the fundaments for most of later Mormonism were constructed. The city plans of the early Mormon gathering places in the East, for example, were models for Salt Lake City and other

FIG. 1. William Warner Major (1804–54), *Brigham and Mary Ann Angell Young and Their Children,* 1845–51. Oil on board, 25" x 33". This painting elevates Brigham Young to the status of a refined country gentleman. The typical standard of refinement in Utah, however, was less opulent.

Utah towns with their wide streets, square blocks, and town house lots for farmers. The precedents for genteel living should have been established at the same time. If refinement was basic, Joseph Smith would have spoken of it and, what is more, lived by it. Hence the relevance of the question: Was Joseph Smith a gentleman?

The modern depictions of Joseph Smith rarely show him as anything but a gentleman. With few exceptions, he appears in high collar with white stock and a dark suit; the only contemporaneous picture shows him in the uniform of a general. We can scarcely conceive of him otherwise, because if not a gentleman he would have been coarse, hardly a fitting character for a religious leader. The natural inclination today is to think that refinement and religion must intermingle. Living in a century when the American middle class has absorbed the standards of genteel culture, we have trouble imagining that gentility could ever be considered alien to true religion.

In the eighteenth century, however, before the middle class as we know it had come into existence, gentility was thought of as a sinful extravagance

for the population as a whole, best left to the gentry and the European aristocracy. Benjamin Franklin felt guilty about replacing a plain earthenware
bowl with chinaware for his breakfast bread and milk, and he chided plain
workmen who tried to appear like gentlemen by living beyond their
means.[5] Lorenzo Dow, the great evangelist after whom Brigham Young's
brother was named, made fun of all genteel practices. Dancing schools
came right out of Babylon, Dow said, and were actually little more than
places "where people were taught 'the important art of hopping and jump-
ing about.'" He condemned the promoters of "Polite Literature" in the form
of romances and novels, which caused people to neglect the Bible. Peter
Cartwright, a pioneer Methodist preacher in the first half of the nineteenth
century, told of a fashionably dressed man who could not find forgiveness
until "with his hands he deliberately opened his shirt bosom, took hold of
his ruffles, tore them off, and threw them down in the straw; and in less
than two minutes God blessed his soul."[6] Writing in his memoirs in 1856,
Cartwright mourned how Methodist simplicity had been lost as the century had gone on. He loved the early days when Methodists "dressed plain;
attended their meetings faithfully, especially preaching, prayer and class
meetings; they wore no jewelry, no ruffles," and "parents did not allow
their children to go to balls or plays; they did not send them to dancing-
schools."[7] A good Methodist, in other words, was plain, not fancy, avoiding
fashionable dress in the belief that gentility stood in the way of heartfelt
religion.

Joseph Smith came out of that tradition. Before his visions set him on
another course, he was "partial to the Methodist sect," at a time when plain
living was still their way (JS–H 1:8). Emma was a Methodist, as were
Brigham Young and many other early converts. They would have understood the passage in the revelation called "the law of the Church" that commanded the Saints to "let all thy garments be plain, and their beauty the
beauty of the work of thine own hands" (D&C 42:40). Those words would
have made sense to Joseph Smith, who did not grow up among genteel
people. Not "well bred" in the conventional sense of being reared as a gentleman, he was part of the mass of log-cabin people to whom the Whig
politicians appealed in the log-cabin campaign of 1840. For the larger part
of his boyhood, his parents, poor tenant farmers, resided among the lower
ranks of the social order, the class of people that included Abraham Lincoln's family. The Smiths were dirt farmers, who worked with their hands
at a time when genteel culture belonged to white-collar workers who
labored with their minds.

But the Smiths' lowly social position and Joseph's connection with the
Methodists do not tell the whole story of his upbringing. Complicating
this picture of a plain-folks family was the spread of middle-class gentility
in the first decades of the nineteenth century, touching the lives of many

farm people, including Joseph Smith's mother. More attuned to cultural pressures than others in the family, Lucy Smith had social ambitions. Around 1819, when the Smiths finally got land of their own in Manchester after fourteen years of tenant farming, she hoped to find a place among the village middle class. Soon after they built their cabin, she happily accepted an invitation to take tea with "some wealthy merchants wives and the minister's lady." Her pleasure turned to chagrin, however, when one of the women innocently declared that "Mrs. [Smith] ought not to live in that log house of her's any longer she deserves a better fate." "Interpreting the comment as a slight," Lucy turned on the circle and excoriated the women for the failings of their husbands and children. Although the Smiths lived in a cabin, she wanted it known that they were the moral equals of anyone in town. As Lucy told the story, she came off the victor in this clash between moral values and gentility, and yet moral respectability was not enough for her. In the next entry, Lucy noted that "about this time we began to make preparations for building a house. The family hired a carpenter to construct a frame house with parlor and central hall," the classic design for middle-class genteel dwellings—even though the ensuing debt overwhelmed their resources and led to the loss of their farm.[8] Lucy wanted a genteel house badly enough to stretch their resources to the breaking point.

Besides his mother's influence in rearing him, Joseph also came under the influence of genteel culture through a few of the early converts. Sidney Rigdon, though afforded only a common school education while he grew up on his father's farm in Pennsylvania, consumed books voraciously while preparing to be a Baptist preacher and retained everything. As the minister of a "respectable" Pittsburgh congregation, he was exposed to middle-class, urban values, which he brought with him into the Church.[9] Refinement was never a major theme of his preaching, but he did find a place for good manners and comely appearance. In an article called "The Saints and the World," published in the *Messenger and Advocate* in 1836, he outlined the work of building Zion and then posed a question: "Now let me ask the saints of the last days, what kind of people must you be, in order that you may accomplish so great a work?" How was Zion to "become the joy and the praise of the whole earth, so that kings shall come to the brightness of her rising?" The people of Zion needed to shine. "Surely, it will be by her becoming more wise, more learned, more refined, and more noble, than the cities of the world, so that she becomes the admiration of the great ones of the earth." Zion would attract attention "by the superiority of her literary institutions, and by a general effort of all the saints to patronize literature in our midst, so that the manners of the saints may be properly cultivated, and their habits correctly formed." Besides the people themselves, "her buildings will have to be more elegant, her palaces more splendid, and her public houses more magnificent." "Neither are we to leave out of the question," Rigdon went on, "the dress of the saints, for this supplies a place also in effecting this great object; the beauty and neatness of their dress is characteristic of the degree of refinement, and decency of a society. The nobles of the earth would not be likely to admire disgraceful apparel, untastefully arranged." Without all this, Zion could not become "the joy and praise of the whole earth."[10]

Although a strong endorsement for refinement, Rigdon's article fell short of making it an article of faith. He promoted correct manners, beautiful dress, and elegant buildings more as means to an end than as a basic value. His aim was to win the admiration and support of earthly powers, not to make the Saints over into ladies and gentlemen as a good in itself. In other moods, Mormon preachers could show their doubts about gentility. A *Times and Seasons* article in support of baptism by immersion expressed doubt about the willingness of refined people to get themselves wet all over. "Enlightened and refined society are not so vulgar as to go down into the water to be baptized. How ridiculously absurd it would be to lead one of the elite of the popular world, muffled in silks and satins, down into the dark waters of the great Mississippi."[11] Lorenzo Dow's and Peter Cartwright's skepticism about fashionable people echoes in those sentences. An old-style ambivalence about gentility is found in Mormonism along with Rigdon's enthusiasm. Refinement was at one moment a desirable polish to make the Saints shine in the world's eyes and at another a worldly pride that hindered acceptance of the gospel.

How did Joseph Smith navigate these crosscurrents in Mormon culture? The eyewitness depictions of the Prophet show him in many lights, but not usually as a standard polished gentleman. Some come close. Emily Partridge Young, one of Joseph's wives, said, "He was all that the word *gentleman* would imply—pure in heart, always striving for right, upholding innocence, and battling for the good of all."[12] While attaching admirable qualities to the term *gentleman,* Emily Young said nothing about the fine manners usually connected to gentility. The Masonic grandmaster who came to Nauvoo in March 1842 for the installation of Masonic officers was surprised at the man he met. Instead of an "ignorant and tyrannical upstart," Joseph Smith was "a sensible, intelligent, companionable and gentlemanly man."[13]

Most observers agreed with the grandmaster that Joseph was "a fine-looking man," but they did not consider him a gentleman. When Joel Hills Johnson met Joseph in 1831, the Prophet himself said, "I suppose you think that I am [a] great green, lubberly fellow," and Johnson observed that the phrase "was an exact representation of his person, being large and tall and not having a particle of beard about his face."[14] A Vermont girl who saw him in Kirtland in 1833 said, "He would better have answered to the character of a 'Davy Crockett,' than to the leader of a band who professed to be followers of the Saviour of mankind."[15] Charlotte Haven, a girl from New Hampshire, lived in Nauvoo through most of 1843. Not a Mormon, she viewed the Prophet with a jaundiced eye. She saw "a large, stout man, youthful in his appearance, with light complexion and hair, and blue eyes set far back in the head," making no note of either polish or crudity in his appearance. His speech was another matter. She had expected, she said, "to be overwhelmed by his eloquence" and was disappointed. He spoke in "a loud voice, and his language and manner were the coarsest possible. His object seemed to be to amuse and excite laughter in his audience." By comparison, Sidney Rigdon struck Haven more favorably: "He has an intelligent countenance, a courteous manner, and speaks grammatically." She judged him "by far the ablest and most cultivated of the Mormons," an indirect comment on the little she knew about Joseph Smith.[16]

Haven's reaction to Joseph Smith's speech was unusual. No one called him a polished speaker, but most were impressed with his effectiveness. Parley Pratt said Joseph was "not polished—not studied—not smoothed and softened by education and refined by art," and yet "he interested and edified, while, at the same time, he amused and entertained his audience; and none listened to him that were ever weary with his discourse." His enemy Eber D. Howe, the antagonistic Painesville, Ohio, newspaper editor, granted that Joseph was "easy, rather fascinating and winning."[17] He had a great knack for the telling rejoinder when he came under verbal attack. A female preacher who came across Joseph in 1831 challenged him to swear in the presence of God that an angel from heaven showed him the golden plates. Joseph replied gently, "I will not swear at all." She demanded, "Are you not ashamed of such pretensions? You, who are no more than an ignorant ploughboy of our land!" Joseph meekly said, "The gift has returned back again, as in former times, to illiterate fishermen."[18]

The comparison with Christ's illiterate fishermen may have summed up Joseph's idea about himself. He did not pretend to oratory and eloquence; fine speeches were left to Sidney Rigdon. Joseph thought of himself more as a plain person with a gift. If called upon, he could get a crowd to laugh, as he seems to have done in Charlotte Haven's hearing, but his tongue also gave forth the mysteries of godliness when he chose. Eliza R. Snow, a refined, graceful person herself who wrote poetry and taught a "select school" for young ladies, lived with the Smiths and watched Joseph's "'daily walk and conversation.'" She found that "his lips ever flowed with instruction and kindness," though capable of "severe rebuke" when moved to defend his people.[19]

Gentleman was not the word Josiah Quincy used to describe Joseph. Son of the Harvard College president and soon to be mayor of Boston himself, Quincy was a thoroughgoing Brahmin when he and Charles Francis Adams paid a call on Joseph Smith in May 1844. Quincy was not unattentive to the question of gentility. In the collection of sketches taken from his journal, Quincy preceded the account of his Nauvoo visit with the story of Andrew Jackson's visit to Boston to receive an honorary degree from Harvard while he was president of the United States. Quincy opened his sketch by rebutting the judgment common among Bostonians that "General Jackson was not what you would call a gentleman!" To the contrary, Quincy declared, "the seventh President was a knightly personage" and "vigorously a gentleman in his high sense of honor and in the natural straightforward courtesies which are easily to be distinguished from the veneer of policy." Quincy put forward this claim against the prevailing intolerance of Jackson by "the Brahmin caste of my native state."[20] Presumably, he had the nerve to say the same of Joseph, whom he greatly admired, had he seen gentlemanly qualities in the Prophet.

Instead he found another basis for his admiration. Joseph appeared to Quincy as a great vital force. He compared Joseph to the Rhode Island congressman Elisha Potter, whom Quincy had met in Washington in 1826. The two of them, Quincy said, emanated "a certain peculiar moral stress and compulsion which I have never felt in the presence of others of their countrymen." Potter, a giant of a man in physical bulk, had "wit and intelligence" in proportion to his size. Though not as large, Joseph left a similar impression. "Both were of commanding appearance, men whom it seemed natural to obey." Potter carried about him "a surplus of vital energy, to relieve the wants of others": "I well remember how the faces about Miss Hyer's dining table were wont to be lighted up when he entered the room." Quincy in passing spoke of Potter as "a gentleman," a word he never applied to Joseph, but the impressive qualities of both of them had nothing to do with refinement.[21]

Quincy and Adams dropped in on Joseph Smith unannounced early one morning. Their steamboat had stopped at the Nauvoo landing after midnight, and they were about to continue upstream after they discovered there was no room at "General Smith's tavern," but a room was found in an old mill that had been converted into a house. They swept "a small army of cockroaches" from the coverlet and slept through the night in their dressing gowns. The next morning, after driving two muddy miles, they saw the Prophet by a three-story frame house surrounded by a white fence:

> Preëminent among the stragglers by the door stood a man of commanding appearance, clad in the costume of a journeyman carpenter when about his work. He was a hearty, athletic fellow, with blue eyes standing prominently out upon his light complexion, a long nose, and a retreating forehead. He wore striped pantaloons, a linen jacket, which had not lately seen the washtub, and a beard of some three days' growth. This was the founder of the religion which had been preached in every quarter of the earth.

While the incongruity of Joseph's appearance and his religious pretensions struck Quincy as slightly humorous, it did not trouble Joseph. Later in the morning, before he accompanied the two visitors on a tour of Nauvoo, Joseph changed into a broadcloth suit, but he had seen no need to dress up earlier to appear on the streets of the city. On this day, he had left off the white stock of the modern portraits and had not bothered to shave his face. The role of prophet, which he never stepped out of, did not require him to appear in the garb of a gentleman. Nor was he embarrassed when caught in undress by two finely attired visitors.

And yet his presence impressed Quincy. "A *fine-looking man* is what the passer-by would instinctively have murmured," he said of the Prophet, "but Smith was more than this, . . . one could not resist the impression that capacity and resource were natural to his stalwart person." Linking him to Potter again, Quincy observed that "of all men I have met, these two seemed best endowed with that kingly faculty which directs, as by intrinsic right, the feeble or confused souls who are looking for guidance." The comment reduced the Nauvoo Mormons to mixed-up weaklings but without devaluing Joseph's character. Although disbelieving everything Joseph said and considering his comments "puerile," Quincy could not resist "the impression of rugged power that was given by the man."[22]

Joseph did not come among his working-class followers as John Wesley did, appearing as an aristocrat with fine skin and smooth hair that awed and inspired common people. On an ordinary day, Joseph stepped out of his house in striped pantaloons, a dirty jacket, and a three days' growth of beard. Nor did he reside in a splendid mansion. After getting by in a cramped log house for three years in Nauvoo, he moved into the Mansion House, where there was more space to entertain visitors.[23] Fenced with white pickets, as Quincy noted, and probably painted, the house was certainly well above the average Nauvoo residence and yet did not function as a mansion when Quincy and Adams visited. Sold to a tavern keeper in January 1844 to help with Joseph's debts, the house did not have the amenities of a mansion on this particular day. As he set about to entertain his distinguished visitors, he was not able to usher them into a parlor where genteel people always entertained important guests; Joseph had to hunt for a space to even sit down.[24] Avoiding the "comfortless" barroom, Joseph opened a door to a room occupied by a woman in bed, shut it, and ran upstairs to another room where three men were sleeping in three beds. The next room had two sleeping occupants, but "the third attempt was somewhat more fortunate, for we had found a room which held but a single bed and a single sleeper. . . . Our host immediately proceeded to the bed, and drew the clothes well over the head of its occupant. He then called a man to make a fire, and begged us to sit down." Without embarrassment, Joseph then discoursed on the Church's history and prospects.[25]

The incident occurred a little over a month before the Prophet's death. Nauvoo had grown into a large city, about as large as Chicago. Immigrants were pouring in at a ferocious rate, and a huge temple was under construction on the bluff overlooking the town. Still, at this late date, Joseph could not entertain important visitors in a parlor, the essential architecture of a gentleman. He talked to them in his pantaloons, sitting in a bedroom next to a concealed (and likely startled) sleeper huddled under the covers. Much as they admired the Prophet's intelligence and personal force, Quincy and Adams could never write a report on Joseph Smith's refinement.

Joseph Smith himself recognized the incongruity and had taken strong measures to end it. Like Sidney Rigdon, he believed the Saints should show a polished face to the world. A January 1841 revelation commanded the Saints to build a hotel at the same time as the temple was going up, "that the weary traveler may find health and safety while he shall contemplate the word of the Lord" (D&C 124:23). Joseph put the case more bluntly when he later was pressing the city to step up its efforts. "There is no place in this city," he told a conference in April 1843, "where men of wealth, character and influence from abroad can go to repose themselves, and it is necessary we should have such a place."[26] He foresaw the arrival of figures like Quincy and Adams and knew they deserved better than a bed covered with cockroaches and a parlor shared with a covered sleeper. Lyman Wight and George Miller got busy in the summer of 1841 to raise money and bring down lumber from Wisconsin to raise the massive structure. The plans called for a three-story brick building composed of two wings, each 120 by 40 feet, enough space for seventy-five rooms plus a suite for Joseph and his family.[27]

In the end, the hotel construction was more than the Saints could manage at the same time as the temple. The hotel was never completed, though not for want of effort on Joseph's part. He insisted the hotel was of equal importance with the temple, though sentiment was all against him. "The building of the Nauvoo House is just as sacred in my view as the Temple," he told the workers in February of 1843. "I want the Nauvoo House built. It *must* be built. Our salvation [as a city] depends upon it." As he put it, the Lord had commanded, "'Build a Temple to my great name, and call the attention of the great, the rich, and the noble.'" But when they came to see the temple, they would ask, "Where shall we lay our heads? In an old log cabin."[28] But the rhetoric was in vain. In the summer of 1843, the project was abandoned with the hotel only partly up, and the next May, Quincy and Adams had to stay in a shanty.

As a comment on the Mormon attitude toward gentility, the failed Nauvoo House made the point exactly. The large plan, the great effort, Joseph's pleadings with the workmen, all attested to his serious interest in presenting his people favorably. How else, as Sidney put it, "is Zion to become the joy and the praise of the whole earth"? Nothing about the city or the Saints should bring shame to the work, moving Joseph to put the hotel, rhetorically at least, on a par with the temple. But when resources ran out, Nauvoo House construction stopped while the Saints worked on the temple up to the last second before their departure, determined to complete it at any cost. Refinement and beauty were means to an end, not, like the temple, the greatest good itself.

Warren Cowdery stated the Mormon position in an 1837 essay on "Manners" in the *Messenger and Advocate*. "I make it a point of morality," Cowdery wrote, "never to find fault with another for his manners. They may be awkward or graceful, blunt or polite, polished or rustic, I care not what they are if the man means well and acts from honest intentions."[29] Joseph Smith would have endorsed those sentiments. He said that he loved a man better "who swears a stream as long as my arm yet deals justice to his neighbors and mercifully deals his substance to the poor, than the long, smooth-faced hypocrite." He spoke of himself as "a huge, rough stone rolling down from a high mountain," polished only when it chipped off a corner by striking something.[30] John D. Lee, a rough-hewn man himself, said Joseph's "countenance was that of a plain, honest man, full of benevolence and philanthropy and void of deceit or hypocrisy."[31]

Joseph Smith's hopes for elevating his people followed along the same line. He certainly did not want to leave them mired in vulgarity and coarseness. Jackson County frontiersmen shocked him in 1831 with their "degradation, leanness of intellect, ferocity, and jealousy"; he mourned for those "who roamed about without the benefit of civilization, refinement, or religion."[32] Joseph envisioned cultural development for the Saints, but not exactly in terms of genteel polish. He used another vocabulary for the assembly that gathered in April 1841 to lay the foundation stones for the Nauvoo temple. The crowd's demeanor lifted his spirits, because he heard no profane language and saw no intoxication:

> We will say we never witnessed a more imposing spectacle than was presented on this occasion, and during the sessions of the conference. Such a multitude of people moving in harmony, in friendship, in dignity, told in a voice not easily misunderstood, that they were a people of intelligence, and virtue and order; in short, that they were Saints; and that the God of love, purity and light, was their God, their Exemplar, and Director; and that they were blessed and happy.[33]

Those were Joseph's words—intelligence, virtue, order, friendship. Nothing about dress, posture, fine manners, fashion. He was more interested in character than personality.

The refinement-in-the-wilderness histories of Utah, then, must be put in a broader context. Refinement there was, most certainly, but more as a product of spreading middle-class gentility than as a result of Mormon teachings. In Mormon culture, refinement was more an aspect of hospitality and public relations than of religion itself. The campaign for gentility conducted in the pages of the *Woman's Exponent* in the 1870s was as much political as moral. Among the Mormons, the highest human ideal was not refinement. The grim bearded faces and gaunt female forms in Anderson's photographs were not incomplete Saints, as the history of refinement implies (fig. 2). Joseph could have sat among them, dressed in workman's clothes, and chatted as comfortably as he talked with visiting Brahmins. He cared more that his people were honest and loyal, true to one another and their faith, than that they throw off gleams from a polished surface. If they slid their food into their mouths on a knife blade, he would not have objected. He never pretended to be a polished gentleman himself and valued a host of other qualities above good manners. From Liberty Jail in March 1839, he pled with the Saints for a reformation of everyone, "both old and young teachers and taugh[t] both high and low rich and poor bond and free Male and female." What he wanted from them was something far simpler and more difficult than refined manners. "Let honesty and sobriety,

FIG. 2. Refinement was not the highest priority for these Utahns posing for photographer George Edward Anderson in the early 1900s.

and cander and solemnity, and virtue, and pureness, and meekness, and simplisity, Crown our heads in every place."[34] He would have asked the same of farm families in desert cabins and of well-dressed ladies and gentlemen on the streets of Salt Lake City.

NOTES

1. Frances Trollope, *Domestic Manners of the Americans* (1836; New York: Howard Wilford Bell, 1904), 16, 19–20, 21–22, 25.

2. Ibid., vi, vii.

3. Richard L. Bushman, *The Refinement of America: Persons, Houses, Cities* (New York: Alfred A. Knopf, 1992), 386–88.

4. Josiah Quincy, *Figures of the Past*, (1883; Boston: Little, Brown, 1926), 229–30.

5. Bushman, *Refinement of America*, 184–85.

6. Quoted in Ibid., 314, 317.

7. Quoted in Ibid., 319.

8. Bushman, *Refinement of America*, 425–26.

9. Richard S. Van Wagoner, *Sidney Rigdon: A Portrait of Religious Excess* (Salt Lake City: Signature Books, 1994), 4–5, 10–11, 29.

10. Sidney Rigdon, "The Saints and the World," *Messenger and Advocate* 3 (December 1836): 421.

11. "Baptism—the Mode of Its Administration . . . ," *Times and Seasons* 4 (September 15, 1843): 321.

12. Hyrum L. Andrus and Helen Mae Andrus, *They Knew the Prophet* (Salt Lake City: Bookcraft, 1974), 173.

13. Joseph Smith Jr., *History of the Church of Jesus Christ of Latter-day Saints,* ed. B. H. Roberts, 2d ed., rev., 7 vols. (Salt Lake City: Deseret Book, 1971), 4:566 (hereafter cited as *History of the Church*).

14. Andrus and Andrus, *They Knew the Prophet*, 29.

15. Elizabeth Allen, *Sketches of Green Mountain Life; with an Autobiography of the Author* (Lowell, Mass.: Nathaniel L. Dayton, 1846).

16. William Mulder and A. Russell Mortensen, eds., *Among the Mormons: Historic Accounts by Contemporary Observers* (New York: Alfred A. Knopf, 1958), 118–19, 120, 123.

17. Quoted in Fawn M. Brodie, *No Man Knows My History: The Life of Joseph Smith* (New York: Alfred A. Knopf, 1945), 103.

18. Quoted in Ibid., 103–4.

19. Linda King Newell and Valeen Tippetts Avery, *Mormon Enigma: Emma Hale Smith: Prophet's Wife, "Elect Lady," Polygamy's Foe, 1804–1879* (Garden City, N.Y.: Doubleday, 1984), 61.

20. Quincy, *Figures of the Past*, 296.

21. Ibid., 231–33.

22. Ibid., 320–22.

23. Robert Flanders, *Nauvoo: Kingdom on the Mississippi* (Urbana: University of Illinois Press, 1965), 175.

24. In a letter written at that time, Quincy said the Mansion House was "about as dirty as the prophet himself." Jed Woodworth, "Josiah Quincy's 1844 Visit with Joseph Smith, " *BYU Studies* 39, no 4 (2000): 86. A month later, John C. Calhoun Jr. visited Joseph in Nauvoo and was entertained in a "drawingroom." Brian Q. Cannon, "John C.

Calhoun, Jr., Meets the Prophet Joseph Smith Shortly before the Departure for Carthage," *BYU Studies* 33, no. 4 (1993): 777.

25. Quincy, *Figures of the Past*, 322.

26. *History of the Church*, 5:328.

27. Flanders, *Nauvoo*, 182–83.

28. *History of the Church*, 5:285.

29. Warren Cowdery, "Manners," *Messenger and Advocate* 3 (February 1837): 463.

30. *History of the Church*, 5:401.

31. Quoted in Brodie, *No Man Knows My History*, 125.

32. *History of the Church*, 1:189.

33. Ibid., 4:331.

34. Dean C. Jessee, ed., *The Personal Writings of Joseph Smith* (Salt Lake City: Deseret Book, 1984), 397.

15

Joseph Smith as Translator

I began work on a cultural biography of Joseph Smith during my year at the Huntington Library in San Marino, California, in 1996. Facing a mountain of material and scores of difficult questions, I looked for a way to crystallize my thinking as I burrowed through the sources. I hit upon the expedient of preparing preliminary sketches like the small paintings that sometimes precede a mural or larger work.

Joseph Smith's entry into the religious world as a translator fascinated me, so I read up on other translators, scurrying about the Huntington learning how Champollion cracked Egyptian. I had no plans for the essay other than as background for the book. The essay was sitting quietly in my files when Bryan Waterman, then a graduate student at Boston University, wrote about the collection of essays he was assembling for The Prophet Puzzle *(Salt Lake City: Signature Books, 1999). I knew I would disagree with some of the essays in the volume but felt my argument spoke for itself, regardless of its companions.*

The books and essays on Joseph Smith's translations, many of them by skeptics who doubt he translated at all, overlook one large question: How did Joseph Smith come to think of himself as a translator? Laying aside the accuracy of the translations, the preceding question asks where the idea of a translation of any kind originated. No other religious young man in nineteenth-century New York—or anyone else for that matter—offered a volume of translated reformed Egyptian as his initial claim on the public's attention. What inspired Joseph Smith to think of himself as a translator? Ethan Smith, author of *View of the Hebrews* (1823), did not translate ancient records to justify his speculations about Native American origins; Joseph Smith did, and historians who think of the Book of Mormon as a nineteenth-century production need to explain why.

The closest precedent is Solomon Spaulding's "Manuscript Found," the work of a sometime preacher and iron master who migrated from Connecticut to New York to Ohio and wrote a purported translation of a supposed Latin document telling about a Roman voyage to the New World. For a time, Eber D. Howe, the hostile Ohio newspaper editor who published *Mormonism Unvailed* [*sic*] in 1834, claimed Spaulding's story was a source for the Book of Mormon.[1] When the manuscript was eventually located and published in 1885, that theory collapsed, but was Spaulding a precedent for the idea of translation?[2] The faint similarities notwithstanding, Spaulding's translated story no more serves as a precedent for Joseph Smith than renowned translations such as Alexander Pope's rendition of *The Iliad*. Spaulding and Pope were learned men who understood the language they translated. A Dartmouth College graduate who knew Latin, Spaulding made no claim to inspiration. The question is not the idea of translation itself—the learned world was filled with translators and translations—but translation without prior training. Why would Joseph Smith think that he could translate when he lacked all the necessary qualifications?

Joseph Smith's enthusiasm for translation deepens the problem of historical explanation. The role of translator did not spin off from the larger task of writing the Book of Mormon and then disappear once the book was finished. Within a few months of its publication, Joseph began to translate the Bible, and after that the books of Abraham and Joseph. His enthusiasm for translation carried over into a passion for Hebrew. He seemed to embrace translation as a fixed element of his religious identity. An early revelation said he was to be called "a seer, a translator, a prophet" in the records of the Church (D&C 21:1). Why did he find the role of translator so congenial when it was so foreign to his education and background?

Other religious young men of that time did not think of themselves as budding translators of scripture. The conventional path for young people with a religious calling led from personal conversion to preaching. Charles Grandison Finney, a contemporary of Joseph Smith and a revivalist in Joseph's area during the time when the Book of Mormon was published, went through experiences much like Joseph's, up to a point. Born in Connecticut in 1792, Finney was studying law in Adams, New York, when he became convinced of his utter sinfulness. In the autumn of 1821, desperate for relief from his guilt, he stole into the woods for a private prayer. Like Joseph Smith, he had his prayer answered and, again like Joseph, had a vision of Jesus Christ. The Savior appeared while Finney was praying in his law office that night. "It seemed as if I met the Lord Jesus Christ face to face." Later in life he decided the vision was "a mental state," but at the time, he said, "It seemed to me that I saw him as I would see any other man. It seemed to me a reality, that he stood before me, and I fell down at his feet and poured out my soul to him."[3]

The desire for forgiveness, the prayer in the woods, the vision of Christ put Joseph Smith and Charles Finney on parallel tracks until 1821, when they abruptly diverged. Finney went on to become the foremost revivalist of his age, converting thousands in towns along the Erie Canal, the famous "burned-over district" that included Palmyra, New York. Later he was installed as president of Oberlin College. Joseph Smith was not particularly notable for his preaching as a young man, did not attract followers that way, and never conducted a revival of the kind Finney would recognize. Instead, at age twenty-three, Joseph translated a lengthy book, virtually another Bible, and made it the foundation of his new religion.

Joseph Smith always subordinated his role as translator to the more encompassing office of prophet. He chose the larger title when he had an opportunity to define himself in February 1831 upon first arriving in Kirtland, Ohio, to meet a new group of followers. In the legendary account, when Joseph jumped from his sleigh after the journey from Palmyra, he grasped storekeeper Newell K. Whitney by the hand and said, "I am Joseph the Prophet"; and so he was to the Saints from then on.[4] But what stood out about his prophethood in 1831 was the translation. The First Vision was scarcely ever mentioned in those years and received only the most glancing reference in the revelations.[5] During the first months in Kirtland, a little more was made of the restoration of the Aaronic Priesthood and the revelation about the New Jerusalem, but these revelations had not been published yet. The tangible evidence of Joseph's divine calling was the Book of Mormon and the miraculous translation of the hieroglyphs. A few years later in 1834 and 1835 when Oliver Cowdery wrote down his memories of Joseph Smith, Oliver still summed up his account by saying that "the translator of the book of Mormon is worthy [of] the appelation of a seer and a prophet of the Lord."[6]

Outsiders saw Joseph in the same light in the early years. The improbability of a translation struck newspapers as being nearly as strange as the gold plates of the Book of Mormon themselves. The first paper to report the "pretended discovery" said the record was "written in ancient characters, impossible to be interpreted by any to whom the special gift has not been imparted by inspiration."[7] Two months later, in August 1829, a Rochester paper gave as much space to the translation process as to the plates. The editor said the "blindly enthusiastic" Martin Harris "went in search of some one, besides the interpreter, who was learned enough to *English* [translate] them." Finding no one, the article went on, "Harris returned, and set Smith to work at interpreting the Bible."[8] Rather than talk about the contents of the Book of Mormon, the editor of the *Painesville Telegraph* in Ohio noted that "it contains about 500 octavo pages, which is said to be translated from Egyptian Hieroglyphics, on metal plates, by one Smith, who was enabled to read the characters by instruction from Angels."[9] The curious fact, doubtless passed along by believers, was that "the said Smith though a man so illiterate that he cannot write, was, by divine inspiration, enabled to give the true interpretation."[10] In newspapers the translation of the Book of Mormon was Joseph's chief claim to notoriety.

Unfazed by the editors' skepticism, Joseph Smith kept on translating even after the Book of Mormon was published. The role of translator of many records evolved out of experiences with the Book of Mormon. A revelation received in April 1829 while the Book of Mormon was still in process broached the possibility of more records yet to come. The additional records were mentioned in a revelation to Oliver Cowdery, who himself had asked for the privilege of translating. Cowdery had watched Joseph turn out page after page of Book of Mormon translation and then settle a question about the state of the apostle John by translating a parchment written by John that apparently Joseph had seen in vision. After that, Cowdery "became exceedingly anxious to have the power to translate bestowed upon him."[11] A revelation told him that he would "receive a knowledge concerning the engravings of old records, which are ancient," and that if he asked, he would "translate and receive knowledge from all those ancient records which have been hid up, that are sacred" (D&C 8:1, 11). The revelation sparked visions of piles of records awaiting translation. After Cowdery's failure to translate, a revelation comforted him with the news that "other records have I, that I will give unto you power that you may assist to translate" (D&C 9:2).

The prospect of more records to translate would not have discouraged Joseph Smith, who apparently enjoyed his unusual gift. The harsh revelation received after 116 pages of Book of Mormon translation were lost in 1828 spoke of translation as a treasure he was in danger of losing unless he heeded God more than man. For "except thou do this, thou shalt be delivered up and become as other men, and have no more gift" (D&C 3:11). The words suggest that, in God's eyes, and probably in Joseph's own, the "sight and power to translate" distinguished the Prophet from other men (D&C 3:12). To lose the gift would devastate his developing prophetic identity and would be akin to losing a vital bodily organ. One can imagine that translating day after day for three months in 1829, dictating hundreds of thousands of words, gave Joseph pleasure. While translating, he was in his "zone," functioning at the peak of his abilities.

Three months after the publication of the Book of Mormon, Joseph went back to translating, this time working on the Bible itself, beginning with Genesis. He started in June 1830 with a revelation to Moses that prefaced the creation story in the first chapter of Genesis. Joseph called his revision and expansion of the scriptures a translation, although he had no ancient text before him other than the King James Bible. In some passages, he altered a few words; in others he interwove a few verses; in the case of Moses' preface and the stories of Enoch, he added many pages of new text. But he summed up the different forms of emendations under the heading of translation, and until 1833 this was his day-to-day work.[12] While he was administering Church affairs and coping with catastrophes and petty personal problems, his main job was to translate the Bible, believing that he was complying with the promise given in the February 1831 revelation: "my scriptures shall be given as I have appointed" (D&C 42:56). When they were completed, they would be printed as the Book of Mormon was. To make sure the translation reached the world, a second temple in Kirtland, intended to match the first in size, was designated for the lot just south of the main temple. Though never built, this second temple was meant for "the work of the printing of the translation of my scriptures" (D&C 94:10).

Joseph completed his work on the Bible in 1833, but in 1835, when Egyptian scrolls fell into his hands, he went back to translating. Until 1842 he worked on these ancient records, which he said contained writings of Abraham and Joseph and which seemed to arrive in fulfillment of the earlier promise to Oliver Cowdery about additional sacred writings to translate.[13] Thus from age seventeen, when he learned about the golden plates, until two years before his death, Joseph Smith translated ancient records in fulfillment of the title given him at the organization of the Church and in defiance of all expectations associated with the translation process in nineteenth-century America.

In the world at large, translation was work for the learned, almost exclusively college-educated men whose educations were distinguished by instruction in classical languages. Boys from ordinary households and girls who attended school learned to write, read, do simple arithmetic, and understand rudimentary geography and history, but not to translate classical texts. Elegant young women learned French, drawing, fancy sewing, and other genteel arts suitable for polishing young women of their class, but only college-bound young men were taught Latin and learned to translate as part of their ordinary recitations. That learning set them apart as gentlemen and was considered useless for anyone else. Ministerial candidates learned Greek and Hebrew to enable them to interpret the scriptures. Those were the realms where translation went on.[14]

Only the most learned of this college-educated class would undertake a translation of scripture. In Joseph Smith's lifetime, a number of scholars retranslated the Bible from Greek or Hebrew, seeking to simplify the language and make the scriptures more accessible. In 1826, for example, Alexander Campbell, the onetime friend of Sidney Rigdon and later critic of the Book of Mormon, published a new version of the New Testament that combined portions of three new translations, selected by Campbell for their intelligibility and their recognition of immersion as the proper mode of baptism.[15] In 1833 Noah Webster, the student of the American language and author of the dictionary, published a translation designed for American audiences.[16] Theirs were only two among a number meant to encourage popular study of the scriptures.[17] But the multitude of new translations only made Joseph's translation more anomalous, for he encroached on work reserved solely for the most learned men of the age. A book about American translations of the Bible said his work contained "the most astonishing claims ever made in connection with the Bible, and the most peculiar alterations of any Bible in English ever published."[18]

At a still more stratospheric level, French scholar Jean-François Champollion first deciphered Egyptian hieroglyphics in 1822 through close study of parallel documents inscribed in three scripts on the Rosetta Stone (fig. 1). Discussion of the hieroglyphs entered into elite American periodicals like the *North American Review* as early as 1823, and a follow-up article in 1829 discussed Champollion's translation in the very year when Joseph Smith was translating the "reformed Egyptian" on the plates. Conceivably news of Champollion's triumph could have reached Palmyra, but only to discourage Joseph Smith, not to encourage him. The translation of the Rosetta Stone was a work of the most advanced scholarship, a *tour de force* of ingenuity and learning. Champollion was a prodigy who delivered a paper on Coptic at age sixteen and was appointed professor of history at the Grenoble lyceum at age eighteen. Later a chair of Egyptology was created in the College de France especially for him.[19] Culturally, Champollion dwelt in another world from the Mormon prophet. Why Joseph thought he could translate Egyptian characters as this savant did is an unanswered question for those who try to explain the prophet's life historically.

The translation problem takes a more subtle form for those who believe Joseph Smith received the assignment to translate from heaven. Latter-day Saints believe that Joseph did not have to think up the idea of translating gold plates; Moroni told him about "two stones in silver bows," called the Urim and Thummim, and said he would find them with the buried plates. By observing that "God <had> prepared them for the purpose of translating the book," Moroni made Joseph's task obvious.[20] The question for believers is not where the notion of translation originated but how Joseph Smith understood the strange work that had been thrust upon him. He surely knew that translation was not work for the uneducated and that his attempt to translate an unknown language invited skepticism. Why did he find the role of translator so congenial when it was so foreign to his education and background?

Courtesy Egypt Exploration Society

FIG. 1. Jean-François Champollion (1790–1832). His translation of Egyptian at a young age let him into scholarly circles and wide acclaim.

Joseph's only contact with the learned world of translation was in 1828 through the visit of Martin Harris to Charles Anthon, the Columbia University classics professor. One of the first outside the family to believe Joseph, Harris understandably wanted verification of Joseph's work, and, like everyone else, he associated translation with learning. The most natural course in his state of half-doubt, half-belief was to ask a learned person what he thought of Joseph Smith's translation. Anthon's and Harris's accounts of the interview differ drastically. Harris said Anthon confirmed the accuracy of the translation at first and then withdrew written certification when told the plates could not be seen because a part was sealed. Anthon said that the characters were a confused medley of awkwardly scrawled figures, and he advised Harris to steer clear of Joseph Smith. Either way, Harris left Anthon convinced that he could not translate the characters and that Joseph Smith could.[21]

The incident came to mean more to Joseph than to Martin Harris, for it was told as the fulfillment of a biblical prophecy in which Joseph figured. Someone, possibly Joseph himself, seized upon a passage in Isaiah 29 about a learned man who was unable to read a sealed book and an unlearned man who received it despite a lack of learning:

> And the vision of all is become unto you as the words of a book that is sealed, which men deliver to one that is learned, saying, Read this, I pray thee: and he saith, I cannot; for it is sealed: And the book is delivered to him that is not learned, saying, Read this, I pray thee: and he saith, I am not learned. (Isa. 29:11–12)

Joseph saw at once that he and Anthon were the two men in the passage, the unlearned and the learned. The idea of fulfilling a biblical prophecy was gratifying. But still more important, the passage defined a role for Joseph. He was to be another kind of translator, one quite different from Anthon and his ilk, a special kind of translator foreseen in the Bible. In the retelling of the Anthon story, the Isaiah language saturated the account. In his 1832 history, Joseph took the pen from the hand of Frederick G. Williams and personally wrote about Anthon and Harris, who, Joseph said,

> came to Su[s]quehanna and said the Lord had shown him that he must go to new York City with some of the c[h]aracters so we proceeded to coppy some of them and he took his Journy to the Eastern Cittys and to the Learned <saying> read this I pray thee and the learned said I cannot but if he would bring the plates they would read it but the Lord had fo<r>bid it and he returned to me and gave them to <me to> translate and I said ~~I said~~ [I] cannot for I am not learned but the Lord had prepared ~~specticke~~ spectacles for to read the Book.[22]

That passage can be read as marking Joseph's liberation from the learned's claims to a monopoly on translation. When Harris returned, Joseph, scantily educated and just twenty-two, could be Isaiah's unlearned man to whom the Lord gave spectacles and a gift to translate a book the learned could not understand.[23]

In the year following Harris's New York visit, Joseph received confirmation of his somewhat precarious identity in the pages of the Book of Mormon. The book had its own translation stones and inspired translators, the most notable being the King Mosiah who was called upon to translate the twenty-four gold plates of the Jaredites (fig. 2). In the Book of Mormon narrative, the records were discovered after the Jaredites' extinction, and the finders of the plates were intensely curious about what happened. Ammon, an adventurer who knew about Mosiah's powers, told the possessors of the plates that the king "has wherewith that he can look, and translate all records that are of ancient date; and it is a gift from God" (Mosiah 8:13).

Joseph Smith, of course, could see himself in that description, for no mention was made of Mosiah's learning or his mastery of other languages. Mosiah had "interpreters" just as Joseph did, and he translated with this gift (Mosiah 8:13). Moreover, according to the Book of Mormon passage, with the command to look in the interpreters went a title; he who looked, "the same is called seer" (Mosiah 8:13). "A seer is a revelator and a prophet also," Ammon explained, "and a gift which is greater can no man have" (Mosiah 8:16). Besides translating, "a seer can know of things which are past, and also of things which are to come, and by them shall all things be revealed." The description opened vistas beyond the work of translating. Through a seer "shall secret things be made manifest, and hidden things shall come to light, and things which are not known shall be made known by them" (Mosiah 8:17). And all of this was not to exalt the seer himself but to advance the work of God. "Thus God has provided a means that man, through faith, might work mighty miracles; therefore he becometh a great benefit to his fellow beings" (Mosiah 8:18).

Joseph could see himself in those words, just as he found himself in Isaiah's unlearned man. He was more than a mere translator. He translated as Mosiah did, as a seer with interpreters rather than a scholar trained in languages. Together the Book of Mormon and Bible passage formed a tradition for Joseph's incongruous position as a translator. Rather than an ignorant man attempting an impossible task, he was a latter-day edition of Mosiah's seer.

The culture of Vermont and upstate New York may have partially prepared Joseph Smith for this peculiar role. He probably knew the meaning of the word *seer* before he came across it in the Book of Mormon. *Seer* appears in scripture as an older name for prophet: "A Prophet was beforetime called a Seer" (1 Sam. 9:9). In the Bible, Samuel was a seer, and the blinding of seers in Isaiah's prophecy went with the closing of the heavens

Courtesy Museum of Art, Brigham Young University

FIG. 2. Minerva Teichert (1888–1976), *Mosiah Interprets the Jaredite*. Oil on Masonite, 36" x 48". The Book of Mormon prophet Mosiah translates a Jaredite stone tablet as a scribe takes down his words. Translation was performed "by the gift and power of God" (Omni 1:21), probably with the aid of interpreters described elsewhere in the Book of Mormon (see Mosiah 8:13).

and the blighting of the earth (1 Chr. 9:22; Isa. 29:10). In non-biblical literature, the word had a religious ring, too. In Alexander Pope's translation of the *Iliad*, for example, there was a "sacred Seer whose comprehensive View The past, the present, and the future knew."[24]

The word had another life in the culture of seventeenth-century magic. John Dee, the seventeenth-century practitioner of hermetic philosophy, worked with a "Prophet or Seer" who looked into stones.[25] But this older meaning was probably not available to Joseph. By the time the culture of magic made its way down through the centuries and into the neighborhood of the Smiths in New York, the word *seer* was not connected with looking into stones for lost treasures. In the affidavits on the Smith family treasure-seeking collected by Doctor Philastus Hurlbut in 1833, the neighbors never used the word *seer* to describe Joseph or the supposed treasure expeditions with his father. The neighbors frequently mentioned the use of a "stone," or a "glass," or a "peep-stone," but never a "seerstone." None of the critical neighbors called Joseph a seer, though they did speak of his "seeing" with a stone.[26] If the word was in use in Palmyra, it likely had too many biblical associations for it to apply to Joseph Smith. The neighbors, trying to denigrate him with their stories of stones, avoided intimations of a holy calling.

Latter-day Saints first applied the word *seer* to Joseph and combined the two words *seer* and *stone*. Martin Harris, David Whitmer, Oliver Cowdery, Brigham Young, and Orson Pratt described Joseph using a "seerstone" to translate and receive revelations.[27] In making the connection, they joined two traditions—the holy calling of seer and the magical practice of divining with a stone. The marriage of the two words in Mormon usage summarized the changes that Joseph had to go through as he moved into his offices of seer, translator, and prophet. The word *seer* elevated the stones, symbolizing the redirection of the Smith family's interest in magic toward a more serious religious end. Joseph put the pursuit of treasure aside in favor of a greater calling, just as Oliver Cowdery gave up working with a divining rod to write for Joseph.[28]

Although treasure-seeking was left behind, the magical culture of the stones played an important part in the development of Joseph's identity as seer and translator. The Christianity of Methodism or Presbyterianism could not have readied him for translation. In conventional Protestant Christianity, learned men translated the Bible, and pious young people became preachers like Finney or Lorenzo Dow, not translators. The treasure-seeking stones from magic culture, by contrast, helped Joseph move step by step into his calling. The scryer of stones looked for the unseen, whether lost objects or buried treasure. Joseph's first reaction when he brought home the Urim and Thummim was delight with the powers of the instrument. It was "ten times Better than I expected," he told Joseph Knight. "I can see any thing: they are Marvelus."[29] Though amazed at the Urim and Thummim's power, he knew from working with his own stones what to expect; he would "see." Although he had obtained one of his early stones from a hole dug for a well and not by a gift from heaven, practice with stones, looking for lost objects and probably for treasure, was an initiation into "seeing" that could be transferred to translation of the gold plates in the stones of the Urim and Thummim. In fact, as work on the Book of Mormon went on, a seerstone took the place of the Urim and Thummim, blending the culture of magic with the divine culture of translation.[30]

As time went by, Joseph played down the place of magic and seerstones in his early life. After publication of the damning affidavits about money digging in Eber Howe's *Mormonism Unvailed* (1834), he knew that involvement with magic would discredit the Church. Conventional Christianity was fighting to protect itself from the Enlightenment critics' charges of superstition, and, to prove their rationality, Christian apologists vented their anger on the remnants of magic carried down from an earlier time when magic and religion mingled. Joseph did not want to make himself a target for attacks that would cripple the work. But neither did he repudiate the stones or deny their powers.[31] In 1843, using language from the New Testament, he taught that a white stone would be given to all entrants into the celestial kingdom, and with that stone "all things pertaining to an higher order of kingdoms even all kingdoms will be made known."[32] The magic culture of his early life, like his inherited Christianity, though transformed, was not obliterated. He must have understood that the stones had prepared him to step into the improbable roles of seer and unlearned translator.

Joseph Smith's development as a translator did not end when he completed the Book of Mormon and relinquished the seerstones. As he went on to the Bible and the Book of Abraham, his methods changed, and interestingly, he moved closer to the learned men whose powers seemed so far beyond him at the start. As he worked on the Bible, he at first made drastic changes in the revelations on Moses and Enoch received in 1830. Later as he went through the book, he appears to have been reading and rereading in search of flawed passages. The changes did not come to him in a flash of insight or a burst of revelation. As Robert Matthews notes in his study of the Joseph Smith Translation, "a passage that had been revised and recorded once was later further revised and recorded. Some passages were revised even a third time."[33] The manuscript shows signs of him searching his mind for the right words, as a more conventional translator might do. He gave up the Urim and Thummim, Orson Pratt later said, because he had become acquainted with "the Spirit of Revelation and Prophecy" and no longer needed its aid.[34] The inspiration worked in his own mind rather than through an external instrument.

The revisions themselves were more like an improved translation, too. Unlike the many additional pages on Moses and Enoch now published as the Book of Moses, the subsequent revisions added a few verses or altered a word or two, clarifying meaning in small ways in the manner of the translations that sought to make the Bible more accessible to readers. Joseph obviously relied on inspiration to make the changes, since he did not work from an ancient text, but many of the changes read like a conventional translator's work.

As he rounded out his revision of the New Testament in 1833, Joseph Smith paradoxically took up the study of Hebrew. After six years of translating the Book of Mormon and the Bible as an unlearned man, Joseph hired a Jewish scholar, Joshua Seixias, to teach Hebrew in Kirtland, Ohio. Joseph the prophet and seer sat down to learn a language from a professor. Moreover, though he never mastered Hebrew, Joseph became an avid pupil.[35] He loved the classes, advanced rapidly considering the little time he had, and began to introduce translations of Hebrew words into his sermons.[36] His excitement about translating as a seer carried over into his conventional study of languages. A revelation given as he began the study instructed him to "become acquainted with all good books, and with languages, tongues, and people" (D&C 90:15)—despite all of his experience of translation by divine gift.

When he began work on the Book of Abraham after the Church had purchased the Egyptian scrolls from Michael Chandler in 1835, Joseph Smith, having no knowledge of Egyptian, had to rely on inspiration to effect a translation. Although the Book of Abraham in part resembles chapters from Genesis, the text went far beyond the Bible in many respects—again a heroic alteration. But even in this reversion to the Book of Mormon methods, Joseph reached out to conventional scholarship. Instead of plunging into translation as he had with the Book of Mormon, he first worked on "translating an alphabet to the Book of Abraham, and arranging a grammar of the Egyptian language as practiced by the ancients."[37] The next year, 1836, Champollion's *Grammaire* of Egyptian, considered to be his greatest scholarly achievement, was published posthumously, and a year earlier Joseph Smith was writing his "Grammar & Alphabet of the Egyptian Language." The manuscript shows an Egyptian character in a ruled column on the left, and opposite on the right a translation. The translations contain whole paragraphs of material for a single character, and, as the grammar went on, blend into the translation that eventually became the Book of Abraham. But on the first page, the grammar lays down rules for understanding Egyptian, using phrases like "parts of speech," and words like "verbs, participles-prepositions, conjunctions, and adverbs," the words of a grammarian and linguist.[38]

The Egyptian Grammar perplexes Latter-day Saints, who have never known whether to consider it an inspired work or exploratory experiments with an alien language.[39] As far as can be told now, Joseph Smith's translations of the Egyptian characters do not conform to modern understanding of their meaning. They came by inspiration, not from a precocious deciphering of hieroglyphics. On the other hand, they have the appearance and in places the language of a grammar and dictionary. The work seems suspended between the world of learning and the world of divine gift. Joseph could never change himself from seer into scholar, but in this document he reached for more conventional mastery, as if he wanted to blend learning with his own special powers.[40]

Near the end of his life, in a rare moment of self-reflection, Joseph told the Saints that he knew his story strained credulity.[41] Like all religious visionaries, he understood his experience as coming from without, not from within; God, angels, the Holy Spirit directed him, not his own genius. But even so, his own creative powers had to organize the visions and divine commands into a coherent human identity. The translation of the Book of Mormon required him to forge an unprecedented self-understanding for an unlearned citizen of the nineteenth century.

He took on the work with great enthusiasm, developing a momentum that propelled him from the Book of Mormon to the Bible and the Book of Abraham. When the plates were first removed from the hill, he told Joseph

Knight that they were "writen in Caracters and I want them translated," and his resolve never wavered.[42] He loved translating and, rather than faltering under the strain of performing the impossible, valiantly labored on. Near the end of his life, he described himself to James Arlington Bennet, the man he sought for his running mate on the 1844 U.S. presidential ticket: "By the power of God I translated the Book of Mormon from hieroglyphics; the knowledge of which was lost to the world: in which wonderful event I stood alone, an unlearned youth, to combat the worldly wisdom, and multiplied ignorance of eighteen centuries."[43] In that statement, made when pressures on him were mounting, we sense the burden of living an incredible life. But those glimpses were rare. For the most part, his faith in his calling and his buoyant spirit carried him through the formidable task of translating indecipherable hieroglyphics.

NOTES

1. Eber D. Howe, *Mormonism Unvailed; or, A Faithful Account of that Singular Imposition and Delusion, from Its Rise to the Present Time* (Painesville, Ohio: By the author, 1834), 278–90.

2. The classic critique of the Spaulding theory is Fawn M. Brodie, *No Man Knows My History: The Life of Joseph Smith, the Mormon Prophet* (New York: Alfred A. Knopf, 1945), 419–33. A more thorough study is Lester E. Bush Jr., "The Spaulding Theory Then and Now," *Dialogue: A Journal of Mormon Thought* 10 (autumn 1977): 40–69. A highly attenuated effort to revive the Spaulding theory is found in David Persuitte, *Joseph Smith and the Origins of the Book of Mormon* (Jefferson, N.C.: McFarland, 1985), 247–55. In an attempt to distance the Book of Mormon from Spaulding's romance, Latter-day Saint scholars recently republished the original manuscript in Solomon Spaulding, *Manuscript Found: The Complete Original "Spaulding Manuscript,"* ed. Kent P. Jackson, vol. 11 in Religious Studies Center Specialized Monograph Series (Provo: Religious Studies Center, Brigham Young University, 1996).

3. Charles G. Finney, *Memoirs of Rev. Charles G. Finney, Written by Himself* (New York: A. S. Barnes, 1867), 9–20.

4. Joseph Smith Jr., *History of The Church of Jesus Christ of Latter-day Saints,* ed. B. H. Roberts, 2d ed., rev., 7 vols. (Salt Lake City: Deseret Book, 1971), 1:146n (hereafter cited as *History of the Church*).

5. Doctrine and Covenants 20:5; James B. Allen, "Emergence of a Fundamental: The Expanding Role of Joseph Smith's First Vision in Mormon Religious Thought," *Journal of Mormon History* 7 (1980): 43–61.

6. Dean C. Jessee, ed., *The Papers of Joseph Smith,* 2 vols. (Salt Lake City: Deseret Book, 1989–92), 1:95.

7. *Wayne Sentinel,* June 26, 1829, reprinted in Francis W. Kirkham, *A New Witness for Christ in America,* 2 vols. (Independence, Mo.: Zion's Printing and Publishing, 1942), 1:148.

8. "Golden Bible," *Rochester Daily Advertiser and Telegraph,* August 31, 1829; reprinted in Kirkham, *New Witness,* 1:151. Compare *Rochester Gem,* September 5, 1829; reprinted in Kirkham, *New Witness,* 1:151–52.

9. "The Golden Bible," *Painesville Telegraph*, November 16, 1830; reprinted in Kirkham, *New Witness*, 1:383.

10. "Beware of Impostors," *Painesville Telegraph*, December 14, 1830; reprinted in Kirkham, *New Witness*, 1:389.

11. Doctrine and Covenants 7; *History of the Church*, 1:35–36.

12. For the whole story of the revision, see Robert J. Matthews, *"A Plainer Translation": Joseph Smith's Translation of the Bible: A History and Commentary* (Provo: Brigham Young University Press, 1985).

13. *History of the Church*, 2:236.

14. Women educational reformers such as Catherine Beecher were beginning to teach Latin in female seminaries in an effort to equalize women's and men's education. Lawrence A. Cremin, *American Education: The National Experience, 1783–1876* (New York: Harper and Row, 1980), 110–11, 140, 144–45, 394, 404.

15. Alexander Campbell, comp., *The Sacred Writings of the Apostles and Evangelists of Jesus Christ, Commonly Styled the New Testament*, translated from the original Greek by George Campbell, James Macknight and Philip Doddridge (Buffaloe, Va.: publisher, 1826). A revised edition was published in 1832.

16. Noah Webster, *The Holy Bible, Containing the Old and New Testaments, in the Common Version with Amendments of the Language* (New Haven, Conn.: Durrie and Peck, 1833).

17. Margaret T. Hills, ed., *The English Bible in America: A Bibliography of Editions of the Bible and the New Testament Published in America, 1777–1957* (New York: American Bible Society and New York Public Library, 1961); E. B. O'Callaghan, *A List of Editions of the Holy Scriptures and Parts Thereof, Printed in America Previous to 1860* (Albany: Musell and Rowland, 1861).

18. P. Marion Simms, *The Bible in America: Versions that Have Played Their Part in the Making of the Republic* (New York: Wilson-Erickson, 1936), 235, 248.

19. Information on Champollion's academic career can be found in virtually any encyclopedia. See, for example, *Encyclopaedia Britannica*, 15th ed., s.v. "Champollion, Jean-François." See also John T. Irwin, *American Hieroglyphics: The Symbol of the Egyptian Hieroglyphics in the American Renaissance* (New Haven, Conn.: Yale University Press, 1980), 4–6, 8; John A. Wilson, *Signs and Wonders Upon Pharaoh: A History of American Egyptology* (Chicago: University of Chicago Press, 1964), 17–19.

20. Jessee, *Papers of Joseph Smith*, 1:278.

21. Richard L. Bushman, *Joseph Smith and the Beginnings of Mormonism* (Urbana: University of Illinois Press, 1984), 86–90.

22. Jessee, *Papers of Joseph Smith*, 1:9.

23. Joseph Knight's telling of Joseph's translation incorporated the same language: "He B[e]ing an unlearned man did not know what to Do. Then the Lord gave him Power to Translate himself. Then ware the Larned men Confounded, for he, By the means he found with the plates, he Could translate those Caricters Better than the Larned." Dean Jessee, "Joseph Knight's Recollection of Early Mormon History," *BYU Studies* 17 (autumn 1976): 35.

24. *The Oxford English Dictionary*, 2d ed., s.v. "seer," citing Pope's 1718 translation (hereafter cited as OED).

25. OED, s.v. "seer"; D. Michael Quinn, *Early Mormonism and the Magic World View*, 2d ed., rev. and enl. (Salt Lake City: Signature Books, 1998), 40.

26. The affidavits on the Smith family collected by Doctor Philastus Hurlbut in 1833 and Arthur Deming in 1885–87 use the words "stone" or "peep-stone," rather than seerstone, though sometimes referring to "seeing" in a stone. Dan Vogel, ed., *Early Mormon Documents*, 3 vols. (Salt Lake City: Signature Books, 1996–2000), 2:24, 32, 35,

38, 41, 43, 60–61, 65–66, 68, 71, 73, 75, 195, 197, 202, 209. The traditional usage of "seer," going back to the seventeenth century and preserved in dictionaries, may have been revived by the Mormons rather than coming out of neighborhood folk magic. Quinn, *Early Mormonism and the Magic World View*, 40.

27. Richard Van Wagoner and Steve Walker, "Joseph Smith: 'The Gift of Seeing,'" *Dialogue: A Journal of Mormon Thought* 15 (summer 1982): 48–68.

28. Richard L. Bushman, "Treasure-Seeking Then and Now," *Sunstone* 11 (September 1987): 5–7. For a brief statement on seerstones, see Richard E. Turley Jr., "Seer Stones," in *Encyclopedia of Mormonism,* ed. Daniel H. Ludlow, 4 vols. (New York: Macmillan, 1992), 3:1293.

29. Quoted in Jessee, "Joseph Knight's Recollection," 33.

30. There is evidence that the translation stone was given him after he lost the Urim and Thummim when the 116 pages disappeared. Van Wagoner and Walker, "Joseph Smith," 54. For an explanation of Joseph Smith's transition between the culture of magic and the culture of translation, see Mark Ashurst-McGee, "A Pathway to Prophethood: Joseph Smith Junior as Rodsman, Village Seer, and Judeo-Christian Prophet" (master's thesis, Utah State University, 2000).

31. Quinn, *Early Mormonism and the Magic World View*, 242–45.

32. Van Wagoner and Walker, "Joseph Smith," 63; D&C 130:9–11.

33. Matthews, *"A Plainer Translation,"* 61.

34. Quoted in ibid., 40.

35. Brodie, *No Man Knows My History*, 169.

36. *History of the Church*, 6:307–8. For an extreme example of using foreign languages, see Brodie, *No Man Knows My History*, 292. Joseph demonstrated his proficiency in Hebrew to Josiah Quincy in April 1844. Josiah Quincy, *Figures of the Past,* (1883; Boston: Little Brown, 1926), 325.

37. *History of the Church*, 2:238.

38. *Joseph Smith's Egyptian Alphabet and Grammar* (Salt Lake City: Modern Microfilm, n.d.).

39. Jay M. Todd, *The Saga of the Book of Abraham* (Salt Lake City: Deseret Book, 1969), 252–55.

40. For comparison of Joseph Smith's translation of the papyri to conventional Egyptology, see the special journal issues devoted to the topic: *Dialogue: A Journal of Mormon Thought* 3 (summer 1968); *Sunstone* 4 (December 1979); and *BYU Studies* 11 (summer 1971).

41. *History of the Church*, 6:317.

42. Joseph Smith, as quoted in Jessee, "Joseph Knight's Recollection," 33.

43. Joseph Smith, as quoted in Van Wagoner and Walker, "Joseph Smith," 50.

16

The "Little, Narrow Prison" of Language: The Rhetoric of Revelation

*Like the essay "Joseph Smith as Translator," this article originated as a prelimi-
nary sketch for my biography of Joseph Smith. In trying to understand Joseph
Smith's revelations, I was looking for ways to explain their effectiveness. I had
always sensed that every text contains worlds, and if we stare long enough at the
text, those worlds will appear to our eyes. Thinking of language as creating a
space helped me to uncover some of those worlds.*

*I was pleased that so much opened up through this approach. I felt that I had
uncovered the existential-religious point that in the end we must decide for
ourselves about the voice of God in scripture. Without recourse to any outside
authority, we must choose to hear and obey or not. I subsequently learned that
Kierkegaard made a similar argument in his nineteenth-century essay "The
Difference between a Genius and an Apostle," in* Without Authority, *ed. and
tr. by Howard V. Hong and Edna H. Hong (Princeton: Princeton University
Press, 1997).*

I want to raise an old question about Joseph Smith's revelations, one
that came up early in Church history when plans were first being made to
publish the compilation of revelations called the Book of Commandments.
The question is about the language of the revelations. Joseph noted in his
history that at the November 1831 conference in Kirtland, Ohio, where publication was approved, "Some conversation was had concerning revelations
and language." This was the occasion when William E. McLellin, apparently the leading critic of the language, was challenged to make a revelation
himself, and failed. Joseph said the elders at the conference all watched
while McLellin made "this vain attempt of a man to imitate the language of
Jesus Christ," noting that "it was an awful responsibility to write in the
name of the Lord."[1]

My interest in the language of the revelations differs from a critic such
as McLellin, who was accused of saying the writing was unworthy of Jesus
Christ. I do not want to open myself to the criticism of having "more learning than sense," as Joseph said of McLellin (fig. 1).[2] I am less interested in
the quality of the language than in its structure: How are these revelations
put together? Rather than feeling they fall below a suitable rhetorical standard, I am impressed with how effective the revelations are and would

Courtesy Church Archives

FIG. 1. William E. McLellin (1806–83). McLellin thought that some of the language in the revelations was beneath the dignity of God but called other portions "some of the most sublime pieces of composition which I ever perused."

like to understand how they work rhetorically. How do they achieve their impact on believing readers? How do they acquire the high seriousness expected of words from the Almighty?

Consider section 4 of the current Doctrine and Covenants, possibly the revelation McLellin tried to imitate. He had been challenged to "seek ye out of the Book of Commandments, even the least that is among them," and try to better it (D&C 67:6). Section 4 fills less than half a page and runs to just seven verses, making it a logical choice. Yet in that brief space, the revelation interweaves phrases found in eight scattered biblical passages—Isaiah, Mark, 1 Corinthians, John, 2 Peter, Matthew, Luke, James—blending them together into a single energetic call to the latter-day work, beginning with words in Isaiah, "Now behold a marvelous work is about to come forth among the children of men" (D&C 4:1; compare Isa. 29:14). Section 4 is a piece of writing not easily tossed off even by an experienced hand.

The problem of language becomes more complex when we remember that the revelatory language was confined to the vocabulary of Joseph Smith. Joseph's comments on the McLellin incident speak of using the "language of Jesus Christ" and of writing "in the name of the Lord," as if the revelations were transcripts from heaven.[3] Yet, at the same time, the preface to the Book of Commandments says that the commandments were given to the Lord's servants "in their weakness, after the manner of their language" (D&C 1:24). The revelations were given in English, not Hebrew or reformed Egyptian. The vocabulary shows few signs of going beyond the diction of a nineteenth-century American common man. The revelations from heaven apparently shone through the mind of Joseph Smith and employed his language to express the messages.

The principle of working "after the manner of their language," meaning the language of the Lord's servants, whatever their weakness, put fairly severe limitations on the rhetoric of the revelations. Joseph had no grounds for claiming special powers of language. He lacked all formal training, of course, having attended school a few months at best. His wife Emma said that he could scarcely write a coherent letter when she married him.[4] Nor had he been exposed to literature—none of the classics of antiquity, no Shakespeare or Pope, likely no Jefferson or Franklin. We know he at least consulted the Bible, but his mother, Lucy, said he had not read it through before he translated the Book of Mormon.[5] We have no glimpses of him, like the young Abraham Lincoln, reading a book by firelight. Manchester did have a lending library, but the Smiths are not known to have patronized it.[6] He is more likely to have read newspapers and almanacs than any other kind of writing.[7] He doubtless heard sermons, though the family did not attend church regularly. The dominant source of Joseph's language must have been the speech of family and neighbors. Speech is not a shallow well of language, as the rich speech of societies with thin printed resources demonstrates; and the Smiths were a verbal family, if his mother's later autobiography is any indication. But overall the sources within Joseph's reach were not plentiful. The plain language available for Joseph's revelatory rhetoric would necessarily ascend to its greatest heights in the words of the English Bible.[8]

Joseph recognized the limits of his language in a November 1832 letter to W. W. Phelps, the editor of the Church newspaper in Missouri. Joseph ended the letter with a prayer for the time when the two of them should "gaze upon eternal wisdom engraven upon the heavens, while the majesty of our God holdeth up the dark curtain until we may read the round of eternity." Then at last, he hoped, they might be delivered "from the little, narrow prison, almost as it were, total darkness of paper, pen and ink; and a crooked, broken, scattered and imperfect language."[9] The words suggest that Joseph envisioned more than he could express and wanted language that was straight and whole rather than crooked and broken. He seemed to feel the same constraints as Moroni, who said the Nephites stumbled "because of the placing of our words" (Ether 12:25, see also verses 23–24). The revelation to the elders at the November 1831 conference, when the question of Joseph's language was raised, said, "His language you have known, and his imperfections you have known," not denying Joseph's imperfections in writing, but only rebuking the elders for looking upon them (D&C 67:5).

Joseph Smith, then, was no Shakespeare or Dickens; he admitted his own limitations, and section 67 implicitly acknowledges them, too. Yet the elders at the November 1831 conference were convinced that "these commandments were given by inspiration of God, and are profitable for all men, and are verily true."[10] Given the circumstances of their composition, the revelations are surprisingly effective down to this day, making the question of the revelations' rhetorical structure all the more interesting.

The revelations in the Doctrine and Covenants take many forms—excerpts from letters, reports of visions, prayers, items of instruction recorded by clerks, formal statements of the Church (fig. 2). Of them all, one type is most characteristic, those I call "classic" revelations. These are the ones where the Lord speaks directly. Most of the revelations up through section 101 in the current Doctrine and Covenants conform to this type. They begin with a formal address from the Lord to a particular audience: an individual, a group of elders, the Church as a whole, or the world at large. For example, the opening sentence of section 42 calls out, "Hearken, O ye elders of my church, who have assembled yourselves together in my name, even Jesus Christ the Son of the living God" (D&C 42:1). We immediately hear the Lord addressing us, the people of the Church. In section 39, James Covill hears the command, "Hearken and listen to the voice of him who is from all eternity to all eternity, the Great I AM, even Jesus Christ" (D&C 39:1). The classic revelations always open with God speaking directly to his listeners.

Many of the revelations were actually received in the presence of the individuals to whom they were addressed, whether a single person or a group. William McLellin, the supposed critic, described how these public revelations were given.

> The scribe seats himself at a desk or table, with pen, ink, and paper. The subject of inquiry being understood, the Prophet and Revelator inquires of God. He spiritually sees, hears, and feels, and then speaks as he is moved upon by the Holy Ghost, the "thus saith the Lord," sentence after sentence, and waits for his amanuenses to write and then read aloud each sentence. Thus they proceed until the revelator says Amen, at the close of what is then communicated. I have known both those men mentioned above [Joseph Smith and David Whitmer], to seat themselves, and without premeditation to thus deliver in broken sentences, some of the most sublime pieces of composition which I ever perused in any book.[11]

McLellin referred to the revelation in this passage as a "thus saith the Lord," suggesting he was impressed with the presence of God's voice in the words.

McLellin must not have been the only one to marvel at these remarkable productions. I am interested in why these words struck him as "sublime," as verily the words of God. Was there anything about their form that helped implant conviction? One way to get at their structure, and thus the rhetorical sources of their power, is by considering a physical analogy— space. Revelations, like all writing, can be thought of as constructing a rhetorical space comparable to the physical spaces where talk takes place. Every text implicitly organizes the source of the words and the intended readers or listeners into a relationship, forming a kind of space that can be compared to actual physical spaces, as a way of identifying the character of the writing. We all know the difference between talking across the kitchen table and meeting around a table in a corporate boardroom. Sports shirts and slacks are suitable for the kitchen versus navy suits in the boardroom;

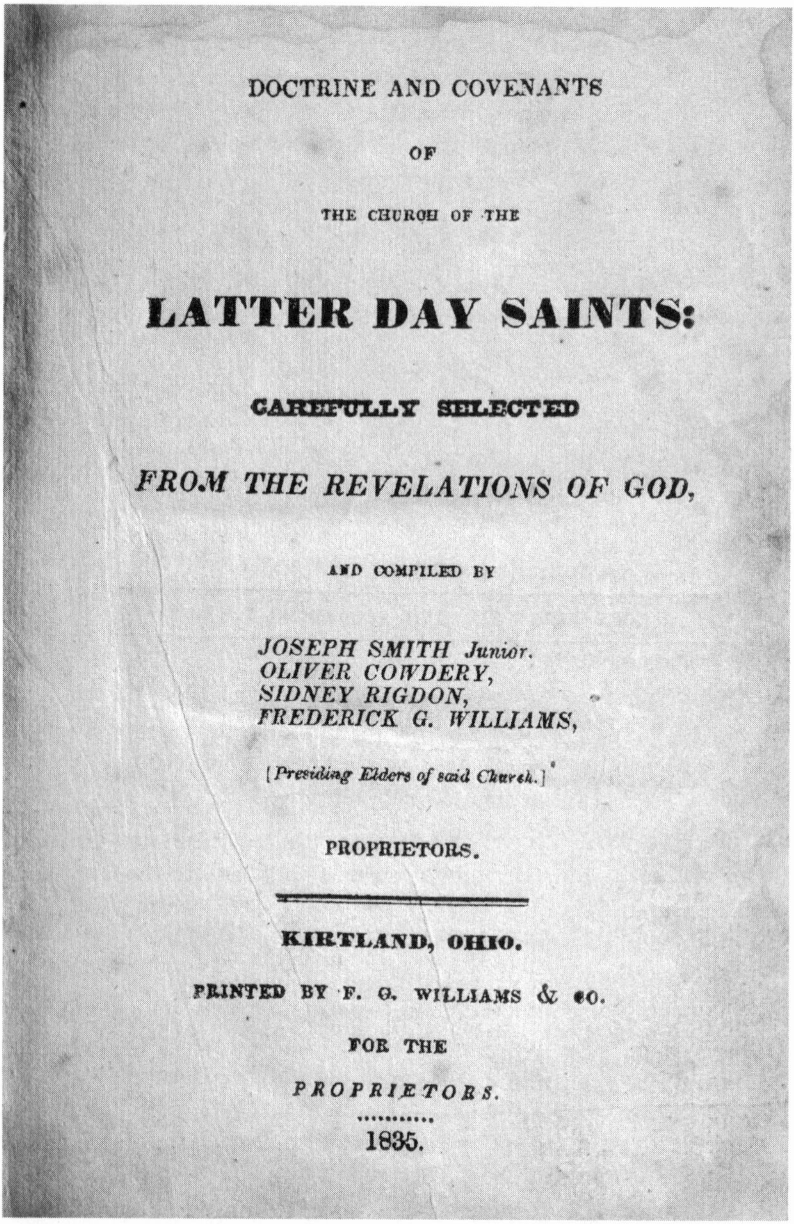

DOCTRINE AND COVENANTS

OF

THE CHURCH OF THE

LATTER DAY SAINTS:

CAREFULLY SELECTED

FROM THE REVELATIONS OF GOD,

AND COMPILED BY

JOSEPH SMITH Junior.
OLIVER COWDERY,
SIDNEY RIGDON,
FREDERICK G. WILLIAMS,

[*Presiding Elders of said Church.*]

PROPRIETORS.

KIRTLAND, OHIO.

PRINTED BY F. G. WILLIAMS & CO.

FOR THE

PROPRIETORS.

1835.

Courtesy L. Tom Perry Special Collections, Brigham Young University

FIG. 2. Title Page, *Doctrine and Covenants* (1835). Joseph Smith selected dozens of his revelations for publication in this work, republished many times and still used by Latter-day Saints today. An earlier edition, *The Book of Commandments*, appeared in 1833.

flowery wallpaper in one and walnut paneling in the other; gossip and personal stories compared to stock valuations and mergers. The circumstances set up quite different relationships among speakers and listeners in the two settings. The place where talk takes place always makes a difference. Think of the differences between a college classroom and a bus stop, a dance floor and the coach's bench on a basketball floor. Each situation sets up roles for the speakers and listeners, prescribes modes of appropriate speech, and establishes relationships among the people in the space. Whoever we may be in other environments, these settings mold our conduct to suit the location.

Similarly, writing sets up rhetorical spaces wherein the relationship of writer (or speaker) and the reader (or listener) are fixed by the writing itself. Although without the stage props of a boardroom table or a navy suit, the writing assigns roles and establishes relationships. An IRS tax form establishes itself as the purveyor of rules that we all are to obey. An autobiography turns readers into intimate acquaintances who are to learn the writer's secrets. A newspaper article brings us dispatches from the front, the reporter assuming that his or her readers want to know everything that is happening in that corner of the world.

Thinking in this vein, we can ask, What kind of rhetorical space do the revelations construct? What relationship do they set up between reader, speaker, and the writer, who is Joseph Smith? The striking feature of Joseph Smith's revelations is the purity of God's voice coming out of the heavens and demanding our attention. The first verse of section 1 speaks with this crystalline clarity: "Hearken, O ye people of my church, saith the voice of him who dwells on high, and whose eyes are upon all men; yea, verily I say: Hearken ye people from afar; and ye that are upon the islands of the sea, listen together" (D&C 1:1). In that passage and through this entire revelation, the Lord alone is speaking, and all readers and hearers are called upon to give heed. *Listen, hearken,* and *hear* are the words with which the classic revelations typically open, and then the voice of God comes right out of the heavens into our ears. From the first word, a relationship is put in place: God speaks to command or inform; we listen.

The voice is pure in that God alone is speaking; Joseph Smith, who spoke the words for God, is totally absent from the rhetorical space. One relationship prevails in these revelations: God speaking to his people. In Isaiah or most of the other Old Testament prophets, the prophet himself repeatedly mediates between the Lord and the people. When we come to passages that begin, "Thus saith the Lord," then we hear the Lord God himself; but before long Isaiah reenters as commentator and teacher, explaining to readers what the Lord implies. Isaiah is our companion and teacher, never far out of the picture. In the Book of Mormon and New Testament, God himself rarely speaks alone in the first person. Most of the scriptures

are sermons or letters by one of the prophets, with only occasional interjections of God's own words. In the Book of Mormon, we come closest to
the unmediated word of God during Nephi's lengthy revelations of world
history. Yet even here, Nephi, for the most part, reports on what he sees.
His person plus the attending angel do most of the talking rather than the
Lord himself.[12]

These guides and mediators disappear in Joseph Smith's revelations.
The Lord speaks directly to his audience, whether one person or the whole
world. "Hearken, my servant John," is the message in section 15 to John
Whitmer, "and listen to the words of Jesus Christ, your Lord and your
Redeemer" (D&C 15:1). That is the interpersonal structure of the rhetoric:
the Lord addresses the reader or listener without any intervening presence.
"Hearken," the reader is told, and then the words come head on. "For
behold I speak unto you with sharpness and with power, for mine arm is
over all the earth" (D&C 16:1–2).

Joseph Smith's authorship, his role as revelator, is obliterated entirely
from this rhetoric, even though the recipient of the revelation may have
actually heard the words come from Joseph's mouth. Though Joseph is
author in the ordinary sense of the word, the voice in the revelation is
entirely separated from the Prophet. In fact, when Joseph figures in the revelation's rhetorical space, he is placed among the listeners. When rebukes
are handed out, he is as likely as anyone to be the target. The first revelation
to be written down, so far as can be told, the current section 3 in the Doctrine and Covenants, was directed entirely against Joseph Smith. Given in
July 1828, after the loss of the 116 pages of Book of Mormon manuscript, the
revelation had no public venue at the time. There was no Church and virtually no followers except for Joseph's own family members and Martin
Harris. In section 3, Joseph stands alone before the Lord to receive a severe
tongue-lashing.

> Remember, remember that it is not the work of God that is frustrated, but the
> work of men;
>
> For although a man may have many revelations, and have power to do many
> mighty works, yet if he boasts in his own strength, and sets at naught the counsels
> of God, and follows after the dictates of his own will and carnal desires, he must
> fall and incur the vengeance of a just God upon him. (D&C 3:3–4)

I consider this revelation an extraordinary rhetorical performance.
Twenty-two-year-old Joseph, probably alone, writes a revelation spoken
purely in the voice of God and directed entirely at Joseph himself, rebuking
him mercilessly for his weakness: "For thou hast suffered the counsel of thy
director to be trampled upon from the beginning" (D&C 3:15). The
Prophet creates *ex nihilo*, out of nothing, a rhetorical space in which God

addresses Joseph as an entirely separate being, and we can only imagine young Joseph, new and inexperienced in his calling, cowering before an angry voice, originating entirely outside of Joseph's mind. All of that happens inside the rhetorical space formed by the revelation.

This rhetorical construction of two distinct persons—the Lord and Joseph Smith—is so real that we are inclined to think a divine being must have stood before Joseph Smith to deliver the scolding. Indeed, the form of the revelations may have shaped the Latter-day imagination more profoundly than we realize. It can be argued that the structure of rhetorical space in the Doctrine and Covenants has even affected the Latter-day Saint tradition of religious painting. Latter-day Saint artists choose different settings to portray God revealing himself than do other Christian artists. The most commonly depicted revelation in the Christian tradition, judging from my informal survey of the art in a few major museums, is Gabriel's appearance to Mary announcing her calling as the mother of Jesus. In these scenes, Gabriel speaks while beams of golden light radiate from heaven on Mary. Less common are representations of the Old Testament prophets or of the authors of the four Gospels, showing them writing while an angel speaks in their ears. Angels or streams of light pouring out of heaven are common mediators in all these scenes.

Latter-day Saint artists are more likely to select scenes where another kind of revelation occurs. Although Joseph Smith received most of his revelations as words or impressions to the mind through the Holy Ghost, Mormon artists most often choose the more tangible First Vision as their archetypical revelation. They represent God and Christ in person in these scenes, in radiant glory, heads turned toward a kneeling Joseph, who hears the words directly from their mouths (fig. 3). God and Christ speak to Joseph, not through him, as do the angels who speak through the Gospel writers. There are no mediators working from God through the angels to the prophet and then to the people. In Latter-day Saint paintings, God personally does the speaking, and the prophet is the hearer. We favor this scene, I believe, because God speaks directly to his people in so many revelations. Because of our familiarity with rhetorical space in the Doctrine and Covenants, Latter-day Saints imagine revelation as an address from God to his Prophet or his people in a pure, first-person voice.

The purity of God's voice in the classic revelations makes a second feature of the revelations' rhetorical space all the more startling: the insertion of mundane matters into the exalted revelations on the doctrine and plans of God. Critical commentators, such as Fawn Brodie, have made fun of the way business details on the Nauvoo House mingle with high religious language about spreading the gospel to the four corners of the earth.[13] In another example of this mixture, section 93 offers a long meditation in the spirit of the first chapter of John, beginning "I am the true light that

"THIS IS MY BELOVED SON, HEAR HIM!"

FIG. 3. Joseph Smith's First Vision (1913). Maker unknown. Leaded stained glass, 84" x 60". Latter-day Saint artists often represent God and Christ speaking without divine mediators to prophets.

lighteth every man that cometh into the world," and going on to declare that "man was also in the beginning with God. Intelligence, or the light of truth, was not created or made, neither indeed can be" (D&C 93:2, 29). These teachings are among Joseph Smith's most provocative and mysterious, and yet within a few verses the revelation rebukes Frederick G. Williams for letting his children get out of hand, and Sidney Rigdon and Joseph are admonished for not keeping their houses in order (D&C 93:41–50). Some revelations include long lists of missionary assignments about who is to accompany whom and where they are to go (D&C 52, for example). In others, the Lord seems to micro-manage the everyday affairs of the Church with all sorts of specific instructions or admonitions to this brother or that, scarcely in keeping with the booming voice of the mighty God. The presence of the mundane matters tempts us to ask: What is that exalted being doing in a revelation to John Whitmer on keeping a history (D&C 47:1), or to Edward Partridge on deeding land to the Saints (D&C 51:3)?

That rhetorical incongruity which offends some religious sensibilities is, in my view, one source of the revelations' effectiveness. The very ease with which the revelations sweep through time and space, forecasting calamities, revealing the depths of God's purposes, and then shedding light upon some named individual with a particular assignment, magnified the revelations' impact. Those humdrum, everyday details of managing the Church are absorbed right into the rhetorical space where God is steering the world toward the Second Coming. In the revelations, we are transported back in history to Adam, Enoch, Moses, carried into deep space where worlds are being created, and then taken forward in time to the descent of Enoch's city. Into this world where God rules and God speaks are brought John Whitmer, Oliver Cowdery, Lyman Wight, Jared Carter, Thomas Marsh, and other specific individuals who were being mobilized for the latter-day work. The lives of plain people are caught up in the same rhetorical space where God's voice speaks of coming calamities and the beginning of the marvelous work and a wonder. The revelations create a rhetorical world in which the Lord God and weak and faltering people work together to bring about the divine purposes. Such language, in my opinion, has the power to change mundane existence into a sacred mission.

Considering that this space is merely constructed by words on a page, why should anyone believe the revelations? Besides considering the purity of God's voice, and the mingling of the mundane with the sublime in these rhetorical spaces, we must ask about the authority of the heavenly voice. How does the speaker in the revelations persuade us to believe? Writers who create other types of rhetorical space use various devices to establish credibility. Novelists usually rely on the verisimilitude of their characters and scenes, describing a believable world in concrete detail and, after winning their readers' confidence in the reality of the story, carrying them off on fantastic adventures. The agricultural experts in the Prophet Joseph's day claimed they were reporting actual experiments in planting corn or working with improved plows, and urged their readers to try the new methods for themselves, making experimentation the basis of their credibility. Evangelical preachers proved their doctrines from the scriptures, relying on the authority of an accepted divine text. Out of all the possible means for establishing credibility, what reasons did the speaker in Joseph Smith's revelations give for believing in the heavenly voice?

The answer is that the voice gives no reasons at all. In one unusual passage, the Lord does speak about reasoning as a man, but then after a few verses the voice returns to the usual declarative mode (D&C 50:10–22). Speaking from the printed pages of the revelation, the voice commands us to hearken and then delivers its message. Authority comes almost entirely from the force of the words themselves. Do they sound like the voice of God heard in the Bible? Is this the way we imagine God speaking? People who listened to the early Mormon missionaries may have measured the message against the standard of the New Testament and judged whether or not the teachings conformed to scripture. Many conversions must have come only after rational evaluation and a comparison of Mormon doctrine with prior beliefs. But none of that reasoning comes from the revelations themselves. The voice of the Lord does not urge people to compare the words of the revelations with biblical teachings or to submit them to any rational test whatsoever. There are no proof texts and only now and then a presentation of evidence. The Lord speaks and demands that people listen. They must then decide for themselves to believe or not, without reference to any outside authority—science, common sense, tradition, the opinions of the educated elite. Within the rhetorical space of the revelation, the hearer is left alone, facing the person behind the pure voice, with the choice to hearken or turn away.[14]

Though forced to choose on their own, without the benefit of outside help, those who hearkened and became Latter-day Saints granted great authority to the revelations. They called them "commandments"—hence the title Book of Commandments—and depended on them for a lead whenever a decision was to be made. In March 1830, when Martin Harris was disillusioned by the slow sales of the Book of Mormon, he told Joseph in a panic, "I want a Commandment." Joseph tried to calm him, but Martin insisted, "I must have a Commandment."[15] He meant that he wanted a revelation from God to reassure him about the future success of the book. Whenever there was uncertainty, people came to Joseph with the same request: get a commandment, they said, meaning a revelation. The Prophet had to tell them, as he told Martin, that they should live by what they had received; it was not a light matter to trouble the Lord for new revelations.

Ezra Booth, the apostate who wrote in detail about his six months' sojourn as a Mormon, said the Church was governed by Joseph's "commandments"—not his commands, but the commandments, or revelations he received about Church governance.[16]

That confidence attests to the power of the rhetorical space formed by the revelations. The people accepted the voice in the revelations as the voice of God, investing in the revelations the highest authority, even above Joseph Smith's counsel. In the revelations, they believed, God himself spoke, not a man. Although the believers trusted and loved the Prophet, the request for a commandment shows they believed in the revelations even more. In them they heard the pure voice of God speaking, not just the voice of Joseph their president and counselor. They had, in other words, accepted the terms of the rhetorical space formed by the revelation. Within that space God spoke directly and forcefully from the heavens with the Prophet himself absent from the space. The believers heard that voice and believed it; in times of stress, they wanted to hear it again. In the bleak fall of 1833, when news of the expulsion from Jackson County was filtering into Kirtland, Frederick G. Williams reported sadly that though Joseph was giving counsel, the Saints had not received any written revelations for a long time.[17] They depended on those powerful words for sustenance and guidance and during a drought longed for them to come again.

We can wonder how Joseph learned to write these revelations in the pure voice of God without pretending to give reasons or depend on outside authority. Whence the certainty of attack in the opening words of the first written revelation? "The works, and the designs, and the purposes of God cannot be frustrated, neither can they come to naught" (D&C 3:1). How did Joseph learn to speak that way at age twenty-two? A few years ago, while I was visiting my daughter-in-law's family in England, the father of the house mentioned Charlotte Brontë's almost miraculous composition of *Jane Eyre* without any prior training as a novelist, and I thought at once of the parallel to Joseph Smith. Could a young genius simply turn out an original and powerful literary production without preparation? I asked if I could look at a biography of Charlotte Brontë, and fortunately their library had one. In the account, I learned that Charlotte, the daughter of a country cleric, began writing stories and essays when she was nine, and she and her sisters put on dramas of their own composition all through their teenage years. Although untrained and certainly precocious, Charlotte had been writing for a decade before the publication of *Jane Eyre*. No such practice runs up to Joseph Smith's literary productions. At most we have Lucy Smith's report on a few weeks of storytelling in the fall of 1823, when Joseph amused the family with tales about ancient America.[18] None of the neighbors who later reported on Smith family character mentioned Joseph's writing or religious speech. In fact, they gave no explanation for the Book of Mormon and the early revelations at all.[19] Like the Book of Mormon, the revelations came out of the blue.

The early revelations present a problem to cultural historians who want to understand Joseph Smith's works as historical productions. They present another kind of problem to today's readers, who, like the first readers of the Book of Commandments, are asked to decide. Will we enter into the revelations' rhetorical space and hearken to the voice of God, or will we turn away and lead our lives in other spaces, heeding voices other than the God of the revelations?

NOTES

1. Joseph Smith Jr., *History of the Church of Jesus Christ of Latter-day Saints*, ed. B. H. Roberts, 2d ed. rev., 7 vols. (Salt Lake City: Deseret Book, 1957), 1:224, 226 (hereafter cited as *History of the Church*).

2. *History of the Church*, 1:226. Mark Grandstaff has argued that McLellin may not have been as critical as we have thought. Mark R. Grandstaff, "Having More Learning Than Sense: William E. McLellin and the Book of Commandments Revisited," *Dialogue: A Journal of Mormon Thought* 26 (winter 1993): 23–48.

3. *History of the Church*, 1:226.

4. Joseph Smith III, "Last Testimony of Sister Emma," *Saints' Herald* 26 (October 1, 1879): 290.

5. Lucy Mack Smith, *Biographical Sketches of Joseph Smith, the Prophet, and His Progenitors for Many Generations* (Liverpool: S. W. Richards, 1853), 84. By Nauvoo, Joseph had accumulated a sizable library, containing works by religious philosophers such as Jonathan Edwards and Thomas Dick, and ancient works by authors such as Epicurus, but there is little evidence his interest in books began in the 1820s. His mother, in fact, reflecting on the early years, said Joseph "seemed much less inclined to the perusal of books than any of the rest of our children, but far more given to meditation and deep study." Smith, *Biographical Sketches*, 84; Nauvoo Library and Literary Institute, Minutes, 33–70, Church Archives, The Church of Jesus Christ of Latter-day Saints, Salt Lake City.

6. After surveying the titles found in the Manchester Library during the early 1800s, Robert Paul concludes that "we can be reasonably certain . . . that young Joseph did not exploit the resources" of his hometown library. Robert Paul, "Joseph Smith and the Manchester (New York) Library," *BYU Studies* 22 (summer 1982): 333–56.

7. Orsamus Turner, the Palmyra newspaperman, recalled that "once a week [Joseph] would stroll into the office of the old *Palmyra Register,* for his father's paper." Orsamus Turner, *History of the Pioneer Settlement of Phelps and Gorham's Purchase, and Morris' Reserve* (Rochester, N.Y.: William Alling, 1851), 214. The *Register* folded in 1821, when Joseph Jr. was just fifteen, and whether he ever read the papers himself is unknown. Turner also remembered Joseph participating in the local "juvenile debating club," which may have passed around texts for consideration. Ibid., 214.

8. D. Michael Quinn has recently challenged the view that the young Joseph Smith's language was generally confined to biblical words and phrases. He asserts that the Book of Mormon and Joseph Smith's early revelations "have correspondences to

words, phrases, and ideas in occult literature." To account for the parallels, Quinn goes to great lengths to show the availability of occult literature in the 1820s in the bookstores of Palymra and neighboring Canandaigua. The heady books advertised in the local newspapers, he concludes, prove Palmyra's "sophisticated reading habits" and belie the "myth" that Joseph Smith "was barely literate with no intellectual curiosity." Quinn implies that Joseph Smith read some of the more advanced books and absorbed their vocabulary. While Quinn's findings deserve more investigation, I believe we must question the assumption that availability means access or dependence. See D. Michael Quinn, *Early Mormonism and the Magic World View*, 2d ed., rev. (Salt Lake City: Signature Books, 1998), 178–236, quotes on 178 and 181.

    9. *History of the Church*, 1:299. The prayer echoed the regrets of Moroni that the Nephites were not "mighty in writing." "When we write we behold our weakness, and stumble because of the placing of our words" (Ether 12:24–25; compare 2 Ne. 33:1). Moroni spoke for every writer in every age, but most poignantly for the prophets who had to bridge the gulf between divine vision and human language.

    10. *History of the Church*, 1:226.

    11. Quoted in Grandstaff, "William E. McLellin and the Book of Commandments," 40. McLellin's admiration of the revelation seems out of keeping with his famous challenge to the quality of the writing.

    12. The relevant passages include 1 Ne. 11–14; 2 Ne. 26–28. The Lord's voice is found in rarer instances such as 2 Ne. 28:17, 30 and 2 Ne. 29.

    13. Fawn M. Brodie, *No Man Knows My History: The Life of Joseph Smith, the Mormon Prophet*, 2d. ed., rev. (New York: Alfred A. Knopf, 1990), 263.

    14. Søren Kierkegaard argued that this is the way of prophets in "The Difference Between a Genius and an Apostle," in Soren Kierkegaard, *Without Authority*, ed. and tr. Howard V. Hong and Edna H. Hong (Princeton, N.J.: Princeton University Press, 1997).

    15. Quoted in Richard L. Bushman, *Joseph Smith and the Beginnings of Mormonism* (Urbana: University of Illinois Press, 1984), 111.

    16. The Booth letters are excerpted in Eber D. Howe, *Mormonism Unvailed; or, A Faithful Account of That Singular Imposition and Delusion, From its Rise to the Present Time* (Painesville, Ohio: By the author, 1834), 177, 181.

    17. *History of the Church*, 1:417.

    18. Smith, *Biographical Sketches*, 84–85.

    19. The accounts of neighbors were published in Howe, *Mormonism Unvailed* and republished in Dan Vogel, ed., *Early Mormon Documents*, 3 vols. (Salt Lake City: Signature Books, 1996–2000), 2:18–77.

17

A Joseph Smith for the Twenty-first Century

I was reluctant at first to include this essay in the collection. It is the last to be completed and the least finished in my mind. The essay was written in 2001 in response to a request from Jill Derr, a Brigham Young University faculty member, to contribute to the Smith Institute symposium she was organizing on writing Mormon biography. She knew I was working on Joseph Smith, and she wanted to give me an opportunity to reflect on the process of doing biography. I felt it was time to look a little more closely at the biographies of Joseph Smith, and so I took the opportunity here.

At the same time I was wrestling with questions of Joseph's significance in American history and how to situate him more accurately. The essay really divides in the middle as I address two questions: one about writing biography, the other about assessing significance. I decided the two were closely enough linked not to strain the listener's credulity. John W. Welch, editor-in-chief at BYU Studies, who attended the symposium, expressed interest in the talk and put Jed Woodworth, an editorial assistant, to work on it. Jed's involvement in this essay may have had something to do with his concurrence in Reid Neilson's suggestion about collecting my essays.

I offer an answer to Joseph Smith's significance here, but I recognize that it is far from complete. We will, I am sure, go on wrestling with Joseph's meaning as we ceaselessly debate the import of all figures with large followings.

Since Henry Caswall published *The Prophet of the Nineteenth Century* in 1843, a year before Joseph Smith's death, nineteen book-length biographies of the Prophet have appeared in print, more than half of them since 1940.[1] They differ wildly in tone and perspective, as might be imagined. Several are still worth considering by serious students of Joseph Smith's life. Among the more notable, I. Woodbridge Riley's *The Founder of Mormonism* is severely critical but ingenious and original, the first biography to attempt a scientific explanation of Joseph Smith's revelations.[2] Fawn Brodie's *No Man Knows My History* is a magnificent piece of journalism that oscillates between snide skepticism and genuine admiration and is always interesting.[3] John Henry Evans's enthusiastic presentation of the Prophet's achievements in *Joseph Smith, an American Prophet* is credited by former Church historian Leonard Arrington with having attracted him to Church history.[4] Donna Hill's balanced but noncommittal *Joseph Smith, the First Mormon* tells a good tale with the benefit of her brother Marvin Hill's extensive knowledge of Joseph Smith's life.[5] Hill's is the biography Latter-day Saints are most likely to recommend to interested friends. Each of these studies deserves attention from anyone seriously interested in Joseph Smith. After more than half a century, *No Man Knows My History* is still considered by most American historians as the best account of Joseph's life. To the surprise of Mormons, many non-Mormon readers think that Brodie presents a sympathetic as well as a revealing picture of Joseph Smith.[6]

We have no reason to think that the writing of biographies about the Prophet will cease as we enter the twenty-first century. Major historical figures always invite reassessment, and interest in Joseph Smith shows no signs of flagging. The relentless growth of the Church makes him more important now than ever. To account for Mormonism's modern success, the mysteries of Joseph Smith have to be plumbed. How are we to understand this extravagant and bold figure whose work has now attracted millions of followers all over the world? How can Joseph be situated in American culture and now in global culture? Why was he so successful? Puzzles such as these are sure to attract biographers in the coming century.

Over the past hundred years, two issues have shaped writing on Joseph Smith, and as we move into the twenty-first century, it may be worth speculating on how these questions will be addressed in the future. May we expect sharp departures, or will the classic questions be answered in the classic ways? The first of these is the question of belief. Until now, the tone and import of a Joseph Smith biography has depended heavily on whether or not the author believed in Joseph's revelations. Will the author's attitude toward the authenticity of the revelations continue to govern the organization of biographies in the future as in the past?

The second issue is the question of significance. What is the place of Mormonism in American history? Where did Mormonism come from? What is its impact? What does Mormonism tell us about America? These questions bear directly on Joseph Smith's life, and the answers are sure to change as our understanding of American culture evolves. The discussion will become even more complicated as Mormonism spreads around the globe. Mormon historians rarely deal with the question of significance, but non-Mormon readers want an answer. Mormon authors should contribute to this speculation as it goes forward rather than leaving the question of significance to outsiders and critics.

Belief and Joseph Smith's Life

The issue of belief was recently posed to me by Alfred Bush, curator of Western Americana at the Firestone Library at Princeton University.

FIG. 1. Joseph Smith and Hyrum Smith. Believing biographers of Joseph Smith are more likely to represent Joseph in words and images consonant with his own stated calling. The engravings shown here, based in part on sketches made in 1842, comprised the frontispiece in George Q. Cannon, *Life of Joseph Smith, the Prophet* (Salt Lake City: Juvenile Instructor Office, 1888). These images show the two Church leaders in a dignified, respectable bearing, underscoring the believers' view of Joseph Smith as a sincere witness and martyr. The images evoked the memory of Joseph and Hyrum together, who "in life . . . were not divided, and in death . . . were not separated" (D&C 135:3).

Because of his Mormon background, Bush is one of the most attentive observers of the Mormon scene and is responsible for a superb collection of Mormon Americana at the Firestone. When he learned I was writing a biography of Joseph Smith, he told me that I must address the question of the historicity of the Book of Mormon. The historian is responsible, Bush insisted, for determining whether or not the book is true history.

I see this as a version of a question that has dominated writing on Joseph Smith from the beginning: Was Joseph Smith a prophet to whom God actually spoke? Were the Book of Mormon and the other revelations—amounting to over 800 pages of writing—from God or were they the fabrications of a human mind? Although Mormons and their critics answer differently, they all deal with this question of authenticity, and the author's answer determines a great deal about how a biography is put together.

The issue of authenticity can be thought of as a governing question. The writer's position on the revelations has consequences far beyond the passages where the revelations themselves are discussed. If the author believes in the revelations, the story is likely to take the following shape:

1. Joseph's character and personality will be conceived positively (fig. 1). A believing author will tend to see Joseph as possessing a character worthy

of a prophet. George Q. Cannon said of the Prophet, "His magnetism was masterful, and his heroic qualities won universal admiration."[7] For these biographers, faults get overlooked and virtues magnified. Critical historians always suspect believing historians of whitewashing Joseph and his family. After my book *Joseph Smith and the Beginnings of Mormonism* appeared, I was asked by one colleague why I had not mentioned Joseph Smith Sr.'s bouts of intoxication. Actually it was a slip in my scholarship, but the critics thought I was covering up. Unbelievers would never make such a mistake. They would be sure to notice Father Smith's somewhat demeaning weakness.

2. Believers will see Joseph's doctrines as unique or at least inspiring. His revelations look like new truth bursting on the earth. John Henry Evans inspired Leonard Arrington because Evans was so upbeat about Joseph's teachings. "Joseph Smith's attraction," Evans wrote, "lay partly in his personality, but mainly in the dynamic power of his religious philosophy."[8] Non-Mormons tend to think that the Book of Mormon is simplistic and easily dismissed.[9] Believers see its profundities and complexities.

3. Among believers there is an inclination toward providential history, that is, to see the hand of the Lord working on the Saints' behalf. They are likely to play up small miracles in everyday life. The Mormon world is filled with God's presence. Consequently, the biography's overall plot line is inclined to be triumphalist. Struggle is a form of testing that brings success in the end. This is God's cause, and it will eventually overcome all opposition.[10]

Skeptics, on the other hand, give the narrative another form:

1. Joseph has to become in some sense a scoundrel. The reason for this is that he pretended to have revelations that the author believes were fabricated. It follows that Joseph deceived his followers by claiming revelation he was not really receiving. He almost inevitably therefore becomes a showman or a con man. This is the way Brodie puts it:

> For Joseph what was a dream one day could become a vision the next, and a reality the day after that. It is doubtful if he ever escaped the memory of the conscious artifice that went into the Book of Mormon, but its phenomenal success must have stifled any troublesome qualms. And at an early period he seems to have reached an inner equilibrium that permitted him to pursue his career with a highly compensated but nevertheless very real sincerity. Certainly a persisting consciousness of guilt over the cunning and deception with which his prophetic career was launched would eventually have destroyed him.[11]

Starting with such assumptions about Joseph Smith's character, one can expect all sorts of relapses into deceptive behavior because a lie lay at the bottom of his life. Joseph becomes morally ambiguous, doing many noble and heroic things but also capable of base behavior—a divided man at his core.[12]

2. Because Joseph's revelations are thought to be a concoction, the skeptical biographer has to locate the sources of the revelations. Where did all the components of the Book of Mormon and the Book of Moses come from? As Brodie puts it, Joseph Smith's theology was "a patchwork of ideas and rituals drawn from every quarter."[13] This assertion leads to a survey of all kinds of source materials, sometimes ranging far into the past in search of precedents for his ideas.[14] Since Joseph wrote so much, it is difficult to locate a source for everything, so these biographers content themselves with a few examples and presume the rest could be accounted for by further searching. Strangely, not much credit is given to Joseph's own imagination and certainly none to God. The skeptics show a peculiar reluctance to suggest Joseph might have had independent genius, even though writing the Book of Mormon in three months is surely one of the greatest writing feats of all time.

3. Along the same line, the skeptic may have to work out the devious means by which Joseph carried off his deceptions. Having to account for the testimonies of the Three and Eight Witnesses, skeptics speculate about making supposed gold plates out of tin or filling a box with sand to make it heavy enough to feel like gold. The requirement of discovering the magician performing his tricks results in the fabrication of events, comparable to the attenuated explanations of the Spaulding theory in the previous century where Sidney Rigdon had to be shown smuggling the manuscript of the Book of Mormon to Joseph.[15]

These contrasting qualities could be elaborated, but they suggest, I hope, how the question of authenticity has shaped the organization and tone of writings about Joseph Smith in the twentieth century. Doubtless the question of authenticity will not die in the twenty-first century, but I believe that this issue has steadily been losing its edge and that a growing body of readers are ready for another depiction of the Prophet. These readers do not want to be caught up in the battles of believers and disbelievers; they are more interested in knowing about an extraordinarily intriguing person.

This group of readers, I suggest, may not be satisfied with the choices that Dan Vogel, one of Joseph's best-informed critics, offers to readers of Joseph Smith biographies. In describing some of the supernatural events in Joseph's early life, Vogel says that we have three choices: (1) Joseph Smith *consciously* deceived people by making up events and lying about them; (2) he *un*consciously deceived people by imagining events and calling them real; (3) he told the truth. Vogel asserts that we cannot believe that Joseph told the truth without abandoning all "rationalist categories of historical investigation."[16] No one can believe rationally in the actuality of supernatural happenings of the kind Joseph claimed for himself. Therefore, he must have been a deceiver, either consciously or unconsciously. Like

Brodie, Vogel leans toward conscious deceit. Vogel believes Joseph Smith knowingly lied by claiming that he translated the Book of Mormon when in fact Joseph was making it up as he went along.

For my hypothetical body of twenty-first-century readers, Vogel's alternatives represent a hard choice. Readers are being asked to consider the revelations as either true or a form of deception. Joseph Smith either spoke for God or duped people. There is no middle ground. Vogel's set of alternatives represents a version of what I would call "the strict Enlightenment," by which I mean a form of Enlightenment thought that forces everything into rational categories of analysis and refuses to admit the validity of any other forms of thought and belief. By this strict standard, Mohammad's vision of Gabriel carrying him to Jerusalem was a form of conscious or unconscious deception. Saint Theresa's transports, Native American vision quests, Saint Paul's encounter with Christ on the road to Damascus—all these and hundreds of other reports of visitations and journeys into heaven are conscious deceptions, or they are the product of the visionaries' imaginations and are thus unconscious deceptions.

The Enlightenment had a word for all these supposed revelations: superstition. Joseph was categorized with a long line of impostors starting with Mohammad and continuing down through the French Prophets and Joanna Southcott, the notorious English prophetess.[17] Enlightened newspaper editors and critics of religion dealt with revelators by classifying them all as frauds and throwing them all on the trash heap together. For many years, Roget's *Thesaurus* listed the Qur'an and Book of Mormon together under "pseudo-revelation" (fig. 2).[18] Joseph Smith, Mohammad, and other extrabiblical prophets could be understood by putting them in the company of impostors through the ages.

In this postmodern era, when the Enlightenment itself has been discredited, many readers may prefer to be less strict in their rationality. Vogel himself thinks of Joseph Smith as a sincere deceiver. He sympathetically concludes, "I suggest Smith really believed he was called of God to preach repentance to a sinful world but that he felt justified in using deception to accomplish his mission more fully."[19] Many readers want to see human life as variegated, strange, and rife with complex possibilities.

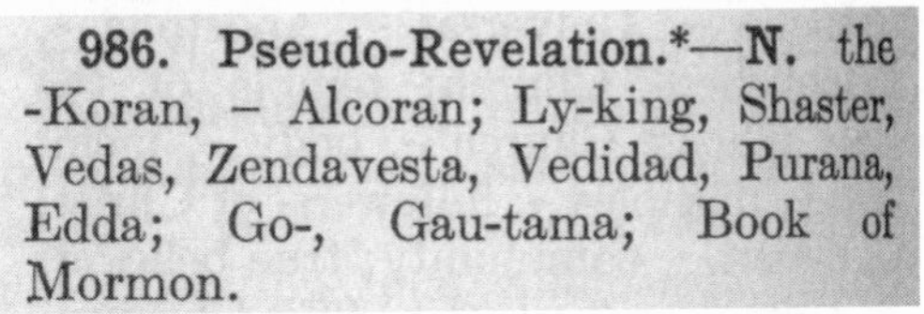

986. Pseudo-Revelation.*—N. the -Koran, – Alcoran; Ly-king, Shaster, Vedas, Zendavesta, Vedidad, Purana, Edda; Go-, Gau-tama; Book of Mormon.

FIG. 2. Entry in Roget's *Thesaurus*, 1935. Enlightenment thinking placed the Book of Mormon and other religious texts and words into categories that marginalized them. Entry 986 of Roget's *Thesaurus* puts the Book of Mormon under "pseudo-revelation." Peter Mark Roget, John Lewis Roget, and Samuel Romilly Roget, *Thesaurus of English Words and Phrases, Authorized American Edition* (New York: Grosset and Dunlap, 1935).

These new readers are open to experiences beyond the ordinary. They want to observe lives that are unlike their own, sometimes in astounding ways. As George Eliot said of the visionary Theresa of Avila, "Who that cares much to know the history of man, and how the mysterious mixture behaves under the varying experiments of Time, has not dwelt, at least briefly, on the life of Saint Theresa."[20] In other words, Theresa's visions take us to the outer reaches of human capacity to places we don't ordinarily go. This desire to explore the varieties of human experience does not require a dissection of every supposedly supernatural event in order to find its rational, scientific basis. We realize now that dissection kills the animal put under the knife. We grant visionaries the benefit of the doubt and acknowledge that they may have had experiences beyond conventional understanding and knowledge. They are part of a grand human effort to discover meaning through poetry, art, and revelation. We can delight in the diversity of human experience and rejoice in all that God has wrought among his children. Modern readers may be willing to allow that Joseph Smith was sincere in saying he had visions and translated the Book of Mormon, and simply want to know more. To call him a deceiver misses the point of visions. In *The American Religion,* the literary critic Harold Bloom, no believer in revealed religion, relished the genius of Joseph Smith's historical revelations without getting bogged down in questions of scientific authenticity.[21]

The common presumption nowadays is that visionaries should not be called "pious frauds," Vogel's term.[22] That broad tolerance has come about partially because of developments outside of Mormon historiography. In a postcolonial time, the accusation that strange religions are superstitions has been discredited by our experience with native peoples. Imperialists once applied the term *superstition* to the religions of colonized populations. Discrediting their religion as superstition was one step in subjecting them. Now, in our effort to see these colonized people on their own terms, we want to give their religions full credit. That transformation in the study of world religions has prepared an audience to give more credence to Joseph Smith. Rather than colonizing him in the name of Enlightenment rationality, we listen more sympathetically. Contemporary readers will look upon Joseph Smith as if they were tolerant ethnographers going among native people. Interested students will want to learn about the world of early Mormonism without disrupting it and get as close as they can to the experience of revelation as Joseph experienced it.

I have presented the passing of the old twentieth-century issue of authenticity as if this were a gain for Mormons. Biographers of Joseph Smith now can write for an audience with broad sympathies who will want to know more about revelation and will not require that it be explained as pious deception. But I wish now to reverse direction and ask if Mormons will be happy with this outcome. Is it an improvement to end the war between believers and unbelievers that raged in the biographies of the twentieth century? The new tolerance permits a believing biographer like myself to present more of Joseph's revelations without fear of running up against a wall of hostile disbelief, but is that advantage counteracted by a blurring of the real issues? Wouldn't believing biographers prefer to have the question of authenticity laid squarely before our readers, even at the cost of having the revelations disputed? Do we want Joseph Smith's challenge to the world to be lost in a haze of a patronizing kindness?

By giving in to tolerance, there is a danger that Mormonism will be treated like voodoo or shamanism—something to examine in excruciating detail and with labored respect, while privately the ethnographers believe these religious manifestations are the product of frenzied minds and a primitive, prescientific outlook. Wouldn't we prefer to be taken seriously enough to be directly opposed rather than condescended to? Right now, the Book of Mormon might aspire to be classed with the Qur'an as the inspired book of a great world religion. Many readers would go with us that far. But are Mormons willing to accept that judgment, or do we want a more exclusive claim on revelation? Many Mormons believe that Joseph Smith and the scriptural revelations are in a class of their own, distinct from Saint Theresa and Mohammad, and would be unhappy to be put on such a list, no matter how distinguished the other visionaries.

One fact in Joseph Smith's history may prevent his complete absorption into the muffling embrace of liberal tolerance, and that fact is the existence of the gold plates. Many modern readers will acknowledge Joseph's sincerity in his more ordinary run of revelations. They can imagine holy words coming into his mind as he wrote, "Hearken, O ye people of my Church" (D&C 1:1). Most of the Doctrine and Covenants fits within the limits of believable revelation—though privately the readers may feel the words came from no greater distance than Joseph's own subconscious. But gold plates, sitting on the table as Joseph translated, shown to witnesses to feel and examine, touched by Emma as she cleaned house? Such a tangible artifact is hard to attribute to a standard religious experience, even in an extraordinary person such as Joseph. With the gold plates, we cross into the realm of deception or psychotic delusion. In the minds of many readers, to see and touch forty pounds of gold plates with ancient writings on them, people had to be either tricked or confused. Joseph turns back into the impostor or self-deluded fanatic.[23]

Here the old issue, then, reasserts itself. The broad-minded reader has to ask, Can it be possible that Joseph Smith did receive the gold plates from an angel? Was he guided by heaven, or was he not? There is no hiding behind the marvelous workings of the human spirit in explaining the plates. Either something fishy was going on, or Joseph did have a visitor from heaven.

The believing biographer here must abandon his tolerant readers to their own devices. The believer cannot help the unbeliever understand and sympathize with Joseph recovering the plates from the hillside. In that moment the issue is joined, the old issue that has hovered over accounts of Joseph's life from the beginning: Did God speak to him or not?

The Significance of Joseph Smith in American History

The second issue, the question of significance, has never been satisfactorily addressed by twentieth-century Mormon biographers. What do Joseph Smith and Mormonism mean in American history? We call him an American prophet; what is his place in American history? What was the impact of his religion? What do Joseph Smith and Mormonism reveal about the nature of American culture?

Mormons have fiddled with answers, but we rarely address the question seriously because it is of little concern to us. The Restoration is of such immense importance in world history that it carries its meaning on the surface as far as we are concerned. In the Restoration, God enters history to prepare the world for the Second Coming of Christ. Compared to that transcendent purpose, Mormonism's place in American history is of secondary concern.

In fact, Latter-day Saints are inclined to reverse the order and place American history in the history of the gospel. We think that Western civilization has been shaped in preparation for the Restoration. The breakup of the medieval church, the rise of learning and free inquiry, the separation of church and state, even a technology like printing are seen as providential preparation for the Restoration. The United States, in the Mormon view, was founded to make a home for the Church.[24]

Unbelievers, of course, are not satisfied with this view of events. They want to wrench Mormonism out of our conspectus and fit it into their own historical schemes, a task that, unfortunately, is not easily accomplished.[25] The trouble is not a paucity of explanations but an overabundance. With so many being offered, how do we choose from among them? They are so diverse, we feel in danger of losing intellectual coherence. Mormonism appears to be so many things it goes out of focus.

Without going into details or evaluation, let me list some of the alternatives for situating Joseph Smith in American history, most of them of recent vintage. Interest in the question of significance has grown as Mormon and non-Mormon historians have become less combative.

1. Dan Vogel argued in *Religious Seekers and the Advent of Mormonism* (1988) that Mormonism derived many of its doctrines and a basic attitude from a tradition of religious seeking going back to Roger Williams. In his later years, Williams believed authority had been lost

and people must wait for God to bring back revelation and authority. Closer to Joseph Smith's time, the Irvingites or Catholic Apostolic Church in England searched for prophetic utterance and appointed apostles according to revelation. Vogel believed Mormons branched out of this Seeker movement.[26]

2. In another study, *Early Mormonism and the Magic World View* (1987), Michael Quinn suggested that many early Mormons saw the world under the spell of magic. Building on the work of Jon Butler and Keith Thomas, historians of American and European magic, Quinn made Joseph Smith into a practitioner of magic whose magical worldview infused his teachings and writings.[27]

3. John Brooke's widely acclaimed *The Refiner's Fire: The Making of Mormon Cosmology, 1644–1844* (1994) discovered in Mormonism a strange brand of philosophy and religion supposedly traceable to Hermes Trismegistus, the mythical ancient-Egyptian theologian. Many scholars have shown how early modern Hermeticism, intermixed with alchemy, flowed into the Rosicrucian movement and Freemasonry. Brooke tried to find Hermeticism in Mormonism and in fact argued for its dominant influence on Joseph Smith's distinctive doctrines.[28]

4. In another vein entirely, Kenneth Winn wrote a volume on Mormonism and Republicanism, *Exiles in a Land of Liberty* (1989), at a time when the social and political ideology of the Revolution seemed to be a key to the understanding of American history.[29]

5. In *Illusions of Innocence: Protestant Primitivism in America, 1630–1875* (1988), Richard Hughes and C. Leonard Allen link Joseph Smith to the Restorationists—those who wished to return to the practices and beliefs of primitive Christianity.[30] Mormons themselves are comfortable with this category. An article of faith states that "we believe in the same organization that existed in the Primitive Church."

6. Earlier, Alice Felt Tyler's *Freedom's Ferment* (1944) placed Joseph Smith among utopian reformers because of the Prophet's plans for the city of Zion, putting him in a class with the Shakers and the founders of Brook Farm. In his massive *Religious History of the American People* (1972), the Yale scholar Sydney E. Ahlstrom accepted Tyler's categorization and inserted a discussion of Mormonism in a chapter titled "The Communitarian Impulse." [31]

7. In *The Democratization of American Christianity* (1989), Nathan Hatch made Mormons exemplars of a democratic impulse among early national Christians. Mormonism attacked cultural elites and returned religious power to ordinary people, linking Joseph Smith to the democratic forces coming out of the Revolution.[32]

8. Grant Underwood's *The Millenarian World of Early Mormonism* (1993) made a persuasive argument for Mormonism as a form of millenarianism.[33]

I have doubtless overlooked explanations, but the list of eight is long enough to make the point. Mormonism cannot be accounted for simply, any more than can the Constitution or other complex phenomena in our history. Each of these books standing alone seems to locate Mormonism satisfactorily, but taken together they show the elusiveness of significance. After reading them all, we see that no simple answer to the initial question can be given. Mormonism is multifaceted, diverse, baroque in its effulgence of meanings.

The problem is further complicated by Mormonism's estrangement from American society. For a movement that purportedly incorporated so many elements from the surrounding culture, Mormonism found itself at odds with that culture over and over again. I don't mean arguments, I mean violence. None of the Saints' American neighbors accepted them for very long. Wherever the Latter-day Saints settled in the nineteenth century, they were rejected like a failed kidney transplant. In New York, Missouri, Illinois, and even Utah, the Saints were attacked by force and compelled to change or die. Far from being fundamentally American, something about Mormonism repulsed large numbers of Americans.[34]

Every attempt to assimilate the Restoration into some schema has to face the possibility that Mormonism was more un-American than American. There is more evidence of Mormonism's alienation from the nineteenth-century United States than of its being a natural outgrowth of American culture. The American connection grows ever more tenuous as Mormonism is increasingly viewed as a world religion. If Mormonism is so American, why the immediate success in nineteenth-century Europe and the rapid twentieth-century growth in Latin America and the Philippines?

I see no way to resolve this problem. I am inclined to increase the confusion rather than clarifying it, by adding still another dimension, but one that explains the conflicts with Americans. One place to start on the question of significance is with the single most important principle of the Restoration—revelation. With the Restoration, God began directing his Church again, speaking to prophets, actively engaging in a work. We cannot say Joseph was the only one who laid claim to revelations. The Free Will Baptists, the Universalists, the Shakers—all had founders who received open visions of God when they were called to their work. But among all these, Joseph was preeminent in the extent of his claims, in the number of his revelations, and in the success of his movement.[35] What was the significance of his reliance on revelation?

All these visionaries, and Joseph most of all, discerned what orthodox Christianity had forgotten—that biblical authority still rests, as it always has, on revelation. The Bible's cultural influence was based on the belief that God revealed himself to prophets. The reason for embracing the Bible was that its words had come from heaven. Christianity had smothered this self-evident fact by relegating revelation to a bygone age, making the Bible an archive rather than a living reality. The significance of Joseph Smith— and other prophets of his time—was their introduction of revelation into the present, renewing contact with the Bible's God.

Reliance on revelation made Joseph Smith appear marginal in American Christianity, but like marginal people before him, Joseph aimed a question at the heart of the culture: Did Christians truly believe in revelation? If believers in the Bible dismissed revelation in the present, could they defend revelation in the past? By 1830, when Joseph came on the scene, the question of revelation had been hotly debated for well over a century. Since the first years of the eighteenth century, rational Christians had been struggling with deists, skeptics, and infidels over the veracity of miracles and the inspiration of the prophets and apostles. In 1829, Alexander Campbell debated with the atheist Robert Owen for an entire week on the question of revelation and miracles.[36] Campbell believed he had proven God's presence in the Bible, but doubt lingered on, and over the course of the nineteenth century, belief in revelation eroded among the educated classes. Through the intellectual wars with skeptics and higher critics, believers steadily lost ground. The loss was only dimly perceived by everyday Christians in Joseph Smith's time, but in the half-century to come, the issue divided divinity schools and shook ordinary people.[37]

Joseph stood against that ebbing current. He prophesied and received revelation exactly as Christians thought Bible prophets did. In effect, he reenacted the writing of the Bible before the Christian world's eyes.[38] Most dismissed him as a charlatan without even bothering to evaluate his doctrine. The people in Palmyra decided the Book of Mormon was bogus before they saw it. Their precipitous condemnation betrayed their doubts about the possibility of revelation. If revelation in the present was so far out of the question that Joseph's claims could be discounted without serious consideration, why believe revelation in the past? After one incredulous visitor marveled that the Mormon Prophet was "nothing but a man," Joseph remarked that "they look upon it as incredible that a man should have any intercourse with his Maker."[39] That was exactly the point. People had lost faith that a person could receive revelation. Joseph's life posed the question: Does God speak to man?[40]

In this sense, Joseph was among the "extremist prophets," as one pair of historians have called them.[41] He forced the question of revelation on a culture struggling with its own faith. Joseph's historical role, as he understood it, was to give God a voice in a world that had stopped listening. "The Gentiles shall say," Nephi wrote in the Book of Mormon, "A Bible! A Bible! We have got a Bible, and there cannot be any more Bible." "O fools," the Lord rejoins, "know ye not . . . that I am the same yesterday, today, and forever; and that I speak forth my words according to mine own pleasure"

(2 Ne. 29:3–4, 7, 9). Not only does the Book of Mormon show that God does "inspire men and call them to his holy work in this age and generation, as well as in generations of old" (D&C 20:11), but the reality of revelation in the present also proves the reality of revelation in the past. One reason for restoring the Book of Mormon, an early revelation said, is to prove "that the holy scriptures are true" (D&C 20:11). In reply to a minister's inquiry about the distinguishing doctrine of Mormonism, Joseph told him, "We believe the Bible, and they do not."[42]

At some level, Joseph's revelations indicate a loss of trust in the Christian ministry. For all their learning and their eloquence, the clergy could not be trusted with the Bible. They did not understand what the book meant. It was a record of revelations, and the ministry had turned it into a handbook. The Bible had become a text to be interpreted rather than an experience to be lived. In the process, the power of the book was lost. In Joseph Smith's 1839 account of the First Vision, that was the charge against the churches. "They teach for doctrines the commandments of men, having a form of godliness, but they deny the power thereof" (JS–H 1:19). It was the power thereof that Joseph and the other visionaries of his time sought to recover. Not getting it from the ministry, they looked for it themselves.

To me, that is Joseph Smith's significance for our time. He stood on the contested ground where the Enlightenment and Christianity confronted one another, and his life posed the question, Do you believe God speaks? Joseph was swept aside, of course, in the rush of ensuing intellectual battles and was disregarded by the champions of both great systems, but his mission was to hold out for the reality of divine revelation and establish one small outpost where that principle survived. Joseph's revelatory principle is not a single revelation serving for all time, as the Christians of his day believed regarding the incarnation of Christ, nor a mild sort of inspiration seeping into the minds of all good people, but specific, ongoing directions from God to his people. At a time when the origins of Christianity were under assault by the forces of Enlightenment rationality, Joseph Smith returned modern Christianity to its origins in revelation.

For that reason, rationalists today are required to attack Joseph Smith's revelations. Mormonism revives all the claims to heavenly authority that the Enlightenment was invented to repulse. Since the Enlightenment is far from dead, a biographer of Joseph Smith cannot escape its skepticism. Even if general readers momentarily suspend disbelief, in the end most of them will not believe. That is a fact in our modern world. Educated believers are in a small minority. We write under a different constellation of intellectual moods and fashions in the twenty-first century, but the rationalist doubts of the twentieth century are still with us.

Despite the prevailing disbelief, some modern readers will enjoy the story of an old-fashioned prophet rising once more. Appalled by the miseries of our time, they may feel that the world is desperate for revelation from a caring God. Rather than dismiss Joseph out of hand as a blatant fraud, they will listen and observe. Is it possible that biblical revelation could be renewed? Could the Enlightenment have shut up the heavens through its disbelief? Must we foreclose the very possibility of divine communication? Those questions, raised by this "modern" prophet, may seem worth pondering by at least a few.

NOTES

1. Henry Caswall, *The Prophet of the Nineteenth Century; or, The Rise, Progress, and Present State of the Mormons, or Latter-day Saints* (London: J. G. F. and J. Rivington, 1843). For a review of Caswall's career, see Craig L. Foster, "Henry Caswall: Anti-Mormon Extraordinaire," *BYU Studies* 35, no. 4 (1995–96): 144–59.

2. I. Woodbridge Riley, *The Founder of Mormonism: A Psychological Study of Joseph Smith, Jr.* (New York: Dodd, Mead, 1902), based on his earlier dissertation, "A Psychological History of Joseph Smith, Jr., the Founder of Mormonism" (Ph.D. diss., Yale University, 1902).

3. Fawn M. Brodie, *No Man Knows My History: The Life of Joseph Smith, the Mormon Prophet* (New York: Alfred A. Knopf, 1945). A revised and enlarged edition was published in 1971. The many book reviews of *No Man Knows My History* are digested in Louis Midgley, "F. M. Brodie—'The Fasting Hermit and Very Saint of Ignorance': A Biographer and Her Legend," *FARMS Review of Books* 8, no. 2 (1996): 147–230.

4. John Henry Evans, *Joseph Smith, an American Prophet* (New York: Macmillan, 1933); Leonard J. Arrington, *Adventures of a Church Historian* (Urbana: University of Illinois Press, 1998), 21.

5. Donna Hill, *Joseph Smith, the First Mormon* (Garden City, N.Y.: Doubleday, 1977).

6. Newell G. Bringhurst, "Applause, Attack, and Ambivalence: Varied Responses to *No Man Knows My History*," in *Reconsidering* No Man Knows My History: *Fawn M. Brodie and Joseph Smith in Retrospect*, ed. Newell G. Bringhurst (Logan: Utah State University Press, 1996), 53–55.

In addition to the five biographies of Joseph Smith already mentioned, my list, arranged chronologically, includes Edward W. Tullidge, *Life of Joseph the Prophet* (New York: Tullidge and Crandall, 1878); George Q. Cannon, *Life of Joseph Smith, the Prophet* (1888; Salt Lake City: Deseret Book, 1986); Thomas Gregg, *The Prophet of Palmyra* (New York: John B. Alden, 1890); Harry M. Beardsley, *Joseph Smith and His Mormon Empire* (Boston: Houghton Mifflin, 1931); Preston Nibley, *Joseph Smith, the Prophet* (Salt Lake City: Deseret Book, 1944); Daryl Chase, *Joseph Smith the Prophet: As He Lives in the Hearts of His People* (Salt Lake City: Deseret Book, 1944); Norma J. Fischer, *Portrait of a Prophet* (Salt Lake City: Bookcraft, 1960); John J. Stewart, *Joseph Smith, the Mormon Prophet* (Salt Lake City: Hawkes, 1966); Carl Carmer, *The Farm Boy and the Angel* (Garden City, N.Y.: Doubleday, 1970); Francis M. Gibbons, *Joseph Smith: Martyr, Prophet of God* (Salt Lake City: Deseret Book, 1977); Richard L. Bushman, *Joseph Smith and the Beginnings of Mormonism* (Urbana: University of Illinois Press, 1984); Norman Rothman,

The Unauthorized Biography of Joseph Smith, Mormon Prophet (Salt Lake City: Norman Rothman Foundation, 1997); William D. Morain, *The Sword of Laban: Joseph Smith, Jr., and the Dissociated Mind* (Washington, D.C.: American Psychiatric Press, 1998); and Heidi S. Swinton, *American Prophet: The Story of Joseph Smith* (Salt Lake City: Shadow Mountain, 1999).

One might also include essay collections such as Hyrum L. Andrus, *Joseph Smith, the Man and the Seer* (Salt Lake City: Deseret Book, 1960); Leon R. Hartshorn, *Joseph Smith: Prophet of the Restoration* (Salt Lake City: Deseret Book, 1970); Larry C. Porter and Susan Easton Black, eds., *The Prophet Joseph Smith: Essays on the Life and Mission of Joseph Smith* (Salt Lake City: Deseret Book, 1988); Truman G. Madsen, *Joseph Smith the Prophet* (Salt Lake City: Bookcraft, 1989); Susan Easton Black and Charles D. Tate Jr., *Joseph Smith: The Prophet, the Man* (Provo: Religious Studies Center, Brigham Young University, 1993); and Davis Bitton, *Images of the Prophet Joseph Smith* (Salt Lake City: Aspen Books, 1996).

7. Cannon, *Life of Joseph Smith*, 20.

8. Evans, *Joseph Smith, an American Prophet*, 211.

9. Paul Conkin concludes that "in a sense, the book is rather simple." Paul K. Conkin, *American Originals: Homemade Varieties of Christianity* (Chapel Hill: University of North Carolina Press, 1997), 168.

10. Concluding his account of Joseph's death, Cannon wrote, "The enemies of truth were sure that they had now destroyed the work. And yet it lives, greater and stronger after the lapse of years! It is indestructible for it is the work of God." Cannon, *Life of Joseph Smith*, 527.

11. Brodie, *No Man Knows My History*, 84–85.

12. Beginning with I. Woodbridge Riley at the beginning of the century, the reflections on Joseph's character took the form of scientific psychological labels. Riley couched "the Final question" as being "Was He Demented or Merely Degenerate?" Riley, *The Founder of Mormonism*, xix. In *Joseph Smith and His Mormon Empire*, Harry Beardsley built on and magnified Riley's speculations about epileptic visions, but he also thought that Joseph was "lazy, tricky, and thoroughly unscrupulous" (42).

13. Brodie, *No Man Knows My History*, 403.

14. No one has stretched further than John L. Brooke, *The Refiner's Fire: The Making of Mormon Cosmology, 1644–1844* (Cambridge: Cambridge University Press, 1994), but it began in earnest with Riley, *The Founder of Mormonism*, 105–73.

15. Among many examples are Beardsley, *Joseph Smith and His Mormon Empire*, 48–52; Brodie, *No Man Knows My History*, 37; and Dan Vogel, "'The Prophet Puzzle' Revisited," in *The Prophet Puzzle: Interpretive Essays on Joseph Smith*, ed. Bryan Waterman (Salt Lake City: Signature Books, 1999), 53.

16. Vogel, " 'The Prophet Puzzle' Revisited,' " 53.

17. J. F. C. Harrison, *The Second Coming: Popular Millenarianism, 1780–1850* (New Brunswick: Rutgers University Press, 1979), 180–88.

18. Compare Peter Mark Roget, *Thesaurus of English Words and Phrases* (New York: Thomas Y. Crowell, 1909), item 986, and Peter Mark Roget, John Lewis Roget, and Samuel Romilly Roget, *Thesaurus of English Words and Phrases*, Authorized American Edition (New York: Grosset and Dunlap, 1935), item 986.

19. Vogel, " 'The Prophet Puzzle' Revisited," 61.

20. George Eliot, *Middlemarch: A Study of Provincial Life* (London: William Blackwood and Sons, 1881), prelude.

21. Harold Bloom, *The American Religion: The Emergence of the Post-Christian Nation* (New York: Simon and Schuster, 1992).

22. Vogel, " 'The Prophet Puzzle' Revisited," 61.

23. My argument here relies heavily on Terryl L. Givens, *By the Hand of Mormon: The American Scripture That Launched a New World Religion* (New York: Oxford University Press, 2002).

24. Joseph Fielding Smith, *The Progress of Man*, 3d ed. (Salt Lake City: Genealogical Society of Utah, 1936), 196–288.

25. For example, Daniel Walker Howe calls the recent attempts of Mormon historians to contextualize their studies in American religious history a "maturation." Daniel Walker Howe, "Protestantism, Voluntarism, and Personal Identity in Antebellum America," in *New Directions in American Religious History*, ed. Harry S. Stout and D. G. Hart (New York: Oxford University Press, 1997), 219.

26. Dan Vogel, *Religious Seekers and the Advent of Mormonism* (Salt Lake City: Signature Books, 1988).

27. D. Michael Quinn, *Early Mormonism and the Magic World View* (Salt Lake City: Signature Books, 1987). A revised and enlarged edition was published in 1998.

28. Brooke, *The Refiner's Fire*, 3–29, 209–61. See also Lance S. Owens, "Joseph Smith: America's Hermetic Prophet," *Gnosis* 35 (spring 1995): 56–64. For a review of responses to *The Refiner's Fire*, see Jan Shipps, *Sojourner in the Promised Land: Forty Years among the Mormons* (Urbana: University of Illinois Press, 2000), 204–17. Reviews include Richard L. Bushman, "The Mysteries of Mormonism," *Journal of the Early Republic* 15, no. 3 (fall 1995): 501–8; William J. Hamblin, Daniel C. Peterson, and George L. Mitton, "Mormon in the Fiery Furnace; or, Loftes Tryk Goes to Cambridge," *FARMS Review of Books* 6, no. 2 (1994–95): 3–58; and the reviews by William J. Hamblin and Davis Bitton in *BYU Studies* 34, no. 4 (1994–95): 167–92.

29. Kenneth H. Winn, *Exiles in a Land of Liberty: Mormons in America, 1830–1846*, Studies in Religion, ed. Charles H. Long (Chapel Hill: University of North Carolina Press, 1989).

30. Richard T. Hughes and C. Leonard Allen, *Illusions of Innocence: Protestant Primitivism in America, 1630–1875* (Chicago: University of Chicago Press, 1988), 133–52.

31. Alice Felt Tyler, *Freedom's Ferment: Phases of American Social History to 1860* (Minneapolis: University of Minnesota Press, 1944), 86–107; Sydney E. Ahlstrom, *A Religious History of the American People* (New Haven: Yale University Press, 1972), 501–9.

32. Nathan O. Hatch, *The Democratization of American Christianity* (New Haven: Yale University Press, 1989).

33. Grant Underwood, *The Millenarian World of Early Mormonism* (Urbana: University of Illinois Press, 1993).

34. This ambiguity is well stated in the summary of early Mormonism in David Brion Davis, *The Great Republic: A History of the American People* (Lexington, Mass.: D. C. Heath, 1977), 532–41.

35. See Richard Lyman Bushman, "The Visionary World of Joseph Smith," *BYU Studies* 37, no. 1 (1997–98): 183–204.

36. *Debate on the Evidences of Christianity; Containing an Examination of "The Social System," and of All the Systems of Skepticism of Ancient and Modern Times, Held in the City of Cincinnati, Ohio, in April 15, 1829; Between Robert Owen and Alexander Campbell* (Cincinnati, Ohio: Robinson and Fairbank, 1829).

37. James Turner, *Without God, without Creed: The Origins of Unbelief in America* (Baltimore: Johns Hopkins University Press, 1985).

38. This line of reasoning is taken from Terryl L. Givens, *The Viper on the Hearth: Mormons, Myths, and the Construction of Heresy* (New York: Oxford University Press, 1997), 82–93.

39. Dean C. Jessee, ed., *The Papers of Joseph Smith*, 2 vols. (Salt Lake City: Deseret Book, 1989–92), 2:66.

40. 2 Ne. 27:23; 28:6; Jacob 4:8; Morm. 8:6; 9:11, 20; Doctrine and Covenants 11:25; Givens, *Viper on the Hearth*, 82–93; Turner, *Without God, without Creed*, 141–67. The philosopher Richard Rorty, representing a modern mentality, has said that over the past three centuries we have learned that "the world does not speak. Only we do." Rorty, quoted in Andrew Delbanco, *The Death of Satan: How Americans Have Lost the Sense of Evil* (New York: Farrar, Straus, and Giroux, 1995), 221.

41. Paul E. Johnson and Sean Wilentz, *The Kingdom of Matthias* (New York: Oxford University Press, 1994), 6, 173.

42. Jessee, *Papers of Joseph Smith*, 2:155, capitalization added.

Reflections on Believing History

Soon after publishing *Joseph Smith and the Beginnings of Mormonism,* I was invited to Notre Dame to discuss the book.[1] Questions were coming from all directions, and one person asked why I had not mentioned that Joseph Smith's father sometimes drank to excess. I was caught off balance because I was not sure why this fact had been omitted. Perhaps I had not been aware of the drinking when I wrote those parts; perhaps I had just overlooked it. The questioner took some satisfaction in my embarrassment, because he thought he had caught me off base as well as off balance. My predilection to defend the character of the Smith family had been revealed, and my conscious or unconscious wish to clean up the record was now plainly evident.

All of my efforts to assure my questioner that I had no objections at all to reporting the father's drunkenness were of course in vain. He had exposed the failings of the believing mind in writing about the subjects of its own belief. He had posed the question all nonbelievers ask of believers like myself. How can you avoid crippling bias when writing about your own faith? For nonbelievers, it seems obvious that a believer cannot be self-critical. Consciously or unconsciously, the believer will suppress disconcerting facts and whitewash reality.

I think the situation of believers who write the history of their own traditions is more complicated than their critics allow. The assumption behind the question is that believers cannot bear to criticize their own tradition or record negative facts because their own faith is at stake. In this view, believers have too much invested. They must either suppress everything negative or spend their energies defending the faith. To attack the tradition and bring it down would undermine their own lives and the lives of their fellow believers. When it comes to presenting evidence, the believer hesitates.

There is some truth to this charge, as far as I am concerned. Mormons are exceptionally exposed on the historical front. Our founding events did not occur in the remote past but in the recent, historically accessible past. As a persecuted minority faith, we have been constantly on the defensive from the beginning. For Mormons, much hinges on the inspiration of Joseph Smith, and so there is a natural impulse to defend his character. Furthermore, it is true that when I write about Joseph I want to affirm the strength of the tradition and the human value of the revelations. I want to assure Mormon readers that their hopes are not in vain. There is a truth in the Mormon scriptures that is worthy to build a life on. My version of Joseph Smith will make him much more admirable than John Brooke's or Fawn Brodie's.

So far, my critics will say, just as we thought, you are a defender of the faith, and we cannot trust your history. I might object on grounds of fairness that all sorts of people these days are advocates of the subjects they write about—feminists, African Americans, historians of liberalism, historians of the left. Richard Rorty says we must even look for positive qualities in American political culture, and build on national virtues instead of deriding them.[2] In other words, everyone who is looking for a usable past will affirm the value or his or her own tradition. Believing historians are no different.

There is a tendency for critics to think that believers work in an isolated and naive mental world. They are prisoners of their faith, isolated from the rough-and-tumble realities of the skeptics. Believers simply cannot grasp the objections to their belief. If they did, the skeptics assume, they would abandon their faith. I have had friendly critics tell me that I must go to the brink with Joseph Smith, that is, break out of my comfortable cocoon and recognize how faulty he was, how incredible his claims, how impossible faith in his revelations really is. In other words, wake up to reality.

But the actual fact is that professional historians today cannot isolate themselves in a cocoon. The questions and doubts of the critics are in the minds of the believers too, right along with their faith. Most modern believing historians are dialogic. They are engaged in constant internal dialogue. They know how the story looks to the faithful, and they also know how it looks to the skeptics. The debate over credibility is waged in their own minds, not just in scholarly debate.

The problem of writing believing history is not naiveté, but constraint. How can you tell a coherent story while being pulled in two directions at the same time? The result of writing under these conditions is a kind of temerity that may take the life out of the history for the simple reason that you can take fewer chances. Writing for one audience alone—either believers or skeptics—permits you to make claims that simply won't hold water if you write for both. A story that seems plausible to a secular audience falls apart when you tell it to Latter-day Saints.

John Brooke's *Refiner's Fire* is a case in point.[3] The book won the Bancroft Prize, got consistently favorable reviews, and is cited frequently these days as an imaginative reconstruction of the Mormon world. But to informed Latter-day Saint readers who know Mormonism well, the book crumbles to dust. Brooke does not describe Mormonism as it is found in the sources, and he forces connections with hermetic philosophy that simply cannot be shown to exist. I had high hopes that the study might turn up an alternative vocabulary for Joseph Smith's visions. But after examining *Refiner's Fire* closely, I knew it would never go down with a Mormon audience. They would say this is not Joseph Smith's Mormonism. As it turned out, the most sophisticated Mormon readers, the ones most open to a book like Brooke's, simply could not swallow the argument. So all the fire and drama of Brooke's book are inaccessible to me.[4]

On the other hand, a story that seems plausible to Latter-day Saints may fall apart when told to a secular audience. Mormons like to believe, for example, that the heavens were sealed until Joseph Smith began receiving revelations. They think that the Christian world had given up on direct communication with God before Joseph Smith. With Joseph, a new dispensation of angelic visitations and open revelation began once more. But as anyone who reads in early-nineteenth-century American religious history knows, people were having dreams and visions all the time. They wrote about them, they depended upon them, they told them to their neighbors. Joseph Smith was one of scores, probably hundreds, of contemporary visionaries. That sets Mormons back a little, but it is a story I must tell.

In my opinion, dialogic thinking is not a fancy name for waffling, nor is it changing your appearance to suit the audience. On the contrary, it requires one to write to all audiences at once. When you write dialogically, all your audiences examine the results simultaneously. You are writing for all your critics and not just the readers before whom you feel most comfortable. You have to discipline yourself to write history you won't back away from under pressure—the opposite of waffling.

The real downside to writing dialogically is that my history seems a little detached to both audiences. I seem to fall short, neither confirming the traditional Mormon view nor making the exciting connections with American culture that secular historians expect. My history lacks a little something. It seems a trifle emaciated.

Looking on the bright side, writing for two audiences does keep one close to the sources. The dialogic historian has to fight on two fronts and have the ammunition to defend himself on both. When I write troubling stories for Latter-day Saints, I must have sources to defend every word. When I talk about revelations and visions to the skeptics, I have to say this is simply what the sources from the time report. In a sense, I am forced to hide behind the source, or to put it more positively, to have strong evidence for everything I claim. A dialogic imagination imposes a kind of mental discipline on history-writing. It has to hew close to the line laid out in the sources. There is less room—not no room, but less room—for speculative flight. For good or ill, dialogic history is less fanciful than history written for one audience only.

There is one other outgrowth of writing with a dialogic imagination. I am, I believe, more aware of the plight of readers and feel compelled to empathize with their predicaments. When Fawn Brodie wrote her brilliant study fifty years ago, she was fleeing Mormonism and had no sympathy for the Mormon reader.[5] She showed no pity as she mowed down the faithful with her account of Joseph Smith. More important, she felt no need to address the objections that Mormon scholars might raise. She was on her way out of the faith and wanted to address the larger world. She played to its prejudices while disregarding believing scholarship. Some believing writers do the opposite. They play to Mormon prejudices while rejecting the larger world.

I do not want to disregard either audience in my Latter-day Saint writings. I know the unbelieving reader wants an explanation of Joseph Smith that will not be forthcoming in my study—not because I am naive but because the believing side of my mind does not find that explanation plausible. That vital part of the story for unbelievers is missing. The best I can do is to turn directly to these readers at certain points and forewarn them about the absences. You won't get those explanations, I said in *Joseph Smith and the Beginnings of Mormonism*; what I can offer is the story as the Mormons themselves experienced it according to their accounts. Never fear, however, you are in my mind as I write.

Contrary to what the critics might think, belief does compel me to discuss the drunkenness of Joseph Smith's father. I not only know they will be wanting to pounce on such omissions, but their criticisms are within my own mind. Dialogic historians like myself cannot leave out embarrassing facts so long as they are part of the historical record. The strict discipline imposed by living in two worlds compels us to tell it all. To believe the history I write, I have to represent all sides.

NOTES

1. Richard L. Bushman, *Joseph Smith and the Beginnings of Mormonism* (Urbana: University of Illinois Press, 1984).

2. Richard Rorty, *Achieving Our Country: Leftist Thought in Twentieth–Century America* (Cambridge, Mass.: Harvard University Press, 1998).

3. John Brooke, *The Refiner's Fire: The Making of Mormon Cosmology, 1644–1844* (New York: Cambridge University Press, 1994).

4. My review of *Refiner's Fire* is published in *Journal of the Early Republic* 15, no. 3 (1995): 501–8. The split reaction to the book is discussed in Jan Shipps, *Sojourner in the Promised Land: Forty Years Among the Mormons* (Urbana: University of Illinois, 2000): 204–17.

5. Fawn M. Brodie, *No Man Knows My History: The Life of Joseph Smith, the Mormon Prophet* (New York: Alfred A. Knopf, 1945).

Index

Aaronic Priesthood, 101, 209, 235
Abraham, book of, 76, 237, 243-44
Abraham, writings of, 237, 243
academia: atmosphere of unbelief, 33-34, 37-38; community of scholars, 40-42; free choice, 35-36; goodness doctrine lacking from, 42-43; hazards, 31, 33, 35; influence on Mormon historians, 8-9; students in, 30-31
"Account of a Trance or a Vision of Sarah Alley" (Alley), 202, 204
achievement, 31-32
Adair, James, 123
Adams, Charles Francis, 225
Adams, John, 48-49, 60n.19
Adams, John Quincy, 118
Age of Reason (Paine), 146
agnosticism, 26, 33-34, 145, 164
Ahlstrom, Sydney E., 271
Allen, C. Leonard, 271
Allen, Ethan, 146
Alley, Sarah, 202, 204, 207, 210
Alma, 51, 55-57, 70, 158
Alma the Younger, 52, 66
American Antiquities and Discoveries in the West (Priest), 123
American Bible Society, 127
American Religion, The (Bloom), 268
American Religions and the Rise of Mormonism (Backman), 11
American Revolution, 271; as heroic resistance, 49-53, 58; popular resistance to monarchy, 53-55; prophecy, 50-52
Amlicites, 86-87
Ammaron, 68, 80-81
Ammon, 69, 89, 240
Anderson, George, 220, 230
Andrew, Laurel, 197n.29
Anthon, Charles, 99, 100, 130, 235, 239
Antichrist, 127
Antimasonry, 66, 95, 118-21, 136n.51, 138n.61. See also Masons
Anti-Nephi-Lehi, 90
apologist scholarship. See Christian apologists
apostasy, 11-12, 72-73, 193

Arrington, Leonard, 173-75, 197n.29, 262-63, 265
articles of faith, 220
Austin, David, 127
authenticity, 264-66

Backman, Milton, 11
baptism, 101, 110, 130, 132, 224
"Barbarism the First Danger" (Bushnell), 218
Barber, John Warner, 180
Barker, James, 11
Barlow, Phil, 20
Beard, Charles, 4-5
belief, xiv, 20-22; atmosphere conducive to, 28; biographies of Smith and, 263-70; Book of Mormon criticism and, 130-33; form of biography and, 264-65; justification for, 23-24, 26; as life-sustaining, 38; overly invested historians, 279-80; self-acceptance and, 34-35; self-criticism and, 279. See also Christian evidences
Ben Israel, Manasseh, 127
Benjamin (King), 69, 74
Bennet, James Arlington, 245
Bennett, James Gordon, 104, 136n.47
Bennett, John C., 188
Benson, Ezra Taft, 34
Bible, 194n.9; American translations of, 237-38; authority of, 272-73; as record of revelations, 273-74; references to Indians in, 125-27; similarities to Book of Mormon, 114-15; Smith's translation of, 236-37, 243
Biographical Sketches of Joseph Smith the Prophet (Smith), 205
biographies, 262-63; authenticity and, 264-66; belief and, 263-70; cultural, 175, 199, 233; form of, 264-65; rationality and, 266-67; significance of, 263, 270-75; sincerity of Smith, 266-68; skeptics and, 265-66; tolerance and, 268-70; twenty-first-century readers, 266-68

Bitton, Davis, 197n.29
Bloch, Marc, 62n.24
Bloom, Harold, xiv, 268
Board of Trade, *189*, 190
Book of Commandments, 209, 248–49, 258. *see also* Doctrine and Covenants; revelations
Book of Mormon: American Revolution prophecy, 50–52; anachronisms in, 115–16; ancient precedents, 57–59; believers in, 130–33; biblical discourse in, 57–58, 122; consistency, 50–52; cursing of Lamanites in, 86–87; deliverance theme, 49–53, 57, 60n.11; enlightenment of people and, 53–55; family story in, 81–85; historicity of, xii–xiii, 47, 264; as imposture, 111–12, 116; influence on Mormonism, 66, 74–75, 131–32; as inspiring, 265; Israelite origin of Indians, 123–30; judgeships, 55–57, 61–62n.21, 62nn.23, 24, 64n.30, 119–22; language of, 74, 77n.12, 109, 233, 238; lawmaking in, 56–57, 64n.30, 122; loss of manuscript, 100, 236, 247n.30, 254; mission to Israel, 126–29; narrative perspective, 107–9, 117, 133n.2; nineteenth-century American culture and, 47–48, 59n.3, 109, 115–16, 126; Old Testament prototypes for, 57–58; pessimism in, 129–30; plot, 107, 116; political passages, 25, 47; psychological view of, xiii–xiv, 79, 83; records in, 67–76, 89; religious arguments against, 110–11; republicanism attributed to, 25–27, 62–63n.24, 121–22, 129; schema of world history in, 70–71, 73–74; skin color in, 86–87; Smith's relationship with, 66–67, 74–76; sources of content, xii–xiii, 95–96; tension between humans and God in, 9–11; title page, 67–68, 102, *108*, 128; translation and, xiii, xiv, 70, 74–76, 80. *See also* Book of Mormon, criticism of; Book of Mormon, recovery of; monarchy
Book of Mormon, criticism of: Campbell's view, 48, 110–11, 113–17, 132, 136n.49, 145, 148; deception thesis, 104–5, 110–12; Dogberry writings, 103–4, 109–14, 116–17, 151–54; early critics, 109–17; explanations for Book of Mormon, 115–17; new critics, 117–30; satires, 109–10, 114. *See also* Book of Mormon
Book of Mormon, recovery of: chronology, 94–95; copyright application, 102;

criticism of, 104–5; events of, 93–94; everyday details, 95–96; loss of manuscript, 98, 100; move to Fayette, NY, 101–2; persons involved, 97–99; pirated excerpts, 103–4; press commentary, 104–5; production rate, 94–95; role of Emma Smith, 97–98. *See also* Book of Mormon
"Book of Mormon and the American Revolution, The" (Bushman), 25
Book of Mormon Authorship Revisited (Reynolds), 93
Book of Revelation, 180
Boudinot, Elias, 84, 123–25, 127–28, 139–40n.82
Brigham Young University, 3, 26, 30, 145, 157, 161
Brodie, Fawn, 103, 117, 152, 175, 255, 262–63, 265–66, 282
Brontë, Charlotte, 259
Brooke, John, 103, 175, 271, 280–81
Bush, Alfred, 263–64
Bushman, Claudia Lauper, *32*, 33, 173
Bushman, Richard Lyman, ix–xvi; visual depictions of, *21, 22, 28, 32*
Bushnell, Horace, 218
Butler, Jon, 271
By the Hand of Mormon: The American Scripture That Launched a New World Religion (Givens), 107

Campbell, Alexander, 48, 110–11, 113–17, 132, 136n.49, 145, 148; Antimasonic theory, 118–21; debate with Owen, 145–46, 151; efforts to discredit Smith, 151–54; on Three Witnesses, 155–56; as translator, 237
Campbell, Thomas, 110, 114, 134–35n.23
Cannon, George Q., 264, 265
Cannon, Mark, 34
capitalism, 169–71, 188–90
Carter, Jared, 131
Cartwright, Peter, 222, 224
Caswall, Henry, 262
Catholic Apostolic Church, 271
Chamberlin, Solomon, 199–201, 205–6, 209–10, 214n.2
Champollion, Jean-François, *238*, 244
Chandler, Michael, 244
Chicago, 187–91
Christ, 43–44, 121; as desirable fruit, 84–85; examination of records, 72–73
Christian apologists, 39, 111–12, 242; Mormon, 39–41, 43

Christian evidences, 26–27, 145; authentication of Biblical miracles, 147–51; credibility of witnesses, 149–51; efforts to discredit Smith, 151–54; internal, 148, 153; Smith's response to, 154–57
church attendance, 167–68
Cincinnati, 180–81, *182*
city planning, 194n.9, 220–21; American, 179–81; City of Zion, 177–79; gathering-city-temple model, 183–85, 193, 195n.12; Nauvoo compared with Chicago, 187–91. *See also* space; temples
civilization, diffusion of, xi, 12
classical figures, 15–16
Cohen, I. B., vii, viii
Cole, Abner (Obediah Dogberry), 103–4, 109–14, 116–17, 151–54
colonized peoples, 268
Columbia University, 32–33
commandments, 258–59
communism, 169–70
Constitution, framers, 4–5
constitutional government, 49, 56–57, 122
conversion, 66, 89–91, 154–55
corporations, 166–68
Covill, James, 251
Cowdery, Oliver, 75–76, 93, 94, *101*–2, 110, 113–14, 130, 209, 235
Cowdery, Warren, 229
Cronon, William, 187–88, 197n.28

Daughters of Utah Pioneers museum, 219–20
deception thesis, 104–5, 110–12, 266–67
Declaration of Independence, 48–49, 53, 88
Dedham, *180*
Dee, John, 241
Deism, 26, 146–47
deliverance theme, 49–53, 57, 60n.11
Delusions: An Analysis of the Book of Mormon (Campbell), 114
democracy, 121, 169–70, 219
democratic politics, 197–98n.38
Democratization of American Christianity, The (Hatch), 271
deprivation, 79, 82–85
Derr, Jill, 262
dialogic thinking, 280–82
Disciples of Christ, 114, 115
dispensation pattern, 11–14, 129
doctrine, 132
Doctrine and Covenants, 131–32, 195n.13, 208–10, 216n.40, 269; revelations in, 249–51; title page, *252. See also* Book of Commandments; revelations

Dogberry, Obediah. *See* Cole, Abner
Domestic Manners of the Americans, The (Trollope), 217–18
Dow, Lorenzo, 222, 224
Dream, or Vision by Samuel Ingalls, A (Ingalls), 202–3

Early Mormonism and the Magic World View (Quinn), 271
Economic Interpretation of the Constitution, An (Beard), 4–5
Egyptian, reformed, 109, 233, 238
Egyptian hieroglyphics, 238, 244
Egyptian scrolls, 237, 244
elections, 56, 63n.26
Eliade, Mircea, xiii
Eliot, George, 268
Emerson, Ralph Waldo, 161
empathetic approach, xiii–xiv
"End of History, The" (Fukuyama), 169
England, Eugene, 166
England, Jews and, 127
Enlightenment thought, 37, 40, 146; biographies and, 266–67; view of visions, 201–2. *See also* skepticism
Enos, 87
Erikson, Erik, xiii, 79
Esplin, Ron, xvi, 175
Essentials in Church History (Smith), 10
Ether, Book of, 13, 102
Evans, John Henry, 262–63, 265
Exiles In a Land of Liberty (Winn), 271
extremist prophets, 273
eyewitnesses, 93, 95, 224–27

family story, 81–85
Fielding, Joseph, 196n.22
Finney, Charles Grandison, 201–2, 214n.5, 234–35
Firestone Library, 263–64
First Nephi (Smith), 82
First Vision, xi, 156, 199, 206–9, 235, 274; paintings of, 255–56. *See also* visionary culture
Footfalls on the Boundary of Another World (Owen), 154
Foundation for Ancient Research and Mormon Studies (FARMS), 39, 93, 107, 157
Founder of Mormonism, The (Riley), 117, 262, 276n.12
framers of Constitution, 4–5
Franklin, Benjamin, 222
free choice, 35–36
Freedom's Ferment (Tyler), 271
free-thought journals, 146
French Revolution, 127

French thought, 40
Freud, Sigmund, xiii
Frey, Joseph S. F. C., 127–28
Fries, Sylvia Doughty, 194n.9
Fukuyama, Francis, 169

Gadiantons, 66, 118, 119–21
gathering-city-temple model, 183–85, 193, 195n.12
gentility: ambivalence about, 222, 224; city plans and, 220–21; European view of American, 217–18; housing and, 227–29; as means to end of building Zion, 223–24; middle-class, 220, 222–23; Mormon view of, 229–31; myth and reality, 219–20; refinement-in-the-wilderness theme, 219–20, 229–30; as sinful, 221–22
Givens, Terryl, x, 107
Gnostics, 12
golden plates, 37–38, 93, 95, 238–39; attempts to view, 100, 102–3; Smith on, 96–97; twenty-first-century readers and, 269–70; viewing of, 155–56. *See also* translation
goodness, 42–43
Gospel Through the Ages (Hunter), 12
government, 121, 219; constitutional, 49, 56–57, 122; rights to, 80–81; true principles of, 53, 55, 60–61n.19
Grammaire (Champollion), 244
"Grammar & Alphabet of the Egyptian Language" (Smith), 244
Grandin, Egbert B., 103, 104
Grand Inquisitor figure, 26, 27
Grand Island, 128
Graves, Thomas, 194n.9
Great Apostasy, 11–12
Greene, John P., 131
Greene, Rhoda, 131

Hamilton, Mark, 177
Hardy, Kenneth, 31–32
Harley, J. B., 176
Harris, Lucy, 95, 98, 100
Harris, Martin, 98, 99, 100, 103, 113, 130; consultation with Anthon, 99, 100, 130, 235, 239; revelations and, 104–5, 258; sells Book of Mormon, 104, 109, 258
Harvard Divinity School, 20, 24, 26, 145
Harvard University, 23–24
Hatch, Nathan, 271
Haven, Charlotte, 225
Hermes Trismegistus, 271
Hermeticism, 271
Hill, Donna, 263
Hill, Gustavus, 185

Hill, Marvin, 263
Hill Cumorah, *iii, 97*
Hinckley, Gordon B., 161
historians, xiv, 5–8, 17; dialogic thinking, 280–82; prophet-historians, 9–10, 52. *See also* Mormon historians
Historical Collections (Barber), 180
history: of the Church, 10–13; cultural values and, 31–32, 79–80; providential, xii, 13–15, 17, 265; psychological influences on, xiii–xiv, 5–6, 79; role of beliefs and values in, xiv, 8; role of records in, 70–72
History of the American Indians, The (Adair), 123
Hofmann letters, 65
Holme, Thomas, 182
Holy Ghost, 164, 165
Hope of Israel (Ben Israel), 127
Howe, Eber D., 94, 112–13, 116–17, 225, 233, 242
Hughes, Richard, 271
Hume, David, 148, 151
Hunter, Milton, 12
Huntington Library, 173, 233
Hurlbut, Doctor Philastus, 94, 116, 117, 241, 246n.26

Iliad (trans. Pope), 241
Illusions of Innocence: Protestant Primitivism in America, 1630–1875 (Hughes and Allen), 271
Indians: as Israelites, 123–29, 138n.73, 139-40nn.82, 84; missions to, 110, 123
inequality, 63–64n.30
Ingalls, Samuel, 202–3
intellectuals, 23, 26, 33–34, 38
internal evidences, 148, 153
Irvingites. *See* Catholic Apostolic Church
Ishmael, 82, 89
Israelites, 71, 77n.8, 81; Book of Mormon mission to, 126–29; Indians as, 123–29, 138n.73, 139-40nn.82, 84; restoration theme, 126–29; ten lost tribes, 125–26
Israel's Advocate, 127

Jackson, Andrew, 118, 138n.61, 162, 219, 226
Jacksonians, 56, 63n.26
Jacob, 85, 128
Jacob, book of, 68–69
Jane Eyre (Brontë), 259
Jaredite record, 70
Jefferson, Thomas, 48–50, 53, 60n.19
Jews, history of, 13
Johnson, Joel Hills, 224
John the Baptist, visitation of, 101, 209

Joseph, writings of, 237
Joseph Smith, an American Prophet (Evans), 262–63
Joseph Smith, the First Mormon (Hill), 263
Joseph Smith and the Beginnings of Mormonism (Bushman), xii–xiii, 27, 107, 175, 265, 279, 282
Joseph Smith's Own Story (Smith), 208
judgeships, 55–57, 61–62n.21, 62nn.23, 24, 64n.30, 88, 121–22; Gadiantons and, 119–20

Kierkegaard, Søren, 268
Kingdom, 162, 165–68
Kirkham, Francis W., 94, 105n.2
Kirtland, Ohio, 110, 113, 235; plan for, 183, *184*, 185
Kishkumen, 119
Knight, Joseph, 98, 101, 104, 210, 244–45, 246n.23
Knight, Newel, 110

Laban, 82
Lafayette, 48, 50
Laman, xiii, 80–82, 84–85, 89
Lamanites, 51; cursing of, 86–87; Gadiantons and, 119–20; mission to, 66, 75, 88–90; national identity, 87–88, 90–92; records and, 70, 73, 79–80; unconverted, 90–91; use of force, 80–88
Lamoni, 87, 89
language: Moroni on, 250, 261n.9; reformed Egyptian, 109, 233, 238; of revelations, 248–50, 260–61n.8; Smith's studies of, 243–44
Latter-day Saints. *See* Mormons
lawmaking, in Book of Mormon, 56–57, 64n.30, 122
Laws (Plato), 192
Lee, John D., 229
Lehi, 13, 14, 68, 81, 84–85, 91, 121, 126
Lehi in the Desert (Nibley), 22, 24, 157
Lemuel, xiii, 81–85, 89
L'Enfant, Pierre Charles, 181, 183
Leslie, Charles, 147
Life, 33
life decisions, 42–43
Life of Joseph Smith (Cannon), 264, 265
Limhi, 51, 69–70
listening to spirit, 164–65
log-cabin culture, 222–23
London Society for Promoting Christianity among the Jews, 127
love, 89–90
Loyalists, 79
Lundquist, John, 186

Machor, James L., 194n.9
magic, 65–66, 241–43, 271
Major, William Warner, 219, 221
"Manuscript Found" (Spaulding), 233–34
market society, 187–92
Marsden, George, x
Marsh, Thomas, 130
Marshall, Elihu, 103
Masons, 118–21, 137n.54, 271. *See also* Antimasonry
masses, the, 22–23
Mather, Increase, 127
Matthews, Robert, 243
Maughan, J. Howard, 22
Maxwell, Neal, 26, 145
McClelland, David, 14, 32
McCormick, Cyrus, 191
McKay, David O., 167
McLellin, William E., 248–49, 251, 261n.11
meetinghouses, 185–86
Messenger and Advocate, 101, 209, 223, 229
Methodists, 216n.39, 222
middle-class American culture, 220, 223–24. *See also* gentility
millenarianism, 271
Millenarian World of Early Mormonism (Underwood), 271
Millennial Harbinger, 114, 151
Miller, George, 228
miracles, xi, 154; authentication of, 147–51; as evidence, 112–13
missions, 21–23, 35, 36; acts of love and generosity, 89–90; to Indians, 110, 123; to Lamanites, 66, 75, 88–90; restoration of Israel, 126–29
Mitchill, Samuel, 99
monarchy, 61n.20, 121–22; abdication of, 54–55, 88; acceptance of, 51–52; enlightened overthrow of, 49, 51; iniquitous monarchs, 55, 58, 63–64n.30; people's demand for, 54, 57–58, 62n.24; popular opposition to, 53–55
Moore, R. Laurence, xiii
moral justification, 16
moral respectability, 223
Morgan, William, 118–20, 137n.54, 137n.59
Mormon, 67, 107–9
Mormon historians, x, 94; apologist scholarship, 39–41, 43; dispensation pattern and, 11–14; framework for, 17–18; influence of academy on, 8–9; inspiration through the Spirit of Christ, 15–17; as overly invested, 279–80; revelation to the prophets, 10–13; significance question and, 263, 270–75. *See also* historians

Mormon History Association, x, 65
Mormonism: converts, 110; institutions of, 165–66; magic and, 65–66; organization of Church, 104, 131; significance of for twenty-first century, 263 270–75
Mormonism Unvailed (Howe), 94, 233, 242
Mormons: church attendance, 167–68; respectability and, 219–20; as unlearned, 111, 134n.20; value of learning to, 31–33; violence against, 272. *See also* gentility
Mormon Sisters (ed. Bushman), 173
Mormon Tabernacle Choir, 32
Moroni, 62–63n.24, 68, 75, 80, 107, 129, 238; on language, 250, 261n.9; visitation of, 209
Mosaic law, 126
Moses, Book of, 76, 243
Mosiah, 25, 56, 69–70, 74, 121, 240
Mosiah, Book of, 69
Mosiah Interprets the Jaredith (Teichert), 241

Napoleon, 127
national traditions, 87–88, 90–92
Nature and Destiny of Man, The (Niebuhr), 15–16
Nature's Metropolis (Cronon), 187–88, 197n.28
Nauvoo, 227–28; Chicago compared with, 187–88; map of, *174;* temple, 185–86, *191,* 192; as temple society, 188–91, 197n.29
Nauvoo House, 195n.14, 227–29, 255
Nephi, 68, 71, 81–82, 89, 91, 107, 121; revelations and, 254, 273–74
Nephihah, 122
Nephites: extended image of earth, 70–71; Gadiantons and, 119–21; government, 47, 51–52; records of, 69–72, 79–80; reunion of, 69–70, 72; use of love and generosity, 89–90; wars with Lamanites, 80–81
New England towns, 179–81, 194n.9
New Harmony, 145
New-Harmony Gazette, 145, 146
New Jerusalem, 180
News from Heaven (Pool), 203
New Testament, translations of, 237
Newton, Isaac, 147
New Witness for God, A (Roberts), 26, 145, 157
New York, political milieu, 48–49
Nibley, Hugh, 12, 14, 22, 24, 26, 39, 61n.21, 63n.24, 90, 145, 157
Niebuhr, Reinhold, 15–17
Noah, Mordecai, 128

Noah (King), 51
Noah's Ark, 123
No Man Knows My History (Brodie), 103, 117, 152, 175, 255, 262–63, 265–66, 282
North American Review, 238

objectivity, x, 39–40, 43
O'Dea, Thomas, 47–48, 59n.3
Ogden, William B., 190–91
Old Testament: prophecies, 99–100, 239–40, 246n.23, 253; prototypes for Book of Mormon, 57–58; providential direction in, 13–14
Omni, Book of, 69
Owen, Robert, 114, 145–46
Owen, Robert Dale, 154

Packer, Boyd K., 30
Pahoran, 119
Painesville Telegraph, 110–11, 114, 225, 235
painting, religious, 221, 255–56, 264
Paley, William, 112, 149–51
Palmyra Reflector, 109, 151, 152
Partridge, Edward, 257
patriotic orations, 48–49, 51, 60n.11, 60–61n.19
Paul, Robert, 260n.6
Penn, William, 182
Peter, James, and John, visitation of, 209
Peterson, Chase, 32
Phelps, W. W., 113, 250
Philadelphia, 179, 181, *182*
physical sciences, 39–40
Plato, 192
Pool, Caleb, 203, 205, 210
Pope, Alexander, 241
positivism, logical, xi, 21, 34, 37–38
postmodernism, 3, 37
Potter, Elisha, 226, 227
power, 176–77, 274; endowment of, 184–85, 195nn.13, 14; temples and, 184–85, 186
Pratt, Orson, 243
Pratt, Parley, 126, 131, 132
President of the High Priesthood, 75
Priest, Josiah, 123, 125
priesthood, 101, 115, 209, 235
Primitive Church, 271
"Proclamation of the First Presidency of the Church to the Saints Scattered Abroad, A" (Smith), 190, 195–96n.15
Progressive Era, 10
proof text method, 67
prophet-historians, 9–10, 52
prophet-kings, 47

Prophet of the Nineteenth Century, The (Caswall), 262
Prophet Puzzle, The (Waterman), 233
prophets, 10–13, 273; false, 148, 151–52; as seers, 240–41
Protestantism, 11, 27, 242
providential history, xii, 13–15, 17, 265
Provo, 3, 30, 145, 173
psychohistory, xiii–xiv, 79
public morality, 162
publishers, 103–4, 204–5, 210
Puritans, 127, 194n.9
Pusey, Nathan, 24

Quincy, Josiah, 219, 225–28, 231n.24
Quinn, D. Michael, 260–61n.8, 271
Quorum of the Twelve, 188–90

Rampton, Calvin, 47
Rampton, Lucybeth, 47
Rathbone, Tim, 94
rationality, xi, 23, 43, 135nn.23, 26, 148; biographies and, 266–67, 274; Christian apologists and, 26, 111–12
reality, 23
recitation ceremony, 69–70
"Recollection" (Knight), 98
records, 75–76; apostasy and, 72–73; ceremony and, 69–70, 72; descent of, 68–69; end of earth and, 71–73; Nephites and, 69–72, 79–80; role in history, 70–72, 77n.8; role in religious culture, 68, 72–73; translation and, 74
Refinement of America, The: Persons, Houses, Cities (Bushman), 217
Refiner's Fire, The: The Making of Mormon Cosmology (Brooke), 271, 280–81
Religion and the Decline of Magic (Thomas), 65
religious culture, role of records in, 68, 72–73
Religious Experience of Norris Stearns, The (Stearns), 205–7
Religious History of the American People (Ahlstrom), 271
religious organizations, 165–66
Religious Seekers and the Advent of Mormonism (Vogel), 270–71
Renaissance culture, 201
Reps, John, 194n.9
republicanism, 271; Book of Mormon and, 25–27, 62–63n.24, 121–22, 129
Republic (Plato), 192
resistance theme, 49–53
restoration, 73, 146, 155, 164, 270, 271; of Aaronic priesthood, 101, 209, 235;

Israel and, 126–29; significance of, 272–73; visionary culture and, 206–7; visionary stories of, 209, 216n.35
revelations, 132–33, 155, 162–65, 181, 183, 243; attempts to imitate, 248–49; authority and, 257–59, 272–73; Bible and, 273–74; biblical mediators, 253–55; classic, 251, 253–55; as commandments, 258–59; dispensation pattern and, 11–12; forms of, 250–57; lack of explanation for, 259–60; language of, 248–50, 260–61n.8; mixture of rhetorical forms, 255–57; modern, 75–76, 132; to the prophets, 10–13; rebukes of Smith, 254–55, 259; religious painting and, 255–56; rhetorical space of, 251–53, 255, 257–58; on rise of Church, 209–11; significance of, 272–74; space and, 251–53, 255, 257–58; on translations, 234, 236–37; vocabulary of Joseph Smith, 249–50. *See also* Book of Commandments; visions
Reynolds, Noel, 93
rhetorical space, 251–58; authority and, 257–59; mixture of forms, 255–57
Rigdon, Sidney, 110, 112, 114, 136n.47, 237, 257; gentility and, 223–24, 225, 228, 229; Spaulding theory and, 116, 266
righteousness, 14–15
Riley, I. Woodbridge, 117, 136n.47, 262, 276n.12
Roberts, B. H., 11, 26, 145, 157
Roman Church, 11
romantics, 15–16
Rorty, Richard, 278n.40
Rosetta Stone, 238
Rosicrucian movement, 271

"Saints and the World, The" (Rigdon), 223
Salt Lake City, 47, 192–93, 220
Schlesinger, Arthur, Jr., 34
schoolbooks, nineteenth-century, 49, 50
Schorske, Carl, 17
Schroeder, Theodore, 137n.56
scientific culture, 163
scientific scholarship, 39–40
Second Coming of Christ, 168, 270
Seeker movement, 270–71
seers, 70, 74, 234, 240–42
seerstones, 74, 77n.13, 97, 102, 246–47n.26; magical culture of, 241–43; Urim and Thummim, 238, 242, 243, 247n.30
Seixas, Joshua, 243
self-interest, 40
self-understanding, 192, 244
Shakers, 271

Shipps, Jan, xviin.12, 27
Short and Easy Method with Deists (Leslie), 147
"Short Sketch of the Life of Solomon Chamberlin, A" (Chamberlin), 200, 212, 214n.2
Silber, John, 32
Simon Peter, 43
skepticism, xi, 23, 41; about visions, 201–2; argument of, 146–47; biographies and, 265–66; modern answers to, 157–58. *See also* Enlightenment
Skousen, Cleon, 13
Smith, Emma, 93, 95, 97–98, 100, 222, 249–50
Smith, Ethan, 67, 95, 124, 125–29, 140n.84, 233
Smith, George A., 130–31
Smith, Hyrum, 101, 131, 200–201, 210, 264
Smith, Joseph, xi; accusations of money digging, 113, 153–54, 242; autobiography, 96; biblical prophecy and, 99–100, 239–40, 246n.23; caricatures of, 110–14; conception of space, 175–76; delivery of golden plates to, 37–38; eyewitness depictions of, 224–27; hunger for knowledge, 31, 243–44; as impostor, 111–12, 116, 266–67; influence in current age, 161–62; literary resources available to, 260nn.5, 6, 7, 260–61n.8; log-cabin culture and, 222–23; magic and, xii, 65–66, 241–43, 271; major principles of teachings, 162; as Mason, 119; Methodist tradition and, 222; nineteenth-century American culture and, 47–48, 59n.3, 109, 115–18, 126; place in visionary culture, 205–6; political milieu, 48–49; as primary source, 94; as prophet, 111–13, 151, 235; relationship with Book of Mormon, 66–67, 74–76; response to critics, 154–57; in role of translator, 234–36, 242–43; self-understanding, 244; significance of for twenty-first century, 263, 270–75; as unlearned, 98–100, 116, 239–40, 246n.23, 259–60; visual depictions of, *264;* vocabulary of, 249–50. *See also* biographies; First Vision; Smith, Joseph, influence of; translation
Smith, Joseph, III, 95
Smith, Joseph, influence of, 161–62, 171–72; Kingdom, 165–68; revelation, 163–65; Zion, 168–71
Smith, Joseph, Sr., 93, 103–4, 130, 205, 265; drinking problem, 279, 282
Smith, Joseph Fielding, 10

Smith, Lucy Mack, 93, *94*, 100, 104, 121, 123, 130, 205, 223, 250, 260n.5
Smith, Samuel, 123, 131
Smith, Solomon, 130
Smith Institute for Latter-day Saint History, Joseph Fielding, vii, xvi, 175, 217, 262
Snow, Eliza R., 225
social environment, 38–40
Some Extraordinary Instances of Divine Guidance and Protection, 202
Soul of the American University, The (Marsden), x
Southcote, Joanna, 111, 152
space, xi, 173; gathering-city-temple model, 183–85, 193, 195n.12; maps and power, 176–77; Mormon forms of, 177–79; orienting function of sacred, 186, 196n.22; over time, 192–93; revelations and, 251–53, 255, 257–58; Smith's conception of, 175–76; temple as primal, 181–87. *See also* city planning
Spaulding, Solomon, 116, 121, 233–34
Spaulding theory, 116, 121, 136nn.47, 49, 233–34, 245n.2, 266
Spirit of Christ, 15–17
spiritualists, 154
standards, 16–17
Star in the West, A (Boudinot), 123–25
Star Wars, 164
Stearns, Norris, 205–7, 210
Stein, Stephen, 27
stones, translation. *See* seerstones
students, as scholars, 30–31
submission, 79, 84
superego, 79, 83
supernatural, Christian disbelief in, 111–12
supernatural intelligences, 164
superstition, visions as, 135n.23, 201–2, 268

Talmage, James, 11
Taylor, John, 200
Teichert, Minerva, 241
temples, 12, 177–78; gathering-city-temple model, 183–85, 193, 195n.12; Kirtland, 237; as model for body, 186; Nauvoo, 185–86, 192; as primal architectural space, 181–87; Salt Lake City, 192–93; society, 188–91, 197n.29; titles for, 181–83. *See also* city planning
testimony, 131, 157–58
Thayre, Ezra, 131
Theresa of Avila, 268
Thesaurus (Roget), 267
Thomas, Keith, 65, 271
Thorowgood, Thomas, 127
Three Witnesses, 22, 113, 155–56, 158, 266

Tiffany's Monthly, 98–99
Tillich, Paul, 24
Times and Seasons, 224
tolerance, 268–70
Toynbee, Arnold, 14
traditions: false, 86–87, 90–92; misunderstanding of, 85, 88–92; national, 87–88, 90–92
Transcendentalists, 199
translation, 70; of Bible, Smith's, 236–37, 243; biblical prophecies about, 99–100, 239–40, 246n.23; Book of Abraham, 76, 237, 243–44; Egyptian scrolls, 237, 244; gift of, 75–76; reformed Egyptian, 109, 233, 238; revelations on, 234, 236–37; by seers, 240–42; seerstones, 74, 77n.13, 246–47n.26; as work for the learned, 237–39
translator, role of, 74, 234
Trollope, Frances, 217–18
truth, 42–43
Tucker, Pomeroy, 94
Twelve Apostles, testimony of, 158
Tyler, Alice Felt, 271

Underwood, Grant, 66, 271–72
Urim and Thummim, 238, 242, 243, 247n.30
utopian reformers, 271

values, early American, 16–17
View of the Evidences of Christianity, A (Paley), 149, *150*, 151
View of the Hebrews (Smith), 67, 95, *124*, 125–29, 233
violence, 92, 272
visionary culture, 199–201, 215n.20, 281; list of pamphlets, 211–13; publishers and, 204–5, 210; Restoration and, 206–7; Smith's differences from, 209–10; as socially neutral, 201–2, 215n.20. *See also* First Vision; visions
visions: apocalyptic, 202–4, 208, 210, 215n.20; intended for public, 204–5; of restoration, 209, 216n.35; as superstition, 201–2; themes, 202–4, 210. *See also* revelations; visionary culture

visitations: of John the Baptist, 101, 209; of Peter, James, and John, 209; unreported, 209, 216n.40
Vogel, Dan, 266–68, 270–71

Wacker, Grant, xi, xii, xiv
Walker, Ron, 217
Walters the Magician, 109–10, 115, 116
Warner, Terry, 26
Washington, D.C., 181, *183*
Waterman, Bryan, 233
Wayne Sentinel, 49, 53, 94, 104, 108
Webster, Noah, 237
Welch, John W., 47, 94, 262
Wentworth, Richard, 34
Wesley, John, 227
Whigs, 222
White, Ellen G., 216n.39
Whitmer, Christian, 200
Whitmer, David, 93, 101–2, *103*
Whitmer, John, 254, 257
Whitmer, Peter, 101, 110; farmhouse of, *102*
Whitney, Newell K., 235
Wight, Lyman, 228
Williams, Frederick G., 177–78, 180, 194n.10, 239, 257, 259
Williams, Roger, 270–71
Winn, Kenneth, 271
Wirt, William, 118
Woman's Exponent, 230
Wonders of Nature and Providence, The (Priest), 123, 125
Woodworth, Jed, vii, 62
work, the, 185, 190, 192, 195–96n.15
world development, 169–70
world religions, 268, 272

Young, Brigham, 97, 131, 165, 185, 192, 219, 220, *221*
Young, Emily Partridge, 224
Young, Phineas, 131

Zarahemla Nephites, 69–70, 72
Zarahemnah, 87
Zeniff, 80, 85
Zion, 162, 168–71, 181; gentility as means to end of, 223–24; plat for City of, 177, *178*